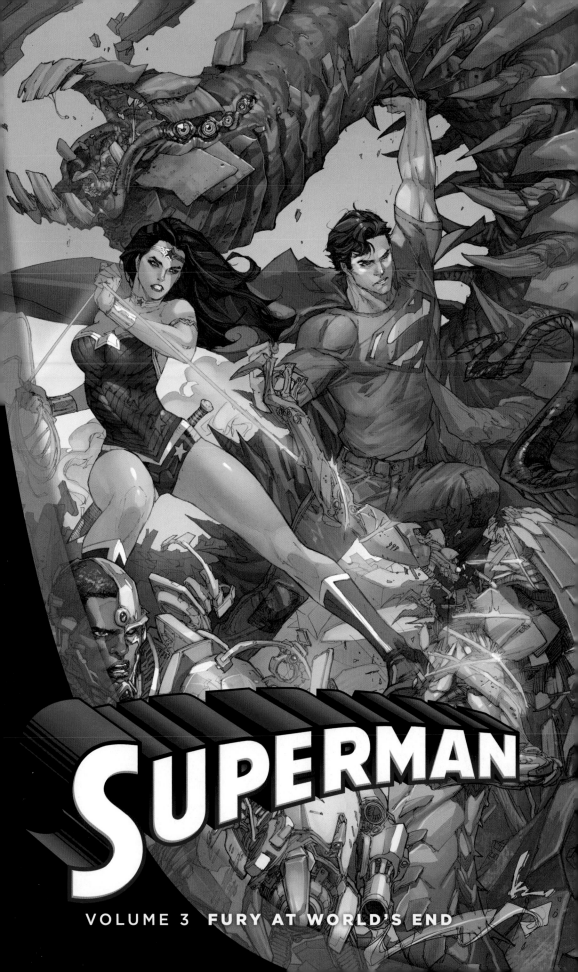

SUPERMAN

VOLUME 3   FURY AT WORLD'S END

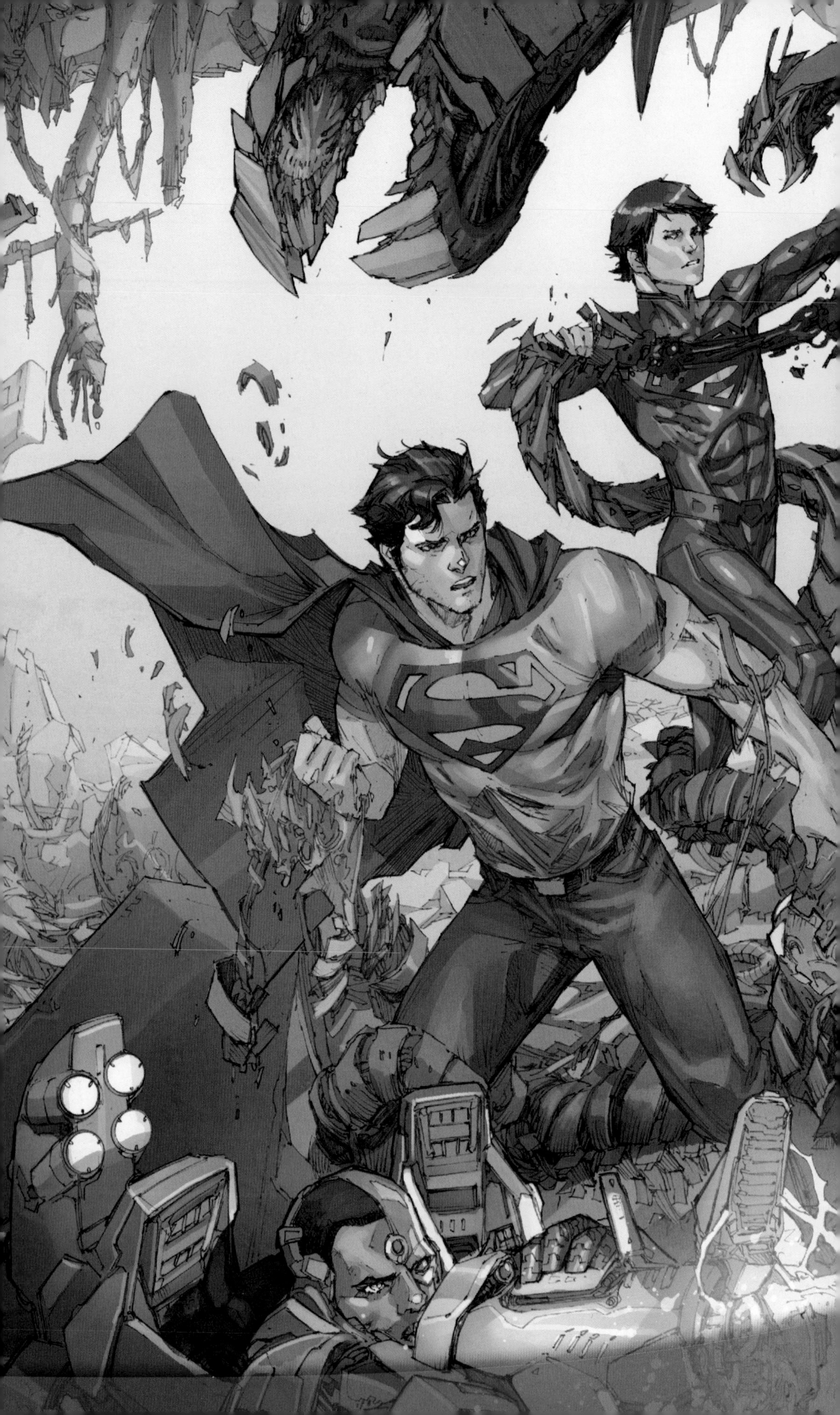

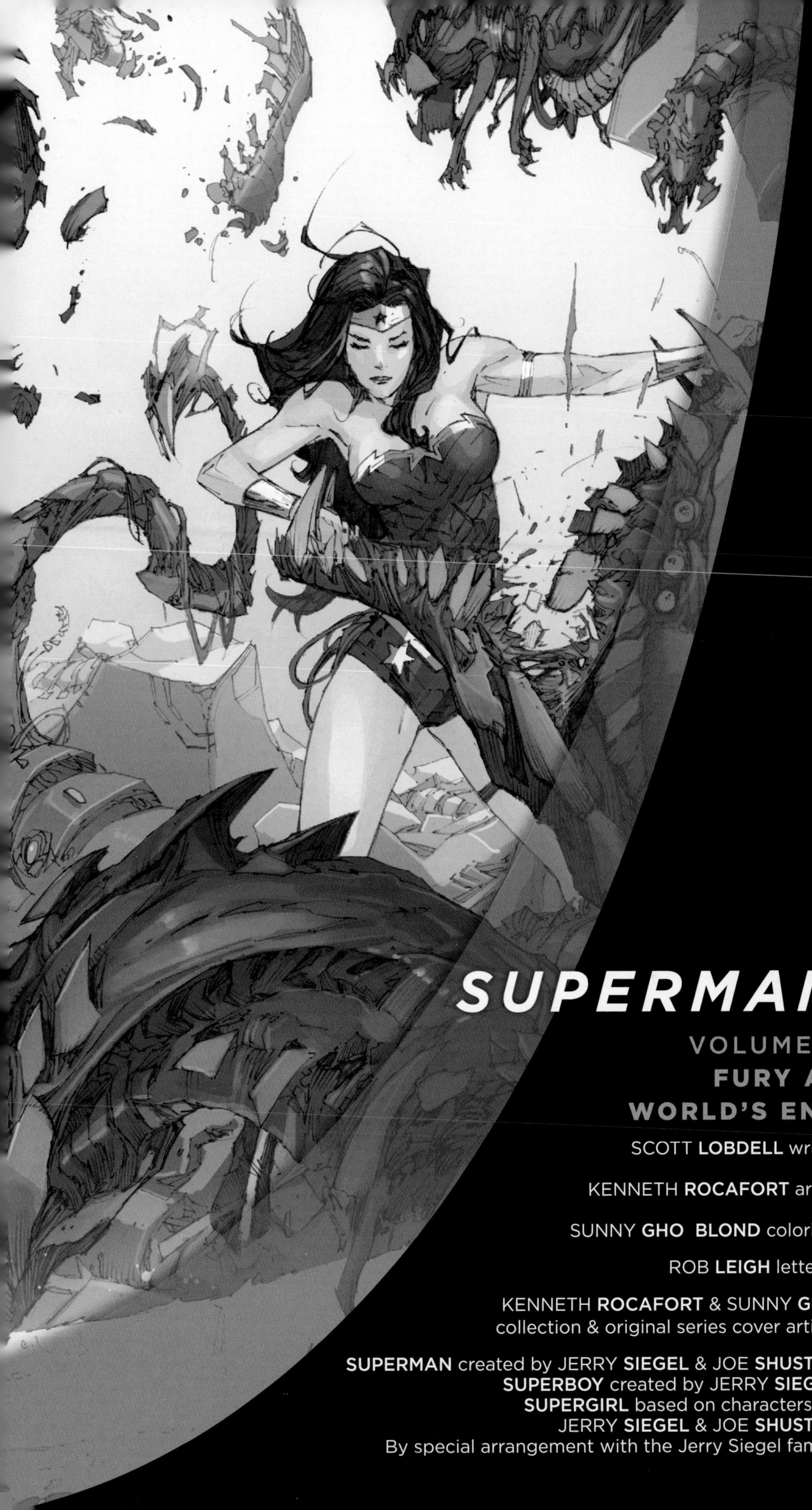

SUPERMAN

VOLUME 3
FURY AT WORLD'S END

SCOTT **LOBDELL** writer

KENNETH **ROCAFORT** artist

SUNNY **GHO BLOND** colorists

ROB **LEIGH** letterer

KENNETH **ROCAFORT** & SUNNY **GHO**
collection & original series cover artists

SUPERMAN created by JERRY **SIEGEL** & JOE **SHUSTER**
SUPERBOY created by JERRY **SIEGEL**
SUPERGIRL based on characters by
JERRY **SIEGEL** & JOE **SHUSTER**
By special arrangement with the Jerry Siegel family

EDDIE BERGANZA Editor – Original Series DARREN SHAN ANTHONY MARQUES Assistant Editors – Original Series
ROWENA YOW Editor ROBBIN BROSTERMAN Design Director – Books ROBBIE BIEDERMAN Publication Design

BOB HARRAS Senior VP – Editor-in-Chief, DC Comics

DIANE NELSON President DAN DIDIO and JIM LEE Co-Publishers GEOFF JOHNS Chief Creative Officer
JOHN ROOD Executive VP – Sales, Marketing and Business Development AMY GENKINS Senior VP – Business and Legal Affairs
NAIRI GARDINER Senior VP – Finance JEFF BOISON VP – Publishing Planning
MARK CHIARELLO VP – Art Direction and Design JOHN CUNNINGHAM VP – Marketing
TERRI CUNNINGHAM VP – Editorial Administration ALISON GILL Senior VP – Manufacturing and Operations
HANK KANALZ Senior VP – Vertigo and Integrated Publishing JAY KOGAN VP – Business and Legal Affairs, Publishing
JACK MAHAN VP – Business Affairs, Talent NICK NAPOLITANO VP – Manufacturing Administration
SUE POHJA VP – Book Sales COURTNEY SIMMONS Senior VP – Publicity BOB WAYNE Senior VP – Sales

SUPERMAN VOLUME 3: FURY AT WORLD'S END

DC Comics, 1700 Broadway, New York, NY 10019
A Warner Bros. Entertainment Company.
Printed by RR Donnelley, Salem, VA, USA. 12/6/13. First Printing.

HC ISBN: 978-1-4012-4320-3
SC ISBN: 978-1-4012-4622-8

Library of Congress Cataloging-in-Publication Data

Lobdell, Scott, author.
Superman Volume 3 : Fury at World's End / Scott Lobdell ; [illustrated by Kenneth Rocafort].
pages cm. — (The New 52!)
"Originally published in single magazine form as SUPERMAN 0, 13-17"—T.p. verso
"Superman created by Jerry Siegel and Joe Shuster."
ISBN 978-1-4012-4320-3 (hardback)
1. Graphic novels. I. Rocafort, Kenneth, illustrator. II. Title. III. Title: Fury at World's End.
PN6728.S9L585 2014
741.5'973—dc23
201303592

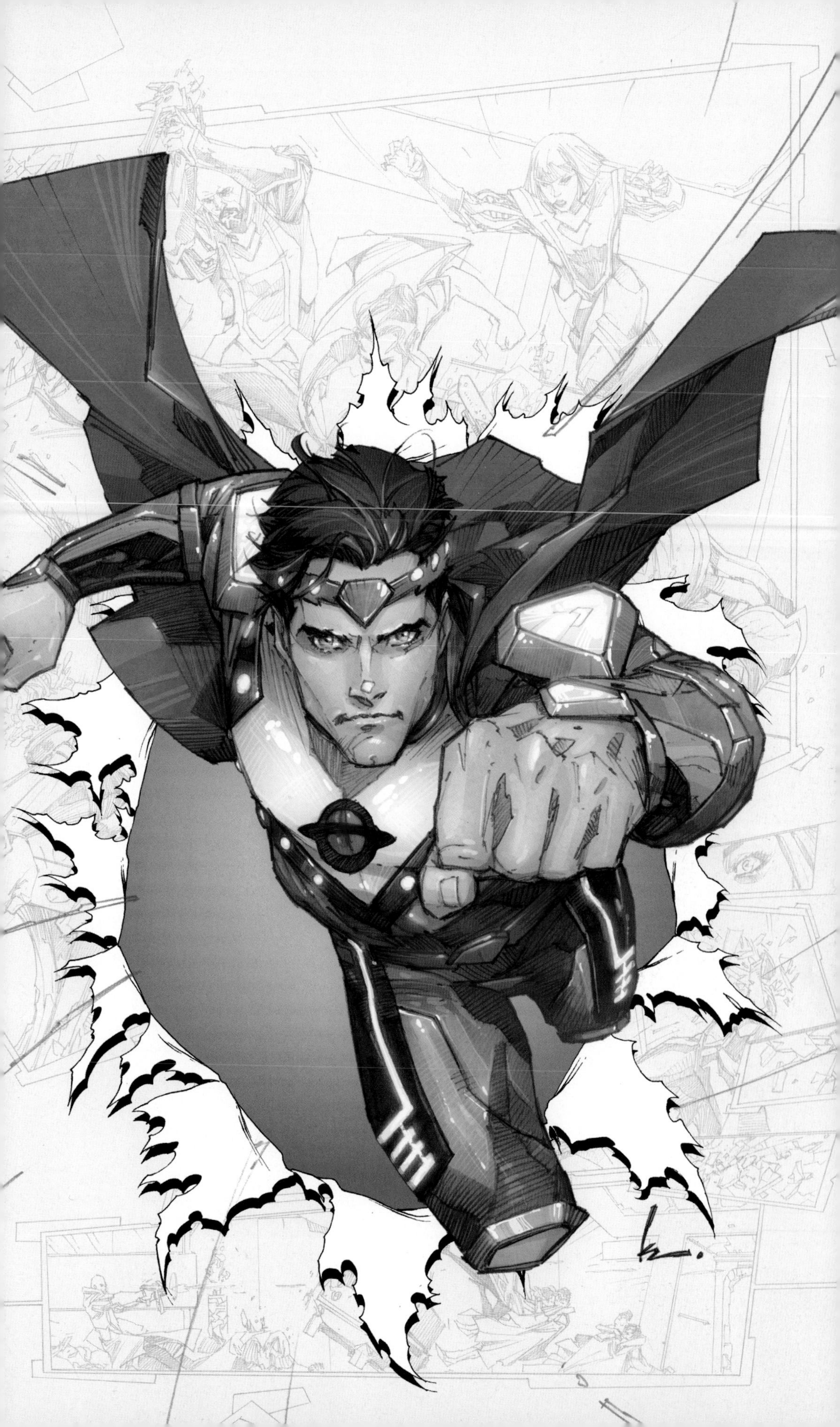

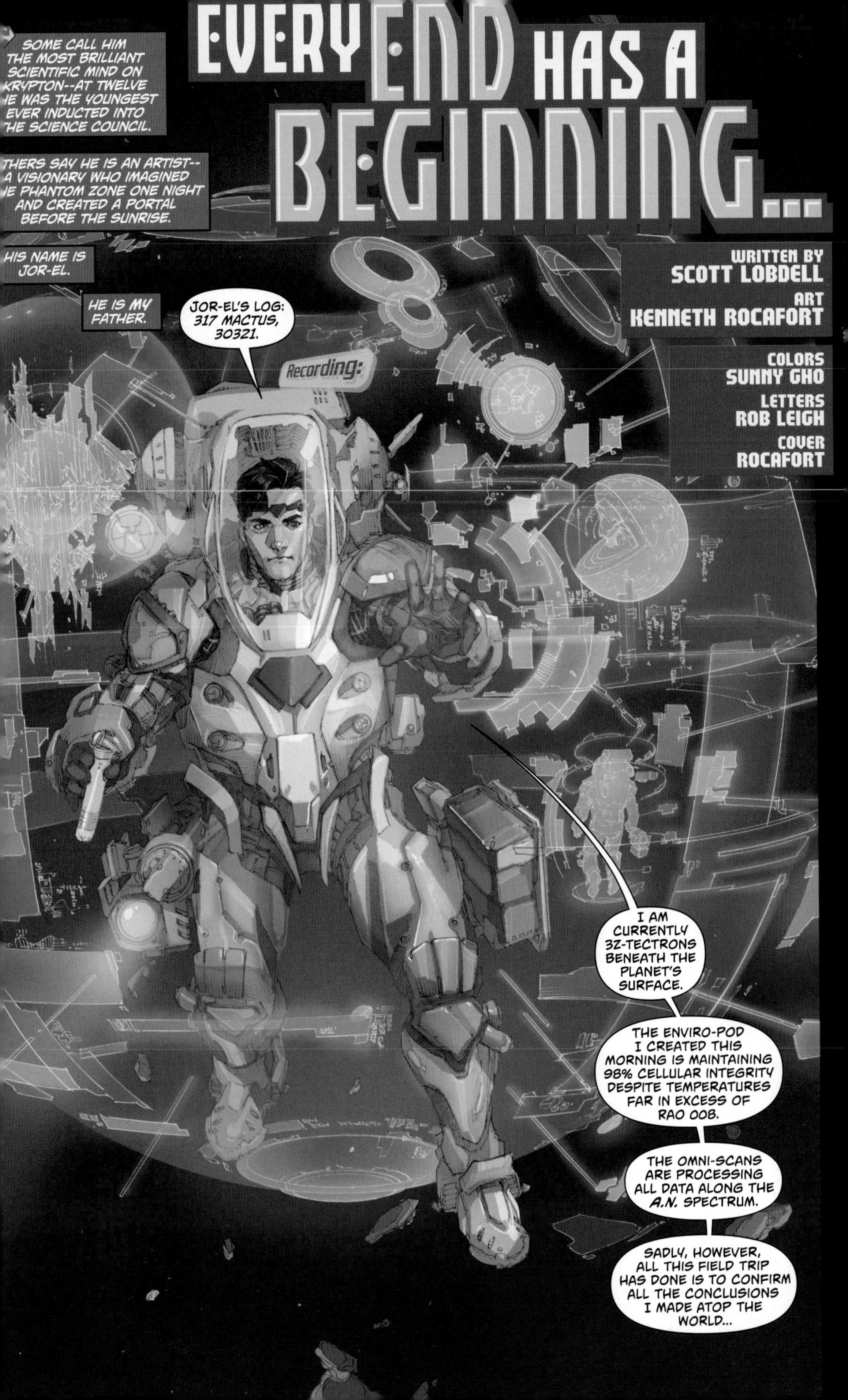
EVERY END HAS A BEGINNING...
SOME CALL HIM THE MOST BRILLIANT SCIENTIFIC MIND ON KRYPTON--AT TWELVE IE WAS THE YOUNGEST EVER INDUCTED INTO HE SCIENCE COUNCIL.
THERS SAY HE IS AN ARTIST-- A VISIONARY WHO IMAGINED IE PHANTOM ZONE ONE NIGHT AND CREATED A PORTAL BEFORE THE SUNRISE.
HIS NAME IS JOR-EL.
HE IS MY FATHER.
JOR-EL'S LOG: 317 MACTUS, 30321.
Recording:
WRITTEN BY SCOTT LOBDELL
ART KENNETH ROCAFORT
COLORS SUNNY GHO
LETTERS ROB LEIGH
COVER ROCAFORT
I AM CURRENTLY 32-TECTRONS BENEATH THE PLANET'S SURFACE.
THE ENVIRO-POD I CREATED THIS MORNING IS MAINTAINING 98% CELLULAR INTEGRITY DESPITE TEMPERATURES FAR IN EXCESS OF RAO 008.
THE OMNI-SCANS ARE PROCESSING ALL DATA ALONG THE A.N. SPECTRUM.
SADLY, HOWEVER, ALL THIS FIELD TRIP HAS DONE IS TO CONFIRM ALL THE CONCLUSIONS I MADE ATOP THE WORLD...

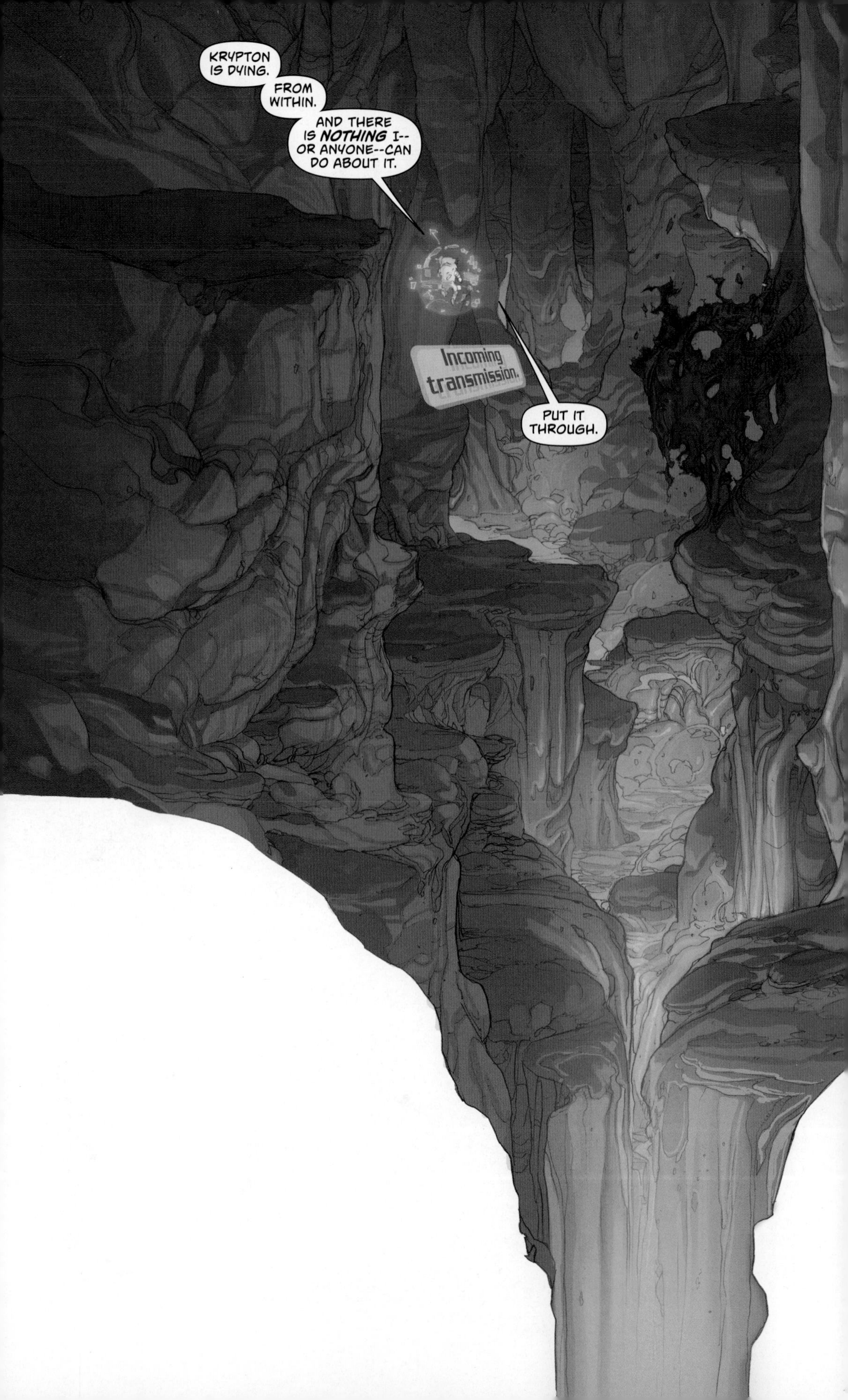
KRYPTON IS DYING.
FROM WITHIN.
AND THERE IS NOTHING I-- OR ANYONE--CAN DO ABOUT IT.
Incoming transmission.
PUT IT THROUGH.

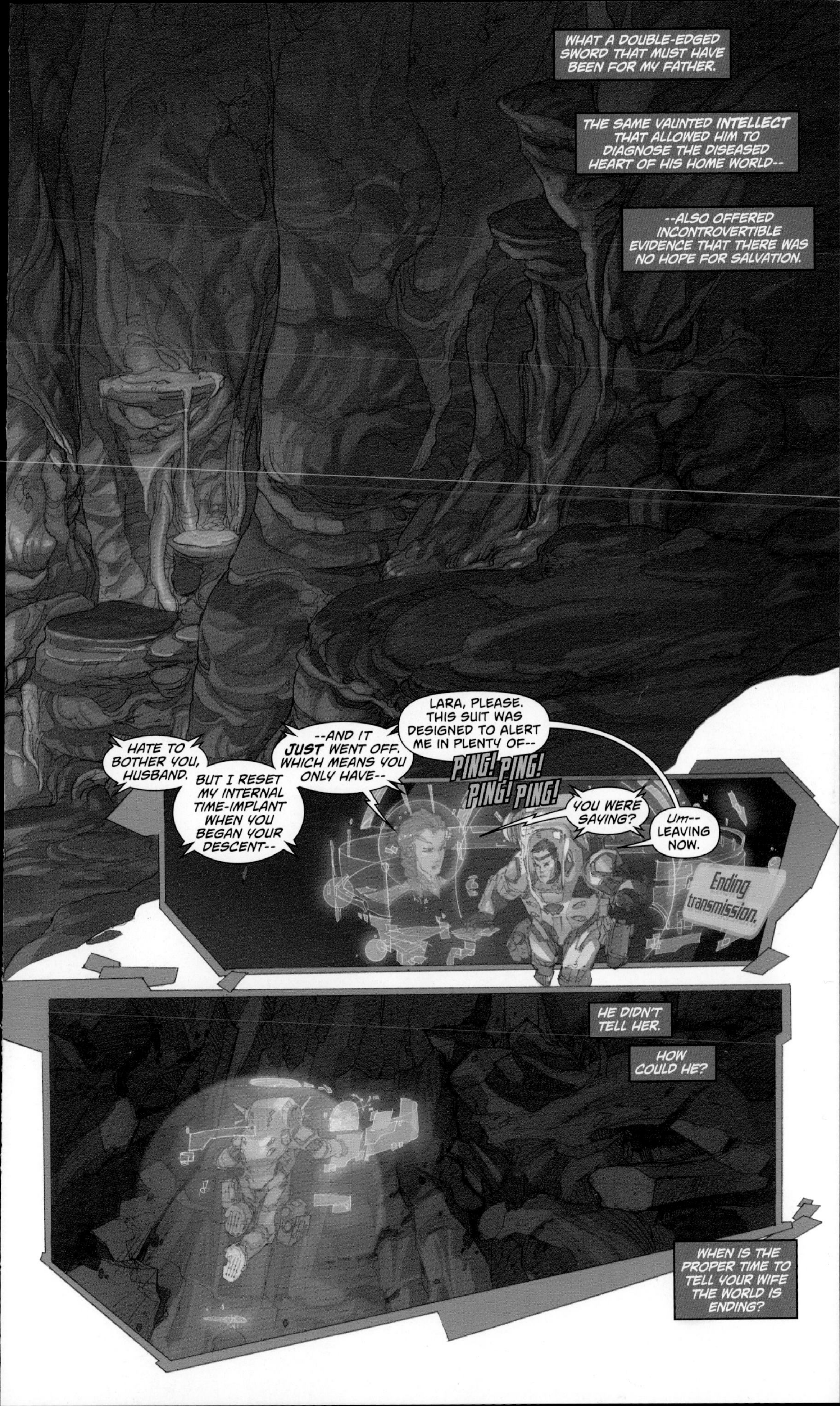
WHAT A DOUBLE-EDGED SWORD THAT MUST HAVE BEEN FOR MY FATHER.
THE SAME VAUNTED INTELLECT THAT ALLOWED HIM TO DIAGNOSE THE DISEASED HEART OF HIS HOME WORLD--
--ALSO OFFERED INCONTROVERTIBLE EVIDENCE THAT THERE WAS NO HOPE FOR SALVATION.
HATE TO BOTHER YOU, HUSBAND.
BUT I RESET MY INTERNAL TIME-IMPLANT WHEN YOU BEGAN YOUR DESCENT--
--AND IT JUST WENT OFF. WHICH MEANS YOU ONLY HAVE--
LARA, PLEASE. THIS SUIT WAS DESIGNED TO ALERT ME IN PLENTY OF--
PING! PING! PING! PING!
YOU WERE SAYING?
UM-- LEAVING NOW.
Ending transmission.
HE DIDN'T TELL HER.
HOW COULD HE?
WHEN IS THE PROPER TIME TO TELL YOUR WIFE THE WORLD IS ENDING?

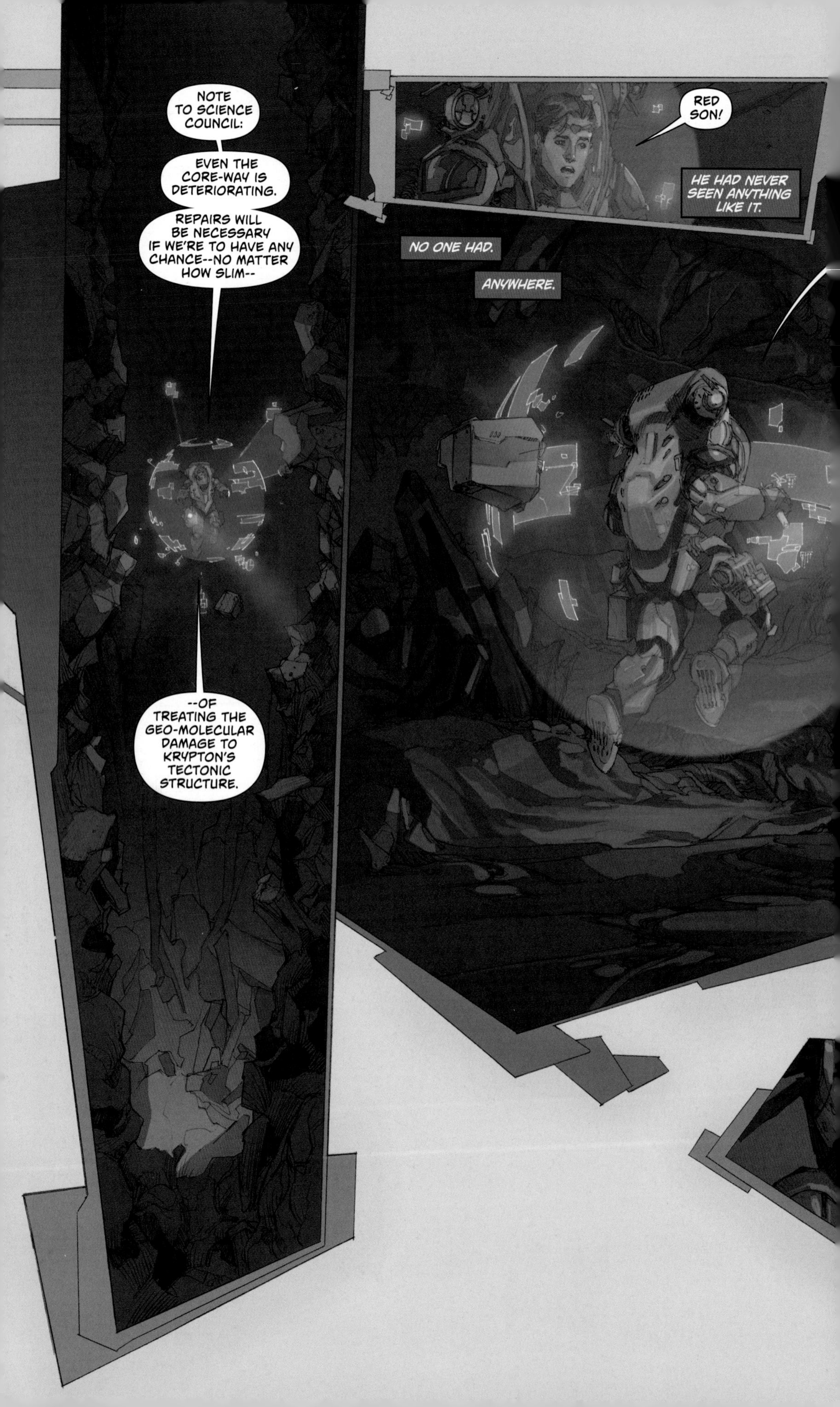
NOTE TO SCIENCE COUNCIL:
EVEN THE CORE-WAY IS DETERIORATING.
REPAIRS WILL BE NECESSARY IF WE'RE TO HAVE ANY CHANCE--NO MATTER HOW SLIM--
--OF TREATING THE GEO-MOLECULAR DAMAGE TO KRYPTON'S TECTONIC STRUCTURE.
RED SON!
HE HAD NEVER SEEN ANYTHING LIKE IT.
NO ONE HAD.
ANYWHERE.

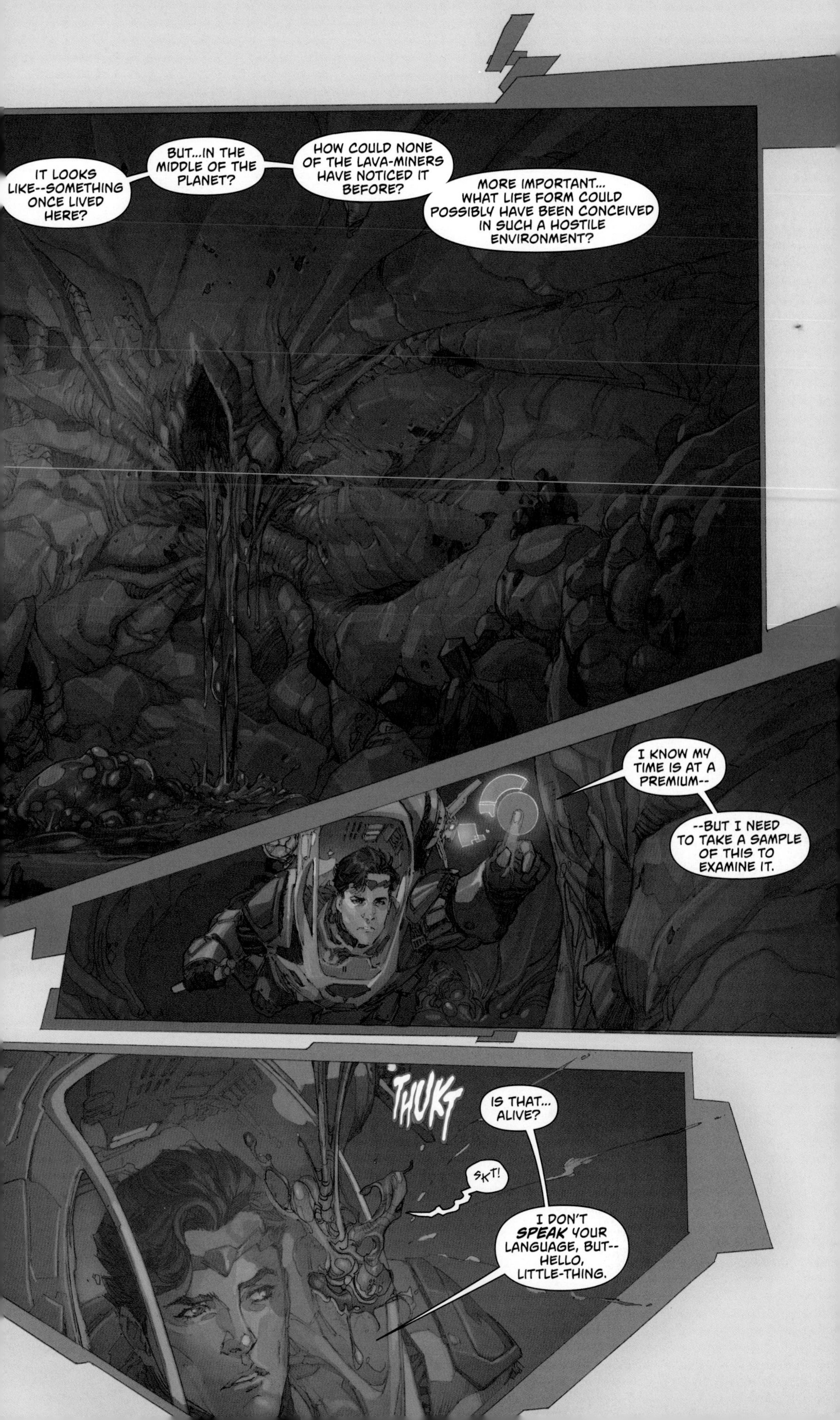
IT LOOKS LIKE--SOMETHING ONCE LIVED HERE?
BUT...IN THE MIDDLE OF THE PLANET?
HOW COULD NONE OF THE LAVA-MINERS HAVE NOTICED IT BEFORE?
MORE IMPORTANT... WHAT LIFE FORM COULD POSSIBLY HAVE BEEN CONCEIVED IN SUCH A HOSTILE ENVIRONMENT?
I KNOW MY TIME IS AT A PREMIUM--
--BUT I NEED TO TAKE A SAMPLE OF THIS TO EXAMINE IT.
THUKT
IS THAT... ALIVE?
SKT!
I DON'T *SPEAK* YOUR LANGUAGE, BUT-- HELLO, LITTLE-THING.

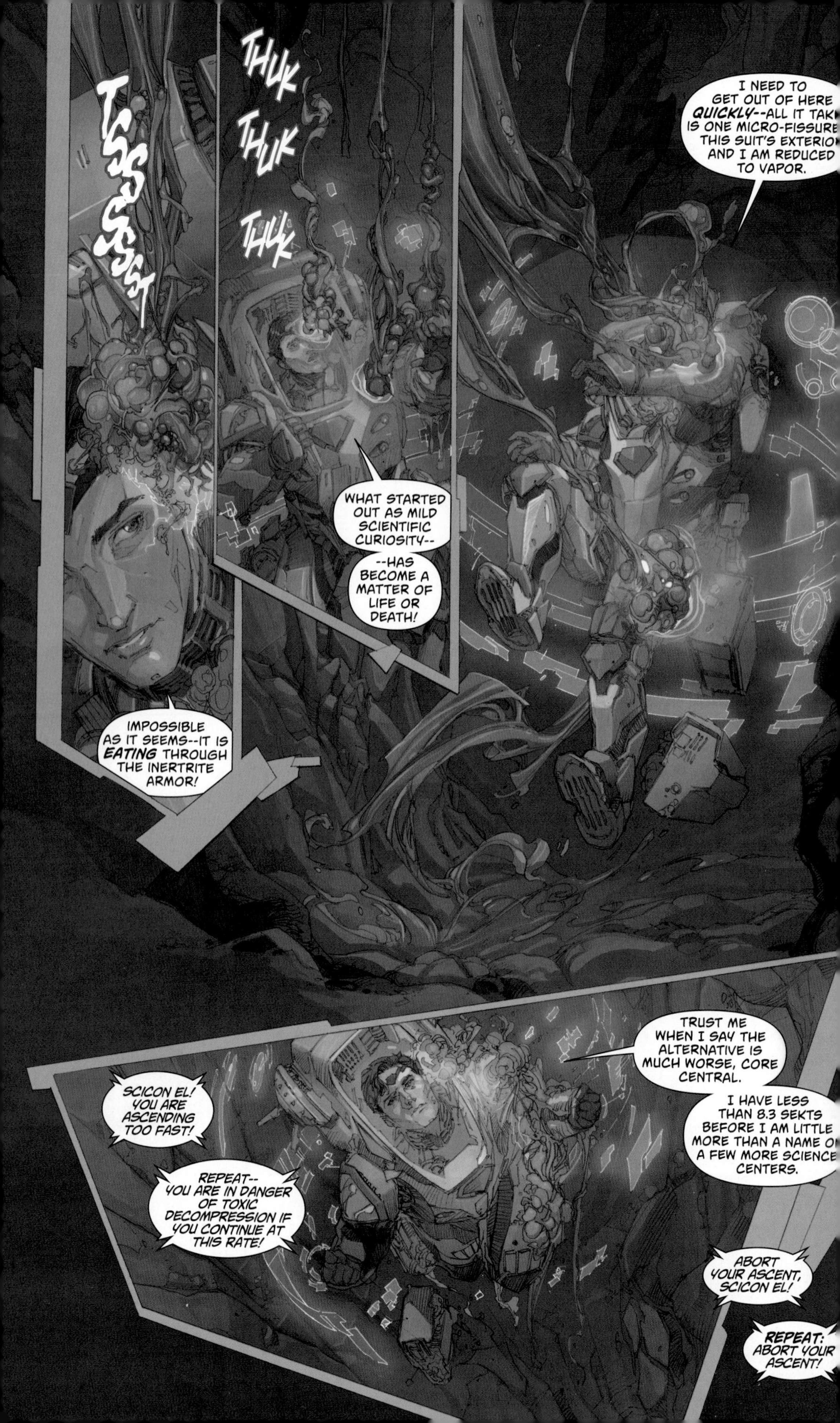
TSSSSSSST
THUK THUK THUK
I NEED TO GET OUT OF HERE QUICKLY--ALL IT TAK IS ONE MICRO-FISSURE THIS SUIT'S EXTERIO AND I AM REDUCED TO VAPOR.
WHAT STARTED OUT AS MILD SCIENTIFIC CURIOSITY--
--HAS BECOME A MATTER OF LIFE OR DEATH!
IMPOSSIBLE AS IT SEEMS--IT IS EATING THROUGH THE INERTRITE ARMOR!
SCICON EL! YOU ARE ASCENDING TOO FAST!
REPEAT-- YOU ARE IN DANGER OF TOXIC DECOMPRESSION IF YOU CONTINUE AT THIS RATE!
TRUST ME WHEN I SAY THE ALTERNATIVE IS MUCH WORSE, CORE CENTRAL.
I HAVE LESS THAN 8.3 SEKTS BEFORE I AM LITTLE MORE THAN A NAME O A FEW MORE SCIENCE CENTERS.
ABORT YOUR ASCENT, SCICON EL!
REPEAT: ABORT YOUR ASCENT!

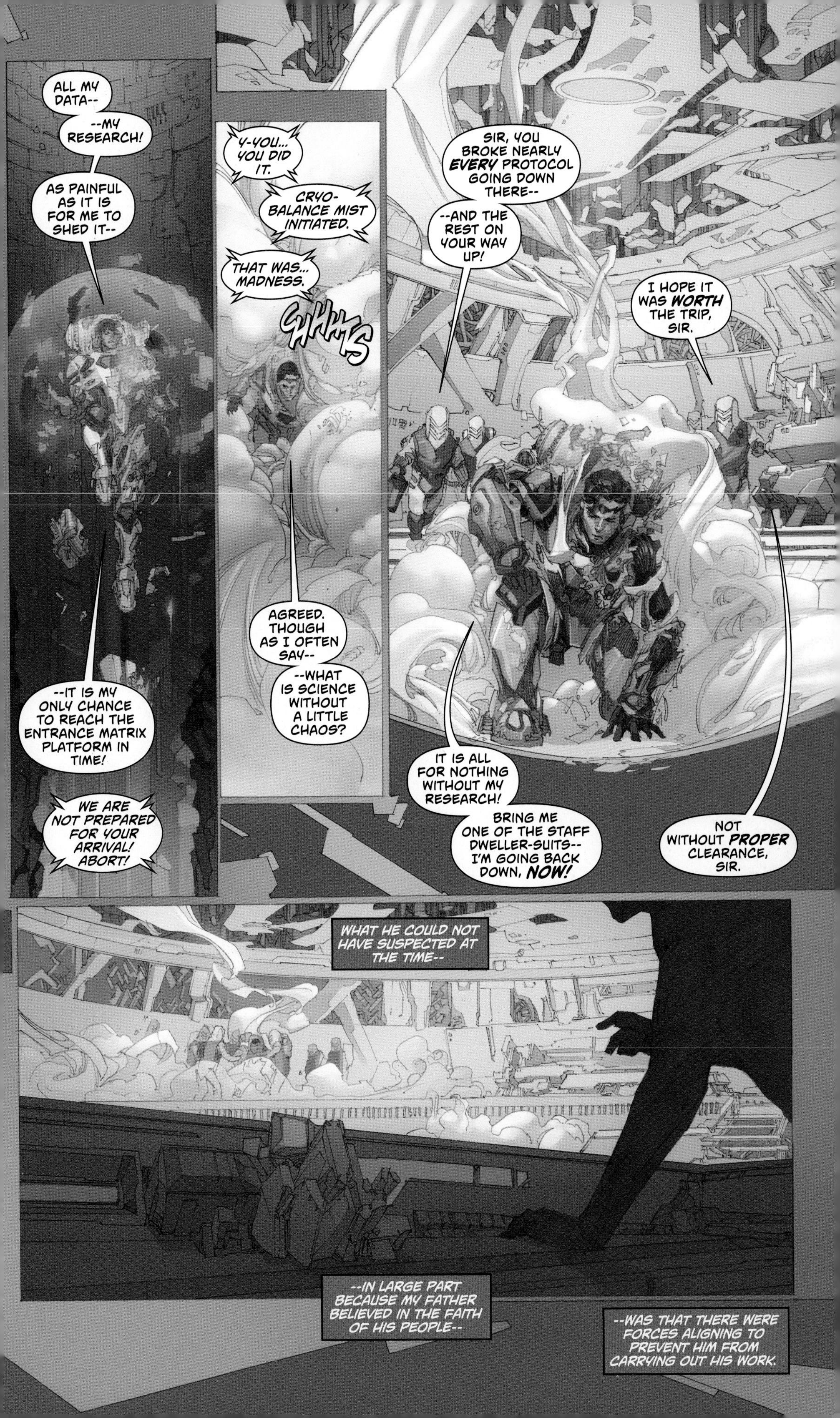

ALL MY DATA--
--MY RESEARCH!
AS PAINFUL AS IT IS FOR ME TO SHED IT--
--IT IS MY ONLY CHANCE TO REACH THE ENTRANCE MATRIX PLATFORM IN TIME!
WE ARE NOT PREPARED FOR YOUR ARRIVAL! ABORT!
Y-YOU... YOU DID IT.
CRYO-BALANCE MIST INITIATED.
THAT WAS... MADNESS.
GHHHTS
AGREED. THOUGH AS I OFTEN SAY--
--WHAT IS SCIENCE WITHOUT A LITTLE CHAOS?
SIR, YOU BROKE NEARLY EVERY PROTOCOL GOING DOWN THERE--
--AND THE REST ON YOUR WAY UP!
I HOPE IT WAS WORTH THE TRIP, SIR.
IT IS ALL FOR NOTHING WITHOUT MY RESEARCH!
BRING ME ONE OF THE STAFF DWELLER-SUITS-- I'M GOING BACK DOWN, NOW!
NOT WITHOUT PROPER CLEARANCE, SIR.
WHAT HE COULD NOT HAVE SUSPECTED AT THE TIME--
--IN LARGE PART BECAUSE MY FATHER BELIEVED IN THE FAITH OF HIS PEOPLE--
--WAS THAT THERE WERE FORCES ALIGNING TO PREVENT HIM FROM CARRYING OUT HIS WORK.

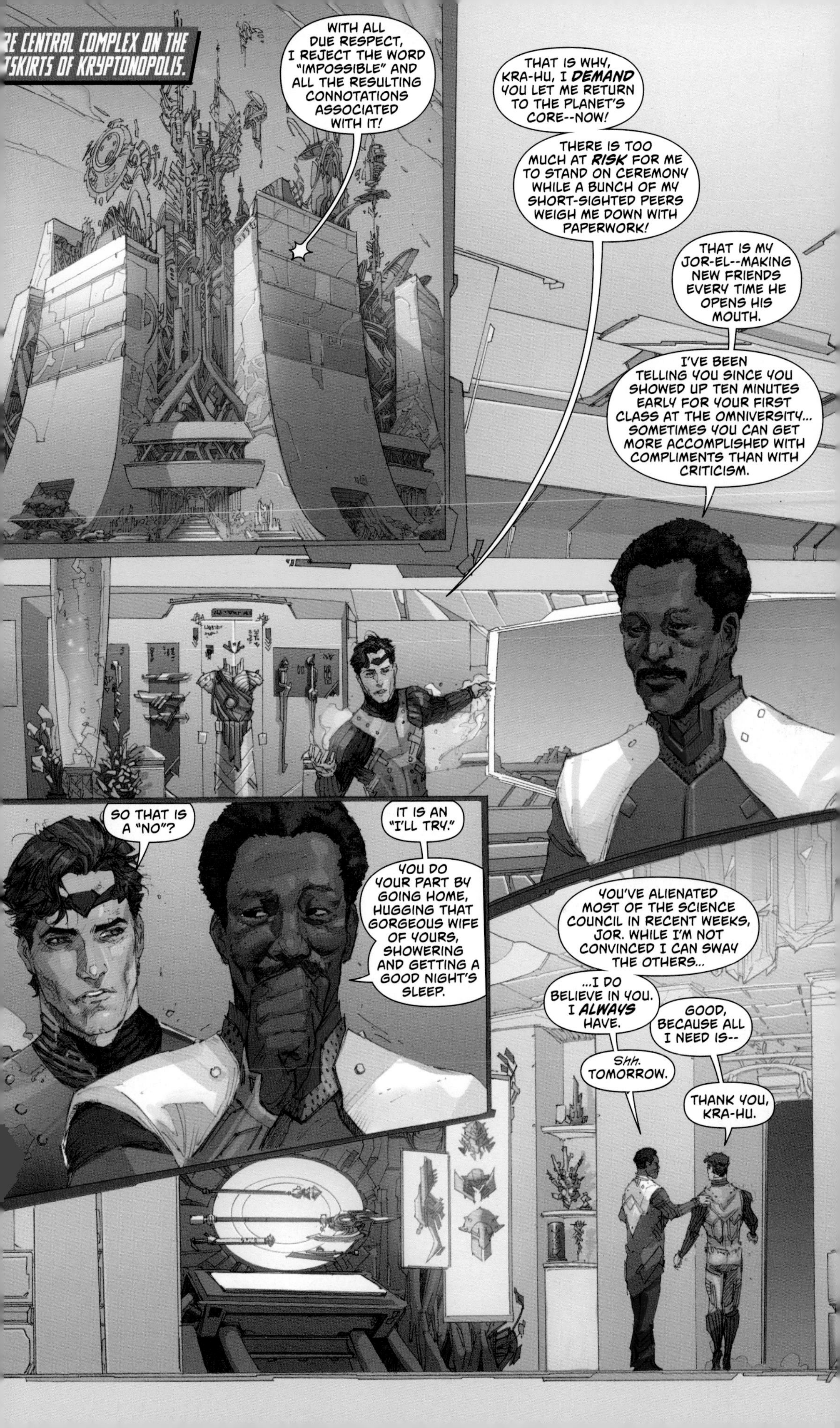

RE CENTRAL COMPLEX ON THE
TSKIRTS OF KRYPTONOPOLIS.
WITH ALL DUE RESPECT, I REJECT THE WORD "IMPOSSIBLE" AND ALL THE RESULTING CONNOTATIONS ASSOCIATED WITH IT!
THAT IS WHY, KRA-HU, I DEMAND YOU LET ME RETURN TO THE PLANET'S CORE--NOW!
THERE IS TOO MUCH AT RISK FOR ME TO STAND ON CEREMONY WHILE A BUNCH OF MY SHORT-SIGHTED PEERS WEIGH ME DOWN WITH PAPERWORK!
THAT IS MY JOR-EL--MAKING NEW FRIENDS EVERY TIME HE OPENS HIS MOUTH.
I'VE BEEN TELLING YOU SINCE YOU SHOWED UP TEN MINUTES EARLY FOR YOUR FIRST CLASS AT THE OMNIVERSITY... SOMETIMES YOU CAN GET MORE ACCOMPLISHED WITH COMPLIMENTS THAN WITH CRITICISM.
SO THAT IS A "NO"?
IT IS AN "I'LL TRY."
YOU DO YOUR PART BY GOING HOME, HUGGING THAT GORGEOUS WIFE OF YOURS, SHOWERING AND GETTING A GOOD NIGHT'S SLEEP.
YOU'VE ALIENATED MOST OF THE SCIENCE COUNCIL IN RECENT WEEKS, JOR. WHILE I'M NOT CONVINCED I CAN SWAY THE OTHERS...
...I DO BELIEVE IN YOU. I ALWAYS HAVE.
GOOD, BECAUSE ALL I NEED IS--
Shh. TOMORROW.
THANK YOU, KRA-HU.

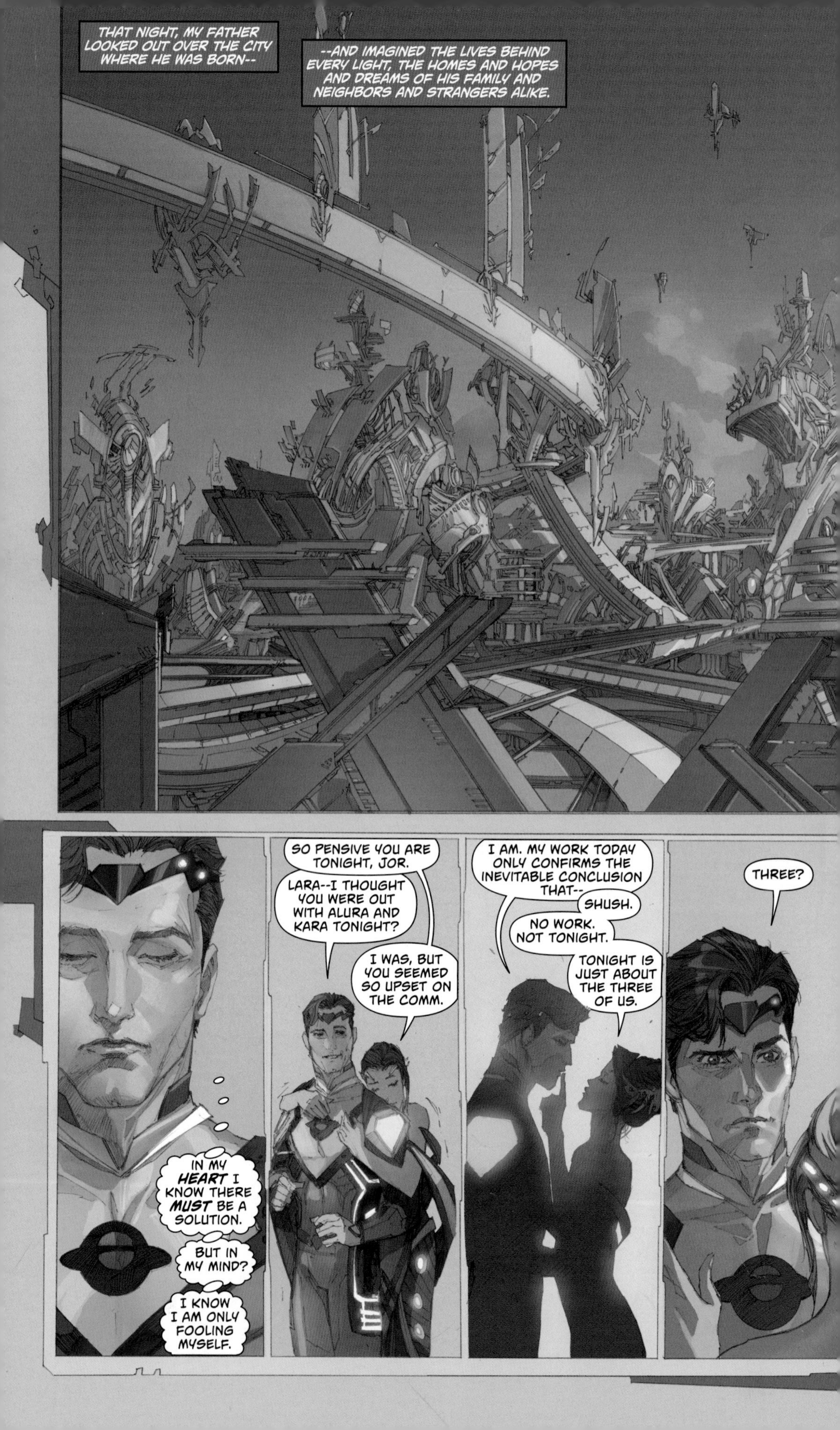

THAT NIGHT, MY FATHER LOOKED OUT OVER THE CITY WHERE HE WAS BORN--
--AND IMAGINED THE LIVES BEHIND EVERY LIGHT, THE HOMES AND HOPES AND DREAMS OF HIS FAMILY AND NEIGHBORS AND STRANGERS ALIKE.
IN MY HEART I KNOW THERE MUST BE A SOLUTION.
BUT IN MY MIND?
I KNOW I AM ONLY FOOLING MYSELF.
SO PENSIVE YOU ARE TONIGHT, JOR.
LARA--I THOUGHT YOU WERE OUT WITH ALURA AND KARA TONIGHT?
I WAS, BUT YOU SEEMED SO UPSET ON THE COMM.
I AM. MY WORK TODAY ONLY CONFIRMS THE INEVITABLE CONCLUSION THAT--
SHUSH.
NO WORK. NOT TONIGHT.
TONIGHT IS JUST ABOUT THE THREE OF US.
THREE?

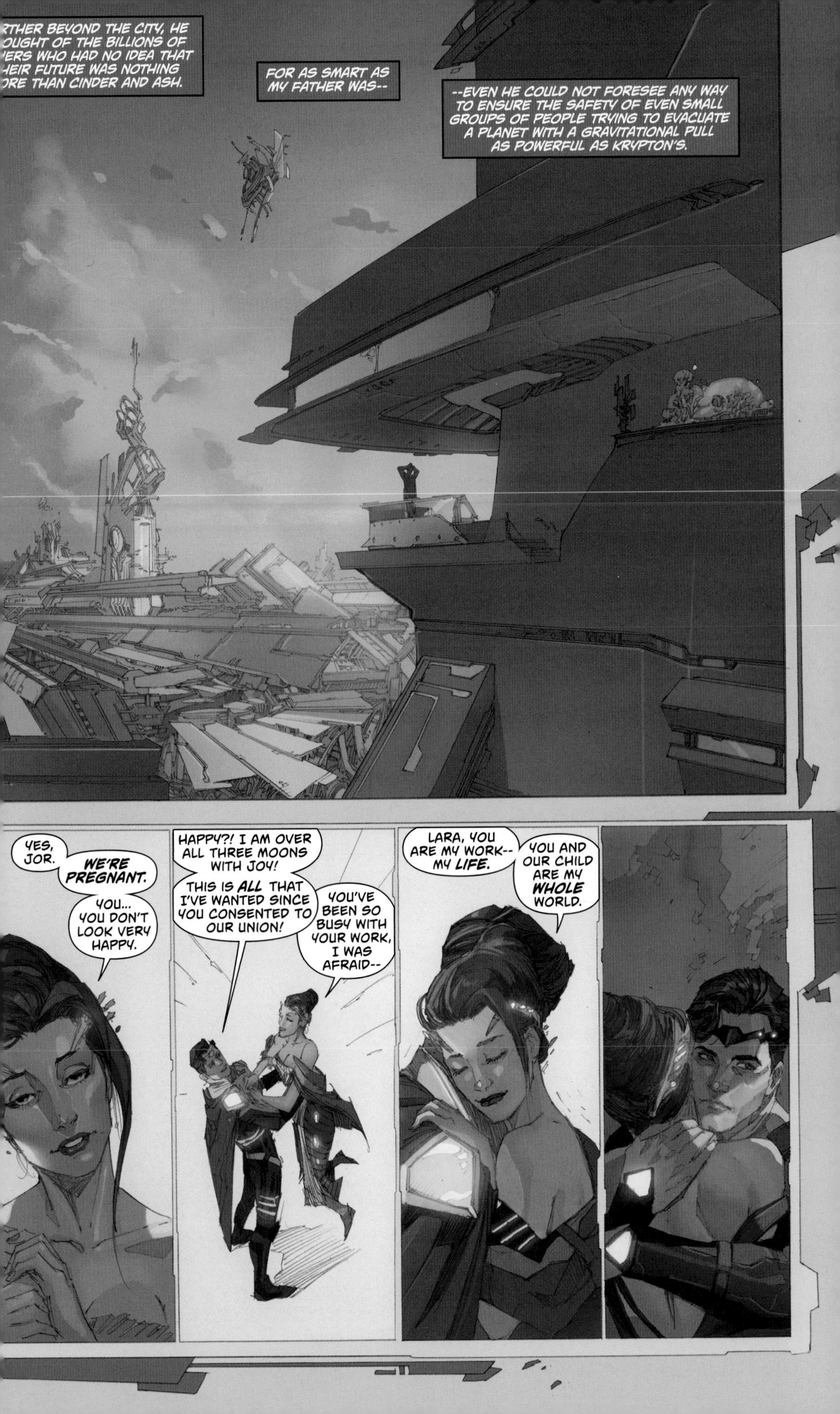
RTHER BEYOND THE CITY, HE OUGHT OF THE BILLIONS OF IERS WHO HAD NO IDEA THAT HEIR FUTURE WAS NOTHING ORE THAN CINDER AND ASH.
FOR AS SMART AS MY FATHER WAS--
--EVEN HE COULD NOT FORESEE ANY WAY TO ENSURE THE SAFETY OF EVEN SMALL GROUPS OF PEOPLE TRYING TO EVACUATE A PLANET WITH A GRAVITATIONAL PULL AS POWERFUL AS KRYPTON'S.
YES, JOR.
WE'RE PREGNANT.
YOU... YOU DON'T LOOK VERY HAPPY.
HAPPY?! I AM OVER ALL THREE MOONS WITH JOY!
THIS IS ALL THAT I'VE WANTED SINCE YOU CONSENTED TO OUR UNION!
YOU'VE BEEN SO BUSY WITH YOUR WORK, I WAS AFRAID--
LARA, YOU ARE MY WORK-- MY LIFE.
YOU AND OUR CHILD ARE MY WHOLE WORLD.

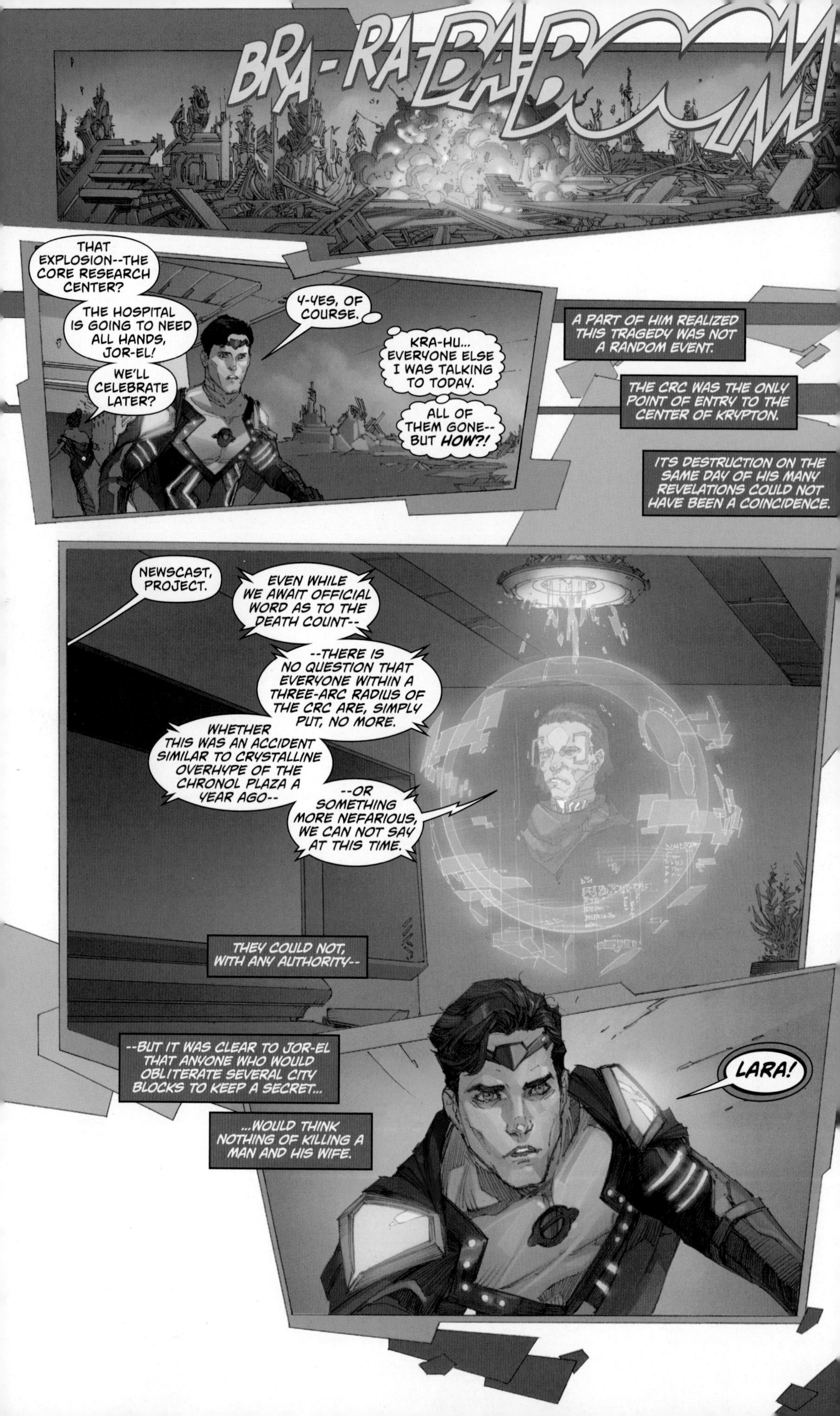
BRA-RA-BABOOM
THAT EXPLOSION--THE CORE RESEARCH CENTER?
THE HOSPITAL IS GOING TO NEED ALL HANDS, JOR-EL!
WE'LL CELEBRATE LATER?
Y-YES, OF COURSE.
KRA-HU... EVERYONE ELSE I WAS TALKING TO TODAY.
ALL OF THEM GONE--BUT HOW?!
A PART OF HIM REALIZED THIS TRAGEDY WAS NOT A RANDOM EVENT.
THE CRC WAS THE ONLY POINT OF ENTRY TO THE CENTER OF KRYPTON.
ITS DESTRUCTION ON THE SAME DAY OF HIS MANY REVELATIONS COULD NOT HAVE BEEN A COINCIDENCE.
NEWSCAST, PROJECT.
EVEN WHILE WE AWAIT OFFICIAL WORD AS TO THE DEATH COUNT--
--THERE IS NO QUESTION THAT EVERYONE WITHIN A THREE-ARC RADIUS OF THE CRC ARE, SIMPLY PUT, NO MORE.
WHETHER THIS WAS AN ACCIDENT SIMILAR TO CRYSTALLINE OVERHYPE OF THE CHRONOL PLAZA A YEAR AGO--
--OR SOMETHING MORE NEFARIOUS, WE CAN NOT SAY AT THIS TIME.
THEY COULD NOT, WITH ANY AUTHORITY--
--BUT IT WAS CLEAR TO JOR-EL THAT ANYONE WHO WOULD OBLITERATE SEVERAL CITY BLOCKS TO KEEP A SECRET...
...WOULD THINK NOTHING OF KILLING A MAN AND HIS WIFE.
LARA!

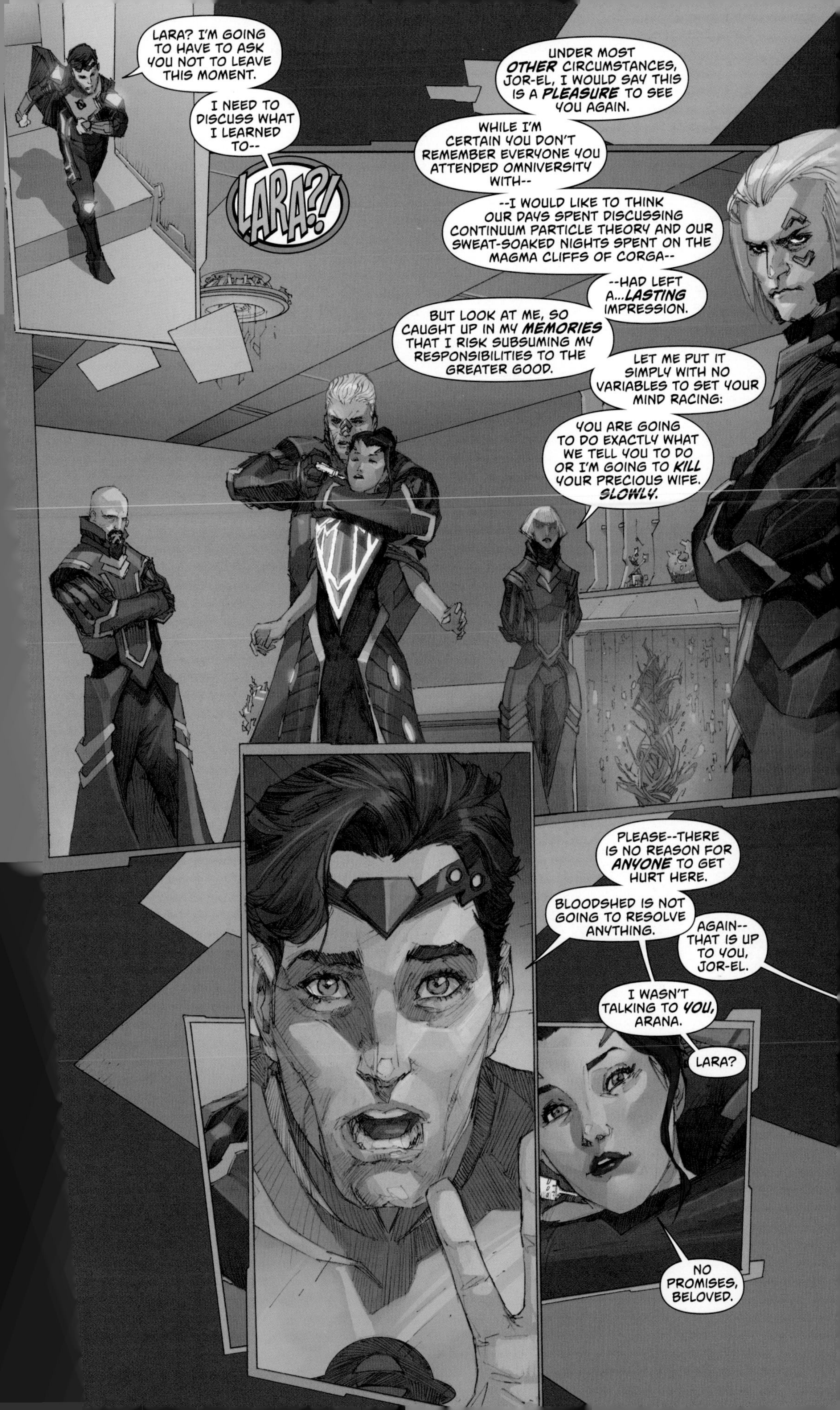

LARA? I'M GOING TO HAVE TO ASK YOU NOT TO LEAVE THIS MOMENT.
I NEED TO DISCUSS WHAT I LEARNED TO--
LARA?!
UNDER MOST OTHER CIRCUMSTANCES, JOR-EL, I WOULD SAY THIS IS A PLEASURE TO SEE YOU AGAIN.
WHILE I'M CERTAIN YOU DON'T REMEMBER EVERYONE YOU ATTENDED OMNIVERSITY WITH--
--I WOULD LIKE TO THINK OUR DAYS SPENT DISCUSSING CONTINUUM PARTICLE THEORY AND OUR SWEAT-SOAKED NIGHTS SPENT ON THE MAGMA CLIFFS OF CORGA--
--HAD LEFT A...LASTING IMPRESSION.
BUT LOOK AT ME, SO CAUGHT UP IN MY MEMORIES THAT I RISK SUBSUMING MY RESPONSIBILITIES TO THE GREATER GOOD.
LET ME PUT IT SIMPLY WITH NO VARIABLES TO SET YOUR MIND RACING:
YOU ARE GOING TO DO EXACTLY WHAT WE TELL YOU TO DO OR I'M GOING TO KILL YOUR PRECIOUS WIFE. SLOWLY.
PLEASE--THERE IS NO REASON FOR ANYONE TO GET HURT HERE.
BLOODSHED IS NOT GOING TO RESOLVE ANYTHING.
AGAIN--THAT IS UP TO YOU, JOR-EL.
I WASN'T TALKING TO YOU, ARANA.
LARA?
NO PROMISES, BELOVED.

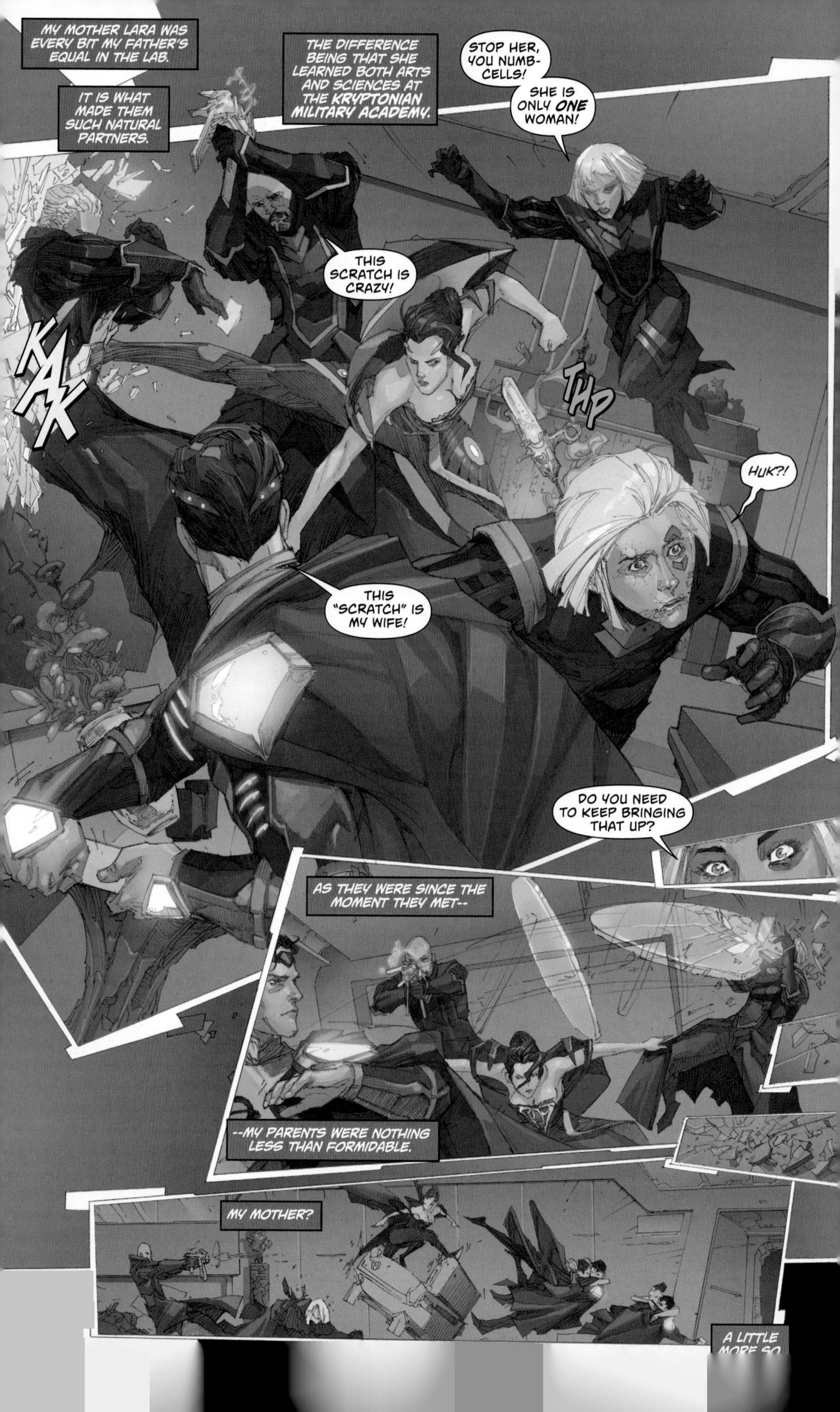
MY MOTHER LARA WAS EVERY BIT MY FATHER'S EQUAL IN THE LAB.
IT IS WHAT MADE THEM SUCH NATURAL PARTNERS.
THE DIFFERENCE BEING THAT SHE LEARNED BOTH ARTS AND SCIENCES AT THE KRYPTONIAN MILITARY ACADEMY.
STOP HER, YOU NUMB-CELLS!
SHE IS ONLY ONE WOMAN!
THIS SCRATCH IS CRAZY!
KAK
THP
HUK?!
THIS "SCRATCH" IS MY WIFE!
DO YOU NEED TO KEEP BRINGING THAT UP?
AS THEY WERE SINCE THE MOMENT THEY MET--
--MY PARENTS WERE NOTHING LESS THAN FORMIDABLE.
MY MOTHER?
A LITTLE MORE SO

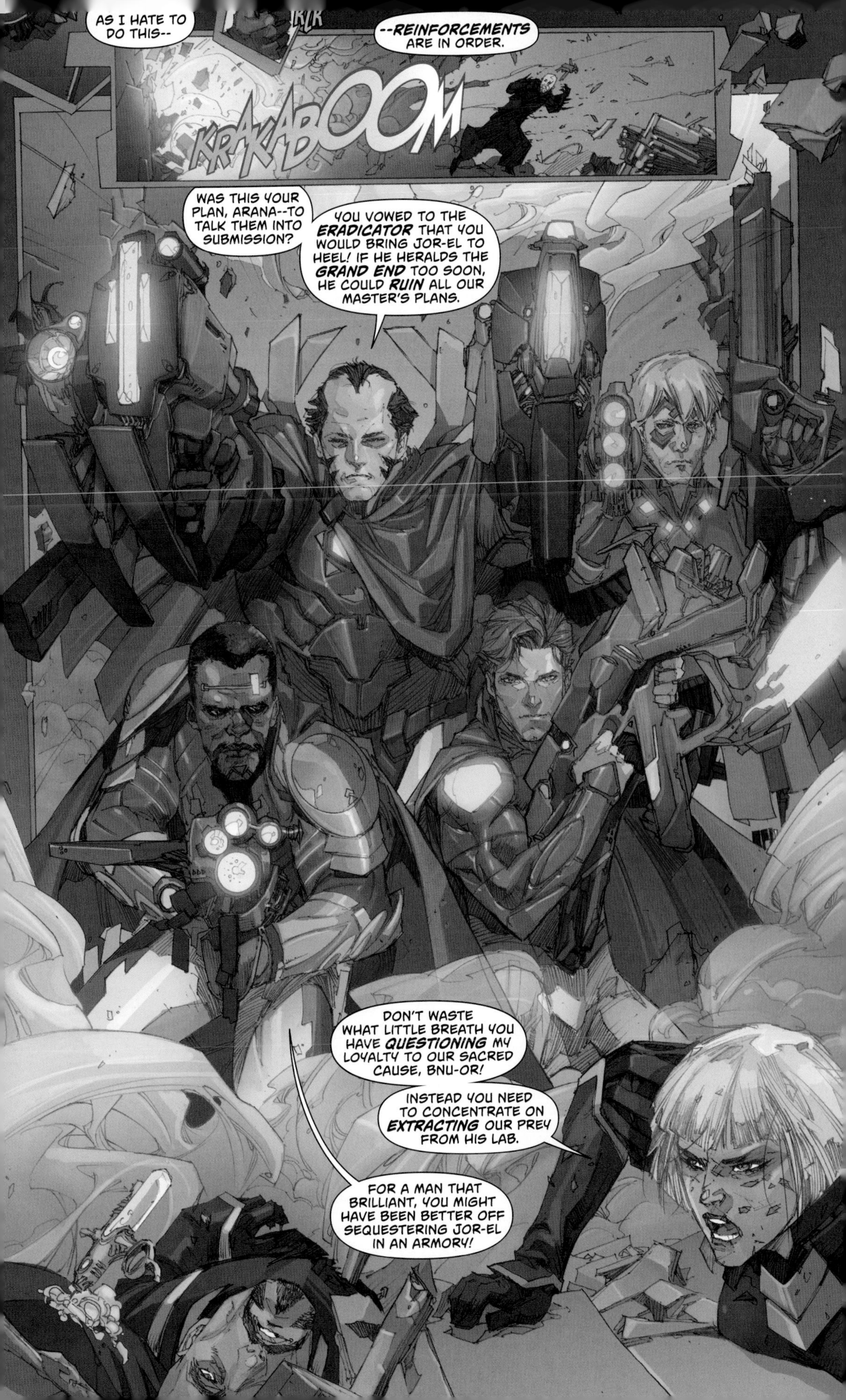
AS I HATE TO DO THIS--
--REINFORCEMENTS ARE IN ORDER.
KRAKABOOM
WAS THIS YOUR PLAN, ARANA--TO TALK THEM INTO SUBMISSION?
YOU VOWED TO THE ERADICATOR THAT YOU WOULD BRING JOR-EL TO HEEL! IF HE HERALDS THE GRAND END TOO SOON, HE COULD RUIN ALL OUR MASTER'S PLANS.
DON'T WASTE WHAT LITTLE BREATH YOU HAVE QUESTIONING MY LOYALTY TO OUR SACRED CAUSE, BNU-OR!
INSTEAD YOU NEED TO CONCENTRATE ON EXTRACTING OUR PREY FROM HIS LAB.
FOR A MAN THAT BRILLIANT, YOU MIGHT HAVE BEEN BETTER OFF SEQUESTERING JOR-EL IN AN ARMORY!

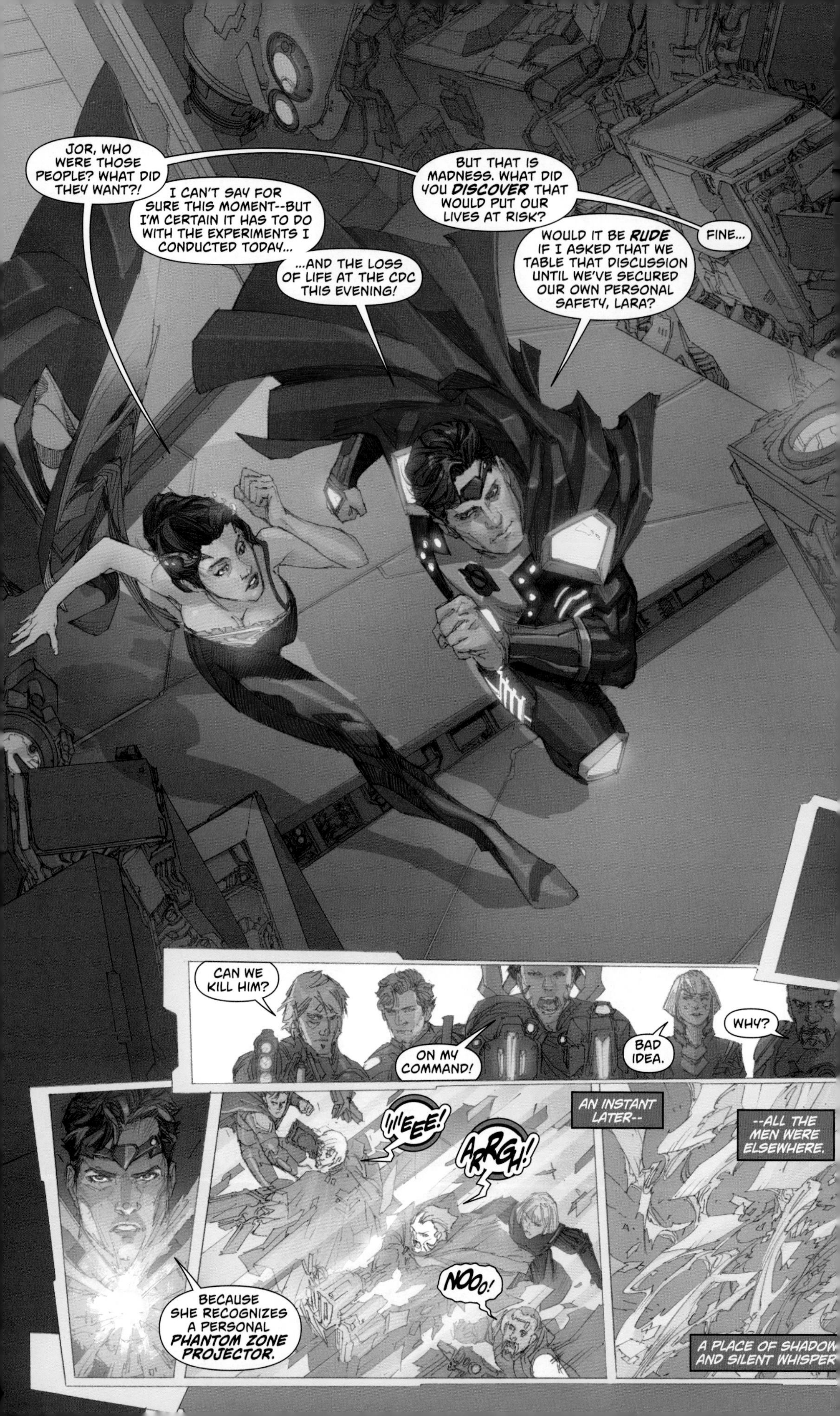
JOR, WHO WERE THOSE PEOPLE? WHAT DID THEY WANT?!
I CAN'T SAY FOR SURE THIS MOMENT--BUT I'M CERTAIN IT HAS TO DO WITH THE EXPERIMENTS I CONDUCTED TODAY...
...AND THE LOSS OF LIFE AT THE CDC THIS EVENING!
BUT THAT IS MADNESS. WHAT DID YOU DISCOVER THAT WOULD PUT OUR LIVES AT RISK?
WOULD IT BE RUDE IF I ASKED THAT WE TABLE THAT DISCUSSION UNTIL WE'VE SECURED OUR OWN PERSONAL SAFETY, LARA?
FINE...
CAN WE KILL HIM?
ON MY COMMAND!
BAD IDEA.
WHY?
BECAUSE SHE RECOGNIZES A PERSONAL PHANTOM ZONE PROJECTOR.
AN INSTANT LATER--
IIIEEE!
ARRGH!
NOOo!
--ALL THE MEN WERE ELSEWHERE.
A PLACE OF SHADOW AND SILENT WHISPER

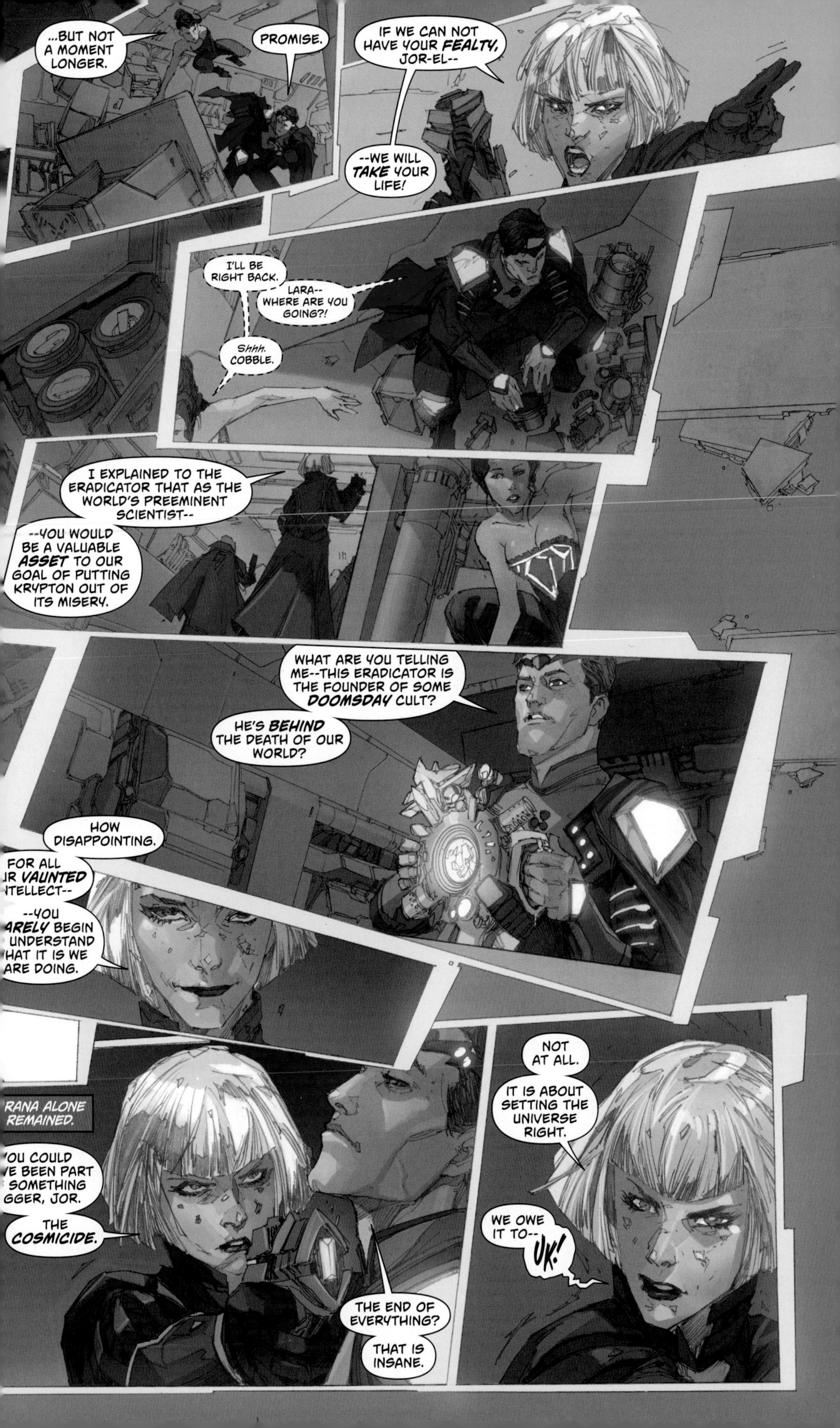

...BUT NOT A MOMENT LONGER.
PROMISE.
IF WE CAN NOT HAVE YOUR FEALTY, JOR-EL--
--WE WILL TAKE YOUR LIFE!
I'LL BE RIGHT BACK.
LARA-- WHERE ARE YOU GOING?!
Shhh. COBBLE.
I EXPLAINED TO THE ERADICATOR THAT AS THE WORLD'S PREEMINENT SCIENTIST--
--YOU WOULD BE A VALUABLE ASSET TO OUR GOAL OF PUTTING KRYPTON OUT OF ITS MISERY.
WHAT ARE YOU TELLING ME--THIS ERADICATOR IS THE FOUNDER OF SOME DOOMSDAY CULT?
HE'S BEHIND THE DEATH OF OUR WORLD?
HOW DISAPPOINTING.
FOR ALL R VAUNTED NTELLECT--
--YOU ARELY BEGIN UNDERSTAND HAT IT IS WE ARE DOING.
RANA ALONE REMAINED.
OU COULD E BEEN PART SOMETHING GGER, JOR.
THE COSMICIDE.
THE END OF EVERYTHING?
THAT IS INSANE.
NOT AT ALL.
IT IS ABOUT SETTING THE UNIVERSE RIGHT.
WE OWE IT TO--
UK!

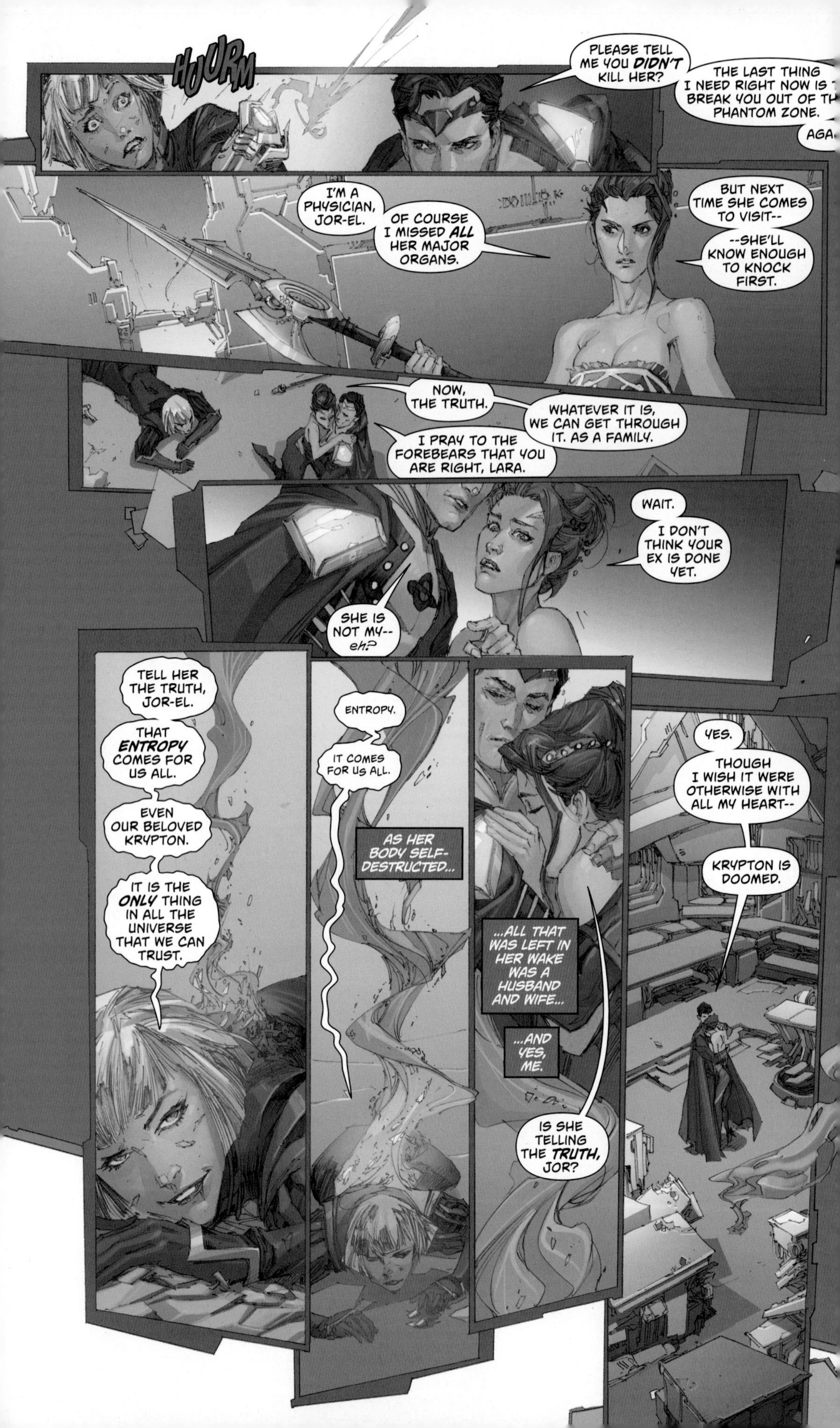
HUURM
PLEASE TELL ME YOU DIDN'T KILL HER?
THE LAST THING I NEED RIGHT NOW IS TO BREAK YOU OUT OF THE PHANTOM ZONE.
AGA
I'M A PHYSICIAN, JOR-EL.
OF COURSE I MISSED ALL HER MAJOR ORGANS.
BUT NEXT TIME SHE COMES TO VISIT--
--SHE'LL KNOW ENOUGH TO KNOCK FIRST.
NOW, THE TRUTH.
WHATEVER IT IS, WE CAN GET THROUGH IT. AS A FAMILY.
I PRAY TO THE FOREBEARS THAT YOU ARE RIGHT, LARA.
WAIT.
I DON'T THINK YOUR EX IS DONE YET.
SHE IS NOT MY-- eh?
TELL HER THE TRUTH, JOR-EL.
THAT ENTROPY COMES FOR US ALL.
EVEN OUR BELOVED KRYPTON.
IT IS THE ONLY THING IN ALL THE UNIVERSE THAT WE CAN TRUST.
ENTROPY.
IT COMES FOR US ALL.
AS HER BODY SELF-DESTRUCTED...
...ALL THAT WAS LEFT IN HER WAKE WAS A HUSBAND AND WIFE...
...AND YES, ME.
IS SHE TELLING THE TRUTH, JOR?
YES.
THOUGH I WISH IT WERE OTHERWISE WITH ALL MY HEART--
KRYPTON IS DOOMED.

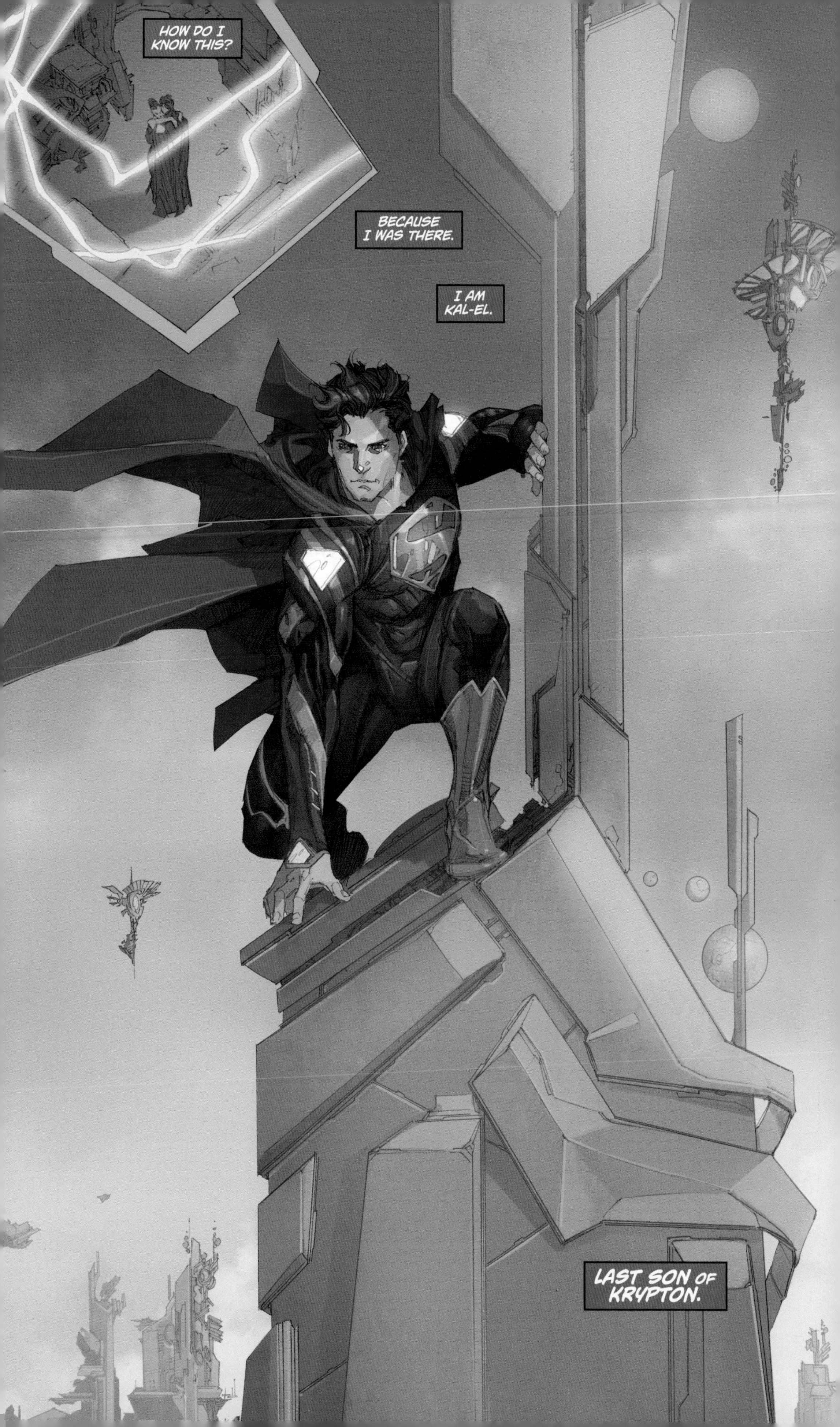
HOW DO I KNOW THIS?
BECAUSE I WAS THERE.
I AM KAL-EL.
LAST SON OF KRYPTON.

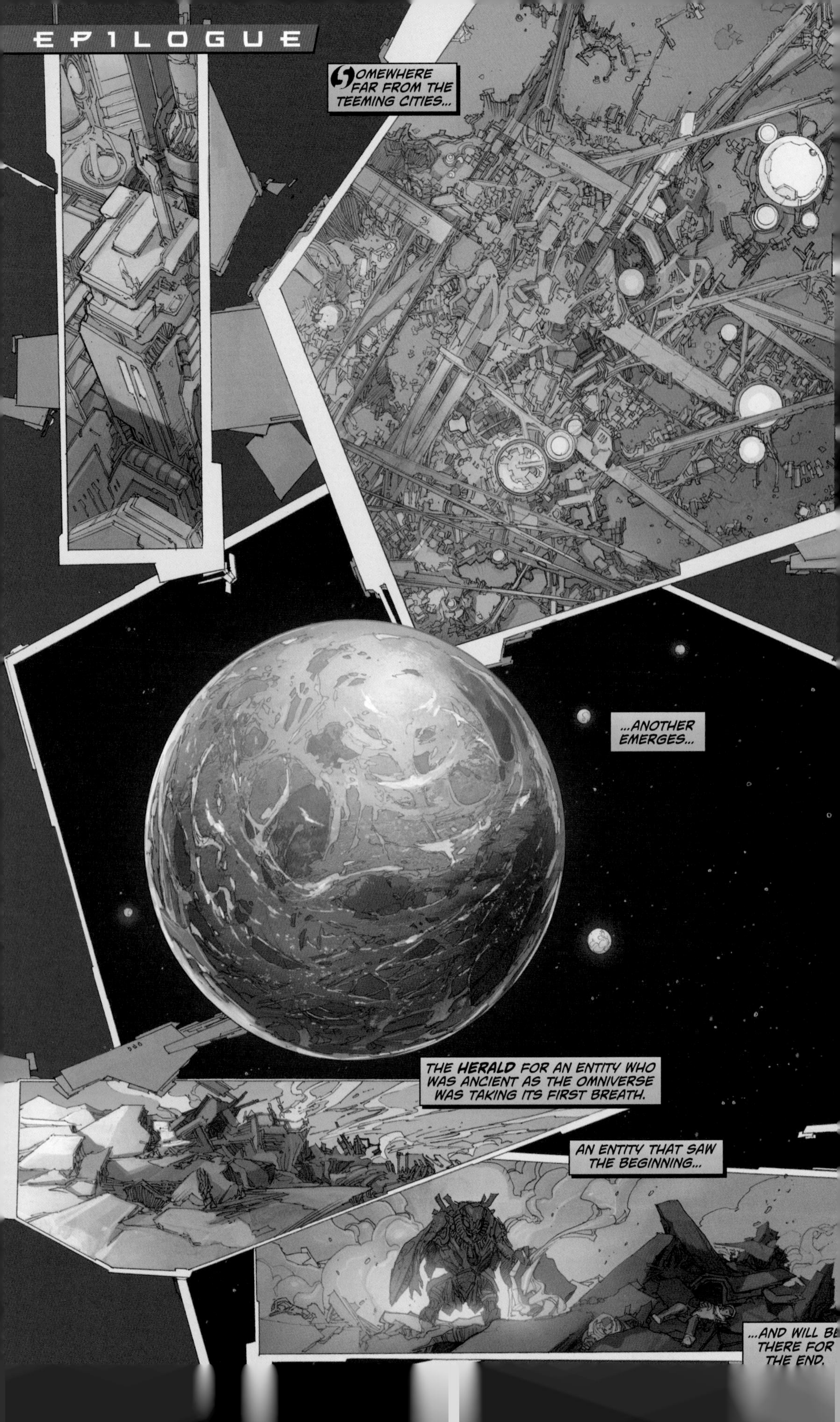
EPILOGUE
SOMEWHERE FAR FROM THE TEEMING CITIES...
...ANOTHER EMERGES...
THE HERALD FOR AN ENTITY WHO WAS ANCIENT AS THE OMNIVERSE WAS TAKING ITS FIRST BREATH.
AN ENTITY THAT SAW THE BEGINNING...
...AND WILL BE THERE FOR THE END.

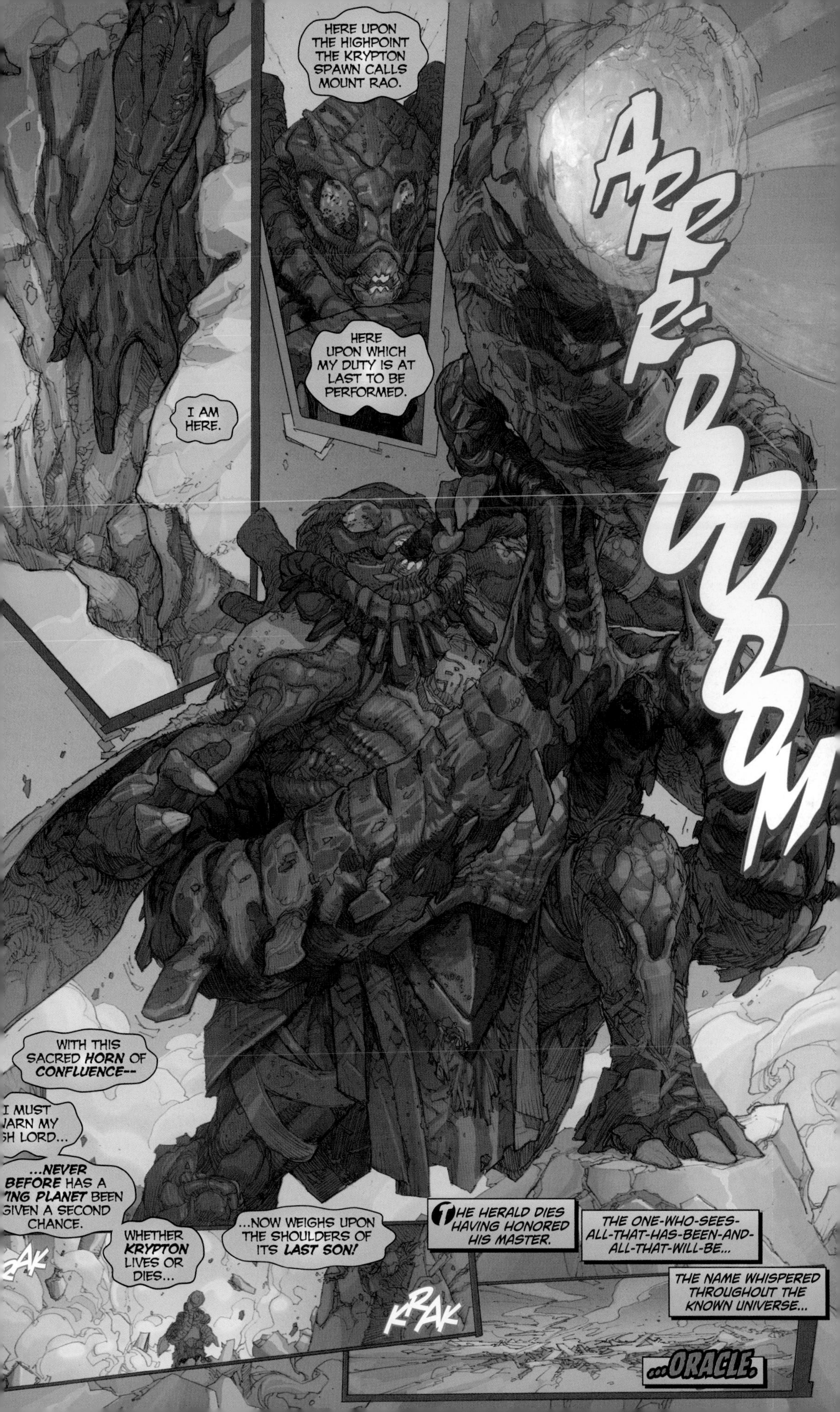
HERE UPON THE HIGHPOINT THE KRYPTON SPAWN CALLS MOUNT RAO.
HERE UPON WHICH MY DUTY IS AT LAST TO BE PERFORMED.
I AM HERE.
ARRR-RROOOOOM
WITH THIS SACRED HORN OF CONFLUENCE--
I MUST WARN MY LORD...
...NEVER BEFORE HAS A PLANET BEEN GIVEN A SECOND CHANCE.
WHETHER KRYPTON LIVES OR DIES...
...NOW WEIGHS UPON THE SHOULDERS OF ITS LAST SON!
KRAK
KRAK
THE HERALD DIES HAVING HONORED HIS MASTER.
THE ONE-WHO-SEES-ALL-THAT-HAS-BEEN-AND-ALL-THAT-WILL-BE...
THE NAME WHISPERED THROUGHOUT THE KNOWN UNIVERSE...
...ORACLE.

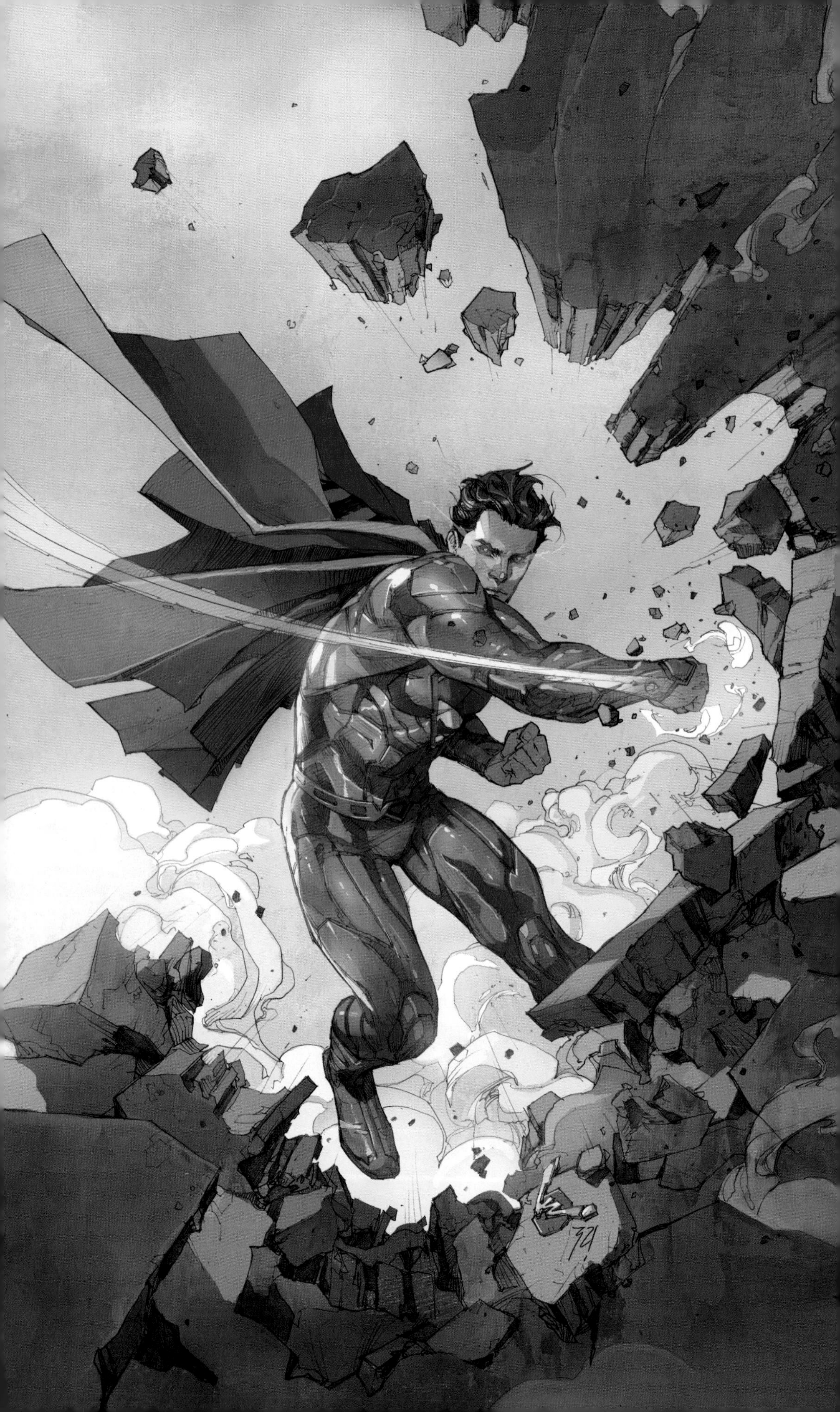

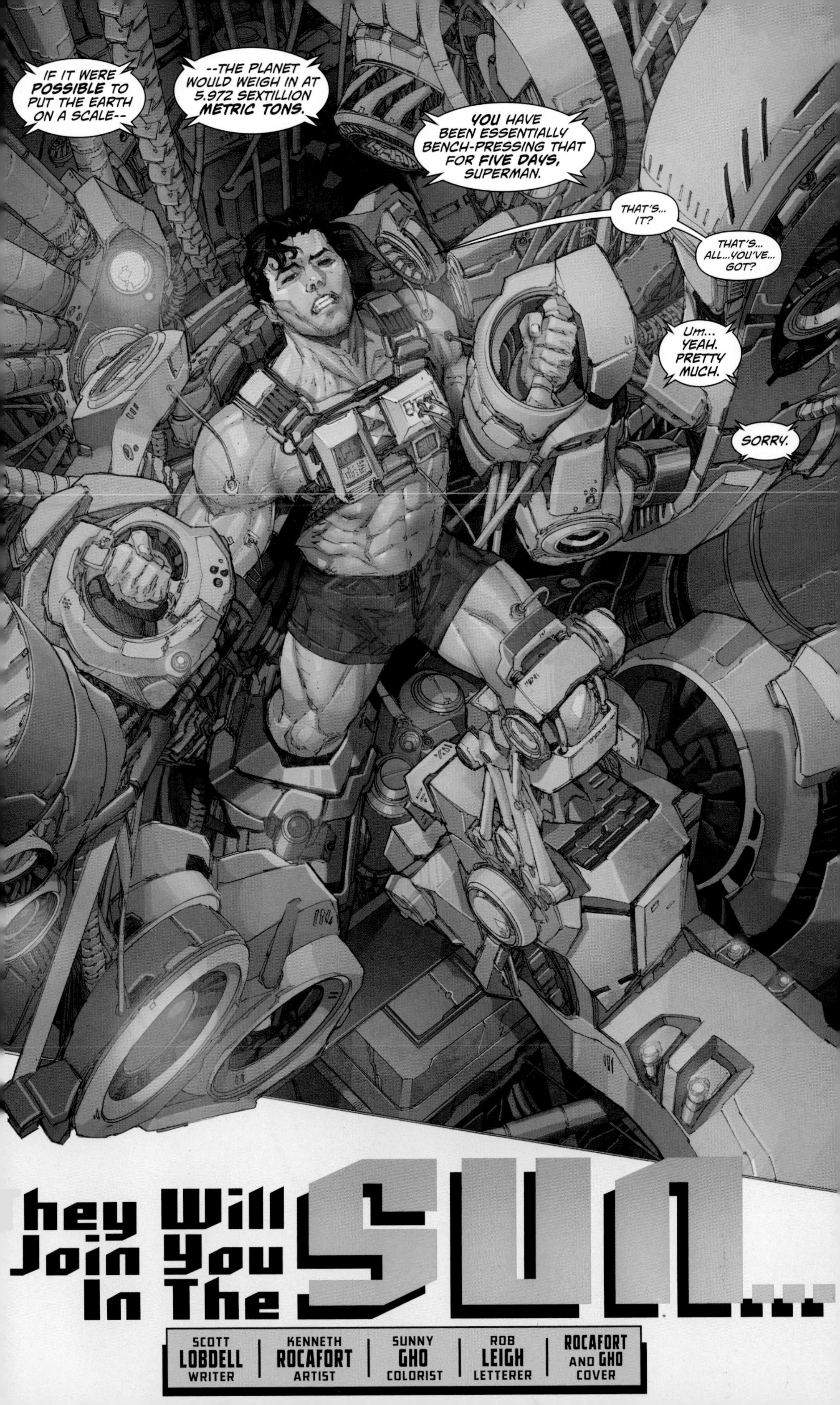
IF IT WERE POSSIBLE TO PUT THE EARTH ON A SCALE--
--THE PLANET WOULD WEIGH IN AT 5.972 SEXTILLION METRIC TONS.
YOU HAVE BEEN ESSENTIALLY BENCH-PRESSING THAT FOR FIVE DAYS, SUPERMAN.
THAT'S... IT?
THAT'S... ALL...YOU'VE... GOT?
Um... YEAH. PRETTY MUCH.
SORRY.
hey Will Join You In The SUN...
SCOTT LOBDELL WRITER
KENNETH ROCAFORT ARTIST
SUNNY GHO COLORIST
ROB LEIGH LETTERER
ROCAFORT AND GHO COVER

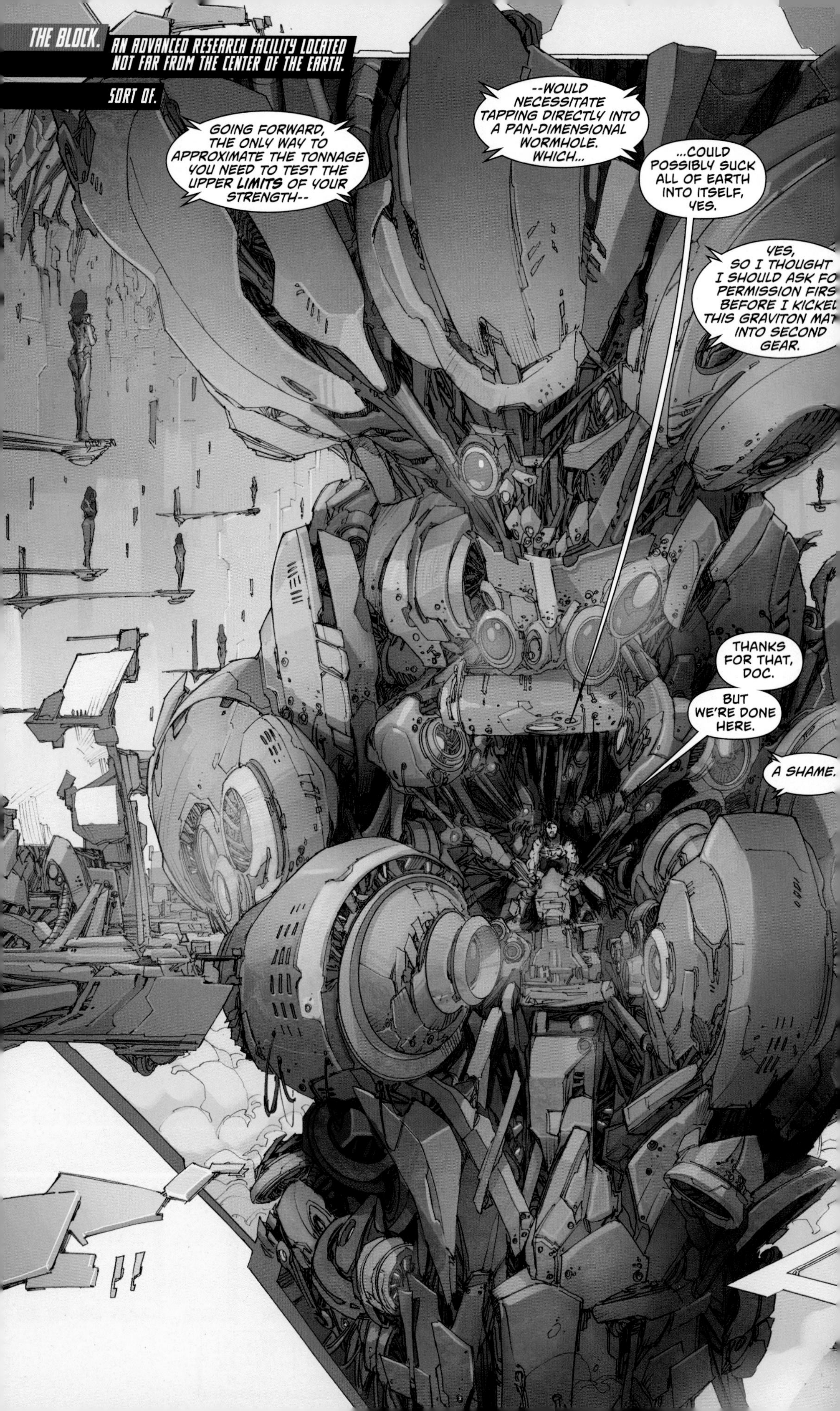
THE BLOCK. AN ADVANCED RESEARCH FACILITY LOCATED NOT FAR FROM THE CENTER OF THE EARTH.
SORT OF.
GOING FORWARD, THE ONLY WAY TO APPROXIMATE THE TONNAGE YOU NEED TO TEST THE UPPER LIMITS OF YOUR STRENGTH--
--WOULD NECESSITATE TAPPING DIRECTLY INTO A PAN-DIMENSIONAL WORMHOLE. WHICH...
...COULD POSSIBLY SUCK ALL OF EARTH INTO ITSELF, YES.
YES, SO I THOUGHT I SHOULD ASK FO PERMISSION FIRS BEFORE I KICKEI THIS GRAVITON MAT INTO SECOND GEAR.
THANKS FOR THAT, DOC.
BUT WE'RE DONE HERE.
A SHAME.

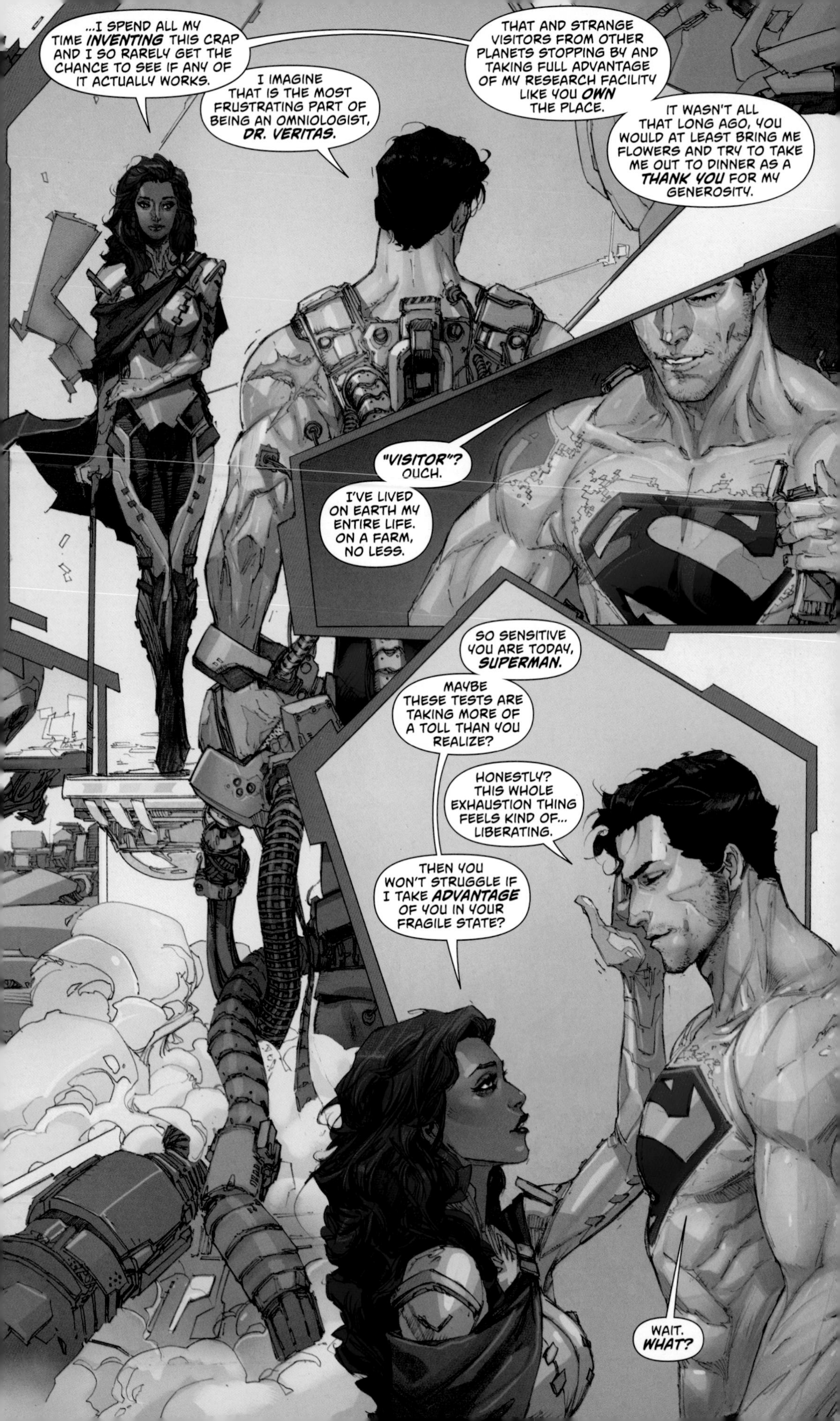
...I SPEND ALL MY TIME *INVENTING* THIS CRAP AND I SO RARELY GET THE CHANCE TO SEE IF ANY OF IT ACTUALLY WORKS.
I IMAGINE THAT IS THE MOST FRUSTRATING PART OF BEING AN OMNIOLOGIST, ***DR. VERITAS.***
THAT AND STRANGE VISITORS FROM OTHER PLANETS STOPPING BY AND TAKING FULL ADVANTAGE OF MY RESEARCH FACILITY LIKE YOU *OWN* THE PLACE.
IT WASN'T ALL THAT LONG AGO, YOU WOULD AT LEAST BRING ME FLOWERS AND TRY TO TAKE ME OUT TO DINNER AS A ***THANK YOU*** FOR MY GENEROSITY.
"VISITOR"? OUCH.
I'VE LIVED ON EARTH MY ENTIRE LIFE. ON A FARM, NO LESS.
SO SENSITIVE YOU ARE TODAY, ***SUPERMAN.***
MAYBE THESE TESTS ARE TAKING MORE OF A TOLL THAN YOU REALIZE?
HONESTLY? THIS WHOLE EXHAUSTION THING FEELS KIND OF... LIBERATING.
THEN YOU WON'T STRUGGLE IF I TAKE ***ADVANTAGE*** OF YOU IN YOUR FRAGILE STATE?
WAIT. ***WHAT?***

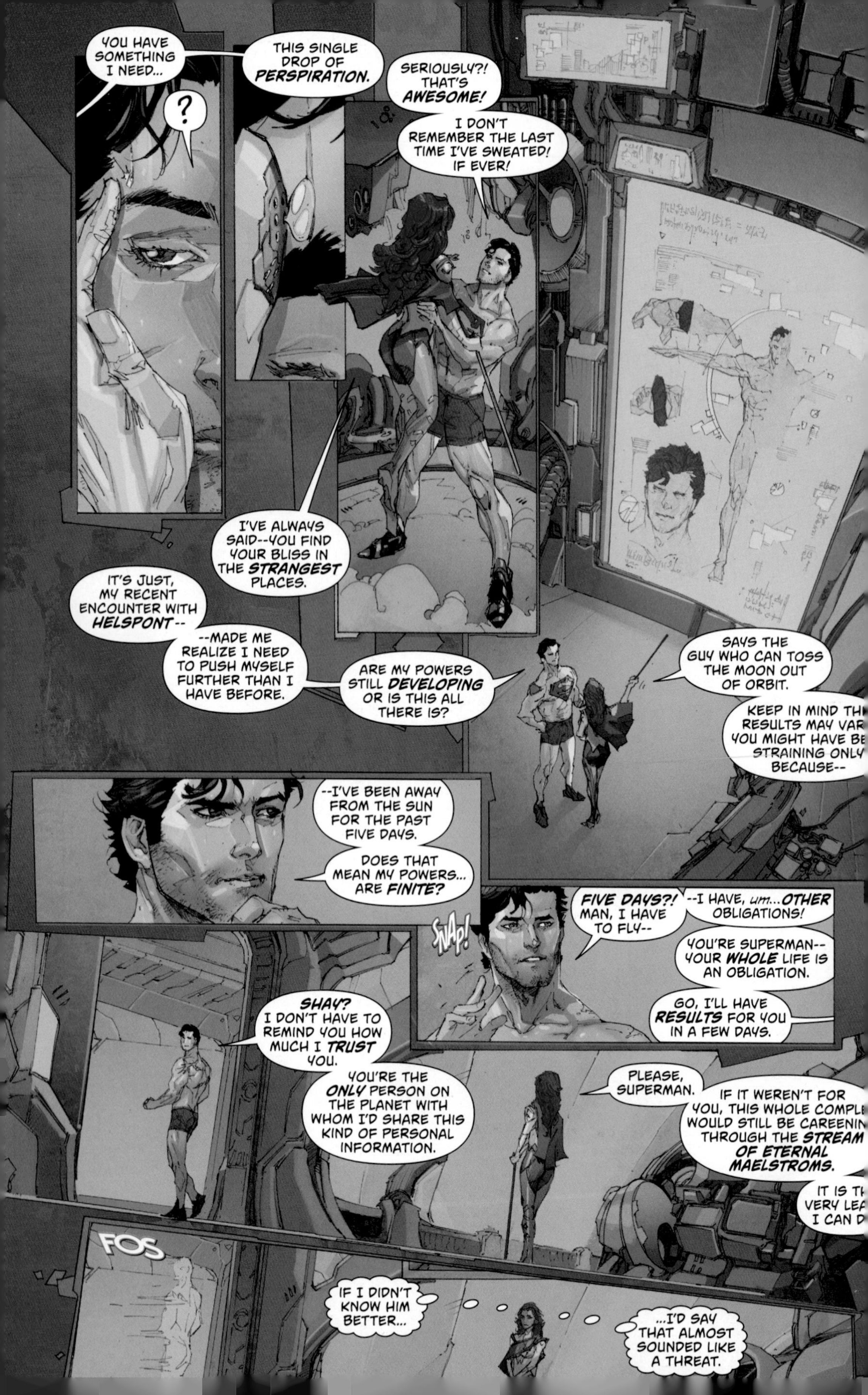

YOU HAVE SOMETHING I NEED...
THIS SINGLE DROP OF PERSPIRATION.
?
SERIOUSLY?! THAT'S AWESOME!
I DON'T REMEMBER THE LAST TIME I'VE SWEATED! IF EVER!
I'VE ALWAYS SAID--YOU FIND YOUR BLISS IN THE STRANGEST PLACES.
IT'S JUST, MY RECENT ENCOUNTER WITH HELSPONT--
--MADE ME REALIZE I NEED TO PUSH MYSELF FURTHER THAN I HAVE BEFORE.
ARE MY POWERS STILL DEVELOPING OR IS THIS ALL THERE IS?
SAYS THE GUY WHO CAN TOSS THE MOON OUT OF ORBIT.
KEEP IN MIND TH RESULTS MAY VAR YOU MIGHT HAVE BE STRAINING ONLY BECAUSE--
--I'VE BEEN AWAY FROM THE SUN FOR THE PAST FIVE DAYS.
DOES THAT MEAN MY POWERS... ARE FINITE?
SNAP!
FIVE DAYS?! MAN, I HAVE TO FLY--
--I HAVE, um...OTHER OBLIGATIONS!
YOU'RE SUPERMAN-- YOUR WHOLE LIFE IS AN OBLIGATION.
GO, I'LL HAVE RESULTS FOR YOU IN A FEW DAYS.
SHAY? I DON'T HAVE TO REMIND YOU HOW MUCH I TRUST YOU.
YOU'RE THE ONLY PERSON ON THE PLANET WITH WHOM I'D SHARE THIS KIND OF PERSONAL INFORMATION.
PLEASE, SUPERMAN.
IF IT WEREN'T FOR YOU, THIS WHOLE COMPLE WOULD STILL BE CAREENIN THROUGH THE STREAM OF ETERNAL MAELSTROMS.
IT IS T VERY LEA I CAN D
FOS
IF I DIDN'T KNOW HIM BETTER...
...I'D SAY THAT ALMOST SOUNDED LIKE A THREAT.

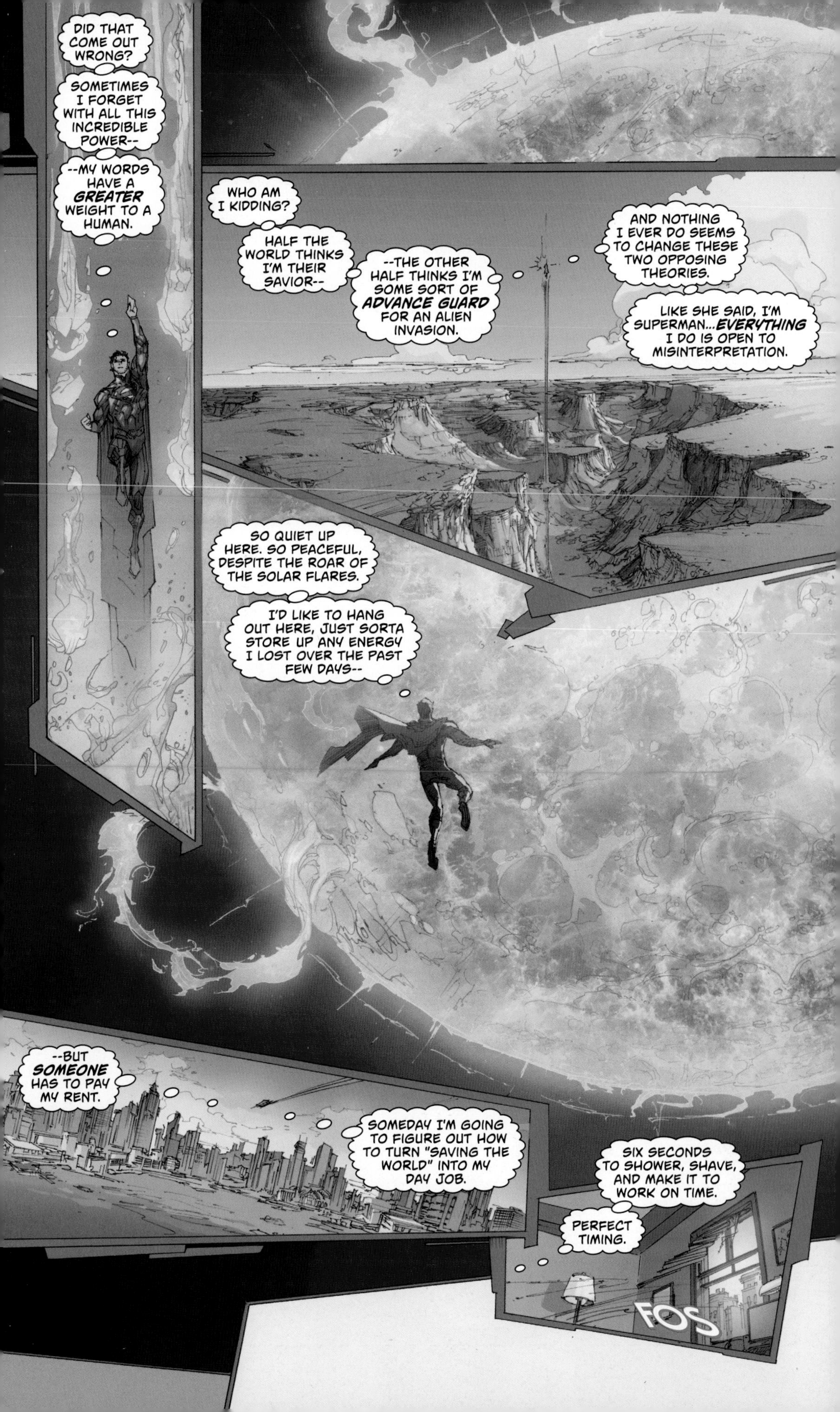
DID THAT COME OUT WRONG?
SOMETIMES I FORGET WITH ALL THIS INCREDIBLE POWER--
--MY WORDS HAVE A GREATER WEIGHT TO A HUMAN.
WHO AM I KIDDING?
HALF THE WORLD THINKS I'M THEIR SAVIOR--
--THE OTHER HALF THINKS I'M SOME SORT OF ADVANCE GUARD FOR AN ALIEN INVASION.
AND NOTHING I EVER DO SEEMS TO CHANGE THESE TWO OPPOSING THEORIES.
LIKE SHE SAID, I'M SUPERMAN...EVERYTHING I DO IS OPEN TO MISINTERPRETATION.
SO QUIET UP HERE. SO PEACEFUL, DESPITE THE ROAR OF THE SOLAR FLARES.
I'D LIKE TO HANG OUT HERE, JUST SORTA STORE UP ANY ENERGY I LOST OVER THE PAST FEW DAYS--
--BUT SOMEONE HAS TO PAY MY RENT.
SOMEDAY I'M GOING TO FIGURE OUT HOW TO TURN "SAVING THE WORLD" INTO MY DAY JOB.
SIX SECONDS TO SHOWER, SHAVE, AND MAKE IT TO WORK ON TIME.
PERFECT TIMING.
FOS

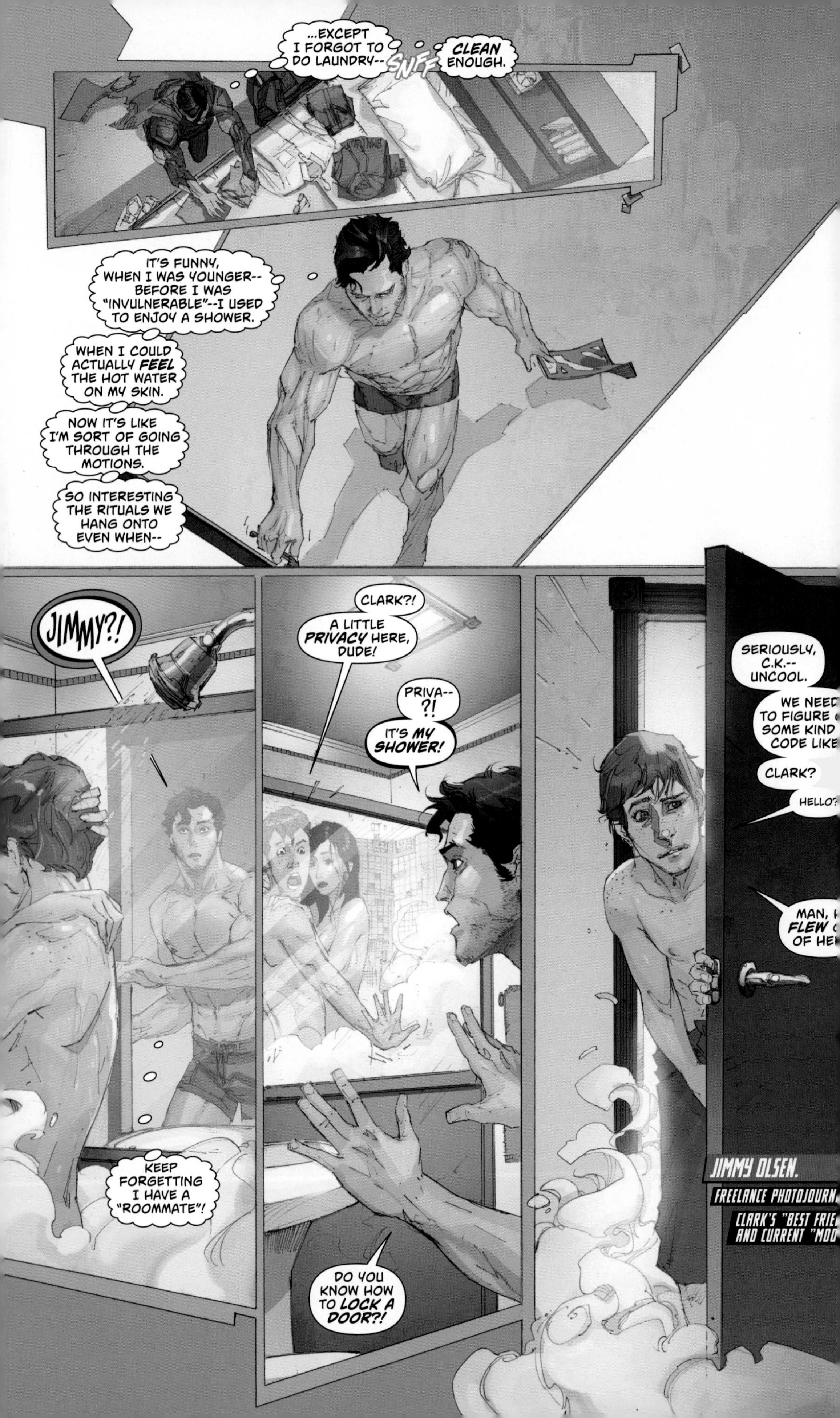

...EXCEPT I FORGOT TO DO LAUNDRY--
SNFF
CLEAN ENOUGH.
IT'S FUNNY, WHEN I WAS YOUNGER--BEFORE I WAS "INVULNERABLE"--I USED TO ENJOY A SHOWER.
WHEN I COULD ACTUALLY FEEL THE HOT WATER ON MY SKIN.
NOW IT'S LIKE I'M SORT OF GOING THROUGH THE MOTIONS.
SO INTERESTING THE RITUALS WE HANG ONTO EVEN WHEN--
JIMMY?!
KEEP FORGETTING I HAVE A "ROOMMATE"!
CLARK?!
A LITTLE PRIVACY HERE, DUDE!
PRIVA--?!
IT'S MY SHOWER!
DO YOU KNOW HOW TO LOCK A DOOR?!
SERIOUSLY, C.K.--UNCOOL.
CLARK?
JIMMY OLSEN.

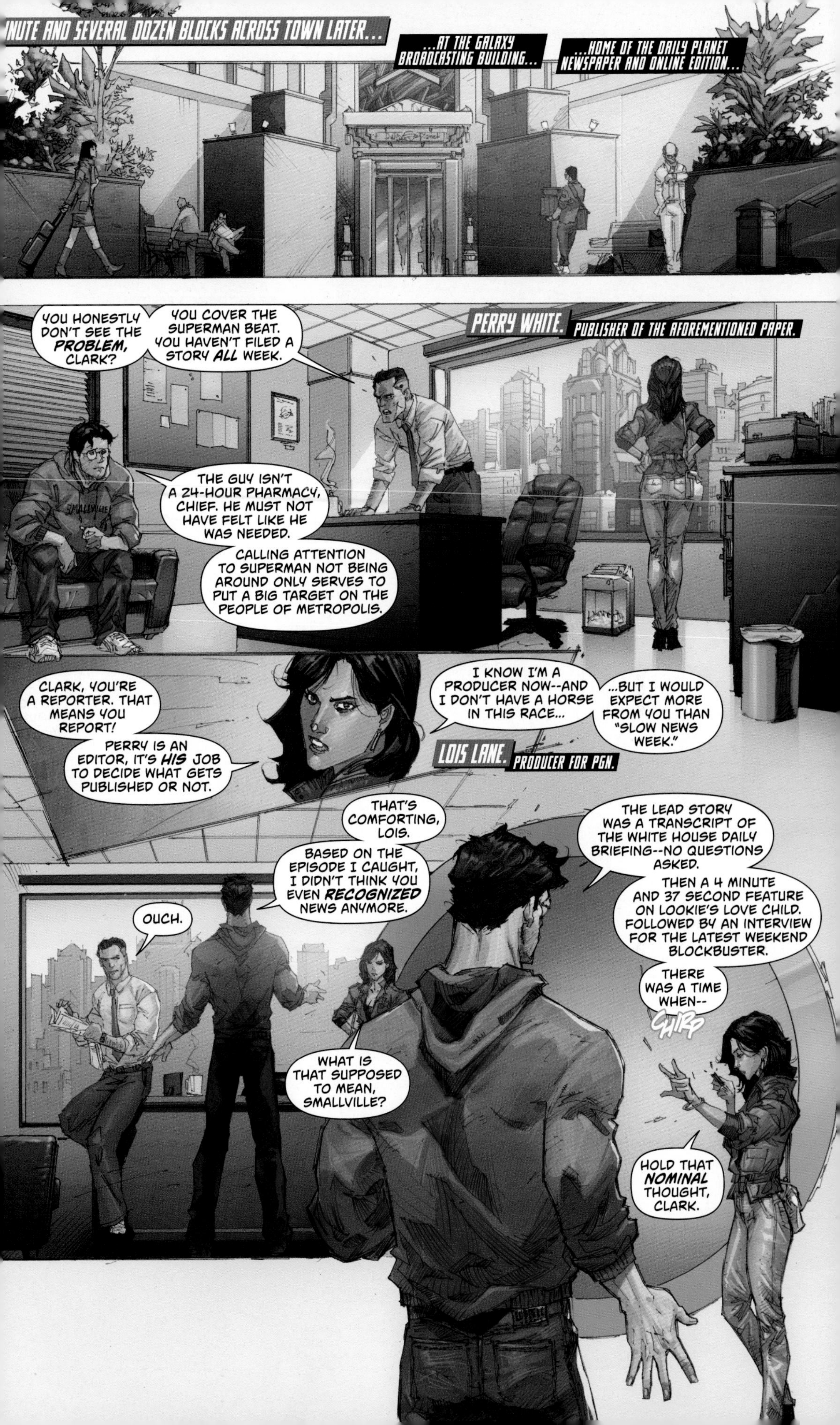
NUTE AND SEVERAL DOZEN BLOCKS ACROSS TOWN LATER...
...AT THE GALAXY BROADCASTING BUILDING...
...HOME OF THE DAILY PLANET NEWSPAPER AND ONLINE EDITION...
YOU HONESTLY DON'T SEE THE PROBLEM, CLARK?
YOU COVER THE SUPERMAN BEAT. YOU HAVEN'T FILED A STORY ALL WEEK.
PERRY WHITE. PUBLISHER OF THE AFOREMENTIONED PAPER.
THE GUY ISN'T A 24-HOUR PHARMACY, CHIEF. HE MUST NOT HAVE FELT LIKE HE WAS NEEDED.
CALLING ATTENTION TO SUPERMAN NOT BEING AROUND ONLY SERVES TO PUT A BIG TARGET ON THE PEOPLE OF METROPOLIS.
CLARK, YOU'RE A REPORTER. THAT MEANS YOU REPORT!
PERRY IS AN EDITOR, IT'S HIS JOB TO DECIDE WHAT GETS PUBLISHED OR NOT.
I KNOW I'M A PRODUCER NOW--AND I DON'T HAVE A HORSE IN THIS RACE...
...BUT I WOULD EXPECT MORE FROM YOU THAN "SLOW NEWS WEEK."
LOIS LANE. PRODUCER FOR PGN.
THAT'S COMFORTING, LOIS.
BASED ON THE EPISODE I CAUGHT, I DIDN'T THINK YOU EVEN RECOGNIZED NEWS ANYMORE.
OUCH.
THE LEAD STORY WAS A TRANSCRIPT OF THE WHITE HOUSE DAILY BRIEFING--NO QUESTIONS ASKED.
THEN A 4 MINUTE AND 37 SECOND FEATURE ON LOOKIE'S LOVE CHILD. FOLLOWED BY AN INTERVIEW FOR THE LATEST WEEKEND BLOCKBUSTER.
THERE WAS A TIME WHEN--
CHIRP
WHAT IS THAT SUPPOSED TO MEAN, SMALLVILLE?
HOLD THAT NOMINAL THOUGHT, CLARK.

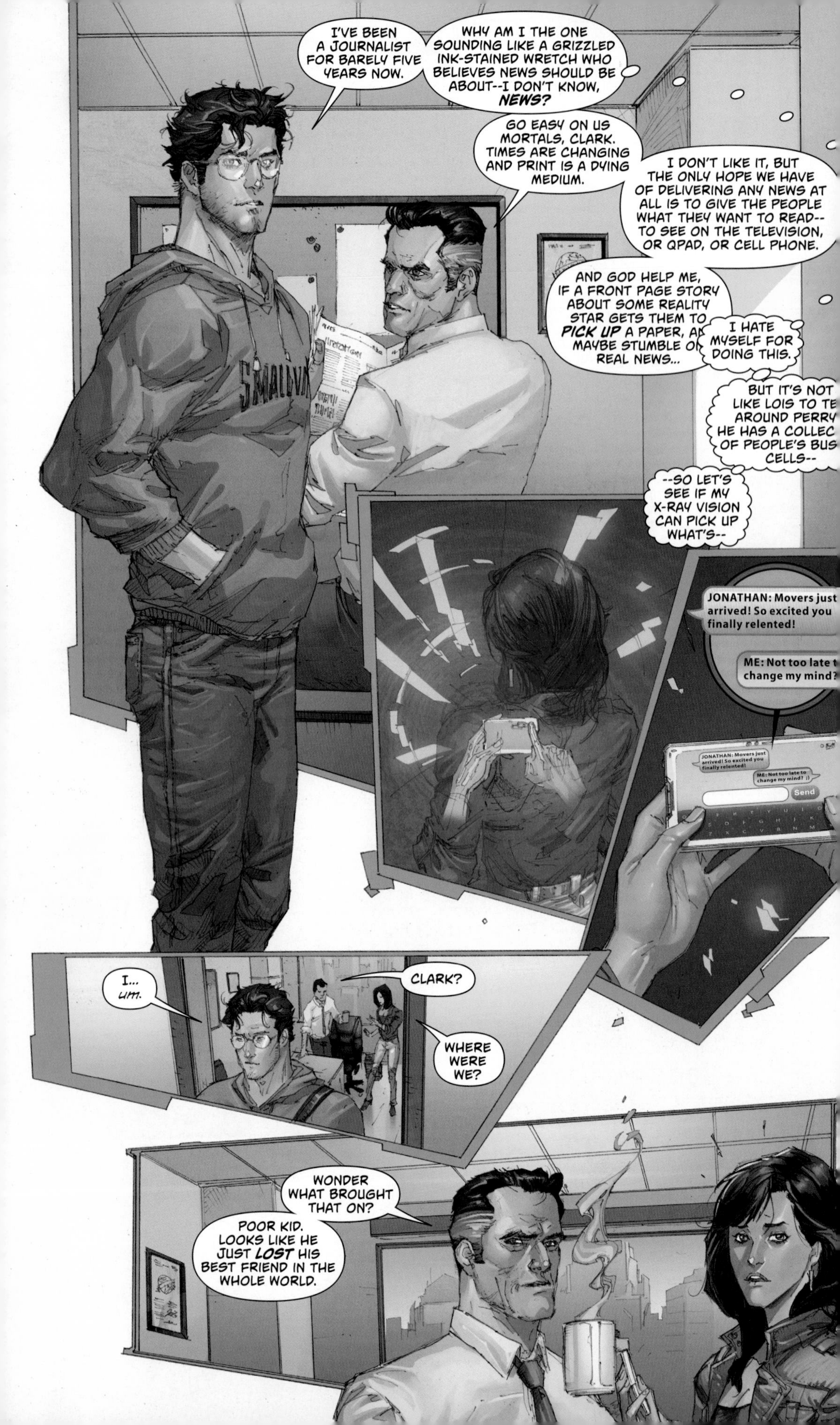
I'VE BEEN A JOURNALIST FOR BARELY FIVE YEARS NOW.
WHY AM I THE ONE SOUNDING LIKE A GRIZZLED INK-STAINED WRETCH WHO BELIEVES NEWS SHOULD BE ABOUT--I DON'T KNOW, NEWS?
GO EASY ON US MORTALS, CLARK. TIMES ARE CHANGING AND PRINT IS A DYING MEDIUM.
I DON'T LIKE IT, BUT THE ONLY HOPE WE HAVE OF DELIVERING ANY NEWS AT ALL IS TO GIVE THE PEOPLE WHAT THEY WANT TO READ-- TO SEE ON THE TELEVISION, OR QPAD, OR CELL PHONE.
AND GOD HELP ME, IF A FRONT PAGE STORY ABOUT SOME REALITY STAR GETS THEM TO PICK UP A PAPER, AN MAYBE STUMBLE ON REAL NEWS...
I HATE MYSELF FOR DOING THIS.
BUT IT'S NOT LIKE LOIS TO TE AROUND PERRY HE HAS A COLLEC OF PEOPLE'S BUS CELLS--
--SO LET'S SEE IF MY X-RAY VISION CAN PICK UP WHAT'S--
JONATHAN: Movers just arrived! So excited you finally relented!
ME: Not too late t change my mind?
Send
I... um.
CLARK?
WHERE WERE WE?
WONDER WHAT BROUGHT THAT ON?
POOR KID. LOOKS LIKE HE JUST LOST HIS BEST FRIEND IN THE WHOLE WORLD.

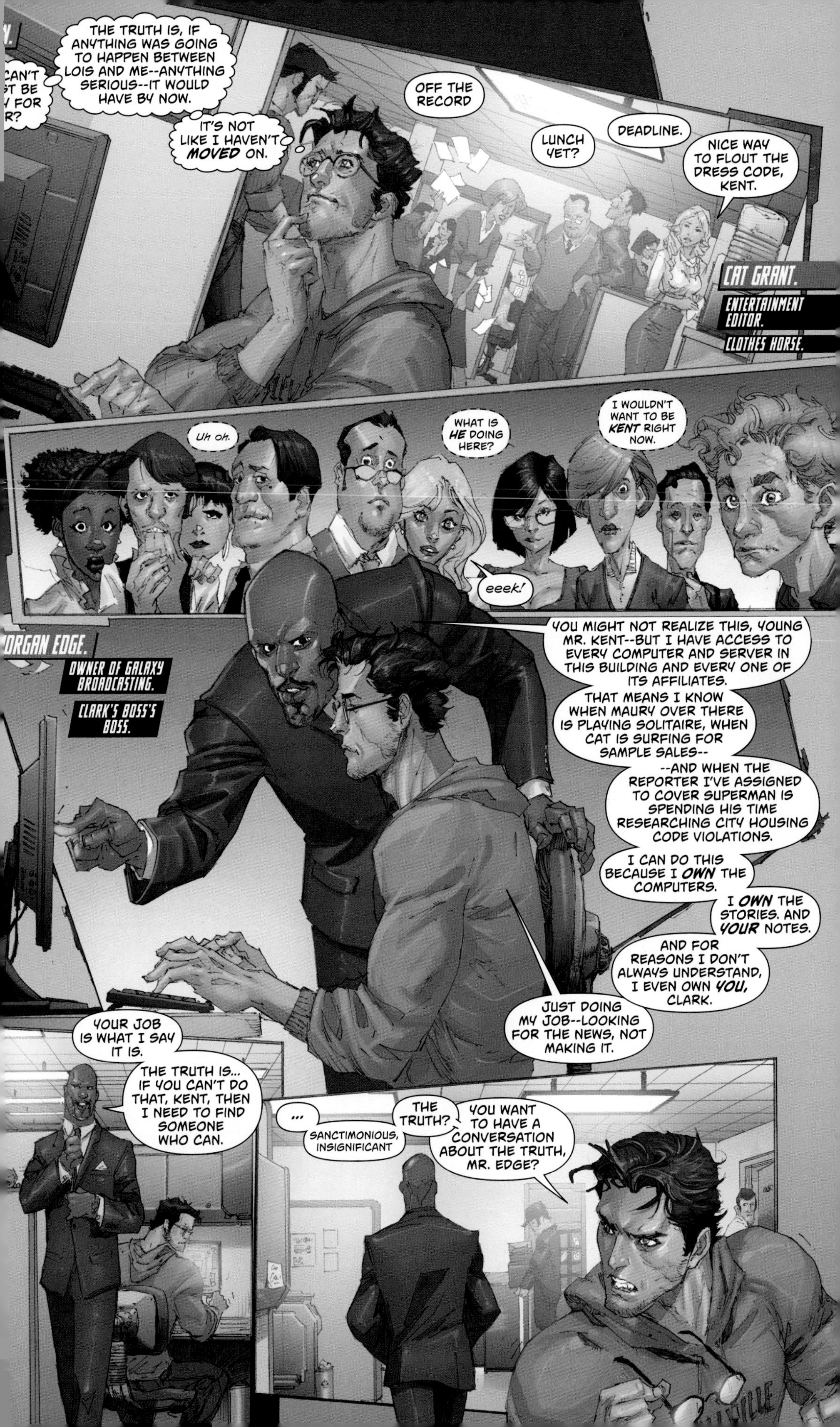

CAN'T
ST BE
FOR
R?
THE TRUTH IS, IF ANYTHING WAS GOING TO HAPPEN BETWEEN LOIS AND ME--ANYTHING SERIOUS--IT WOULD HAVE BY NOW.
IT'S NOT LIKE I HAVEN'T MOVED ON.
OFF THE RECORD
LUNCH YET?
DEADLINE.
NICE WAY TO FLOUT THE DRESS CODE, KENT.
CAT GRANT.
ENTERTAINMENT EDITOR.
CLOTHES HORSE.
Uh oh.
WHAT IS HE DOING HERE?
I WOULDN'T WANT TO BE KENT RIGHT NOW.
eeek!
ORGAN EDGE.
OWNER OF GALAXY BROADCASTING.
CLARK'S BOSS'S BOSS.
YOU MIGHT NOT REALIZE THIS, YOUNG MR. KENT--BUT I HAVE ACCESS TO EVERY COMPUTER AND SERVER IN THIS BUILDING AND EVERY ONE OF ITS AFFILIATES.
THAT MEANS I KNOW WHEN MAURY OVER THERE IS PLAYING SOLITAIRE, WHEN CAT IS SURFING FOR SAMPLE SALES--
--AND WHEN THE REPORTER I'VE ASSIGNED TO COVER SUPERMAN IS SPENDING HIS TIME RESEARCHING CITY HOUSING CODE VIOLATIONS.
I CAN DO THIS BECAUSE I OWN THE COMPUTERS.
I OWN THE STORIES. AND YOUR NOTES.
AND FOR REASONS I DON'T ALWAYS UNDERSTAND, I EVEN OWN YOU, CLARK.
JUST DOING MY JOB--LOOKING FOR THE NEWS, NOT MAKING IT.
YOUR JOB IS WHAT I SAY IT IS.
THE TRUTH IS... IF YOU CAN'T DO THAT, KENT, THEN I NEED TO FIND SOMEONE WHO CAN.
...
SANCTIMONIOUS, INSIGNIFICANT
THE TRUTH?
YOU WANT TO HAVE A CONVERSATION ABOUT THE TRUTH, MR. EDGE?

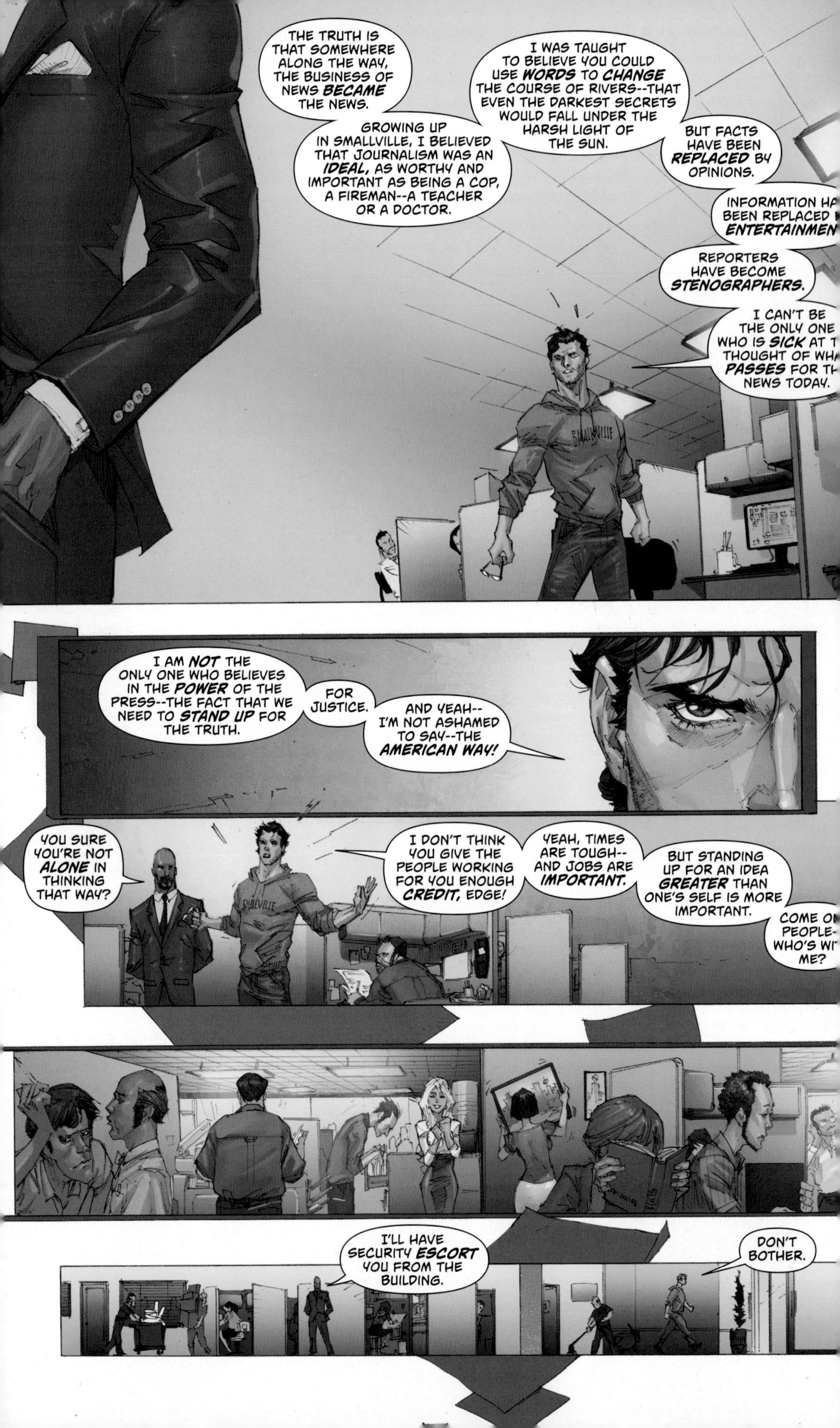
THE TRUTH IS THAT SOMEWHERE ALONG THE WAY, THE BUSINESS OF NEWS BECAME THE NEWS.
GROWING UP IN SMALLVILLE, I BELIEVED THAT JOURNALISM WAS AN IDEAL, AS WORTHY AND IMPORTANT AS BEING A COP, A FIREMAN--A TEACHER OR A DOCTOR.
I WAS TAUGHT TO BELIEVE YOU COULD USE WORDS TO CHANGE THE COURSE OF RIVERS--THAT EVEN THE DARKEST SECRETS WOULD FALL UNDER THE HARSH LIGHT OF THE SUN.
BUT FACTS HAVE BEEN REPLACED BY OPINIONS.
INFORMATION HA BEEN REPLACED ENTERTAINMEN
REPORTERS HAVE BECOME STENOGRAPHERS.
I CAN'T BE THE ONLY ONE WHO IS SICK AT T THOUGHT OF WH PASSES FOR TH NEWS TODAY.
I AM NOT THE ONLY ONE WHO BELIEVES IN THE POWER OF THE PRESS--THE FACT THAT WE NEED TO STAND UP FOR THE TRUTH.
FOR JUSTICE.
AND YEAH-- I'M NOT ASHAMED TO SAY--THE AMERICAN WAY!
YOU SURE YOU'RE NOT ALONE IN THINKING THAT WAY?
I DON'T THINK YOU GIVE THE PEOPLE WORKING FOR YOU ENOUGH CREDIT, EDGE!
YEAH, TIMES ARE TOUGH-- AND JOBS ARE IMPORTANT.
BUT STANDING UP FOR AN IDEA GREATER THAN ONE'S SELF IS MORE IMPORTANT.
COME O PEOPLE- WHO'S WI ME?
I'LL HAVE SECURITY ESCORT YOU FROM THE BUILDING.
DON'T BOTHER.

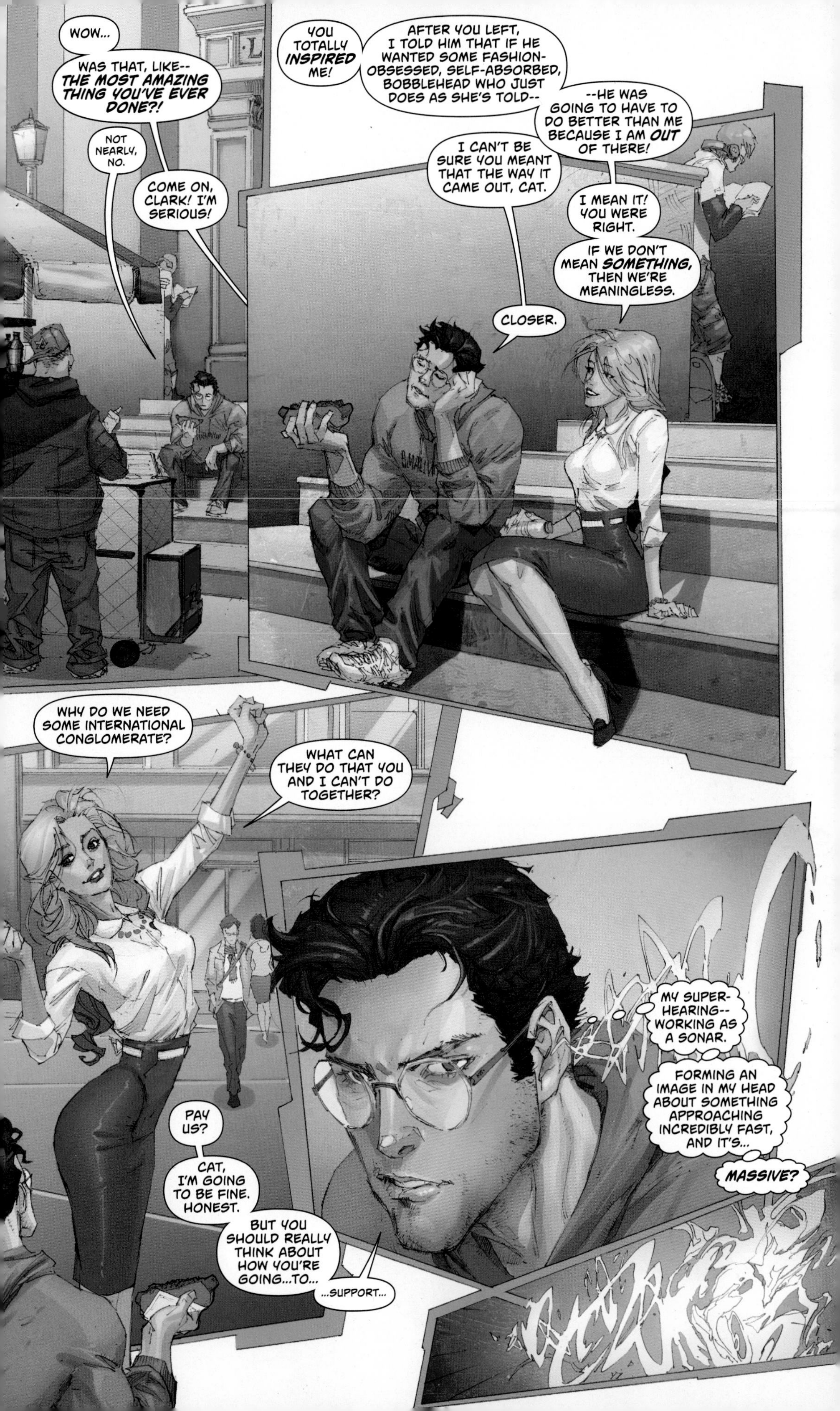
WOW...
WAS THAT, LIKE-- THE MOST AMAZING THING YOU'VE EVER DONE?!
NOT NEARLY, NO.
COME ON, CLARK! I'M SERIOUS!
YOU TOTALLY INSPIRED ME!
AFTER YOU LEFT, I TOLD HIM THAT IF HE WANTED SOME FASHION-OBSESSED, SELF-ABSORBED, BOBBLEHEAD WHO JUST DOES AS SHE'S TOLD--
--HE WAS GOING TO HAVE TO DO BETTER THAN ME BECAUSE I AM OUT OF THERE!
I CAN'T BE SURE YOU MEANT THAT THE WAY IT CAME OUT, CAT.
I MEAN IT! YOU WERE RIGHT.
IF WE DON'T MEAN SOMETHING, THEN WE'RE MEANINGLESS.
CLOSER.
WHY DO WE NEED SOME INTERNATIONAL CONGLOMERATE?
WHAT CAN THEY DO THAT YOU AND I CAN'T DO TOGETHER?
PAY US?
CAT, I'M GOING TO BE FINE. HONEST.
BUT YOU SHOULD REALLY THINK ABOUT HOW YOU'RE GOING...TO...
...SUPPORT...
MY SUPER-HEARING--WORKING AS A SONAR.
FORMING AN IMAGE IN MY HEAD ABOUT SOMETHING APPROACHING INCREDIBLY FAST, AND IT'S...
MASSIVE?

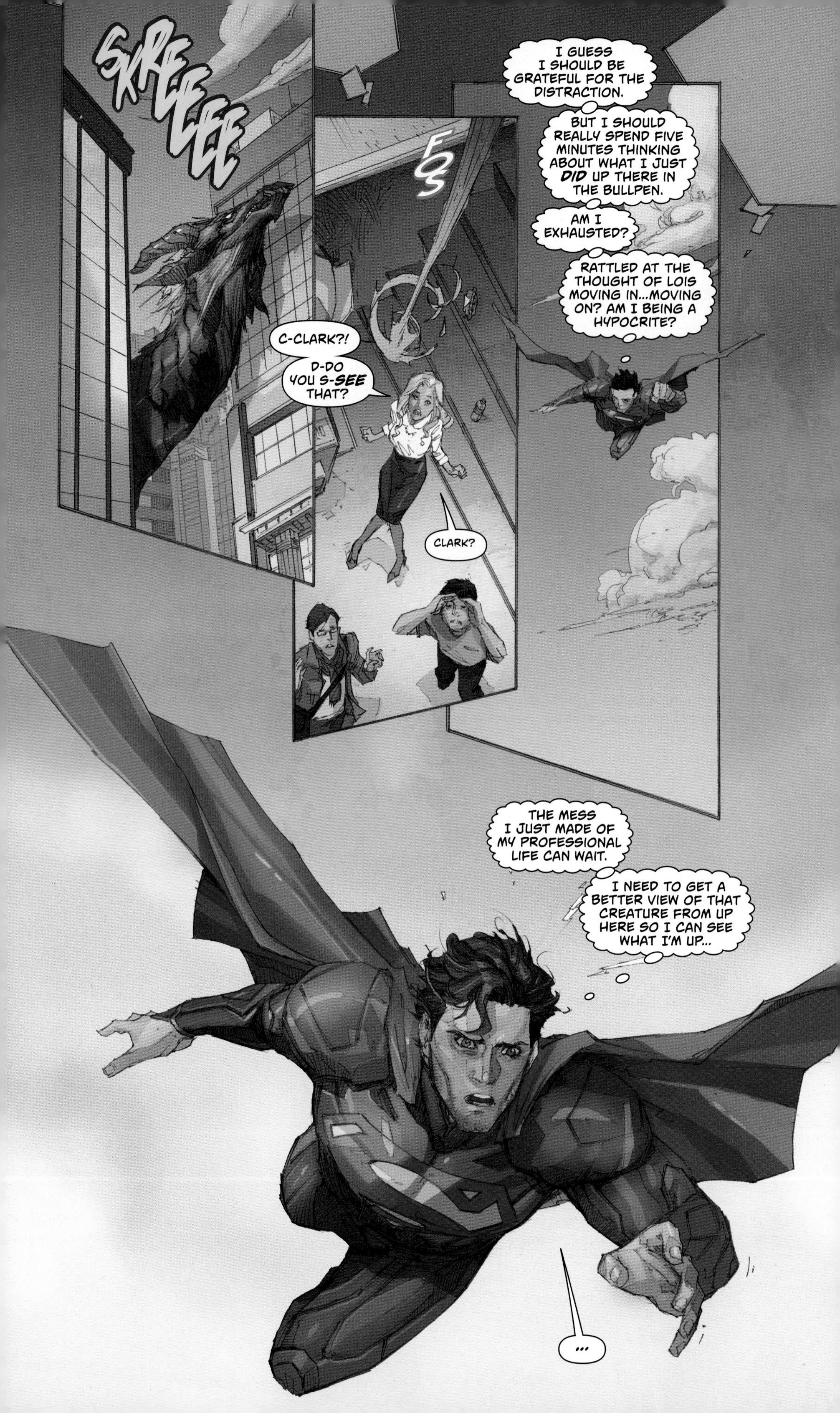
SKREEEEE
FOS
C-CLARK?!
D-DO YOU S-SEE THAT?
CLARK?
I GUESS I SHOULD BE GRATEFUL FOR THE DISTRACTION.
BUT I SHOULD REALLY SPEND FIVE MINUTES THINKING ABOUT WHAT I JUST DID UP THERE IN THE BULLPEN.
AM I EXHAUSTED?
RATTLED AT THE THOUGHT OF LOIS MOVING IN...MOVING ON? AM I BEING A HYPOCRITE?
THE MESS I JUST MADE OF MY PROFESSIONAL LIFE CAN WAIT.
I NEED TO GET A BETTER VIEW OF THAT CREATURE FROM UP HERE SO I CAN SEE WHAT I'M UP...
...

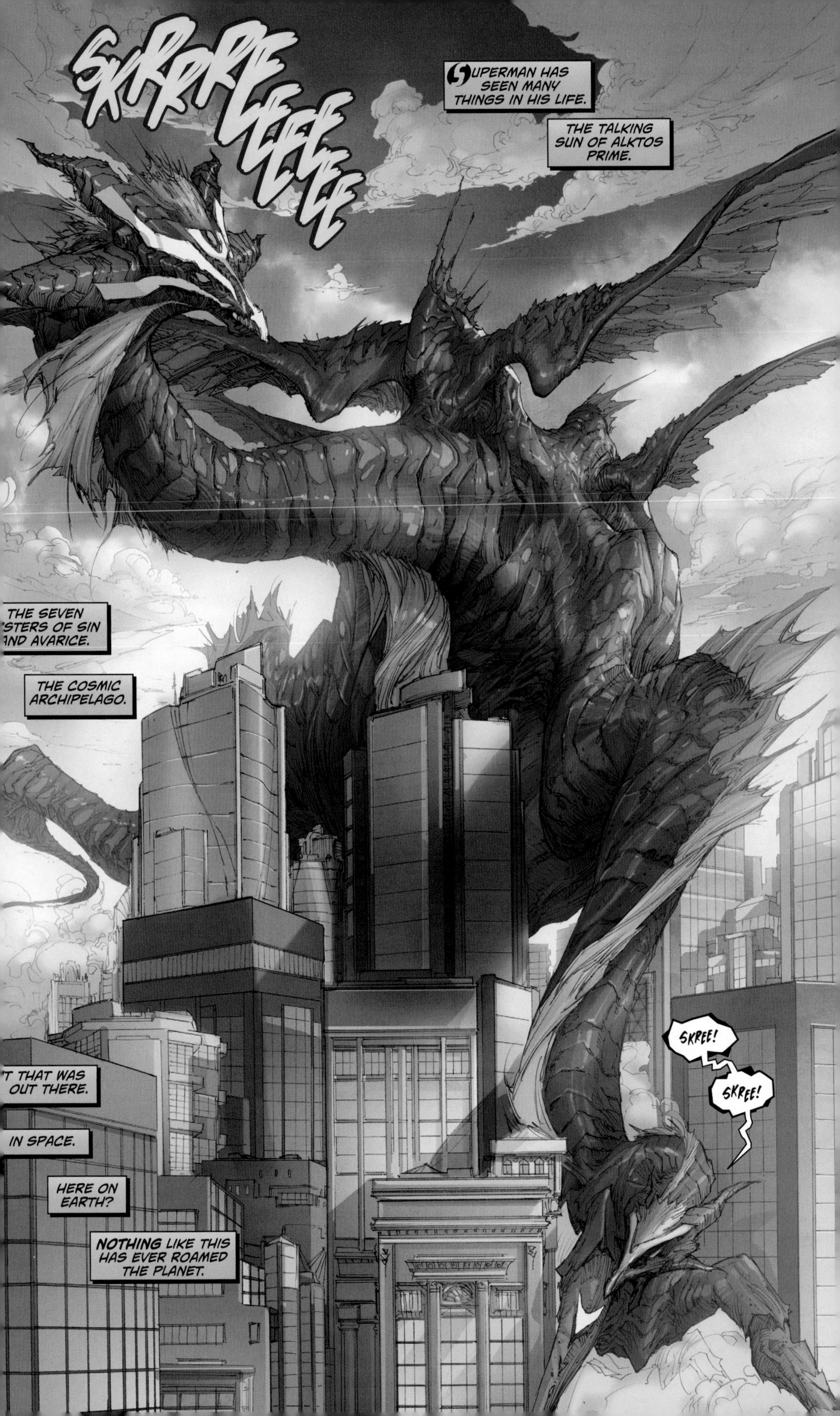
SKRRREEEEEEE
SUPERMAN HAS SEEN MANY THINGS IN HIS LIFE.
THE TALKING SUN OF ALKTOS PRIME.
THE SEVEN ...STERS OF SIN AND AVARICE.
THE COSMIC ARCHIPELAGO.
...T THAT WAS OUT THERE.
IN SPACE.
HERE ON EARTH?
NOTHING LIKE THIS HAS EVER ROAMED THE PLANET.
SKREE!
SKREE!

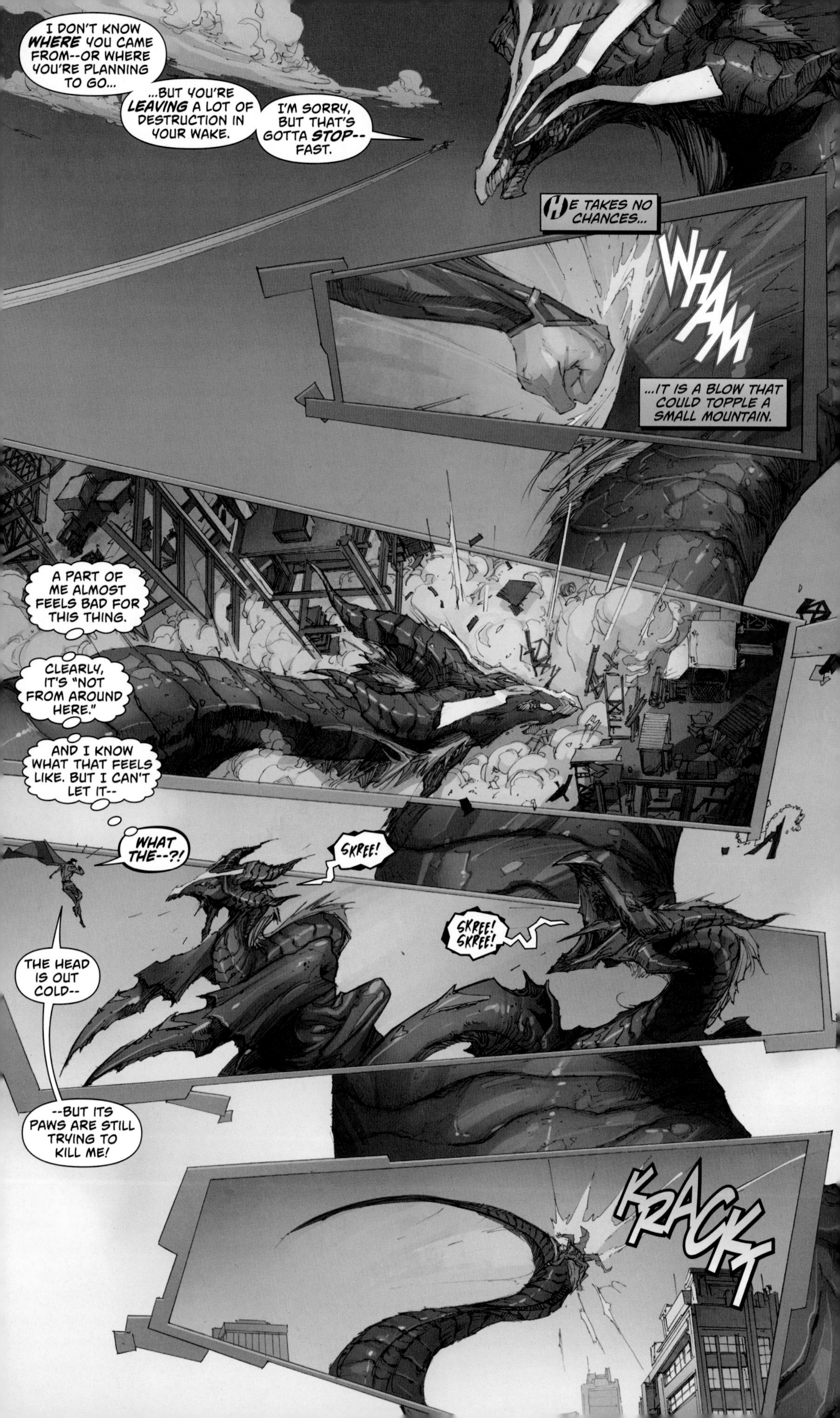

I DON'T KNOW WHERE YOU CAME FROM--OR WHERE YOU'RE PLANNING TO GO...
...BUT YOU'RE LEAVING A LOT OF DESTRUCTION IN YOUR WAKE.
I'M SORRY, BUT THAT'S GOTTA STOP--FAST.
HE TAKES NO CHANCES...
WHAM
...IT IS A BLOW THAT COULD TOPPLE A SMALL MOUNTAIN.
A PART OF ME ALMOST FEELS BAD FOR THIS THING.
CLEARLY, IT'S "NOT FROM AROUND HERE."
AND I KNOW WHAT THAT FEELS LIKE. BUT I CAN'T LET IT--
WHAT THE--?!
SKREE!
SKREE! SKREE!
THE HEAD IS OUT COLD--
--BUT ITS PAWS ARE STILL TRYING TO KILL ME!
KRACK

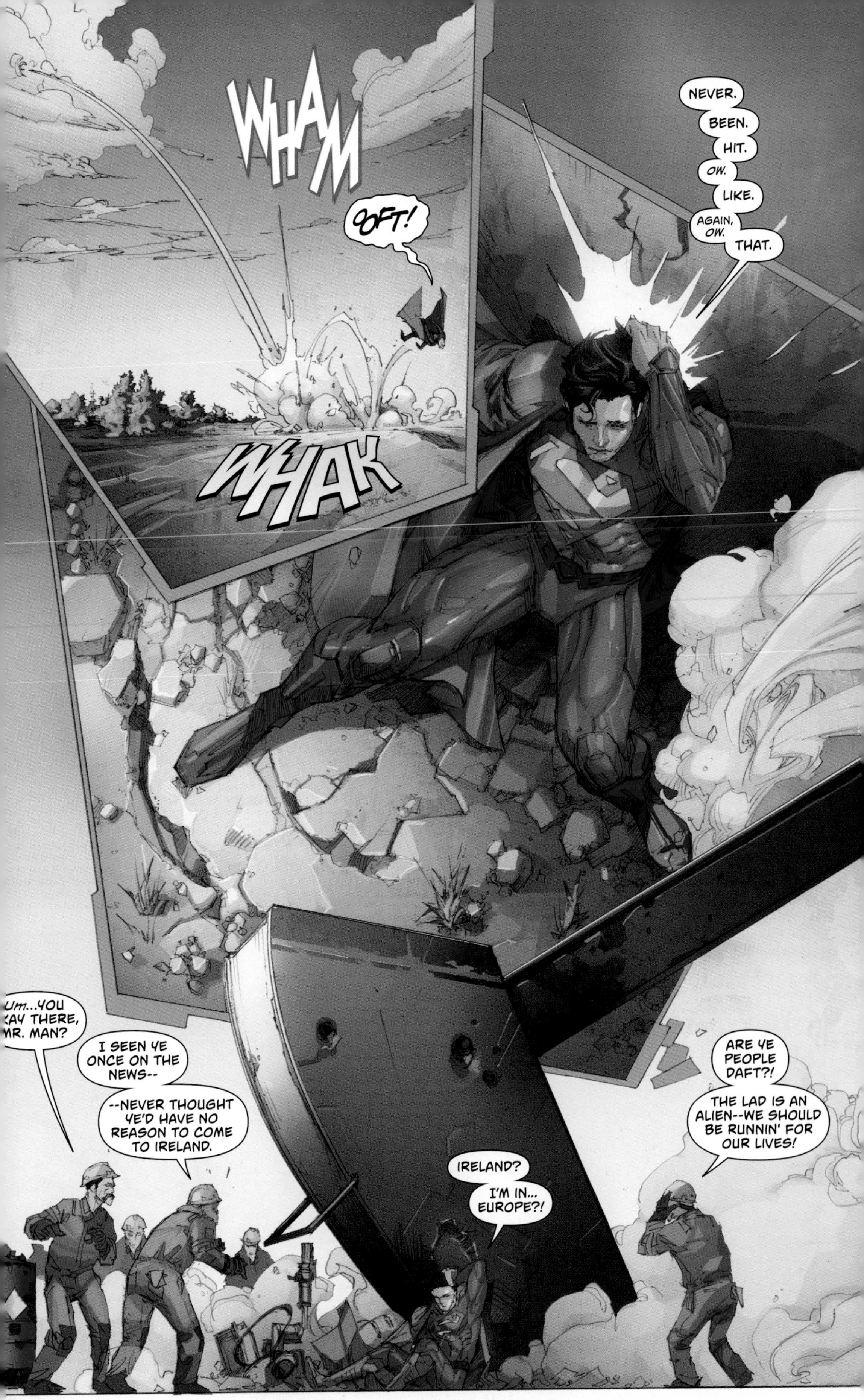
WHAM
OOFT!
WHAK
NEVER.
BEEN.
HIT.
OW.
LIKE.
AGAIN, OW.
THAT.
UM...YOU KAY THERE, MR. MAN?
I SEEN YE ONCE ON THE NEWS--
--NEVER THOUGHT YE'D HAVE NO REASON TO COME TO IRELAND.
IRELAND?
I'M IN... EUROPE?!
ARE YE PEOPLE DAFT?!
THE LAD IS AN ALIEN--WE SHOULD BE RUNNIN' FOR OUR LIVES!

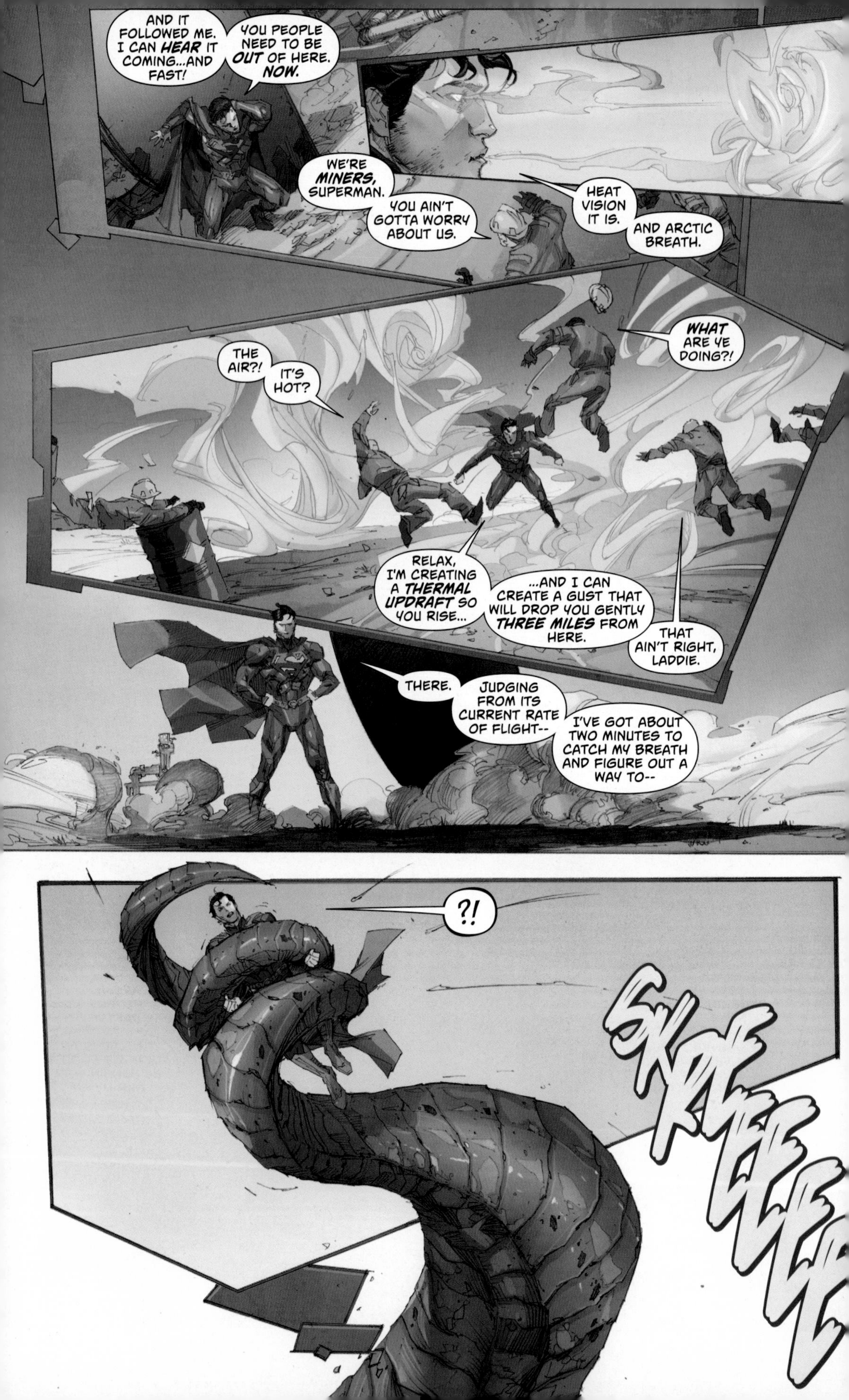
AND IT FOLLOWED ME. I CAN HEAR IT COMING...AND FAST!
YOU PEOPLE NEED TO BE OUT OF HERE. NOW.
WE'RE MINERS, SUPERMAN.
YOU AIN'T GOTTA WORRY ABOUT US.
HEAT VISION IT IS.
AND ARCTIC BREATH.
THE AIR?!
IT'S HOT?
WHAT ARE YE DOING?!
RELAX, I'M CREATING A THERMAL UPDRAFT SO YOU RISE...
...AND I CAN CREATE A GUST THAT WILL DROP YOU GENTLY THREE MILES FROM HERE.
THAT AIN'T RIGHT, LADDIE.
THERE.
JUDGING FROM ITS CURRENT RATE OF FLIGHT--
I'VE GOT ABOUT TWO MINUTES TO CATCH MY BREATH AND FIGURE OUT A WAY TO--
?!
SKREEEEE

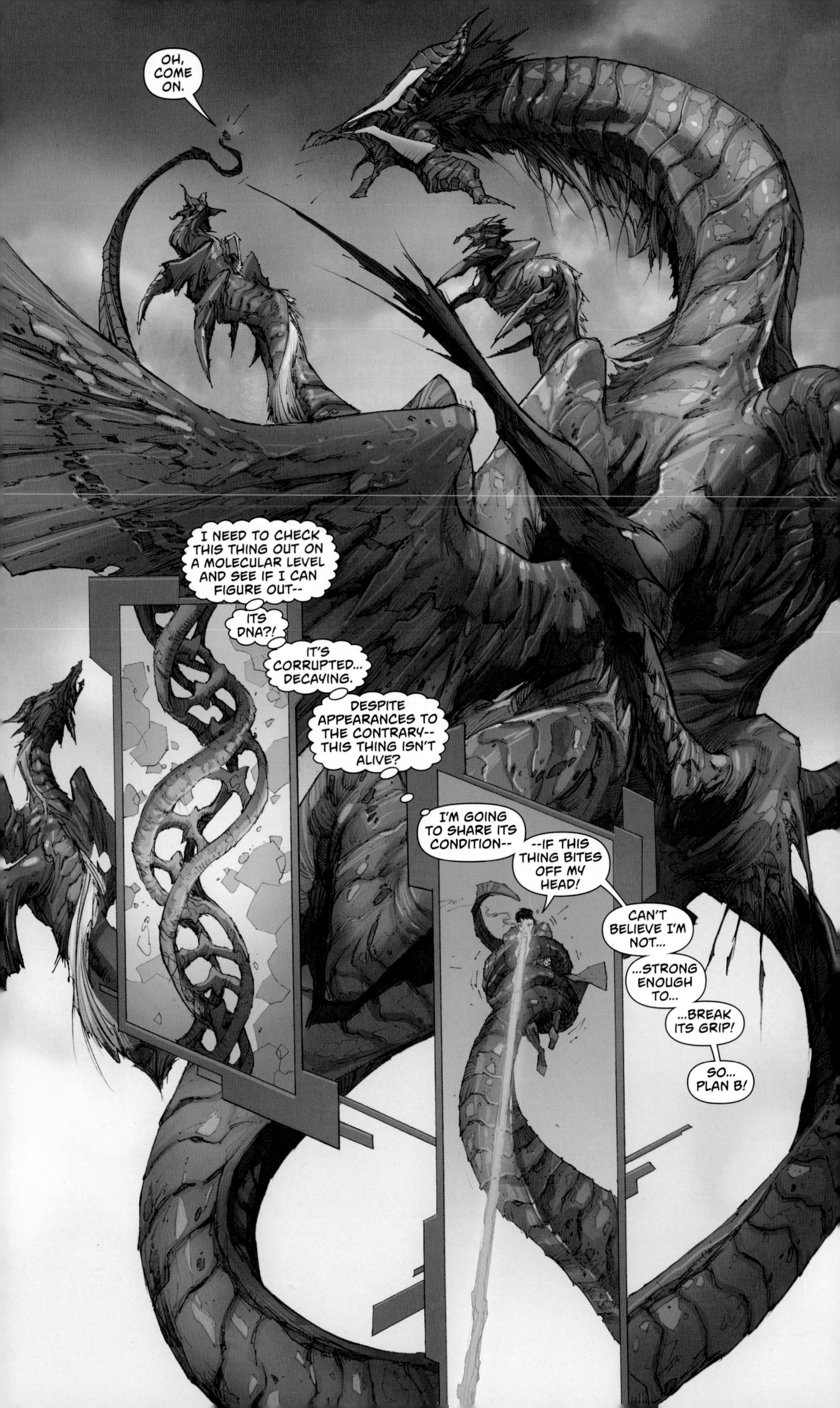
OH, COME ON.
I NEED TO CHECK THIS THING OUT ON A MOLECULAR LEVEL AND SEE IF I CAN FIGURE OUT--
ITS DNA?!
IT'S CORRUPTED... DECAYING.
DESPITE APPEARANCES TO THE CONTRARY-- THIS THING ISN'T ALIVE?
I'M GOING TO SHARE ITS CONDITION--
--IF THIS THING BITES OFF MY HEAD!
CAN'T BELIEVE I'M NOT...
...STRONG ENOUGH TO...
...BREAK ITS GRIP!
SO... PLAN B!

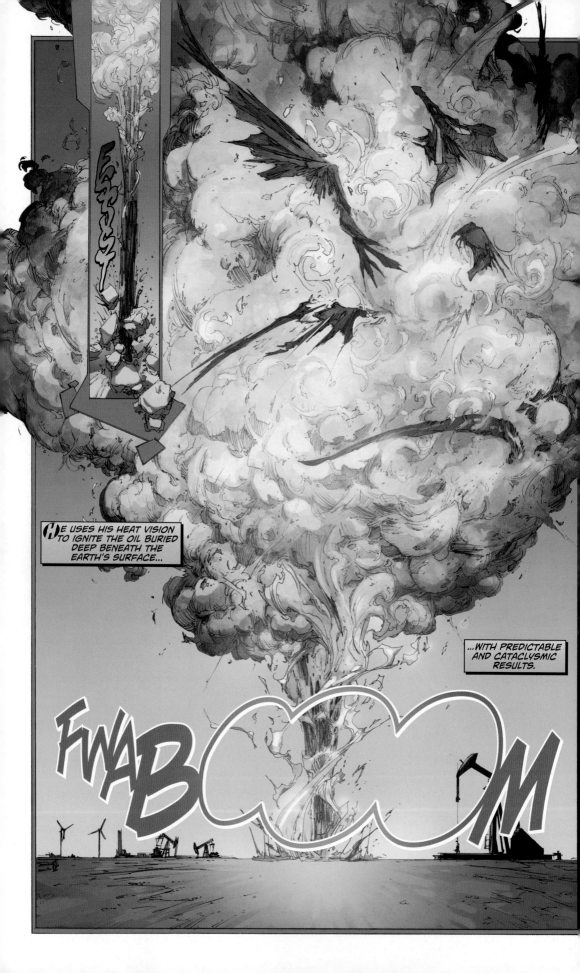

HE USES HIS HEAT VISION TO IGNITE THE OIL BURIED DEEP BENEATH THE EARTH'S SURFACE...

...WITH PREDICTABLE AND CATACLYSMIC RESULTS.

FWABCOOM

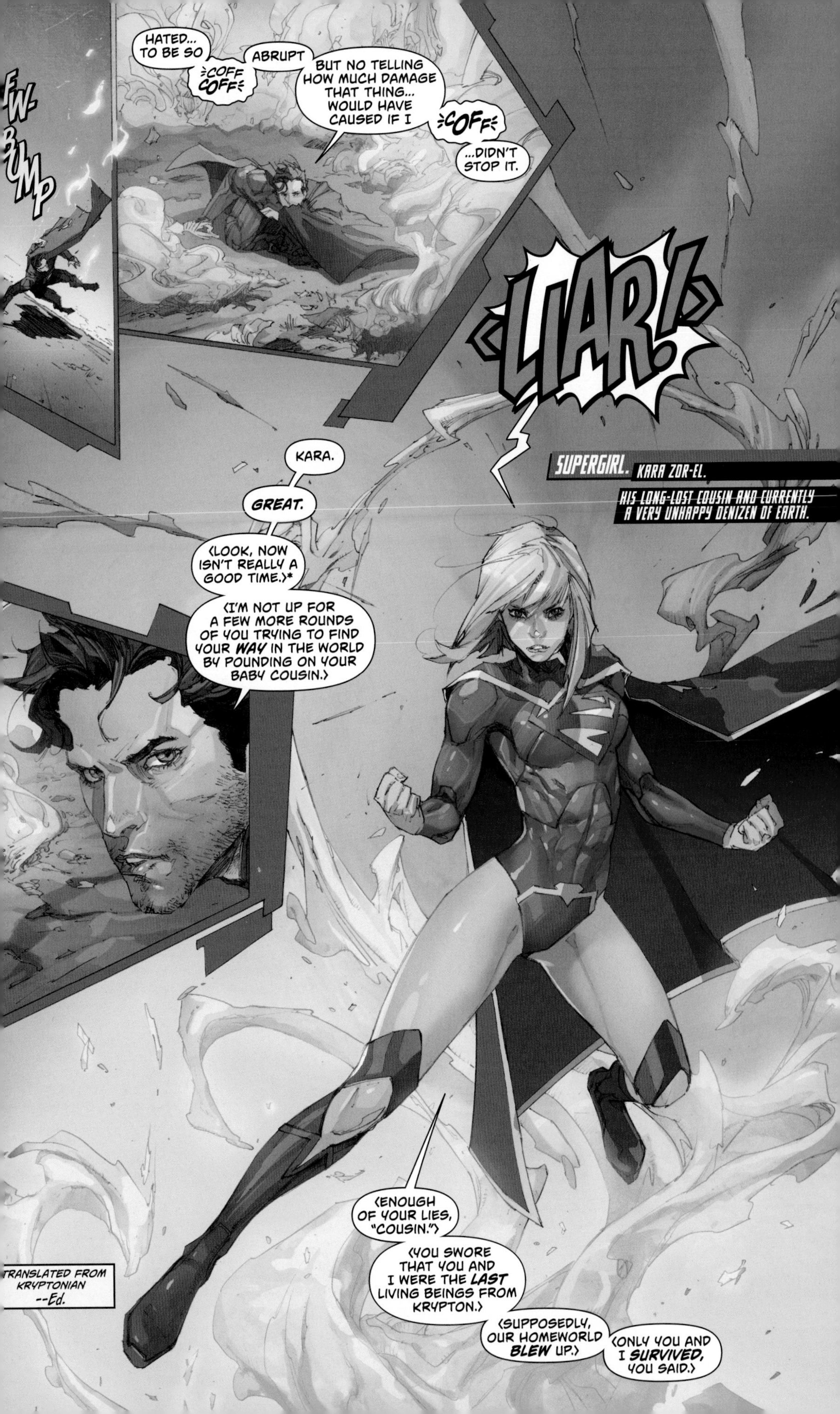
FW-BUMP
HATED... TO BE SO
ABRUPT
COFF COFF
BUT NO TELLING HOW MUCH DAMAGE THAT THING... WOULD HAVE CAUSED IF I
COFF
...DIDN'T STOP IT.
LIAR!
SUPERGIRL. KARA ZOR-EL.
HIS LONG-LOST COUSIN AND CURRENTLY A VERY UNHAPPY DENIZEN OF EARTH.
KARA.
GREAT.
‹LOOK, NOW ISN'T REALLY A GOOD TIME.›*
‹I'M NOT UP FOR A FEW MORE ROUNDS OF YOU TRYING TO FIND YOUR WAY IN THE WORLD BY POUNDING ON YOUR BABY COUSIN.›
‹ENOUGH OF YOUR LIES, "COUSIN."›
‹YOU SWORE THAT YOU AND I WERE THE LAST LIVING BEINGS FROM KRYPTON.›
‹SUPPOSEDLY, OUR HOMEWORLD BLEW UP.›
‹ONLY YOU AND I SURVIVED, YOU SAID.›
*TRANSLATED FROM KRYPTONIAN --Ed.

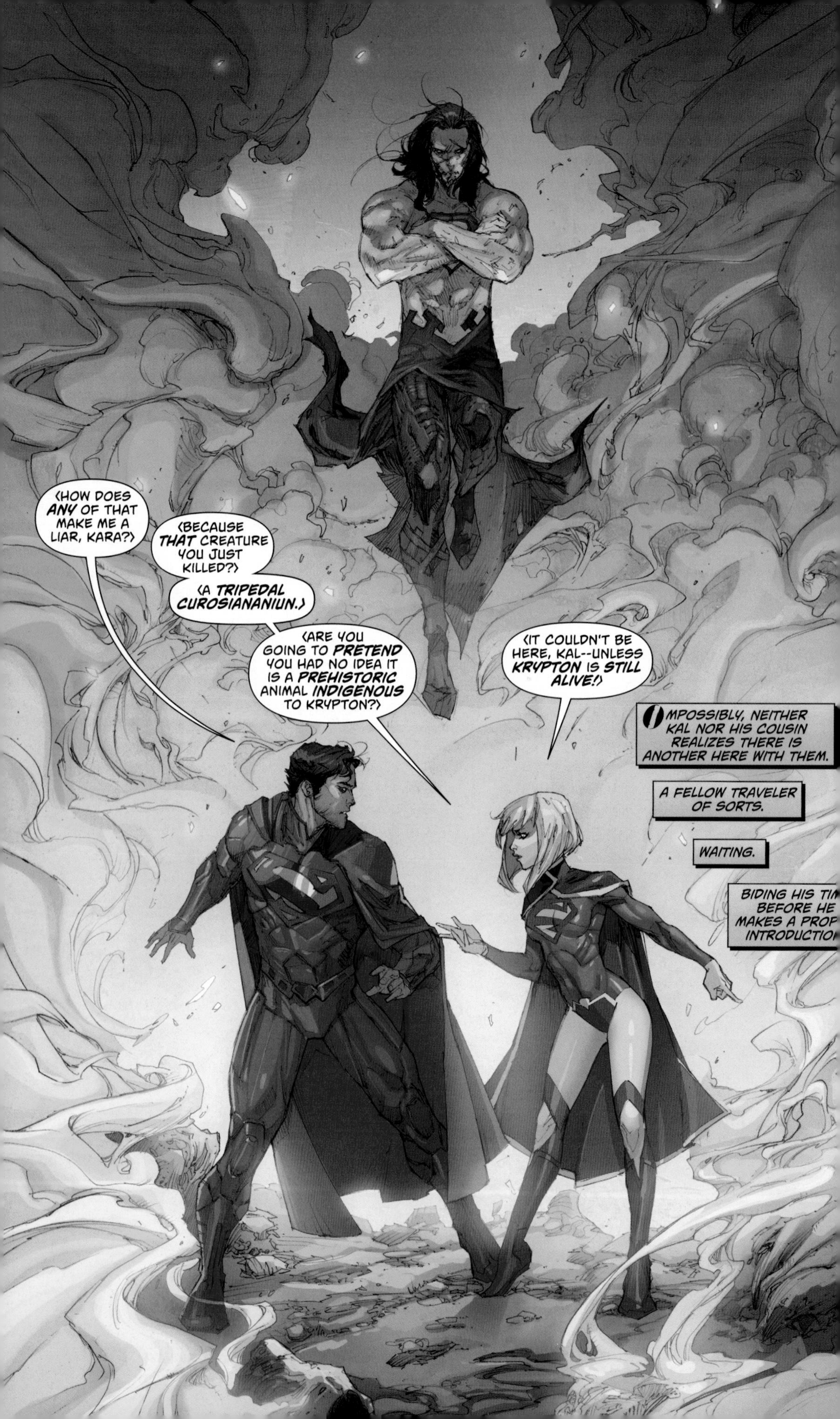

‹HOW DOES ANY OF THAT MAKE ME A LIAR, KARA?›
‹BECAUSE THAT CREATURE YOU JUST KILLED?›
‹A TRIPEDAL CUROSIANANIUN.›
‹ARE YOU GOING TO PRETEND YOU HAD NO IDEA IT IS A PREHISTORIC ANIMAL INDIGENOUS TO KRYPTON?›
‹IT COULDN'T BE HERE, KAL--UNLESS KRYPTON IS STILL ALIVE!›
IMPOSSIBLY, NEITHER KAL NOR HIS COUSIN REALIZES THERE IS ANOTHER HERE WITH THEM.
A FELLOW TRAVELER OF SORTS.
WAITING.

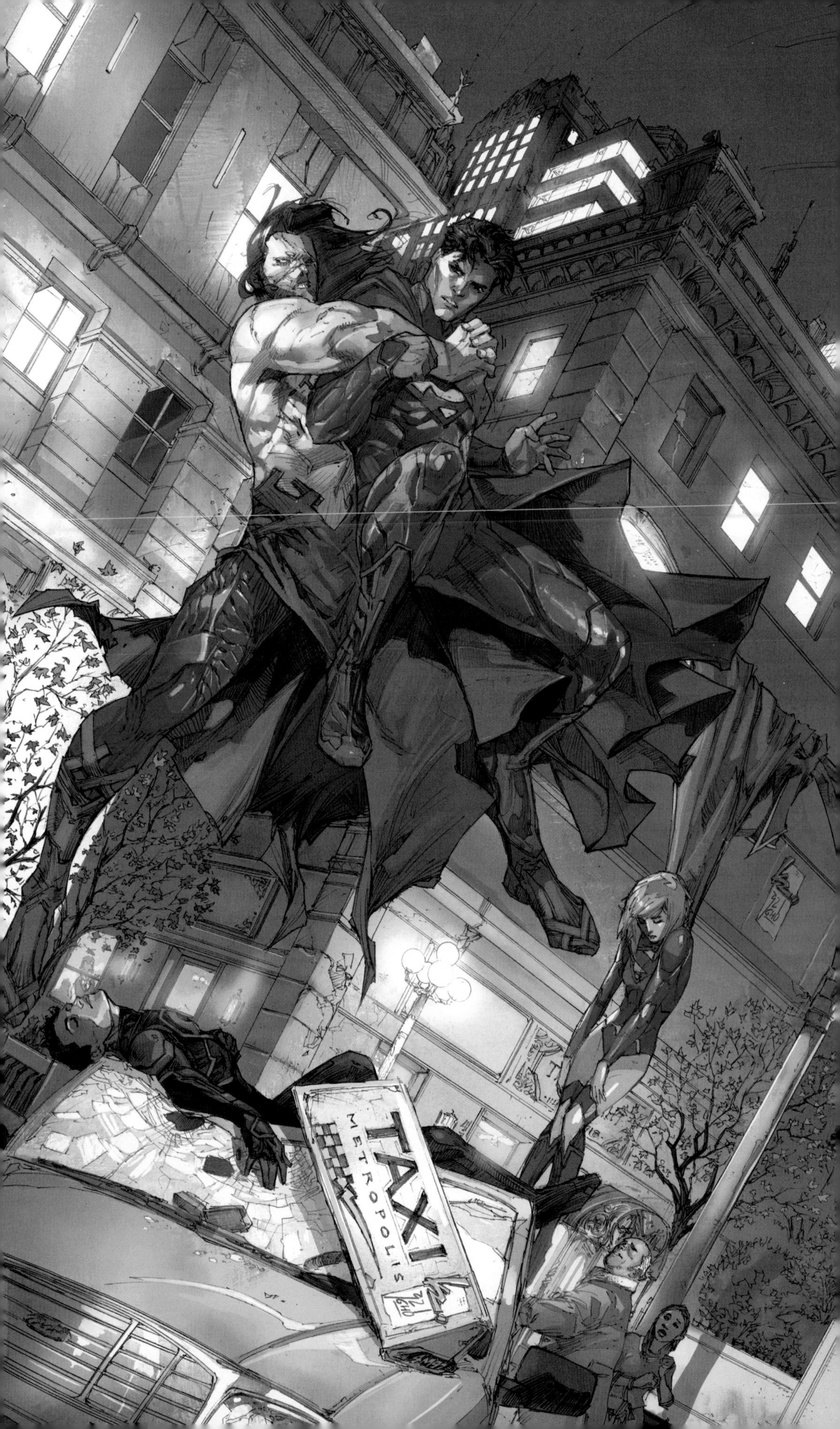
TAXI
METROPOLIS

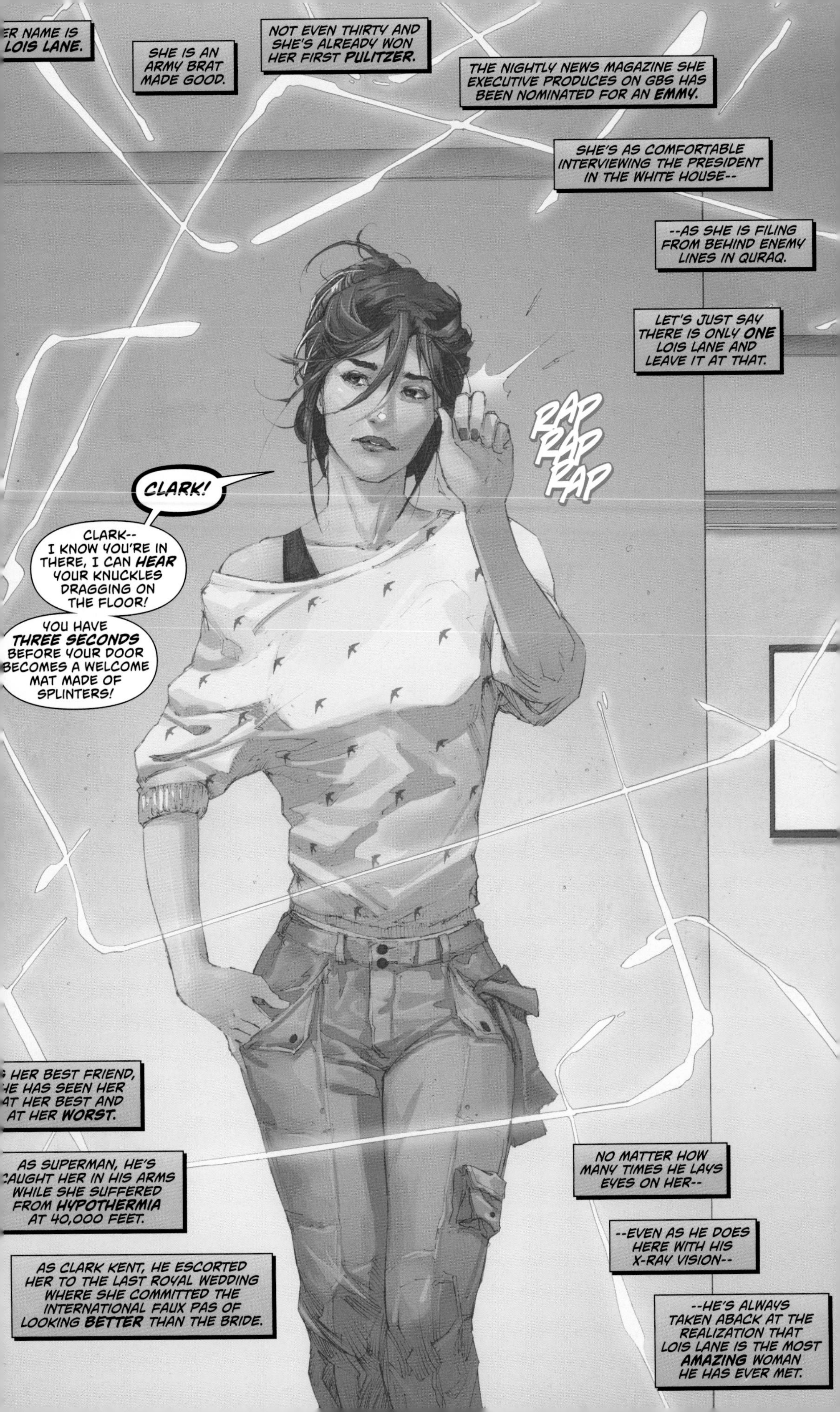
ER NAME IS LOIS LANE.
SHE IS AN ARMY BRAT MADE GOOD.
NOT EVEN THIRTY AND SHE'S ALREADY WON HER FIRST PULITZER.
THE NIGHTLY NEWS MAGAZINE SHE EXECUTIVE PRODUCES ON GBS HAS BEEN NOMINATED FOR AN EMMY.
SHE'S AS COMFORTABLE INTERVIEWING THE PRESIDENT IN THE WHITE HOUSE--
--AS SHE IS FILING FROM BEHIND ENEMY LINES IN QURAQ.
LET'S JUST SAY THERE IS ONLY ONE LOIS LANE AND LEAVE IT AT THAT.
RAP RAP RAP
CLARK!
CLARK-- I KNOW YOU'RE IN THERE, I CAN HEAR YOUR KNUCKLES DRAGGING ON THE FLOOR!
YOU HAVE THREE SECONDS BEFORE YOUR DOOR BECOMES A WELCOME MAT MADE OF SPLINTERS!
S HER BEST FRIEND, HE HAS SEEN HER AT HER BEST AND AT HER WORST.
AS SUPERMAN, HE'S CAUGHT HER IN HIS ARMS WHILE SHE SUFFERED FROM HYPOTHERMIA AT 40,000 FEET.
AS CLARK KENT, HE ESCORTED HER TO THE LAST ROYAL WEDDING WHERE SHE COMMITTED THE INTERNATIONAL FAUX PAS OF LOOKING BETTER THAN THE BRIDE.
NO MATTER HOW MANY TIMES HE LAYS EYES ON HER--
--EVEN AS HE DOES HERE WITH HIS X-RAY VISION--
--HE'S ALWAYS TAKEN ABACK AT THE REALIZATION THAT LOIS LANE IS THE MOST AMAZING WOMAN HE HAS EVER MET.

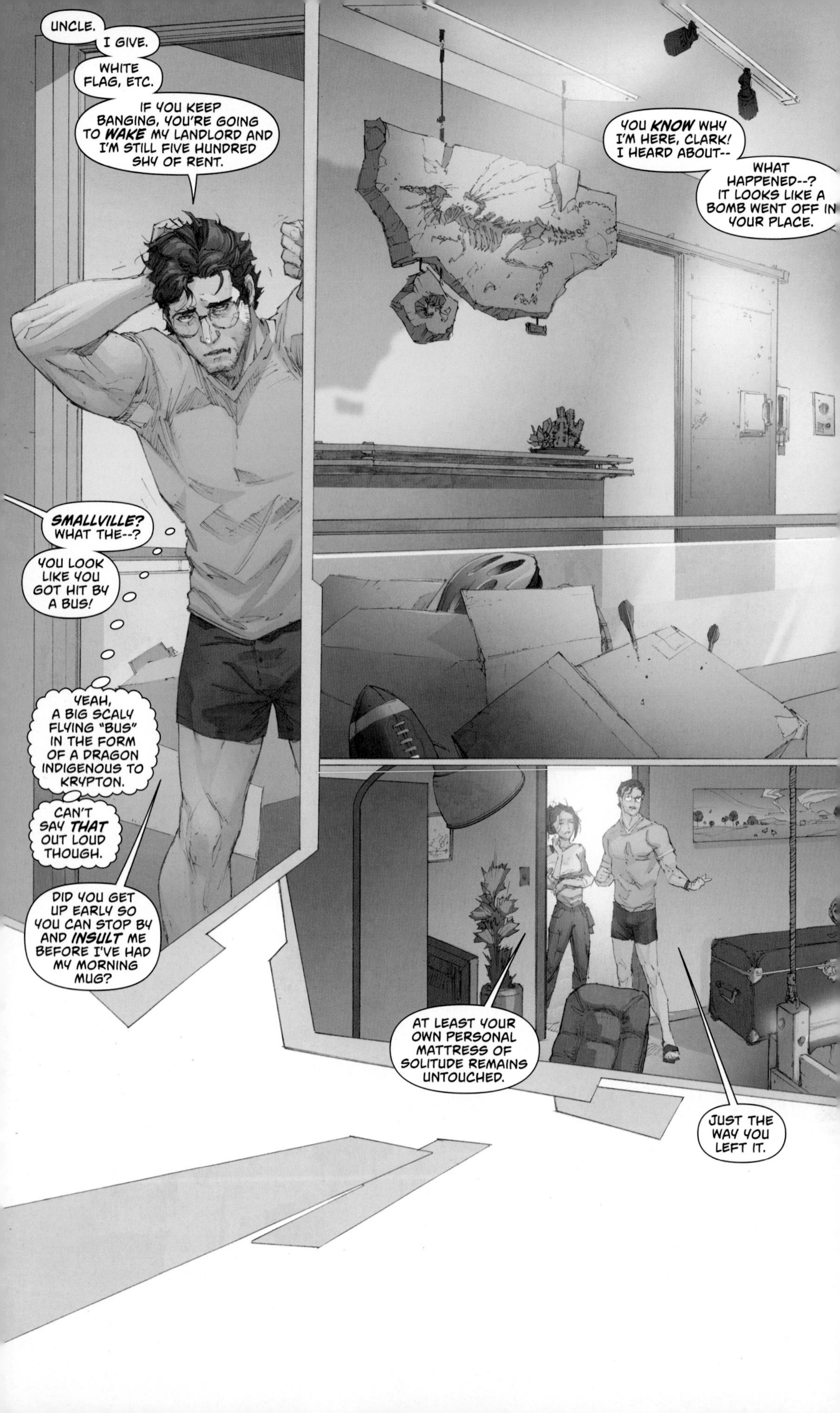
UNCLE.
I GIVE.
WHITE FLAG, ETC.
IF YOU KEEP BANGING, YOU'RE GOING TO WAKE MY LANDLORD AND I'M STILL FIVE HUNDRED SHY OF RENT.
YOU KNOW WHY I'M HERE, CLARK! I HEARD ABOUT--
WHAT HAPPENED--? IT LOOKS LIKE A BOMB WENT OFF IN YOUR PLACE.
SMALLVILLE? WHAT THE--?
YOU LOOK LIKE YOU GOT HIT BY A BUS!
YEAH, A BIG SCALY FLYING "BUS" IN THE FORM OF A DRAGON INDIGENOUS TO KRYPTON.
CAN'T SAY THAT OUT LOUD THOUGH.
DID YOU GET UP EARLY SO YOU CAN STOP BY AND INSULT ME BEFORE I'VE HAD MY MORNING MUG?
AT LEAST YOUR OWN PERSONAL MATTRESS OF SOLITUDE REMAINS UNTOUCHED.
JUST THE WAY YOU LEFT IT.

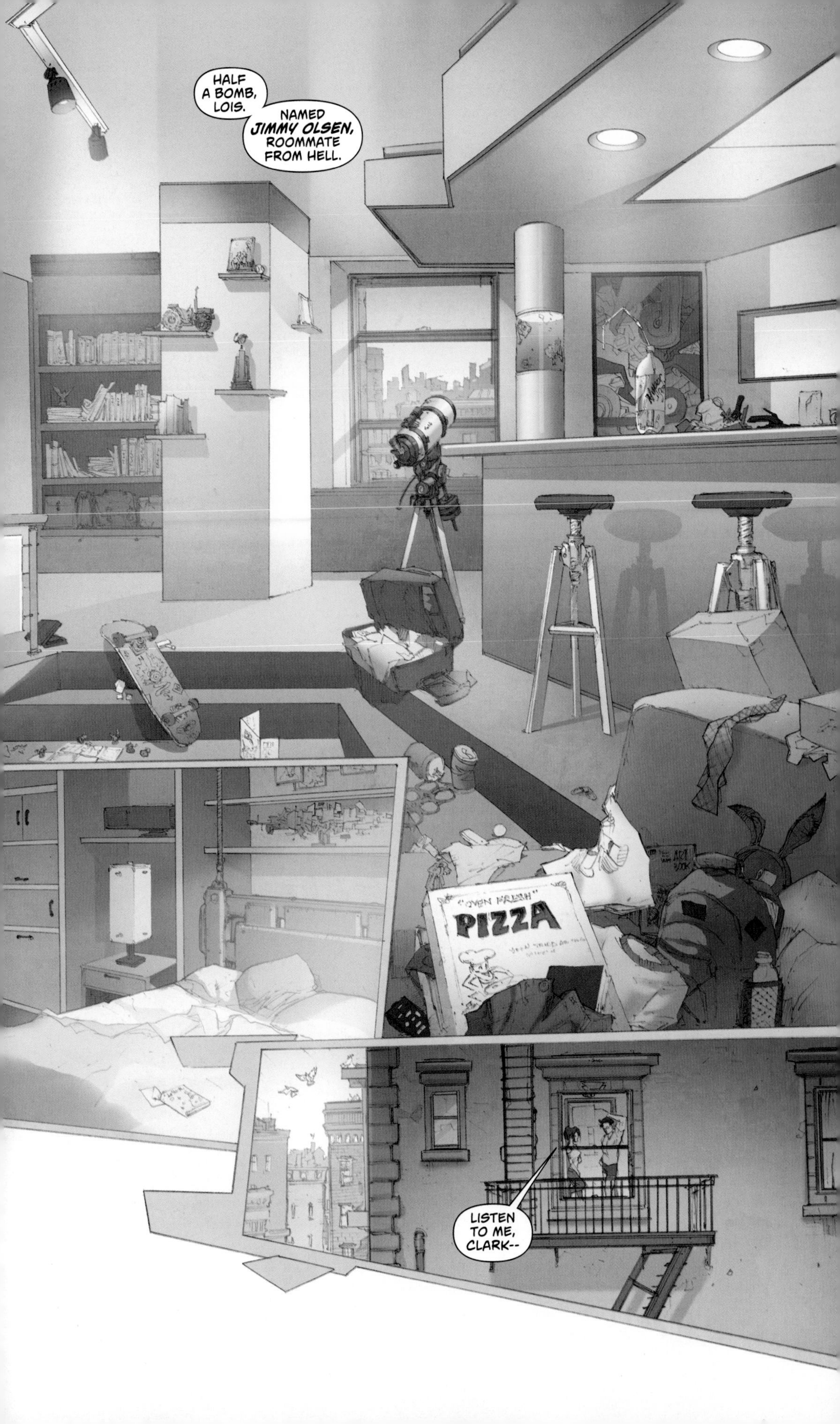
HALF A BOMB, LOIS.
NAMED JIMMY OLSEN, ROOMMATE FROM HELL.
"OVEN FRESH" PIZZA
LISTEN TO ME, CLARK--

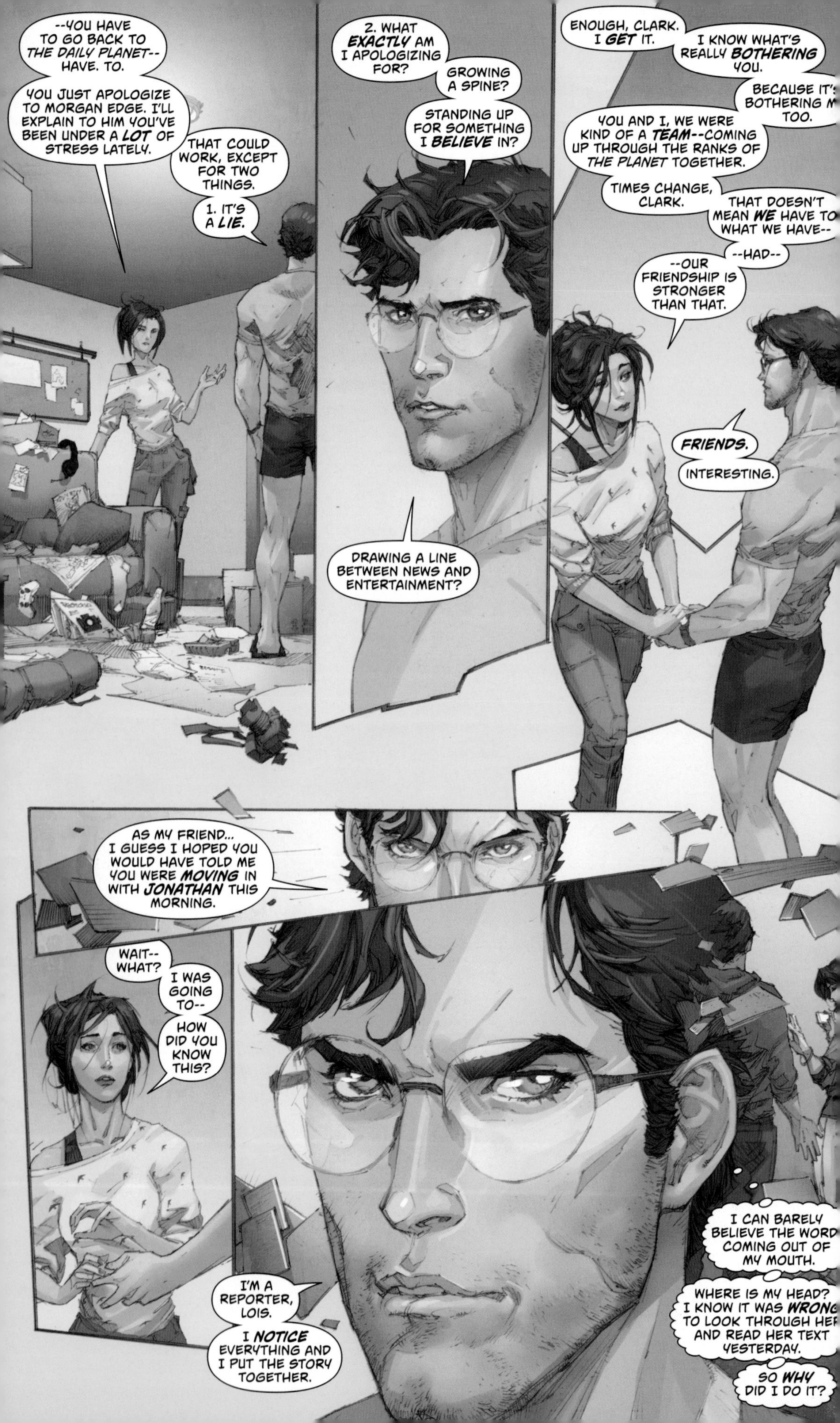

--YOU HAVE TO GO BACK TO THE DAILY PLANET-- HAVE. TO.
YOU JUST APOLOGIZE TO MORGAN EDGE. I'LL EXPLAIN TO HIM YOU'VE BEEN UNDER A LOT OF STRESS LATELY.
THAT COULD WORK, EXCEPT FOR TWO THINGS.
1. IT'S A LIE.
2. WHAT EXACTLY AM I APOLOGIZING FOR?
GROWING A SPINE?
STANDING UP FOR SOMETHING I BELIEVE IN?
DRAWING A LINE BETWEEN NEWS AND ENTERTAINMENT?
ENOUGH, CLARK. I GET IT.
I KNOW WHAT'S REALLY BOTHERING YOU.
YOU AND I, WE WERE KIND OF A TEAM--COMING UP THROUGH THE RANKS OF THE PLANET TOGETHER.
TIMES CHANGE, CLARK.
--OUR FRIENDSHIP IS STRONGER THAN THAT.
FRIENDS.
INTERESTING.
AS MY FRIEND... I GUESS I HOPED YOU WOULD HAVE TOLD ME YOU WERE MOVING IN WITH JONATHAN THIS MORNING.
WAIT-- WHAT?
I WAS GOING TO--
HOW DID YOU KNOW THIS?
I'M A REPORTER, LOIS.
I NOTICE EVERYTHING AND I PUT THE STORY TOGETHER.

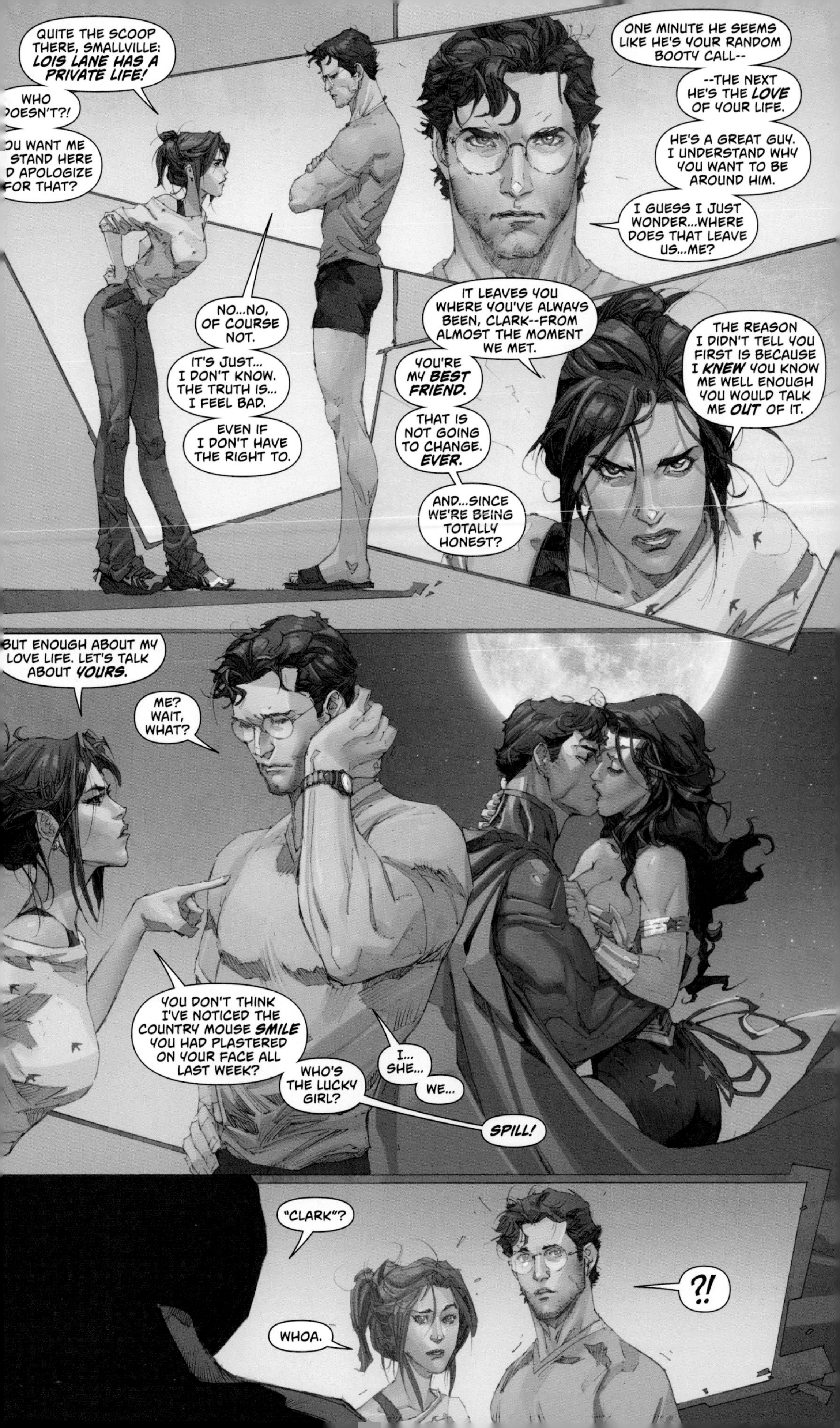

QUITE THE SCOOP THERE, SMALLVILLE: LOIS LANE HAS A PRIVATE LIFE!
WHO DOESN'T?!
YOU WANT ME TO STAND HERE AND APOLOGIZE FOR THAT?
ONE MINUTE HE SEEMS LIKE HE'S YOUR RANDOM BOOTY CALL--
--THE NEXT HE'S THE LOVE OF YOUR LIFE.
HE'S A GREAT GUY. I UNDERSTAND WHY YOU WANT TO BE AROUND HIM.
I GUESS I JUST WONDER...WHERE DOES THAT LEAVE US...ME?
NO...NO, OF COURSE NOT.
IT'S JUST... I DON'T KNOW. THE TRUTH IS... I FEEL BAD.
EVEN IF I DON'T HAVE THE RIGHT TO.
IT LEAVES YOU WHERE YOU'VE ALWAYS BEEN, CLARK--FROM ALMOST THE MOMENT WE MET.
YOU'RE MY BEST FRIEND.
THAT IS NOT GOING TO CHANGE. EVER.
AND...SINCE WE'RE BEING TOTALLY HONEST?
THE REASON I DIDN'T TELL YOU FIRST IS BECAUSE I KNEW YOU KNOW ME WELL ENOUGH YOU WOULD TALK ME OUT OF IT.
BUT ENOUGH ABOUT MY LOVE LIFE. LET'S TALK ABOUT YOURS.
ME? WAIT, WHAT?
YOU DON'T THINK I'VE NOTICED THE COUNTRY MOUSE SMILE YOU HAD PLASTERED ON YOUR FACE ALL LAST WEEK?
I... SHE...
WE...
WHO'S THE LUCKY GIRL?
SPILL!
"CLARK"?
WHOA.
?!

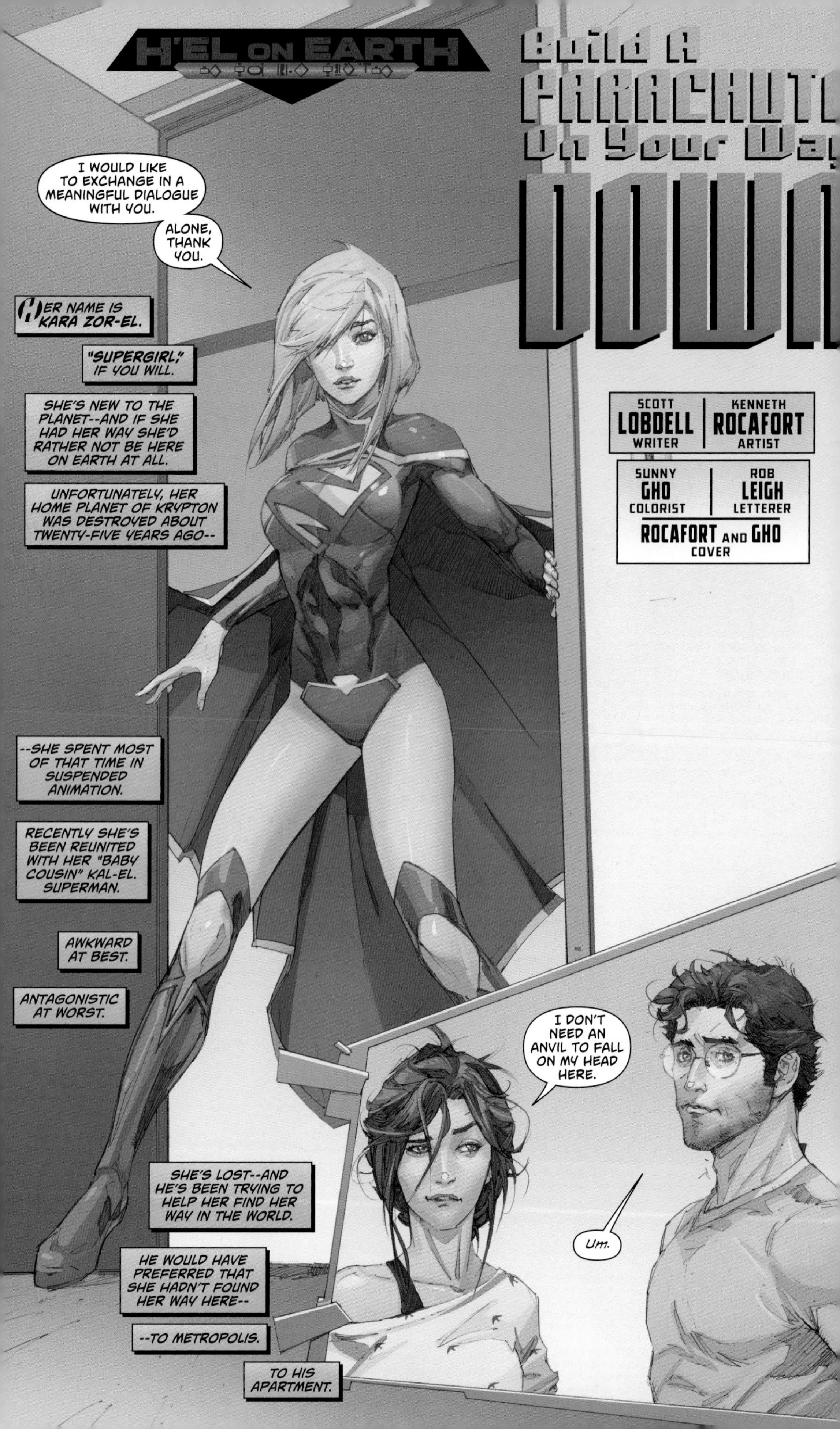

H'EL ON EARTH
Build A PARACHUTE On Your Way DOWN
I WOULD LIKE TO EXCHANGE IN A MEANINGFUL DIALOGUE WITH YOU.
ALONE, THANK YOU.
HER NAME IS KARA ZOR-EL.
"SUPERGIRL," IF YOU WILL.
SHE'S NEW TO THE PLANET--AND IF SHE HAD HER WAY SHE'D RATHER NOT BE HERE ON EARTH AT ALL.
UNFORTUNATELY, HER HOME PLANET OF KRYPTON WAS DESTROYED ABOUT TWENTY-FIVE YEARS AGO--
SCOTT LOBDELL WRITER
KENNETH ROCAFORT ARTIST
SUNNY GHO COLORIST
ROB LEIGH LETTERER
ROCAFORT AND GHO COVER
--SHE SPENT MOST OF THAT TIME IN SUSPENDED ANIMATION.
RECENTLY SHE'S BEEN REUNITED WITH HER "BABY COUSIN" KAL-EL. SUPERMAN.
AWKWARD AT BEST.
ANTAGONISTIC AT WORST.
I DON'T NEED AN ANVIL TO FALL ON MY HEAD HERE.
SHE'S LOST--AND HE'S BEEN TRYING TO HELP HER FIND HER WAY IN THE WORLD.
Um.
HE WOULD HAVE PREFERRED THAT SHE HADN'T FOUND HER WAY HERE--
--TO METROPOLIS.
TO HIS APARTMENT.

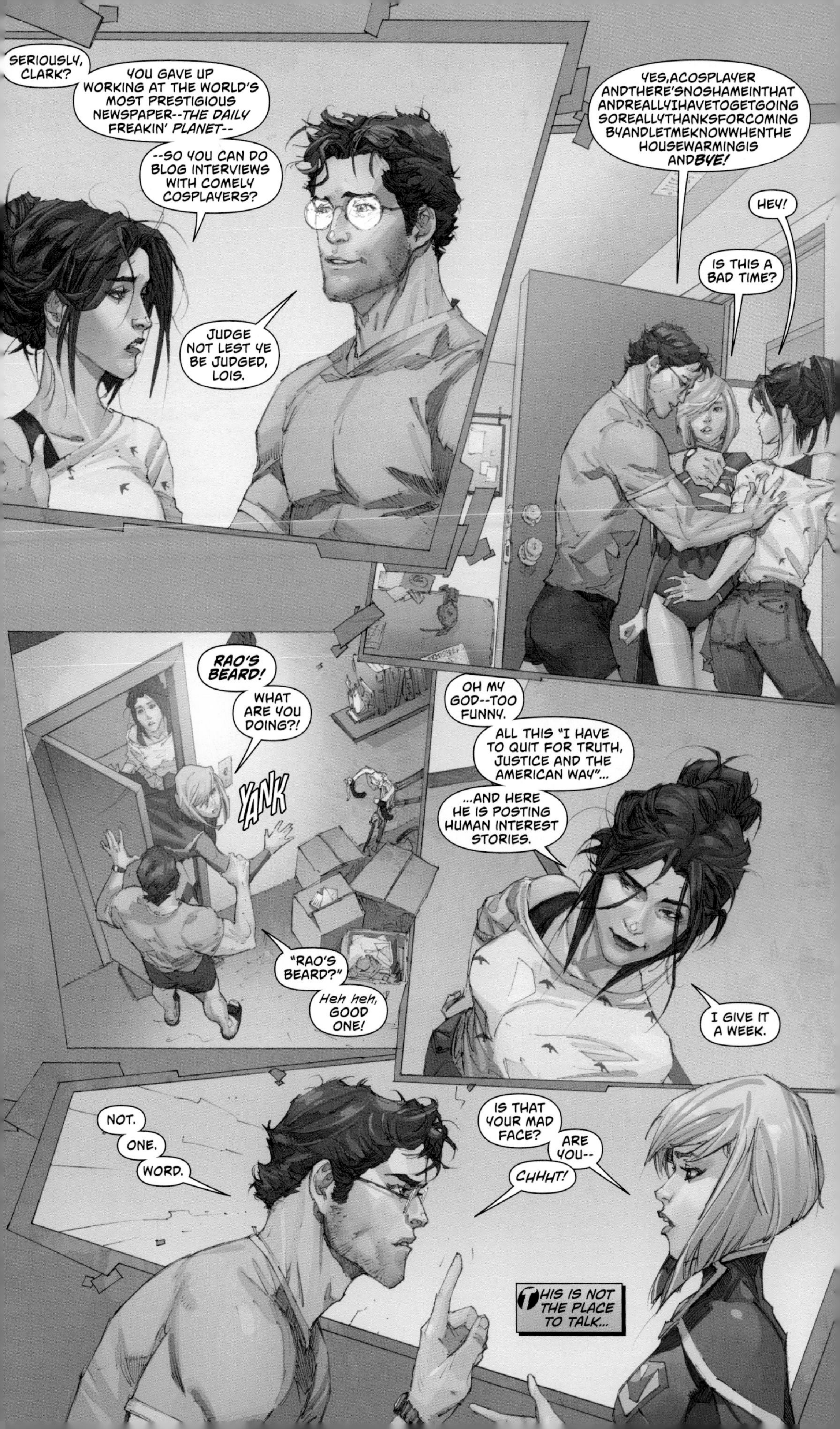

SERIOUSLY, CLARK?
YOU GAVE UP WORKING AT THE WORLD'S MOST PRESTIGIOUS NEWSPAPER--*THE DAILY* FREAKIN' *PLANET*--
--SO YOU CAN DO BLOG INTERVIEWS WITH COMELY COSPLAYERS?
JUDGE NOT LEST YE BE JUDGED, LOIS.
YES,ACOSPLAYER ANDTHERE'SNOSHAMEINTHAT ANDREALLYIHAVETOGETGOING SOREALLYTHANKSFORCOMING BYANDLETMEKNOWWHENTHE HOUSEWARMINGIS AND*BYE!*
HEY!
IS THIS A BAD TIME?
RAO'S BEARD!
WHAT ARE YOU DOING?!
YANK
"RAO'S BEARD?"
Heh heh, GOOD ONE!
OH MY GOD--TOO FUNNY.
ALL THIS "I HAVE TO QUIT FOR TRUTH, JUSTICE AND THE AMERICAN WAY"...
...AND HERE HE IS POSTING HUMAN INTEREST STORIES.
I GIVE IT A WEEK.
NOT.
ONE.
WORD.
IS THAT YOUR MAD FACE?
ARE YOU--
CHHHT!
THIS IS NOT THE PLACE TO TALK...

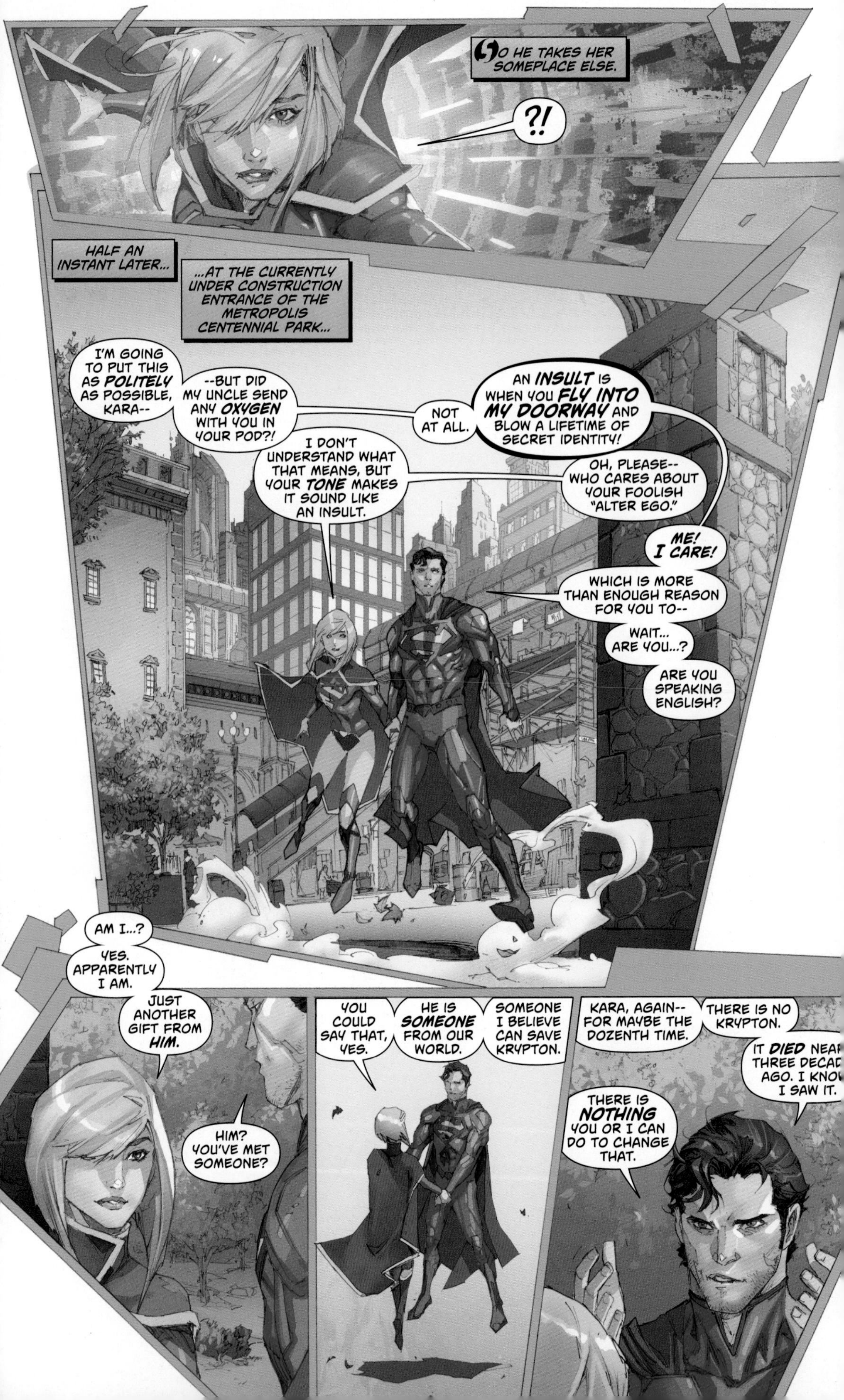
SO HE TAKES HER SOMEPLACE ELSE.
?!
HALF AN INSTANT LATER...
...AT THE CURRENTLY UNDER CONSTRUCTION ENTRANCE OF THE METROPOLIS CENTENNIAL PARK...
I'M GOING TO PUT THIS AS POLITELY AS POSSIBLE, KARA--
--BUT DID MY UNCLE SEND ANY OXYGEN WITH YOU IN YOUR POD?!
I DON'T UNDERSTAND WHAT THAT MEANS, BUT YOUR TONE MAKES IT SOUND LIKE AN INSULT.
NOT AT ALL.
AN INSULT IS WHEN YOU FLY INTO MY DOORWAY AND BLOW A LIFETIME OF SECRET IDENTITY!
OH, PLEASE-- WHO CARES ABOUT YOUR FOOLISH "ALTER EGO."
ME! I CARE!
WHICH IS MORE THAN ENOUGH REASON FOR YOU TO--
WAIT... ARE YOU...?
ARE YOU SPEAKING ENGLISH?
AM I...?
YES. APPARENTLY I AM.
JUST ANOTHER GIFT FROM HIM.
HIM? YOU'VE MET SOMEONE?
YOU COULD SAY THAT, YES.
HE IS SOMEONE FROM OUR WORLD.
SOMEONE I BELIEVE CAN SAVE KRYPTON.
KARA, AGAIN-- FOR MAYBE THE DOZENTH TIME.
THERE IS NO KRYPTON.
IT DIED NEAR THREE DECAD AGO. I KNOW I SAW IT.
THERE IS NOTHING YOU OR I CAN DO TO CHANGE THAT.

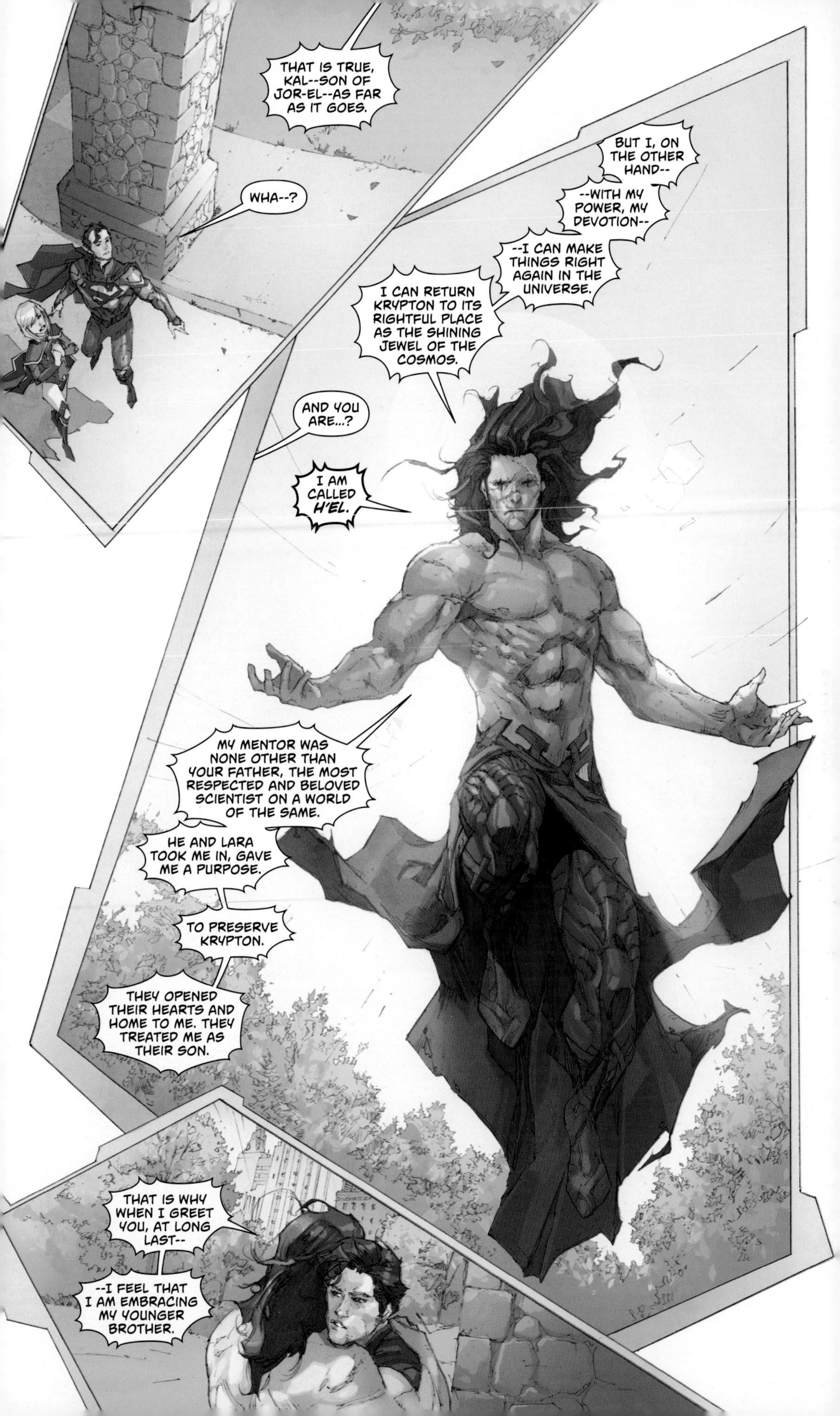

THAT IS TRUE, KAL--SON OF JOR-EL--AS FAR AS IT GOES.
WHA--?
BUT I, ON THE OTHER HAND--
--WITH MY POWER, MY DEVOTION--
--I CAN MAKE THINGS RIGHT AGAIN IN THE UNIVERSE.
I CAN RETURN KRYPTON TO ITS RIGHTFUL PLACE AS THE SHINING JEWEL OF THE COSMOS.
AND YOU ARE...?
I AM CALLED *H'EL*.
MY MENTOR WAS NONE OTHER THAN YOUR FATHER, THE MOST RESPECTED AND BELOVED SCIENTIST ON A WORLD OF THE SAME.
HE AND LARA TOOK ME IN, GAVE ME A PURPOSE.
TO PRESERVE KRYPTON.
THEY OPENED THEIR HEARTS AND HOME TO ME. THEY TREATED ME AS THEIR SON.
THAT IS WHY WHEN I GREET YOU, AT LONG LAST--
--I FEEL THAT I AM EMBRACING MY YOUNGER BROTHER.

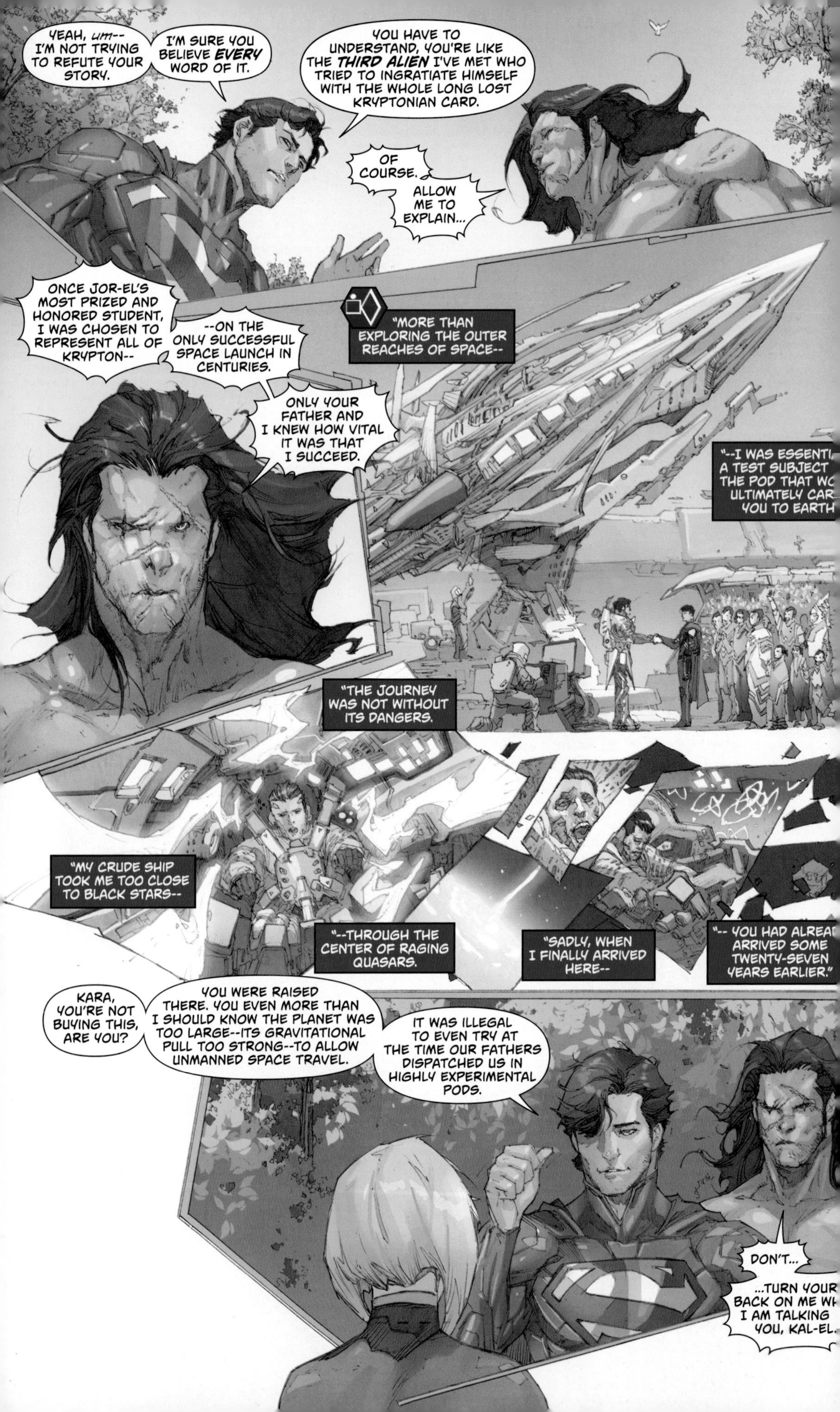
YEAH, UM-- I'M NOT TRYING TO REFUTE YOUR STORY.
I'M SURE YOU BELIEVE EVERY WORD OF IT.
YOU HAVE TO UNDERSTAND, YOU'RE LIKE THE THIRD ALIEN I'VE MET WHO TRIED TO INGRATIATE HIMSELF WITH THE WHOLE LONG LOST KRYPTONIAN CARD.
OF COURSE.
ALLOW ME TO EXPLAIN...
ONCE JOR-EL'S MOST PRIZED AND HONORED STUDENT, I WAS CHOSEN TO REPRESENT ALL OF KRYPTON--
--ON THE ONLY SUCCESSFUL SPACE LAUNCH IN CENTURIES.
ONLY YOUR FATHER AND I KNEW HOW VITAL IT WAS THAT I SUCCEED.
"MORE THAN EXPLORING THE OUTER REACHES OF SPACE--
"--I WAS ESSENTI A TEST SUBJECT THE POD THAT WO ULTIMATELY CAR YOU TO EARTH
"THE JOURNEY WAS NOT WITHOUT ITS DANGERS.
"MY CRUDE SHIP TOOK ME TOO CLOSE TO BLACK STARS--
"--THROUGH THE CENTER OF RAGING QUASARS.
"SADLY, WHEN I FINALLY ARRIVED HERE--
"-- YOU HAD ALREA ARRIVED SOME TWENTY-SEVEN YEARS EARLIER."
KARA, YOU'RE NOT BUYING THIS, ARE YOU?
YOU WERE RAISED THERE. YOU EVEN MORE THAN I SHOULD KNOW THE PLANET WAS TOO LARGE--ITS GRAVITATIONAL PULL TOO STRONG--TO ALLOW UNMANNED SPACE TRAVEL.
IT WAS ILLEGAL TO EVEN TRY AT THE TIME OUR FATHERS DISPATCHED US IN HIGHLY EXPERIMENTAL PODS.
DON'T...
...TURN YOUR BACK ON ME WH I AM TALKING YOU, KAL-EL.

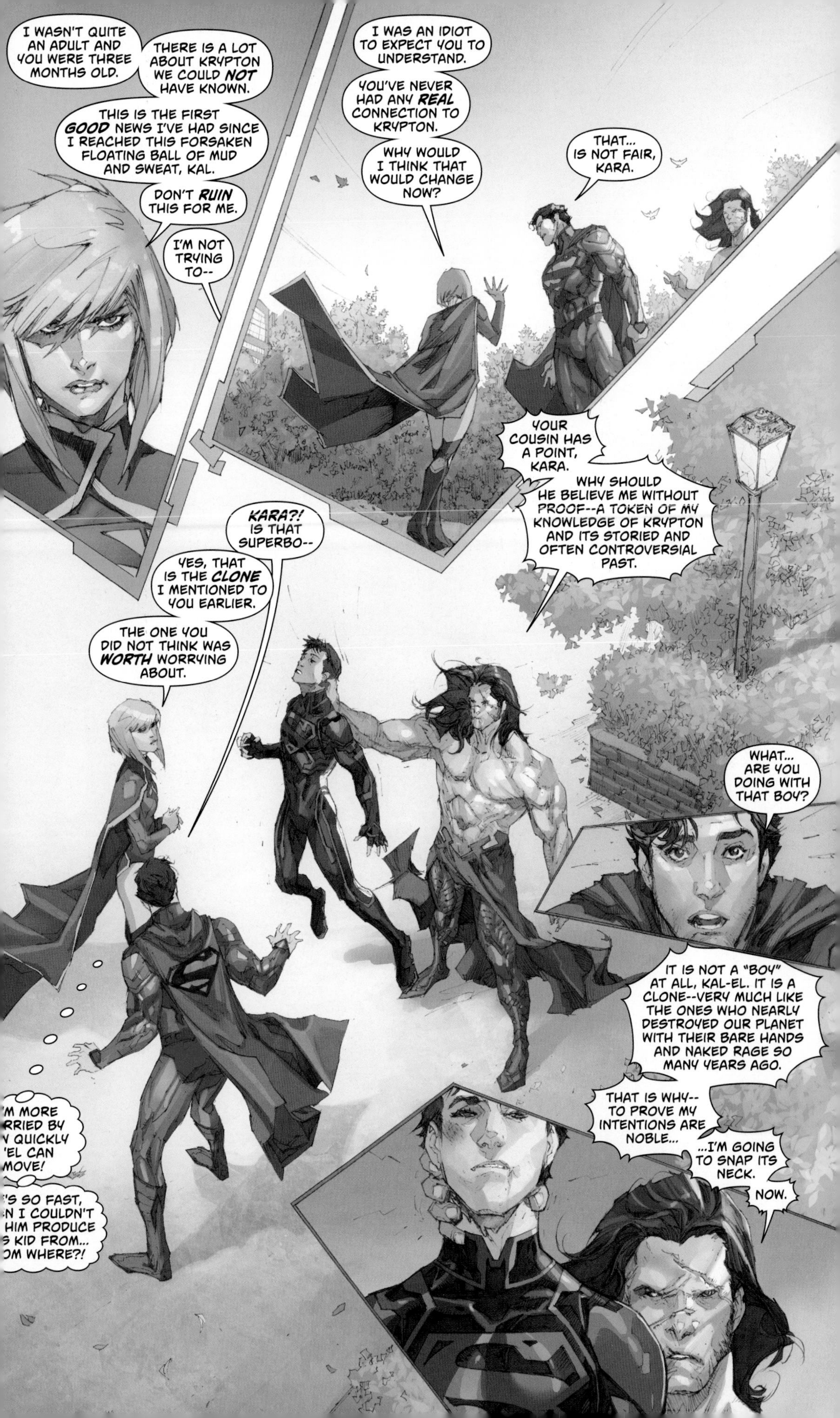
I WASN'T QUITE AN ADULT AND YOU WERE THREE MONTHS OLD.
THERE IS A LOT ABOUT KRYPTON WE COULD NOT HAVE KNOWN.
THIS IS THE FIRST GOOD NEWS I'VE HAD SINCE I REACHED THIS FORSAKEN FLOATING BALL OF MUD AND SWEAT, KAL.
DON'T RUIN THIS FOR ME.
I'M NOT TRYING TO--
I WAS AN IDIOT TO EXPECT YOU TO UNDERSTAND.
YOU'VE NEVER HAD ANY REAL CONNECTION TO KRYPTON.
WHY WOULD I THINK THAT WOULD CHANGE NOW?
THAT... IS NOT FAIR, KARA.
YOUR COUSIN HAS A POINT, KARA.
WHY SHOULD HE BELIEVE ME WITHOUT PROOF--A TOKEN OF MY KNOWLEDGE OF KRYPTON AND ITS STORIED AND OFTEN CONTROVERSIAL PAST.
KARA?! IS THAT SUPERBO--
YES, THAT IS THE CLONE I MENTIONED TO YOU EARLIER.
THE ONE YOU DID NOT THINK WAS WORTH WORRYING ABOUT.
'M MORE RRIED BY N QUICKLY 'EL CAN MOVE!
'S SO FAST, N I COULDN'T HIM PRODUCE S KID FROM... OM WHERE?!
WHAT... ARE YOU DOING WITH THAT BOY?
IT IS NOT A "BOY" AT ALL, KAL-EL. IT IS A CLONE--VERY MUCH LIKE THE ONES WHO NEARLY DESTROYED OUR PLANET WITH THEIR BARE HANDS AND NAKED RAGE SO MANY YEARS AGO.
THAT IS WHY--TO PROVE MY INTENTIONS ARE NOBLE...
...I'M GOING TO SNAP ITS NECK.
NOW.

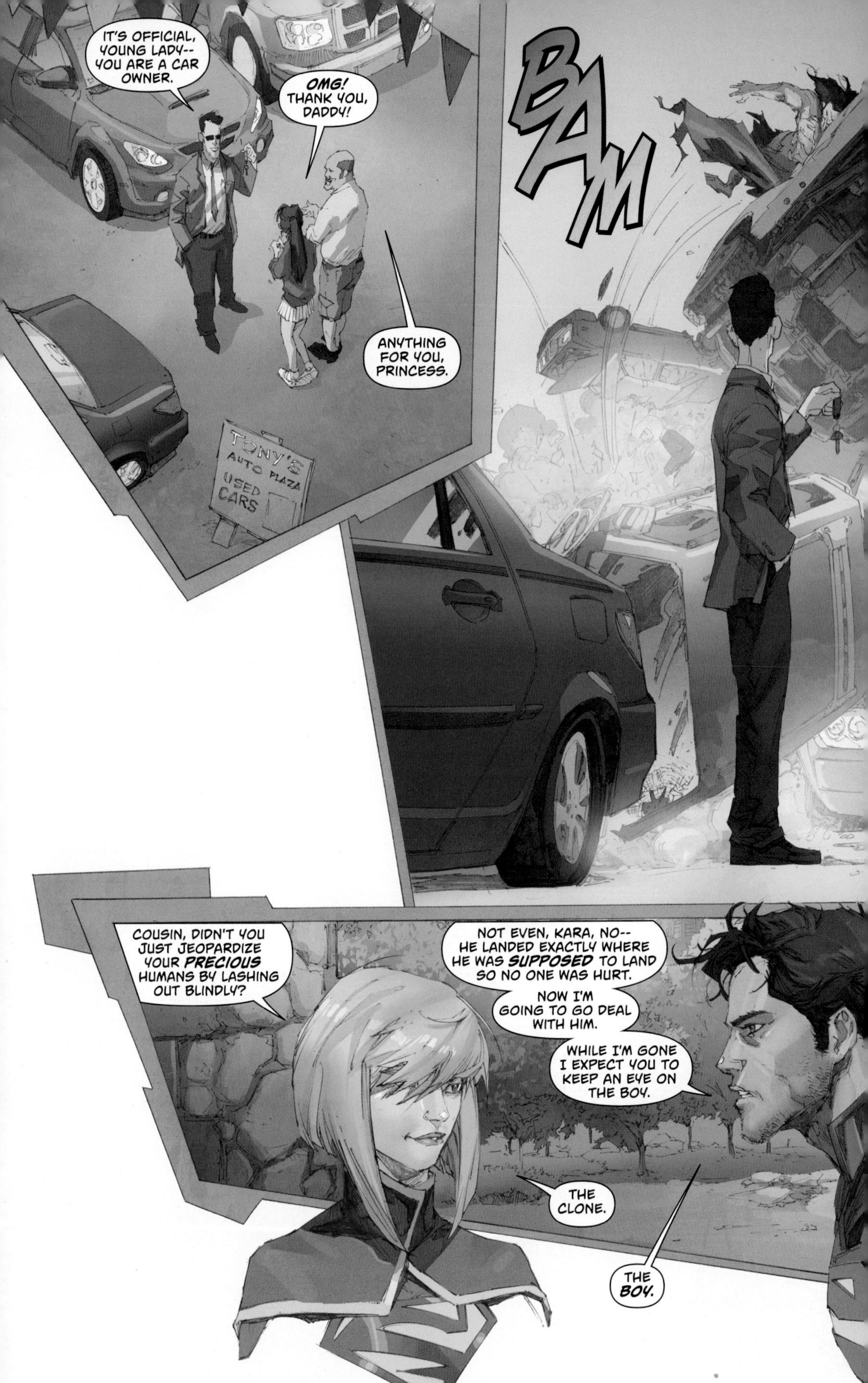
IT'S OFFICIAL, YOUNG LADY-- YOU ARE A CAR OWNER.
OMG! THANK YOU, DADDY!
ANYTHING FOR YOU, PRINCESS.
TONY'S AUTO PLAZA USED CARS
BAM
COUSIN, DIDN'T YOU JUST JEOPARDIZE YOUR PRECIOUS HUMANS BY LASHING OUT BLINDLY?
NOT EVEN, KARA, NO-- HE LANDED EXACTLY WHERE HE WAS SUPPOSED TO LAND SO NO ONE WAS HURT.
NOW I'M GOING TO GO DEAL WITH HIM.
WHILE I'M GONE I EXPECT YOU TO KEEP AN EYE ON THE BOY.
THE CLONE.
THE BOY.

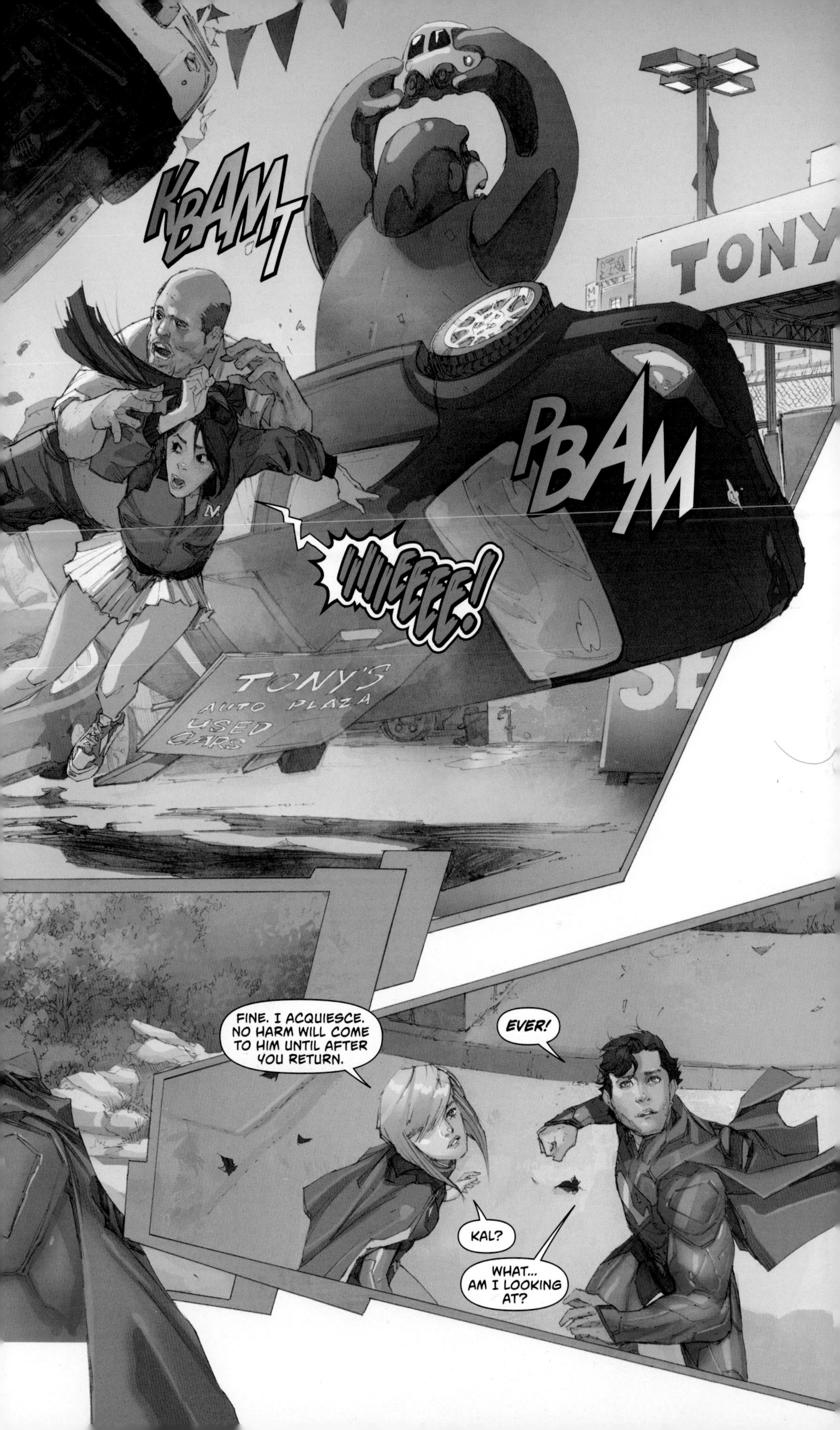

KBAM
TONY
PBAM
IIIIIEEEE!
TONY'S AUTO PLAZA USED CARS
FINE. I ACQUIESCE. NO HARM WILL COME TO HIM UNTIL AFTER YOU RETURN.
EVER!
KAL?
WHAT... AM I LOOKING AT?

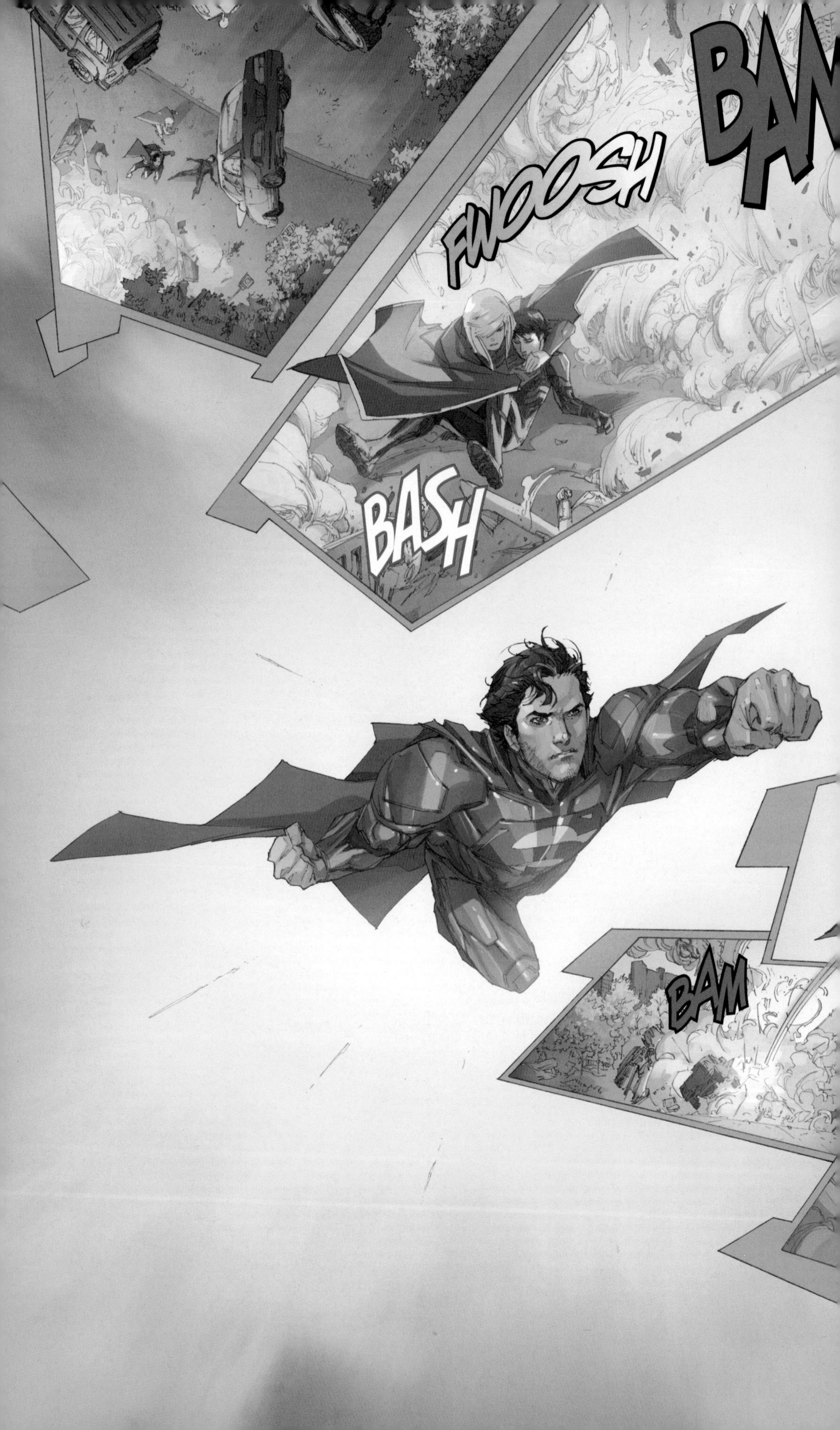
BAM
FWOOSH
BASH
BAM

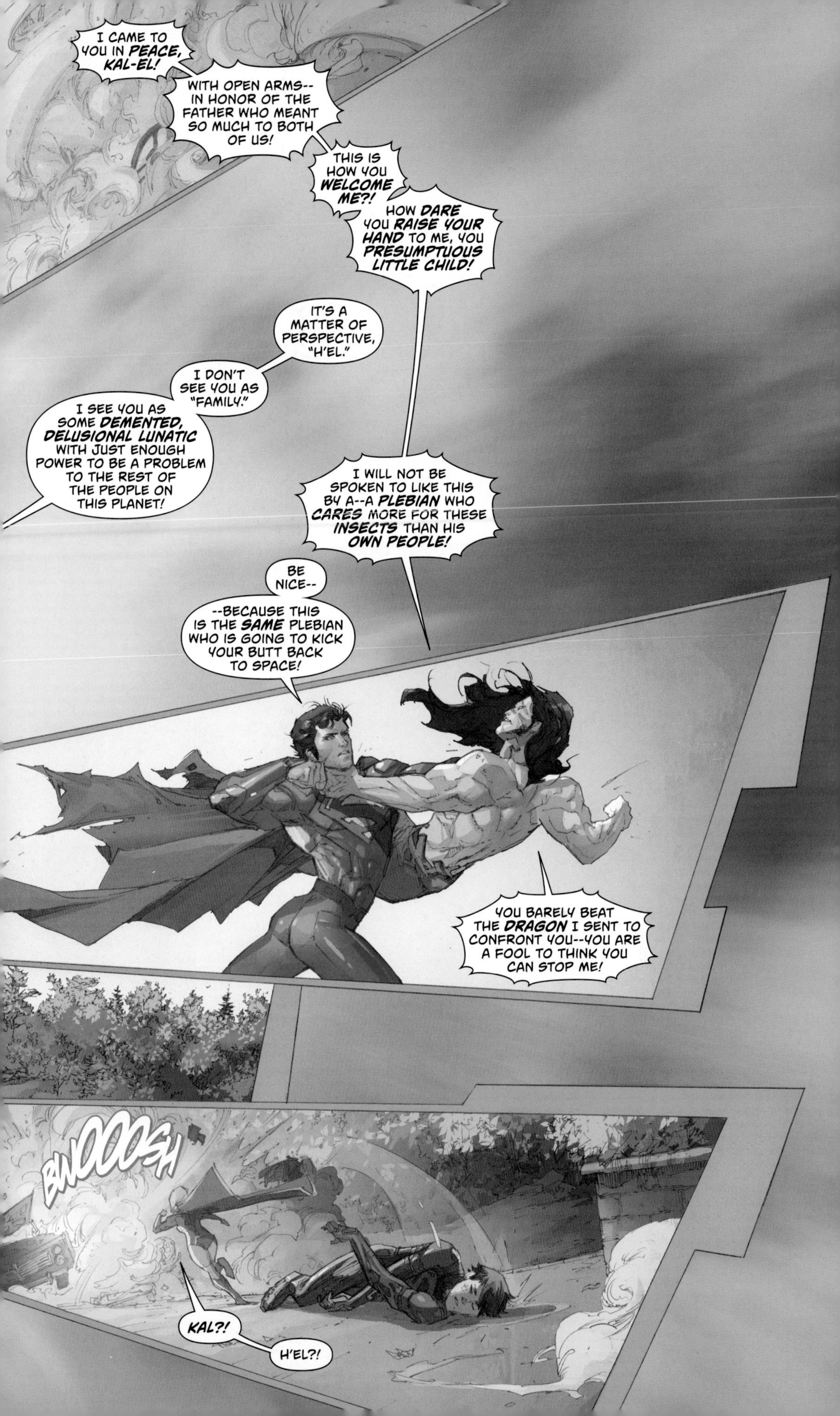
I CAME TO YOU IN PEACE, KAL-EL!
WITH OPEN ARMS-- IN HONOR OF THE FATHER WHO MEANT SO MUCH TO BOTH OF US!
THIS IS HOW YOU WELCOME ME?!
HOW DARE YOU RAISE YOUR HAND TO ME, YOU PRESUMPTUOUS LITTLE CHILD!
IT'S A MATTER OF PERSPECTIVE, "H'EL."
I DON'T SEE YOU AS "FAMILY."
I SEE YOU AS SOME DEMENTED, DELUSIONAL LUNATIC WITH JUST ENOUGH POWER TO BE A PROBLEM TO THE REST OF THE PEOPLE ON THIS PLANET!
I WILL NOT BE SPOKEN TO LIKE THIS BY A--A PLEBIAN WHO CARES MORE FOR THESE INSECTS THAN HIS OWN PEOPLE!
BE NICE--
--BECAUSE THIS IS THE SAME PLEBIAN WHO IS GOING TO KICK YOUR BUTT BACK TO SPACE!
YOU BARELY BEAT THE DRAGON I SENT TO CONFRONT YOU--YOU ARE A FOOL TO THINK YOU CAN STOP ME!
BWOOOSH
KAL?!
H'EL?!

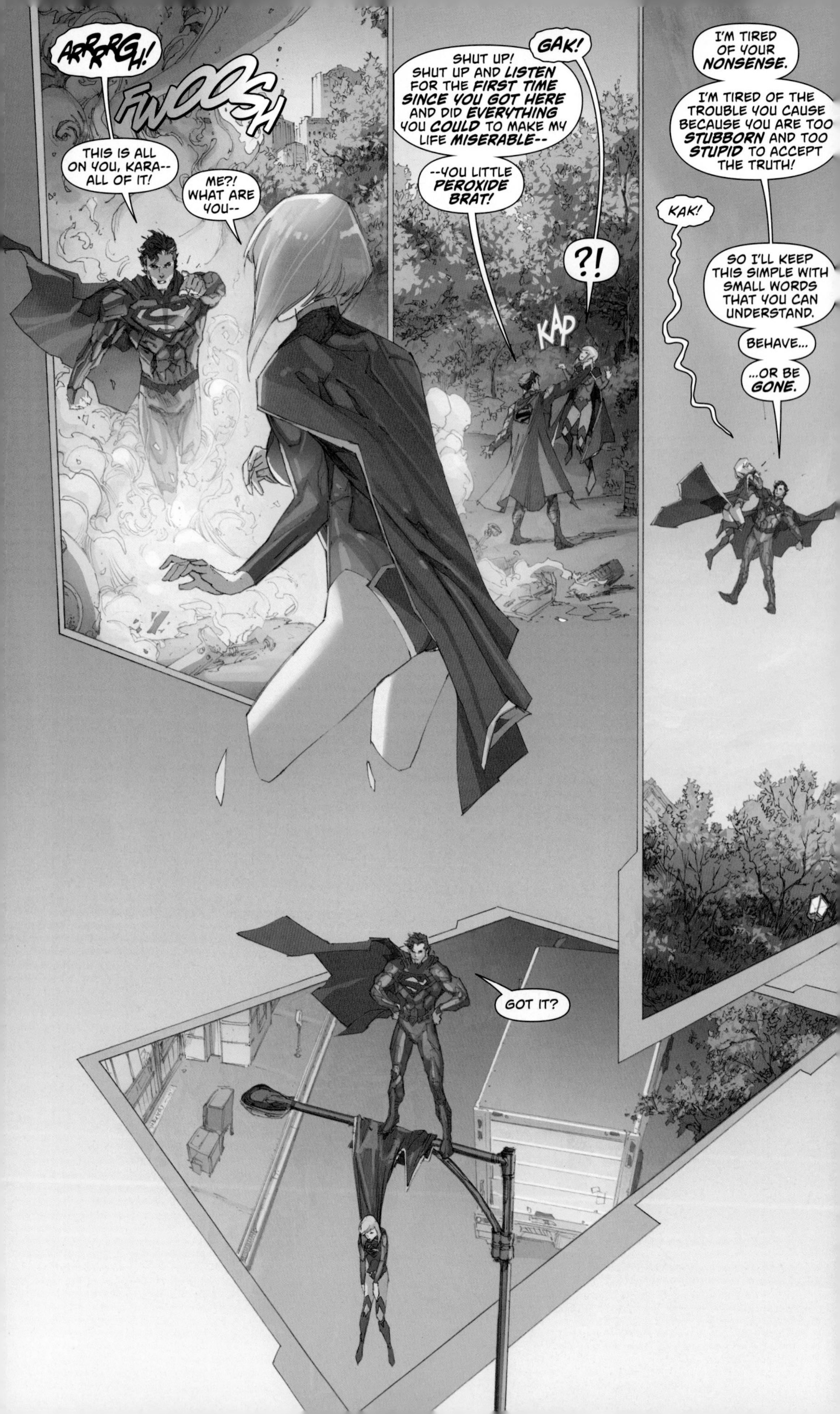

ARRRRGH!
FWOOSH
THIS IS ALL ON YOU, KARA-- ALL OF IT!
ME?! WHAT ARE YOU--
SHUT UP! SHUT UP AND LISTEN FOR THE FIRST TIME SINCE YOU GOT HERE AND DID EVERYTHING YOU COULD TO MAKE MY LIFE MISERABLE--
--YOU LITTLE PEROXIDE BRAT!
GAK!
?!
KAP
I'M TIRED OF YOUR NONSENSE.
I'M TIRED OF THE TROUBLE YOU CAUSE BECAUSE YOU ARE TOO STUBBORN AND TOO STUPID TO ACCEPT THE TRUTH!
KAK!
SO I'LL KEEP THIS SIMPLE WITH SMALL WORDS THAT YOU CAN UNDERSTAND.
BEHAVE...
...OR BE GONE.
GOT IT?

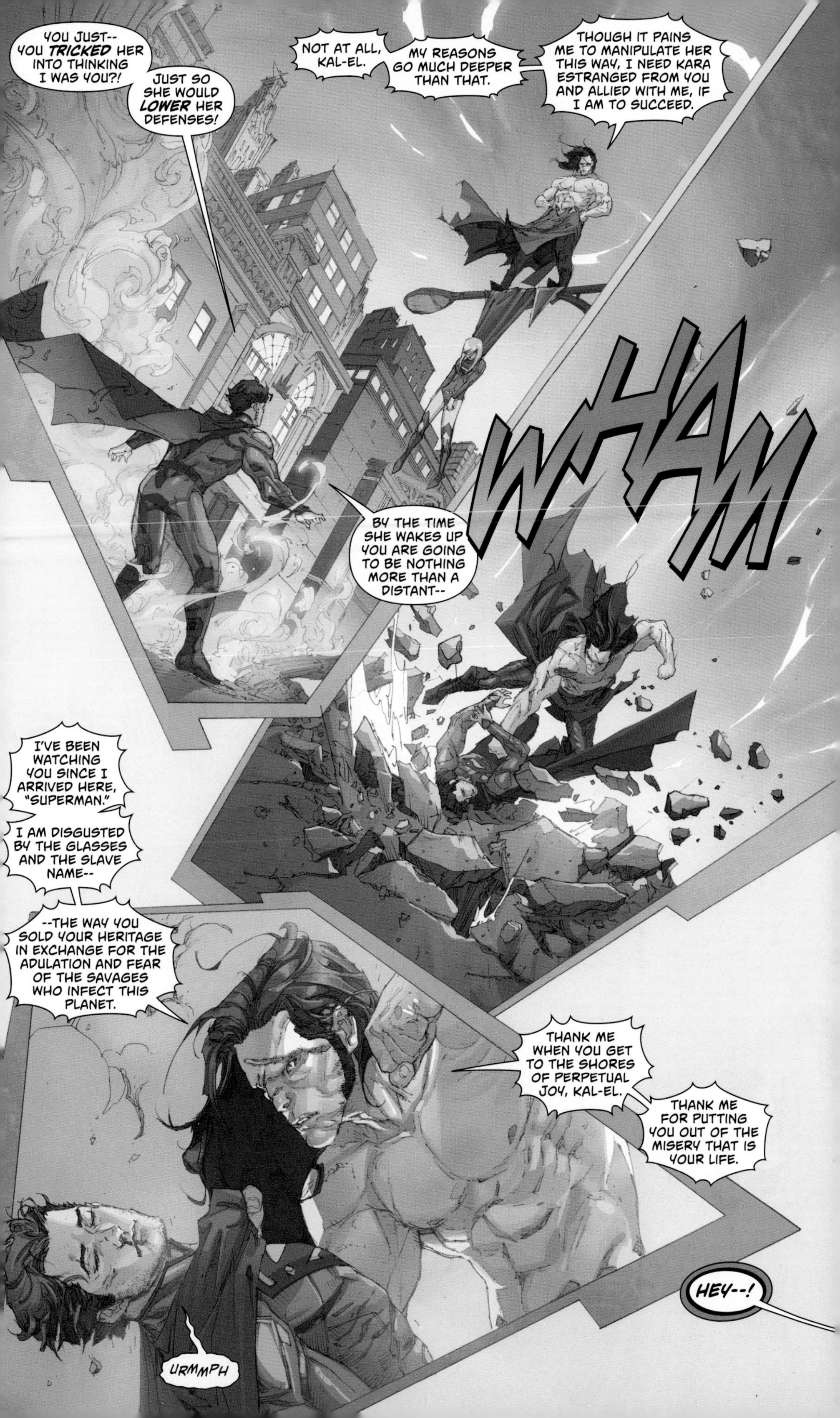
YOU JUST-- YOU **TRICKED** HER INTO THINKING I WAS YOU?!
JUST SO SHE WOULD **LOWER** HER DEFENSES!
NOT AT ALL, KAL-EL.
MY REASONS GO MUCH DEEPER THAN THAT.
THOUGH IT PAINS ME TO MANIPULATE HER THIS WAY, I NEED KARA ESTRANGED FROM YOU AND ALLIED WITH ME, IF I AM TO SUCCEED.
BY THE TIME SHE WAKES UP YOU ARE GOING TO BE NOTHING MORE THAN A DISTANT--
WHAM
I'VE BEEN WATCHING YOU SINCE I ARRIVED HERE, "SUPERMAN."
I AM DISGUSTED BY THE GLASSES AND THE SLAVE NAME--
--THE WAY YOU SOLD YOUR HERITAGE IN EXCHANGE FOR THE ADULATION AND FEAR OF THE SAVAGES WHO INFECT THIS PLANET.
THANK ME WHEN YOU GET TO THE SHORES OF PERPETUAL JOY, KAL-EL.
THANK ME FOR PUTTING YOU OUT OF THE MISERY THAT IS YOUR LIFE.
HEY--!
URMMPH

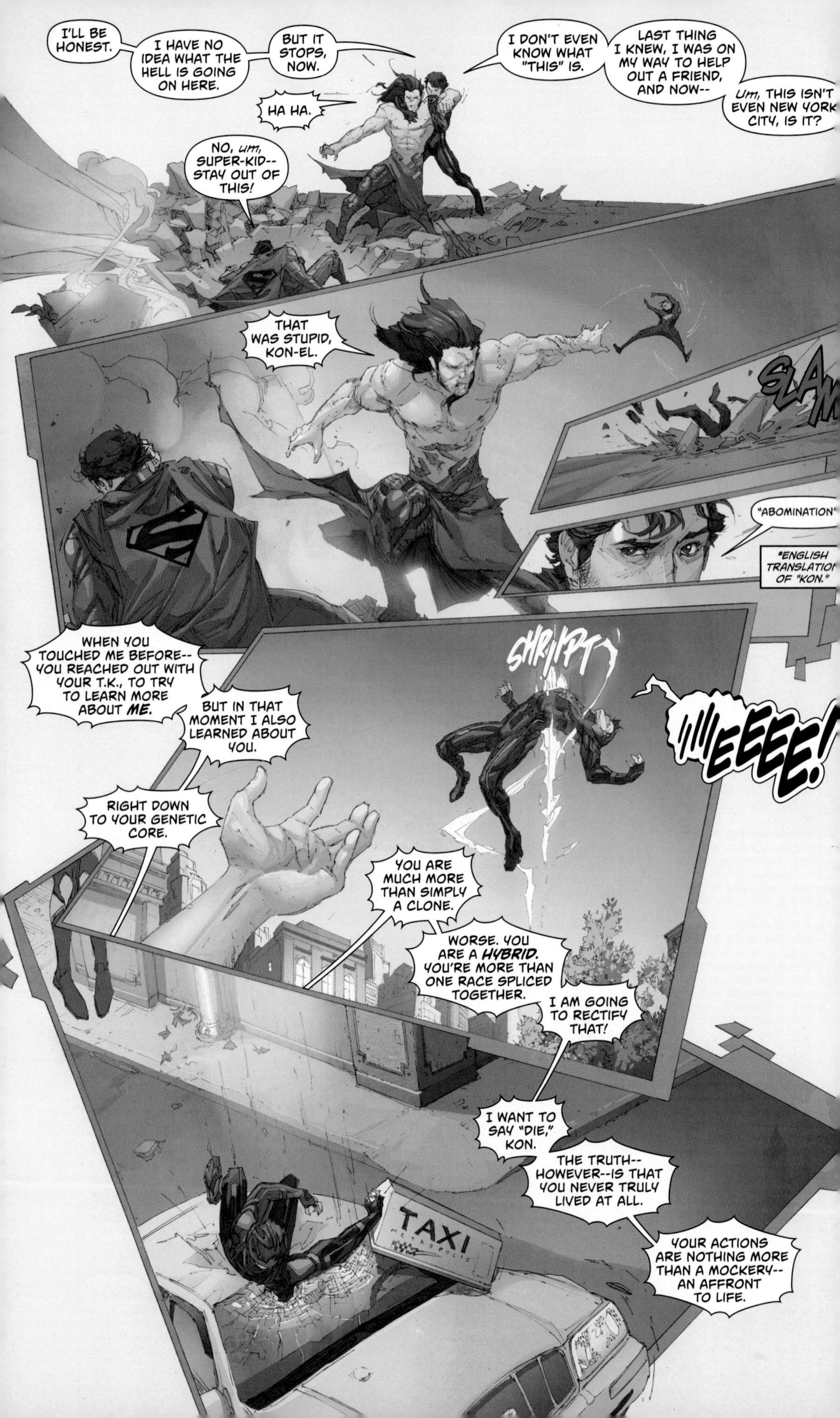
I'LL BE HONEST.
I HAVE NO IDEA WHAT THE HELL IS GOING ON HERE.
BUT IT STOPS, NOW.
I DON'T EVEN KNOW WHAT "THIS" IS.
LAST THING I KNEW, I WAS ON MY WAY TO HELP OUT A FRIEND, AND NOW--
UM, THIS ISN'T EVEN NEW YORK CITY, IS IT?
HA HA.
NO, UM, SUPER-KID--STAY OUT OF THIS!
THAT WAS STUPID, KON-EL.
SLAM
"ABOMINATION"*
*ENGLISH TRANSLATION OF "KON."
WHEN YOU TOUCHED ME BEFORE--YOU REACHED OUT WITH YOUR T.K., TO TRY TO LEARN MORE ABOUT ME.
BUT IN THAT MOMENT I ALSO LEARNED ABOUT YOU.
SHRIIPT
IIIIIEEEEE!
RIGHT DOWN TO YOUR GENETIC CORE.
YOU ARE MUCH MORE THAN SIMPLY A CLONE.
WORSE. YOU ARE A HYBRID. YOU'RE MORE THAN ONE RACE SPLICED TOGETHER.
I AM GOING TO RECTIFY THAT!
I WANT TO SAY "DIE," KON.
THE TRUTH--HOWEVER--IS THAT YOU NEVER TRULY LIVED AT ALL.
TAXI
METROPOLIS
YOUR ACTIONS ARE NOTHING MORE THAN A MOCKERY--AN AFFRONT TO LIFE.

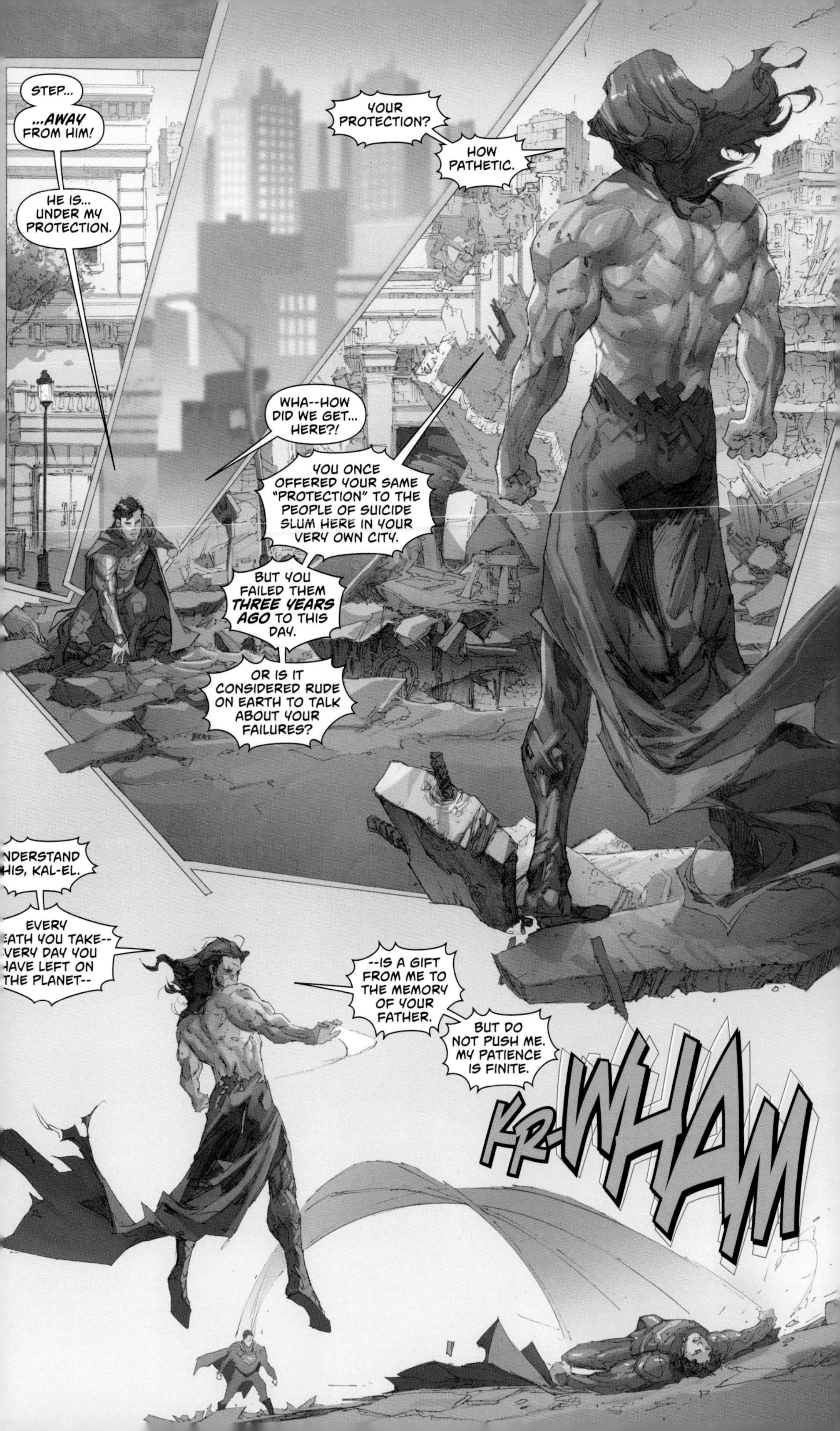
STEP...
...AWAY FROM HIM!
HE IS... UNDER MY PROTECTION.
YOUR PROTECTION?
HOW PATHETIC.
WHA--HOW DID WE GET... HERE?!
YOU ONCE OFFERED YOUR SAME "PROTECTION" TO THE PEOPLE OF SUICIDE SLUM HERE IN YOUR VERY OWN CITY.
BUT YOU FAILED THEM THREE YEARS AGO TO THIS DAY.
OR IS IT CONSIDERED RUDE ON EARTH TO TALK ABOUT YOUR FAILURES?
NDERSTAND HIS, KAL-EL.
EVERY EATH YOU TAKE-- VERY DAY YOU HAVE LEFT ON THE PLANET--
--IS A GIFT FROM ME TO THE MEMORY OF YOUR FATHER.
BUT DO NOT PUSH ME. MY PATIENCE IS FINITE.
KR-WHAM

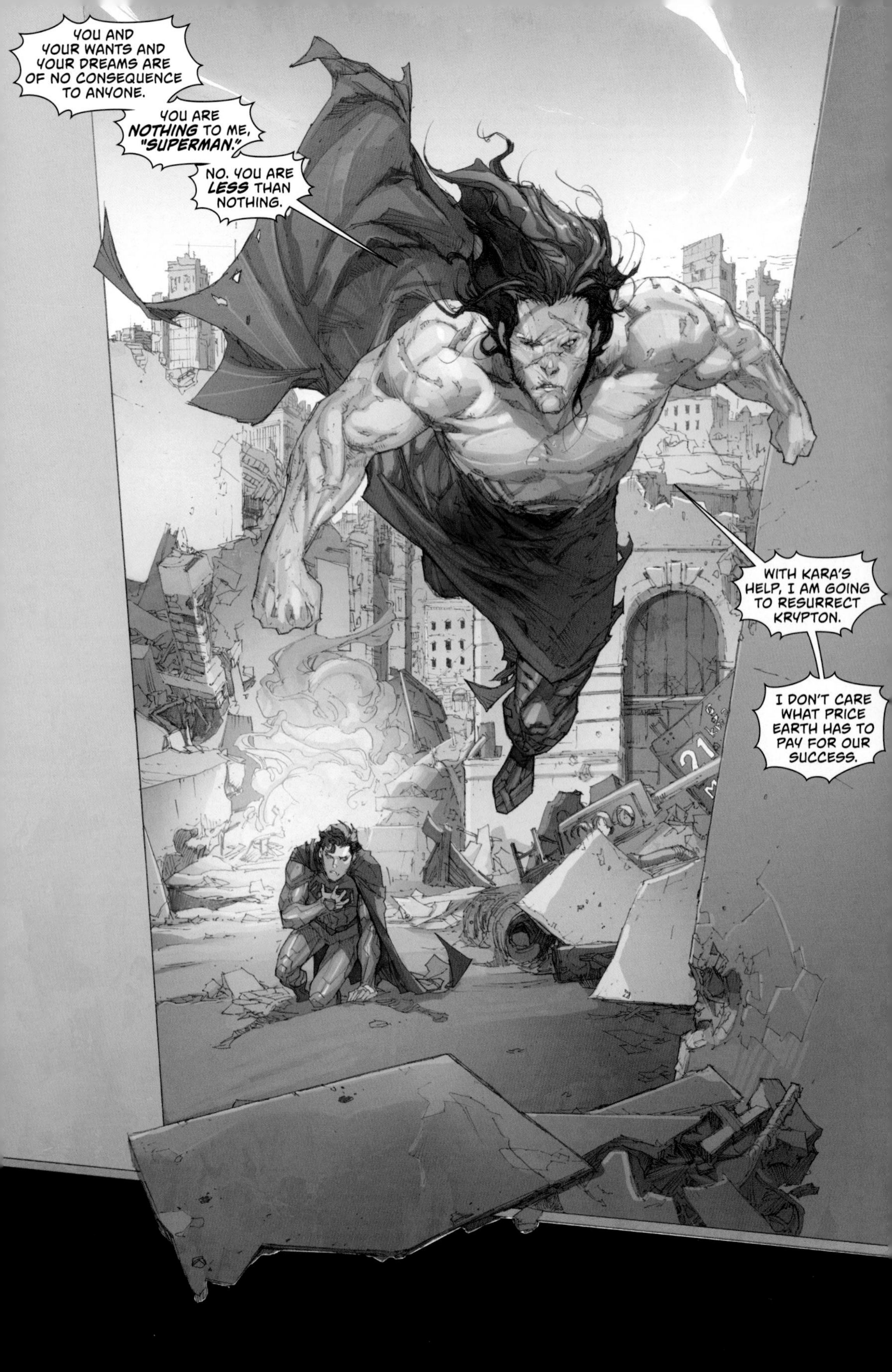
YOU AND YOUR WANTS AND YOUR DREAMS ARE OF NO CONSEQUENCE TO ANYONE.
YOU ARE NOTHING TO ME, "SUPERMAN."
NO. YOU ARE LESS THAN NOTHING.
WITH KARA'S HELP, I AM GOING TO RESURRECT KRYPTON.
I DON'T CARE WHAT PRICE EARTH HAS TO PAY FOR OUR SUCCESS.

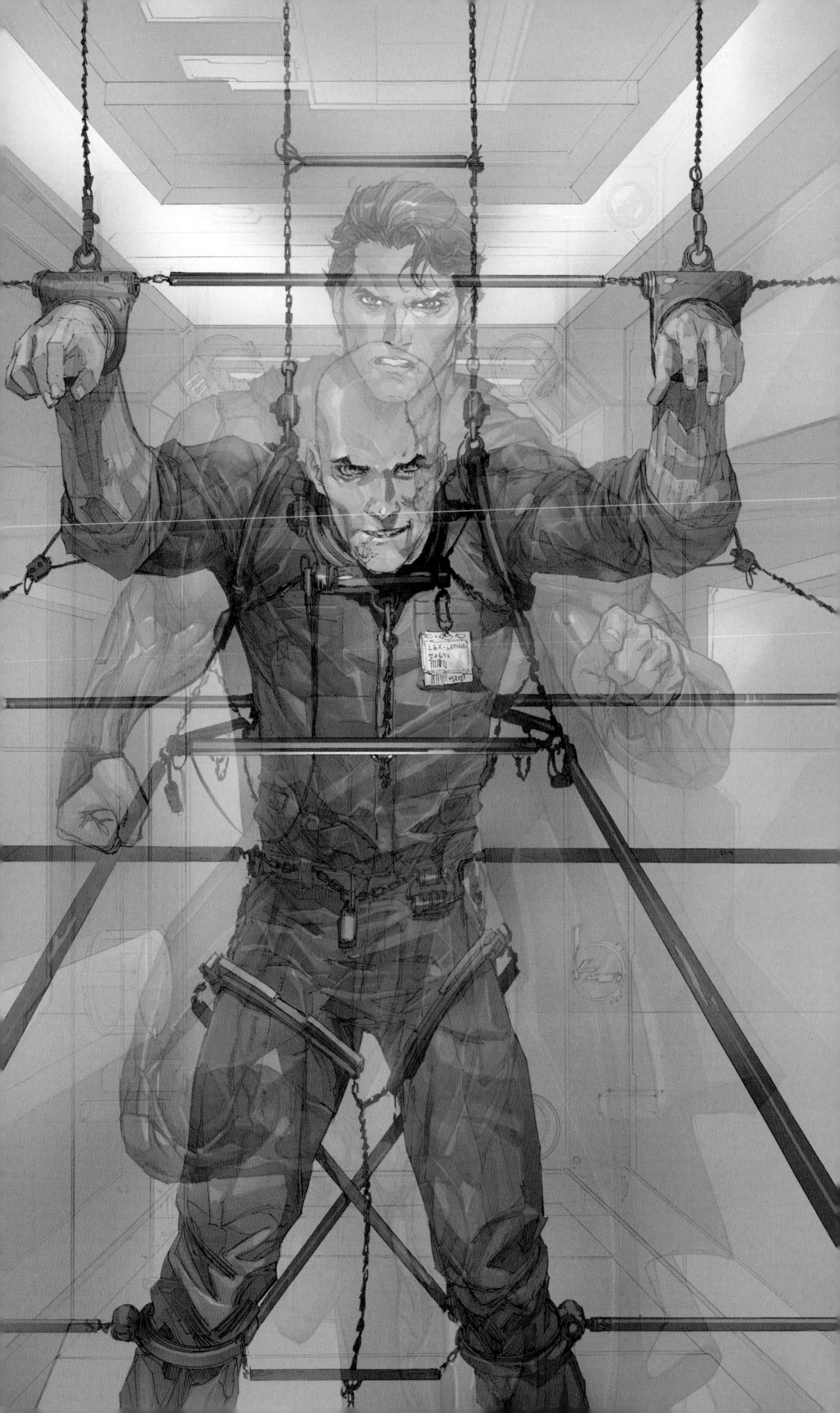
LEX-LUTHOR

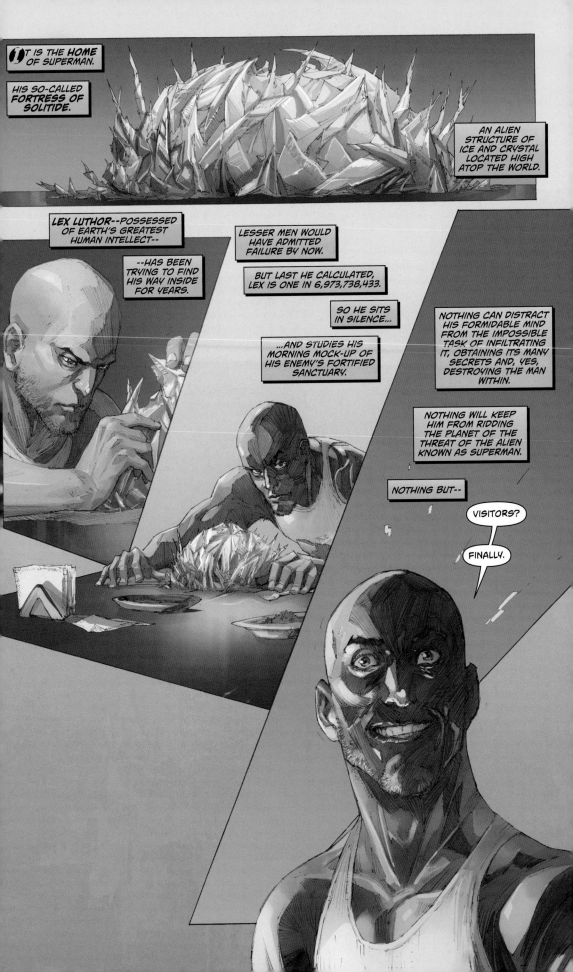

IT IS THE HOME OF SUPERMAN.

HIS SO-CALLED FORTRESS OF SOLITIDE.

AN ALIEN STRUCTURE OF ICE AND CRYSTAL LOCATED HIGH ATOP THE WORLD.

LEX LUTHOR--POSSESSED OF EARTH'S GREATEST HUMAN INTELLECT--

--HAS BEEN TRYING TO FIND HIS WAY INSIDE FOR YEARS.

LESSER MEN WOULD HAVE ADMITTED FAILURE BY NOW.

BUT LAST HE CALCULATED, LEX IS ONE IN 6,973,738,433.

SO HE SITS IN SILENCE...

...AND STUDIES HIS MORNING MOCK-UP OF HIS ENEMY'S FORTIFIED SANCTUARY.

NOTHING CAN DISTRACT HIS FORMIDABLE MIND FROM THE IMPOSSIBLE TASK OF INFILTRATING IT, OBTAINING ITS MANY SECRETS AND, YES, DESTROYING THE MAN WITHIN.

NOTHING WILL KEEP HIM FROM RIDDING THE PLANET OF THE THREAT OF THE ALIEN KNOWN AS SUPERMAN.

NOTHING BUT--

VISITORS?

FINALLY.

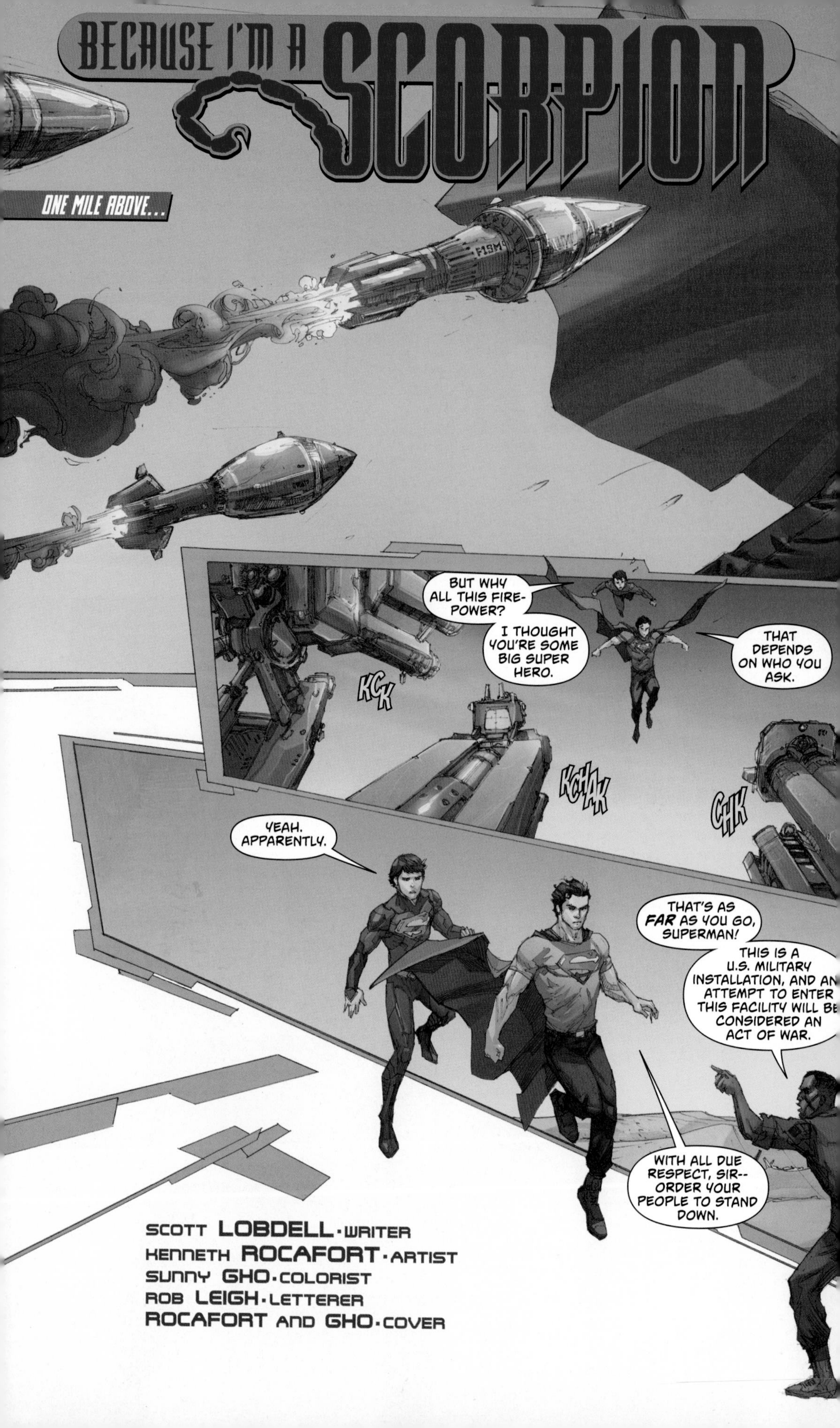

BECAUSE I'M A SCORPION
ONE MILE ABOVE...
BUT WHY ALL THIS FIRE-POWER?
I THOUGHT YOU'RE SOME BIG SUPER HERO.
THAT DEPENDS ON WHO YOU ASK.
KCK
KCHAK
CHK
YEAH. APPARENTLY.
THAT'S AS FAR AS YOU GO, SUPERMAN!
THIS IS A U.S. MILITARY INSTALLATION, AND AN ATTEMPT TO ENTER THIS FACILITY WILL BE CONSIDERED AN ACT OF WAR.
WITH ALL DUE RESPECT, SIR-- ORDER YOUR PEOPLE TO STAND DOWN.
SCOTT LOBDELL · WRITER
KENNETH ROCAFORT · ARTIST
SUNNY GHO · COLORIST
ROB LEIGH · LETTERER
ROCAFORT AND GHO · COVER

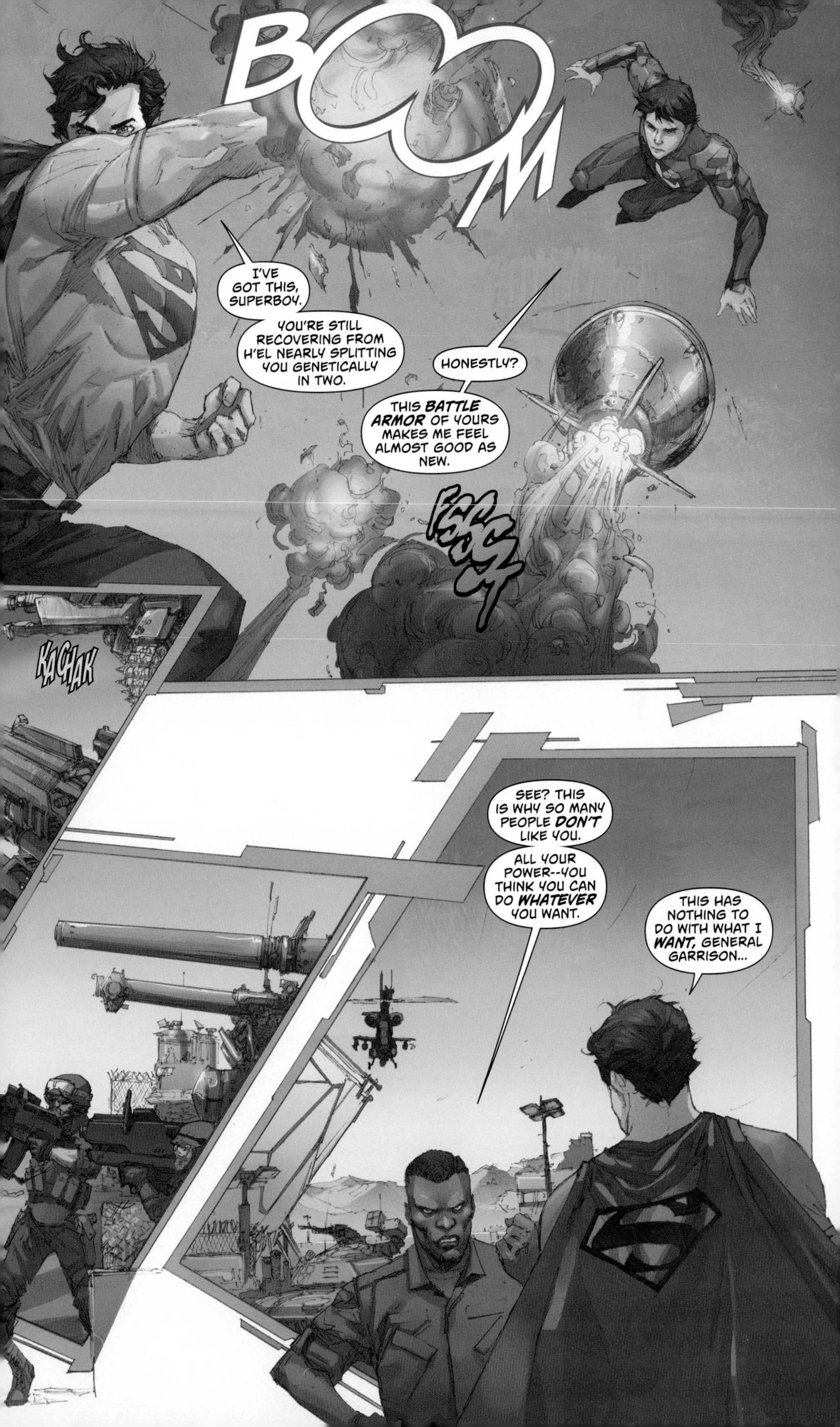
BOOM
I'VE GOT THIS, SUPERBOY.
YOU'RE STILL RECOVERING FROM H'EL NEARLY SPLITTING YOU GENETICALLY IN TWO.
HONESTLY?
THIS BATTLE ARMOR OF YOURS MAKES ME FEEL ALMOST GOOD AS NEW.
KACHAK
SEE? THIS IS WHY SO MANY PEOPLE DON'T LIKE YOU.
ALL YOUR POWER--YOU THINK YOU CAN DO WHATEVER YOU WANT.
THIS HAS NOTHING TO DO WITH WHAT I WANT, GENERAL GARRISON...

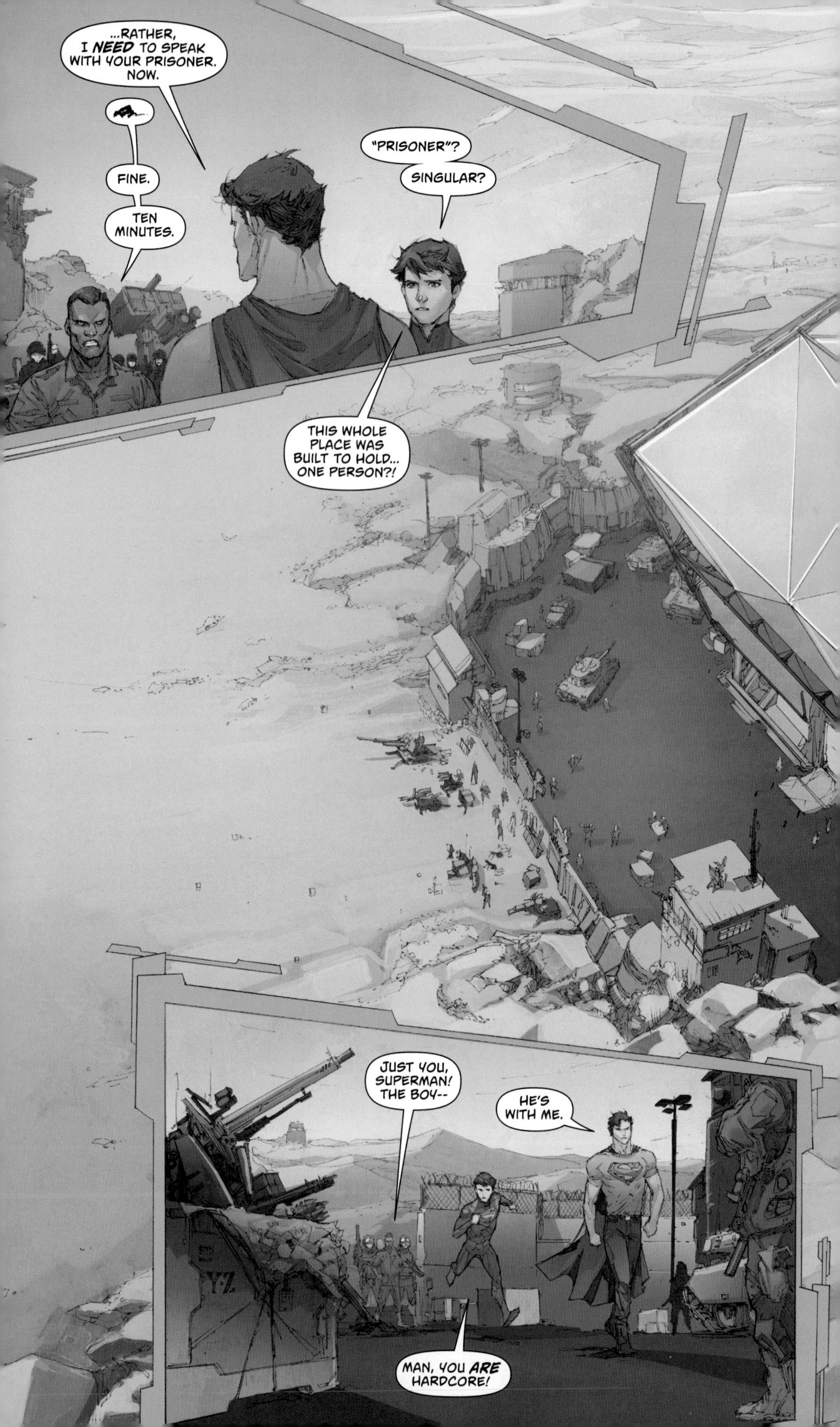
...RATHER, I NEED TO SPEAK WITH YOUR PRISONER. NOW.
FINE.
TEN MINUTES.
"PRISONER"?
SINGULAR?
THIS WHOLE PLACE WAS BUILT TO HOLD... ONE PERSON?!
JUST YOU, SUPERMAN! THE BOY--
HE'S WITH ME.
MAN, YOU ARE HARDCORE!

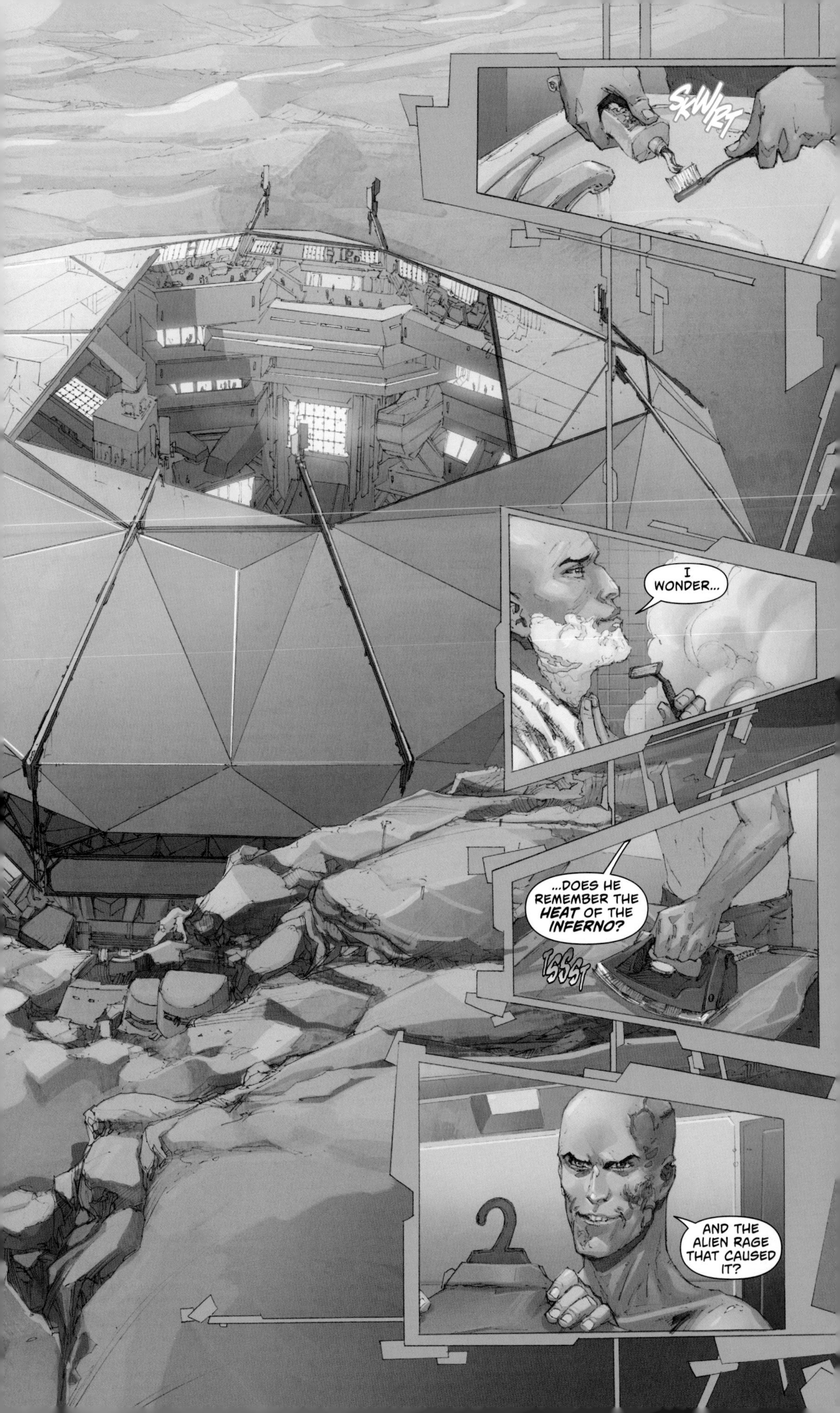
SKWIRT
I WONDER...
...DOES HE REMEMBER THE HEAT OF THE INFERNO?
TSSST
AND THE ALIEN RAGE THAT CAUSED IT?

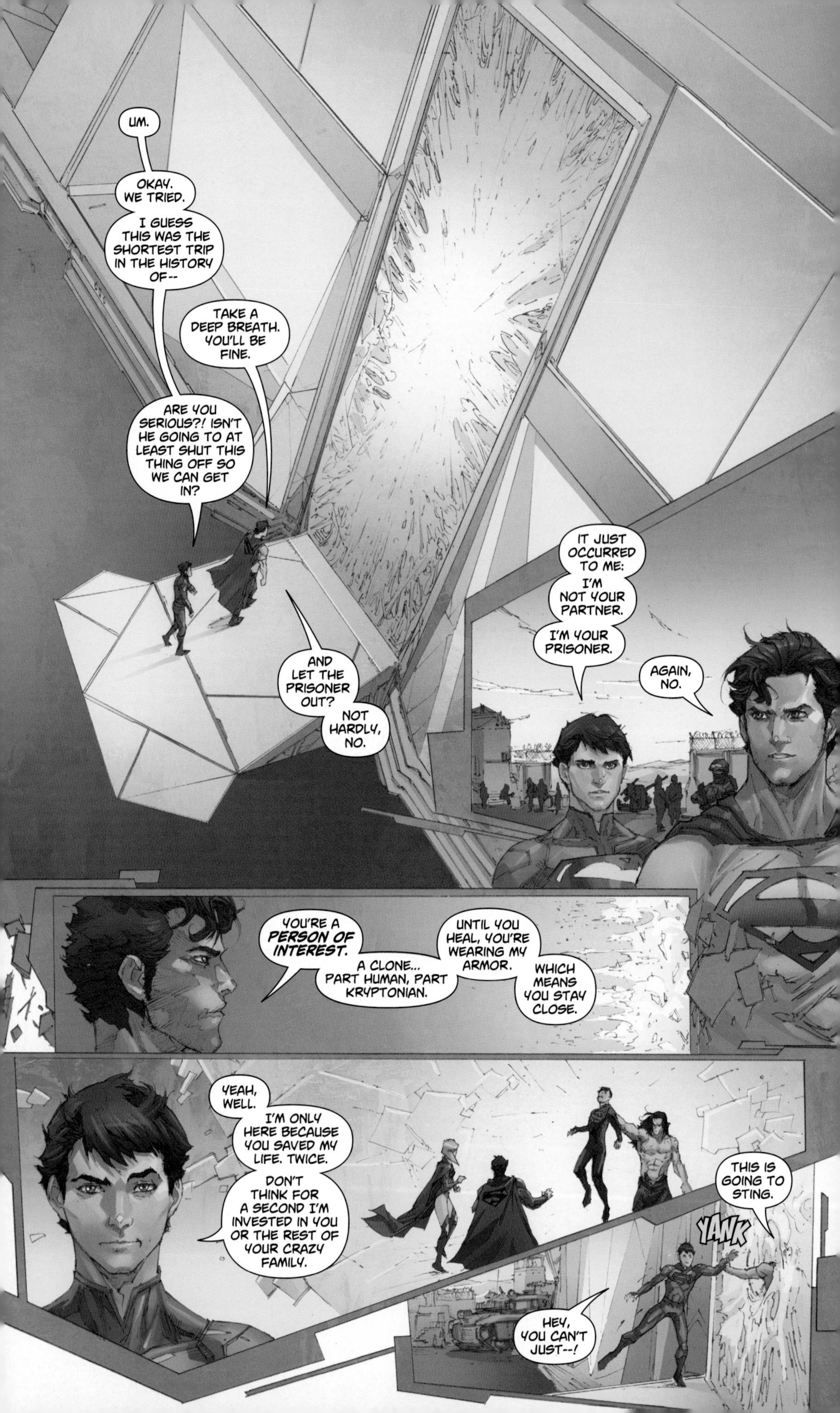
UM.
OKAY. WE TRIED.
I GUESS THIS WAS THE SHORTEST TRIP IN THE HISTORY OF--
TAKE A DEEP BREATH. YOU'LL BE FINE.
ARE YOU SERIOUS?! ISN'T HE GOING TO AT LEAST SHUT THIS THING OFF SO WE CAN GET IN?
AND LET THE PRISONER OUT?
NOT HARDLY, NO.
IT JUST OCCURRED TO ME:
I'M NOT YOUR PARTNER.
I'M YOUR PRISONER.
AGAIN, NO.
YOU'RE A PERSON OF INTEREST.
A CLONE... PART HUMAN, PART KRYPTONIAN.
UNTIL YOU HEAL, YOU'RE WEARING MY ARMOR.
WHICH MEANS YOU STAY CLOSE.
YEAH, WELL.
I'M ONLY HERE BECAUSE YOU SAVED MY LIFE. TWICE.
DON'T THINK FOR A SECOND I'M INVESTED IN YOU OR THE REST OF YOUR CRAZY FAMILY.
THIS IS GOING TO STING.
YANK
HEY, YOU CAN'T JUST--!

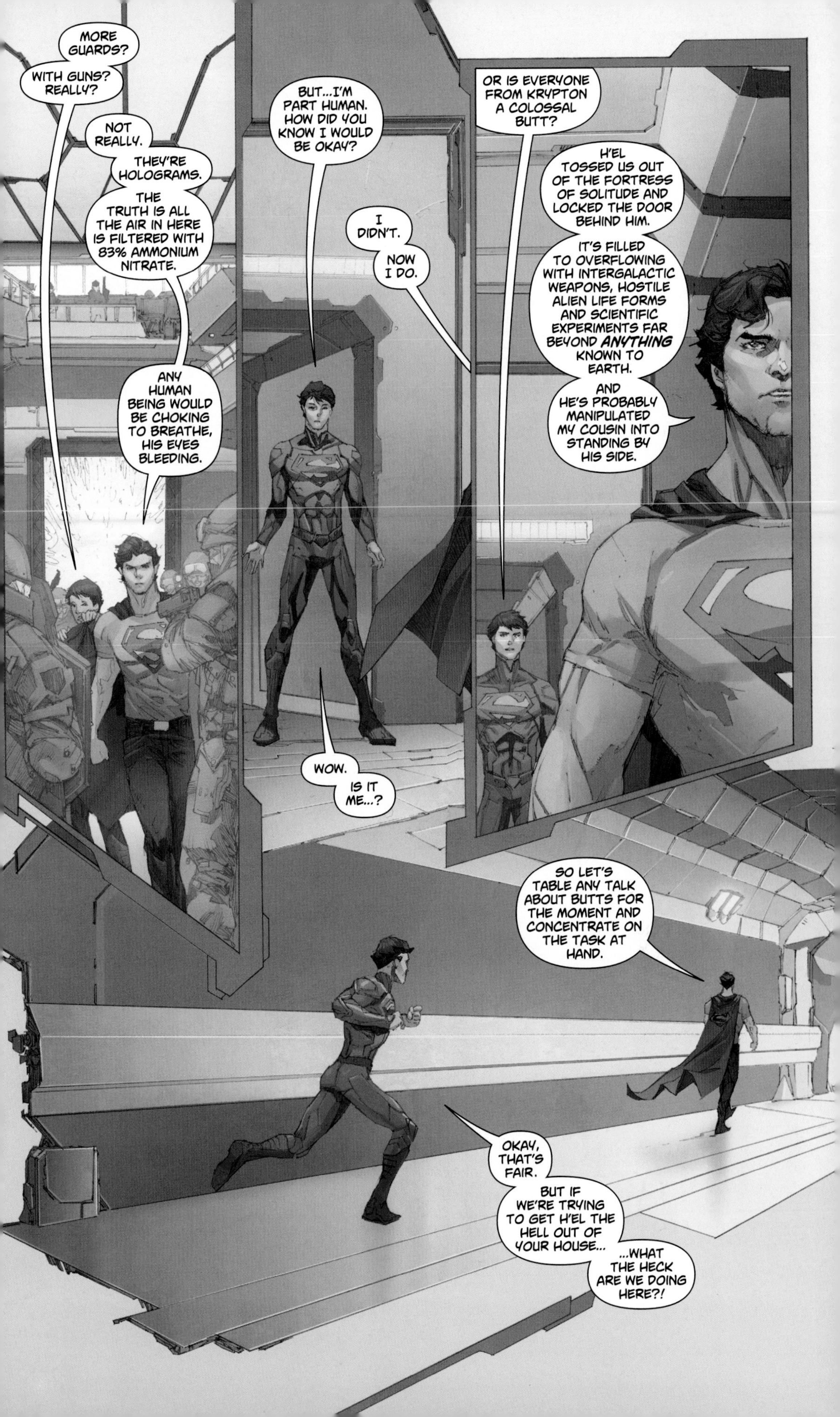
MORE GUARDS?
WITH GUNS? REALLY?
NOT REALLY.
THEY'RE HOLOGRAMS.
THE TRUTH IS ALL THE AIR IN HERE IS FILTERED WITH 83% AMMONIUM NITRATE.
ANY HUMAN BEING WOULD BE CHOKING TO BREATHE, HIS EYES BLEEDING.
BUT...I'M PART HUMAN. HOW DID YOU KNOW I WOULD BE OKAY?
I DIDN'T.
NOW I DO.
WOW.
IS IT ME...?
OR IS EVERYONE FROM KRYPTON A COLOSSAL BUTT?
H'EL TOSSED US OUT OF THE FORTRESS OF SOLITUDE AND LOCKED THE DOOR BEHIND HIM.
IT'S FILLED TO OVERFLOWING WITH INTERGALACTIC WEAPONS, HOSTILE ALIEN LIFE FORMS AND SCIENTIFIC EXPERIMENTS FAR BEYOND ANYTHING KNOWN TO EARTH.
AND HE'S PROBABLY MANIPULATED MY COUSIN INTO STANDING BY HIS SIDE.
SO LET'S TABLE ANY TALK ABOUT BUTTS FOR THE MOMENT AND CONCENTRATE ON THE TASK AT HAND.
OKAY, THAT'S FAIR.
BUT IF WE'RE TRYING TO GET H'EL THE HELL OUT OF YOUR HOUSE...
...WHAT THE HECK ARE WE DOING HERE?!

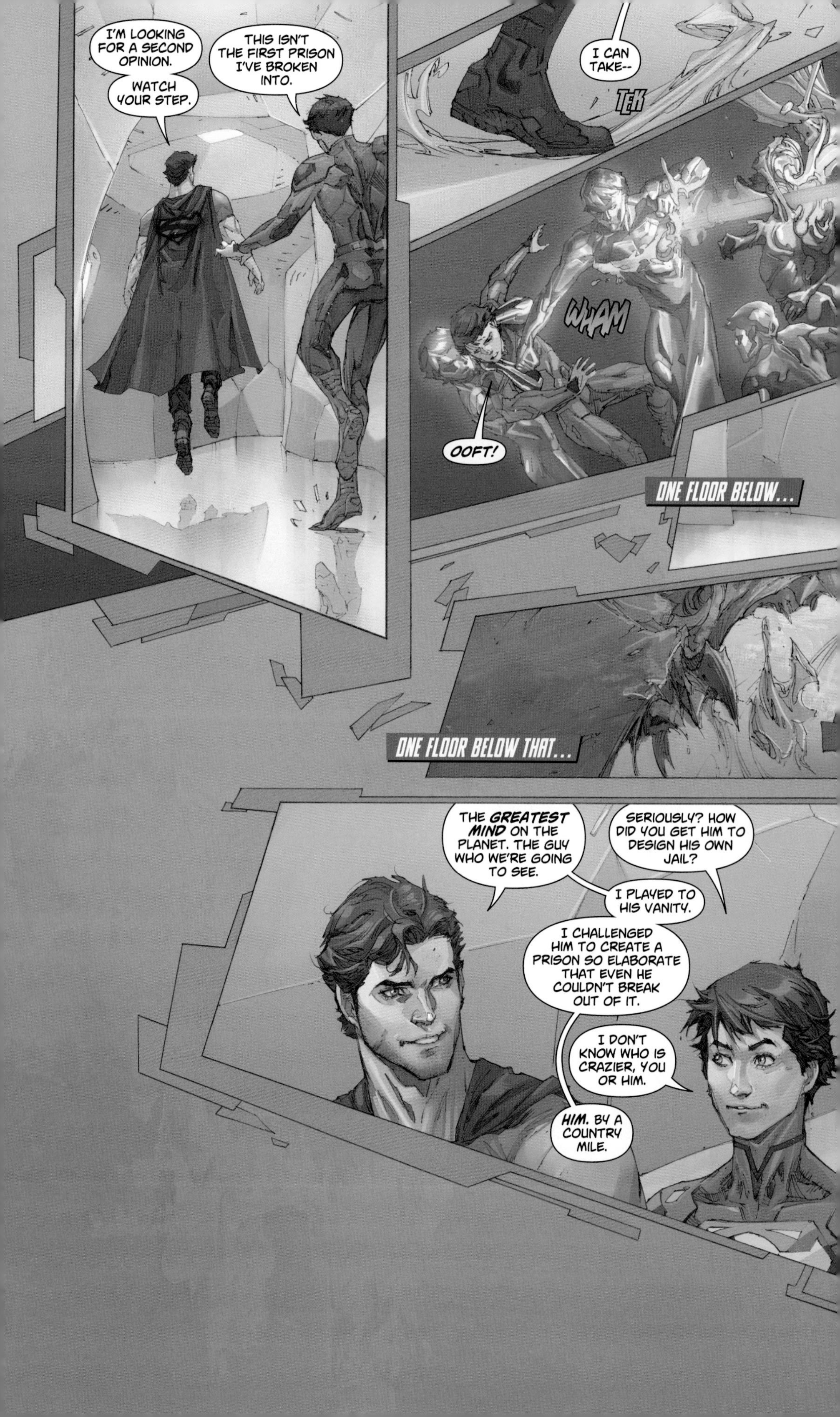
I'M LOOKING FOR A SECOND OPINION.
WATCH YOUR STEP.
THIS ISN'T THE FIRST PRISON I'VE BROKEN INTO.
I CAN TAKE--
TEK
WHAM
OOFT!
ONE FLOOR BELOW...
ONE FLOOR BELOW THAT...
THE GREATEST MIND ON THE PLANET. THE GUY WHO WE'RE GOING TO SEE.
SERIOUSLY? HOW DID YOU GET HIM TO DESIGN HIS OWN JAIL?
I PLAYED TO HIS VANITY.
I CHALLENGED HIM TO CREATE A PRISON SO ELABORATE THAT EVEN HE COULDN'T BREAK OUT OF IT.
I DON'T KNOW WHO IS CRAZIER, YOU OR HIM.
HIM. BY A COUNTRY MILE.

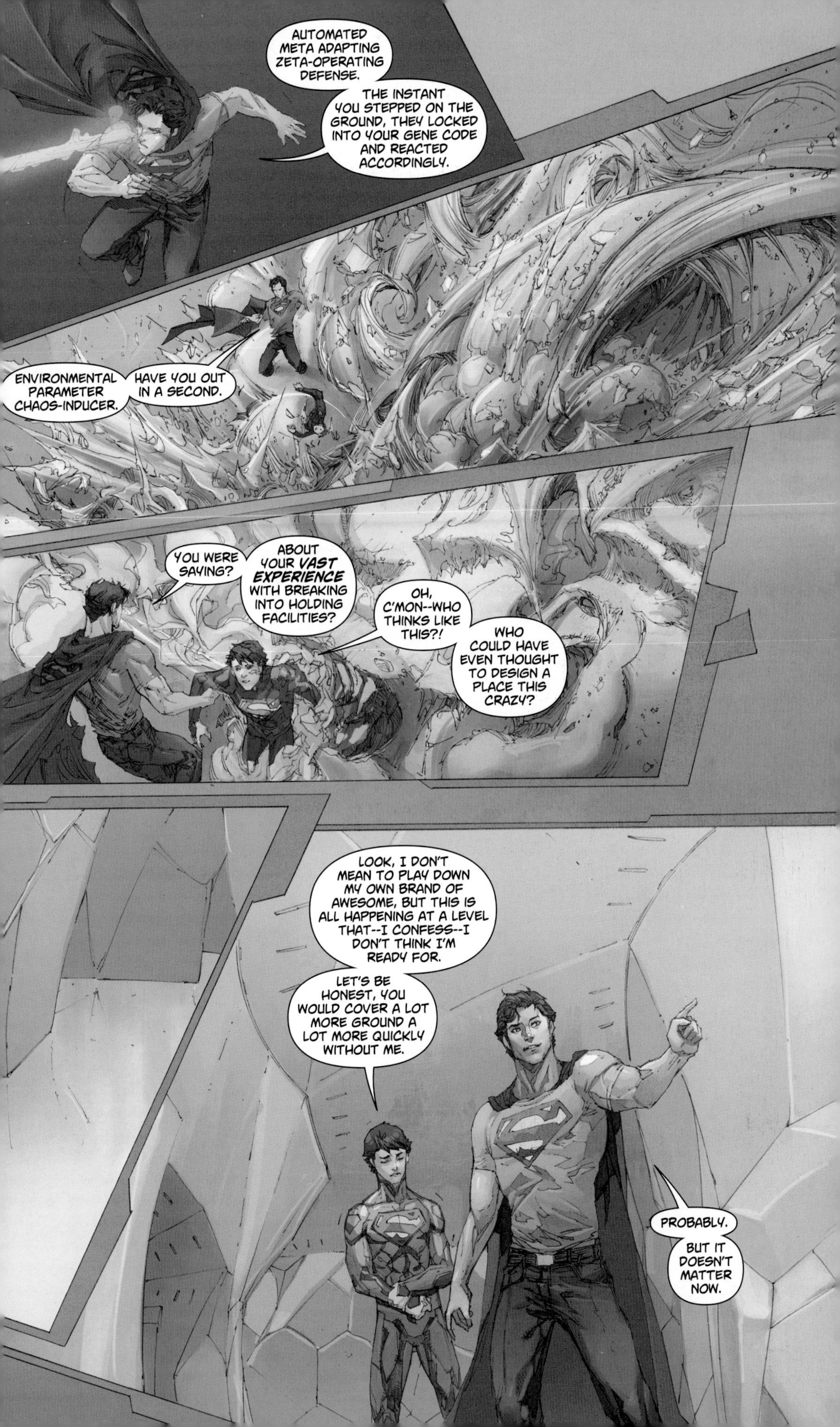
AUTOMATED META ADAPTING ZETA-OPERATING DEFENSE.
THE INSTANT YOU STEPPED ON THE GROUND, THEY LOCKED INTO YOUR GENE CODE AND REACTED ACCORDINGLY.
ENVIRONMENTAL PARAMETER CHAOS-INDUCER.
HAVE YOU OUT IN A SECOND.
YOU WERE SAYING?
ABOUT YOUR ***VAST EXPERIENCE*** WITH BREAKING INTO HOLDING FACILITIES?
OH, C'MON--WHO THINKS LIKE THIS?!
WHO COULD HAVE EVEN THOUGHT TO DESIGN A PLACE THIS CRAZY?
LOOK, I DON'T MEAN TO PLAY DOWN MY OWN BRAND OF AWESOME, BUT THIS IS ALL HAPPENING AT A LEVEL THAT--I CONFESS--I DON'T THINK I'M READY FOR.
LET'S BE HONEST, YOU WOULD COVER A LOT MORE GROUND A LOT MORE QUICKLY WITHOUT ME.
PROBABLY.
BUT IT DOESN'T MATTER NOW.

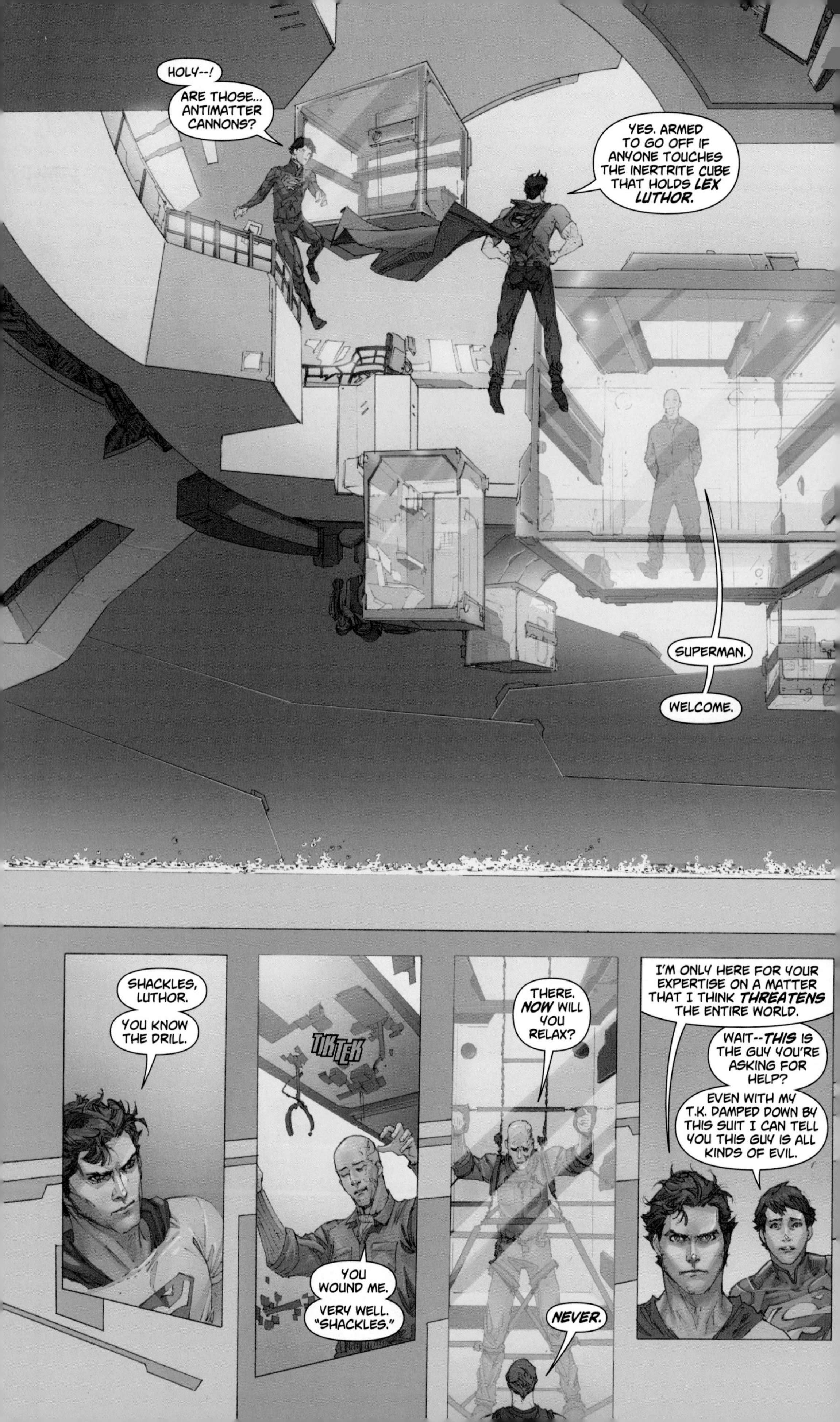
HOLY--!
ARE THOSE... ANTIMATTER CANNONS?
YES. ARMED TO GO OFF IF ANYONE TOUCHES THE INERTRITE CUBE THAT HOLDS *LEX LUTHOR.*
SUPERMAN.
WELCOME.
SHACKLES, LUTHOR.
YOU KNOW THE DRILL.
TIKTEK
YOU WOUND ME.
VERY WELL. "SHACKLES."
THERE. *NOW* WILL YOU RELAX?
NEVER.
I'M ONLY HERE FOR YOUR EXPERTISE ON A MATTER THAT I THINK *THREATENS* THE ENTIRE WORLD.
WAIT--*THIS* IS THE GUY YOU'RE ASKING FOR HELP?
EVEN WITH MY T.K. DAMPED DOWN BY THIS SUIT I CAN TELL YOU THIS GUY IS ALL KINDS OF EVIL.

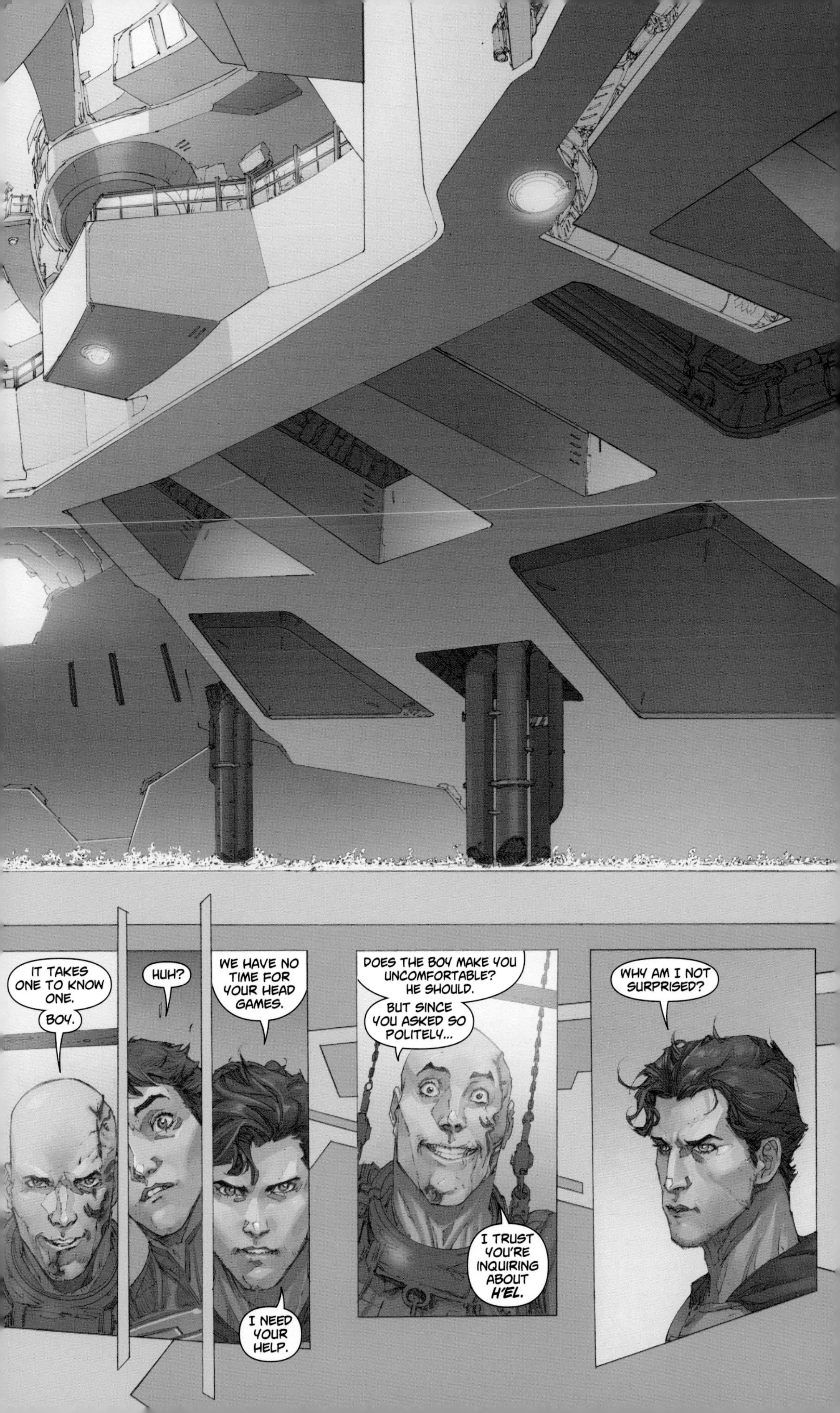
IT TAKES ONE TO KNOW ONE.
BOY.
HUH?
WE HAVE NO TIME FOR YOUR HEAD GAMES.
I NEED YOUR HELP.
DOES THE BOY MAKE YOU UNCOMFORTABLE? HE SHOULD.
BUT SINCE YOU ASKED SO POLITELY...
I TRUST YOU'RE INQUIRING ABOUT H'EL.
WHY AM I NOT SURPRISED?

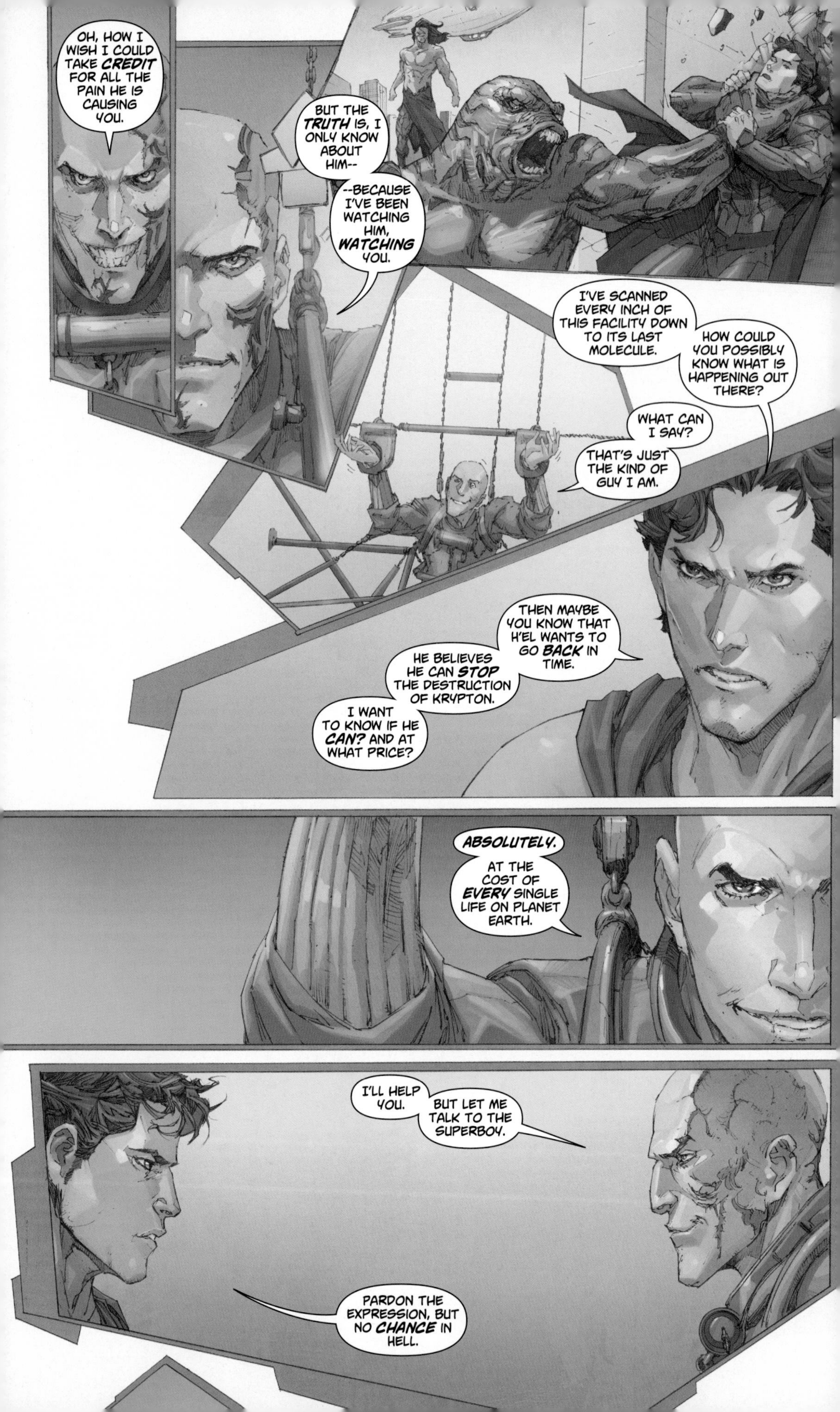
OH, HOW I WISH I COULD TAKE CREDIT FOR ALL THE PAIN HE IS CAUSING YOU.
BUT THE TRUTH IS, I ONLY KNOW ABOUT HIM--
--BECAUSE I'VE BEEN WATCHING HIM, WATCHING YOU.
I'VE SCANNED EVERY INCH OF THIS FACILITY DOWN TO ITS LAST MOLECULE.
HOW COULD YOU POSSIBLY KNOW WHAT IS HAPPENING OUT THERE?
WHAT CAN I SAY?
THAT'S JUST THE KIND OF GUY I AM.
THEN MAYBE YOU KNOW THAT H'EL WANTS TO GO BACK IN TIME.
HE BELIEVES HE CAN STOP THE DESTRUCTION OF KRYPTON.
I WANT TO KNOW IF HE CAN? AND AT WHAT PRICE?
ABSOLUTELY.
AT THE COST OF EVERY SINGLE LIFE ON PLANET EARTH.
I'LL HELP YOU.
BUT LET ME TALK TO THE SUPERBOY.
PARDON THE EXPRESSION, BUT NO CHANCE IN HELL.

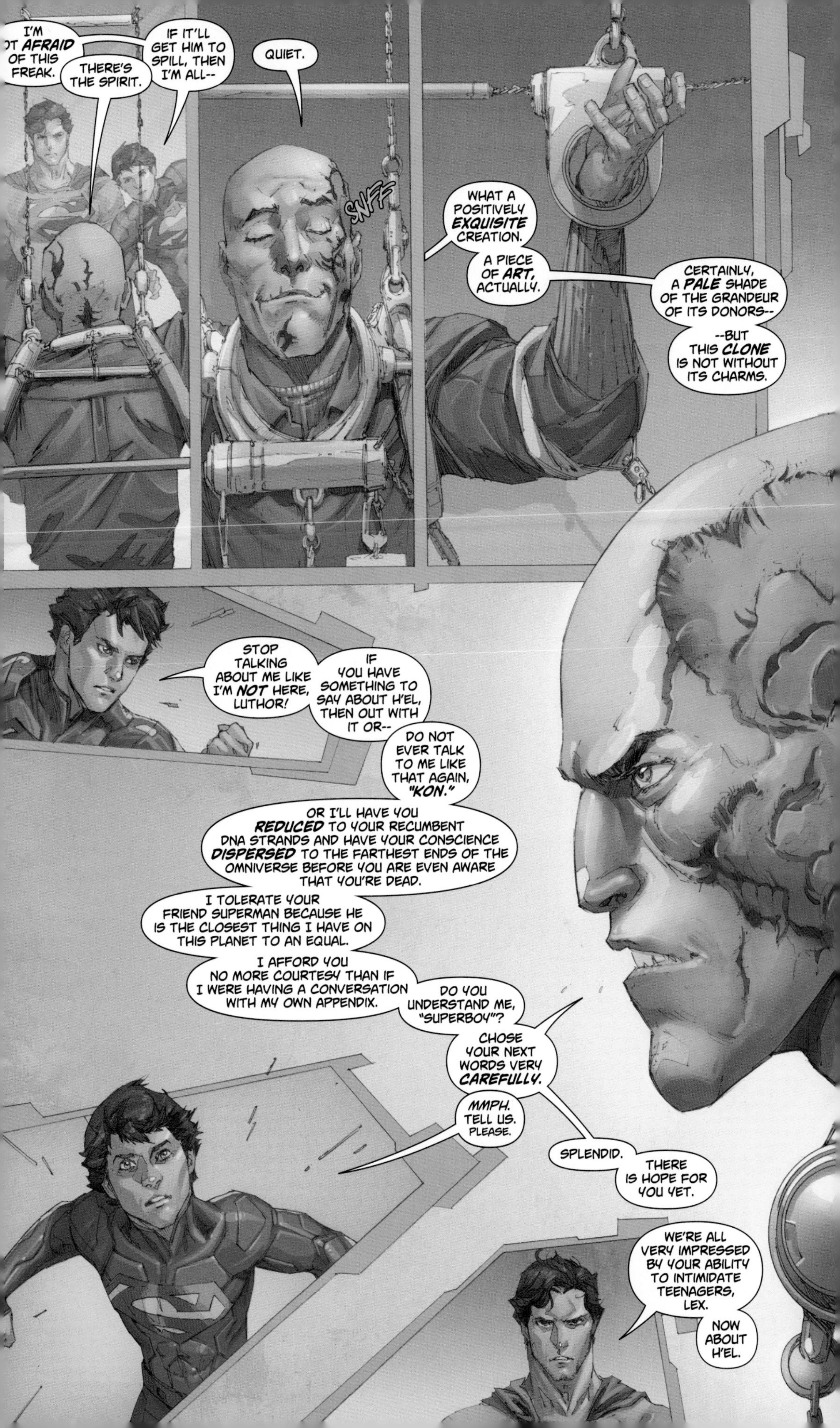
I'M NOT AFRAID OF THIS FREAK.
THERE'S THE SPIRIT.
IF IT'LL GET HIM TO SPILL, THEN I'M ALL--
QUIET.
SNIFF
WHAT A POSITIVELY EXQUISITE CREATION.
A PIECE OF ART, ACTUALLY.
CERTAINLY, A PALE SHADE OF THE GRANDEUR OF ITS DONORS--
--BUT THIS CLONE IS NOT WITHOUT ITS CHARMS.
STOP TALKING ABOUT ME LIKE I'M NOT HERE, LUTHOR!
IF YOU HAVE SOMETHING TO SAY ABOUT H'EL, THEN OUT WITH IT OR--
DO NOT EVER TALK TO ME LIKE THAT AGAIN, "KON."
OR I'LL HAVE YOU REDUCED TO YOUR RECUMBENT DNA STRANDS AND HAVE YOUR CONSCIENCE DISPERSED TO THE FARTHEST ENDS OF THE OMNIVERSE BEFORE YOU ARE EVEN AWARE THAT YOU'RE DEAD.
I TOLERATE YOUR FRIEND SUPERMAN BECAUSE HE IS THE CLOSEST THING I HAVE ON THIS PLANET TO AN EQUAL.
I AFFORD YOU NO MORE COURTESY THAN IF I WERE HAVING A CONVERSATION WITH MY OWN APPENDIX.
DO YOU UNDERSTAND ME, "SUPERBOY"?
CHOSE YOUR NEXT WORDS VERY CAREFULLY.
MMPH. TELL US. PLEASE.
SPLENDID.
THERE IS HOPE FOR YOU YET.
WE'RE ALL VERY IMPRESSED BY YOUR ABILITY TO INTIMIDATE TEENAGERS, LEX.
NOW ABOUT H'EL.

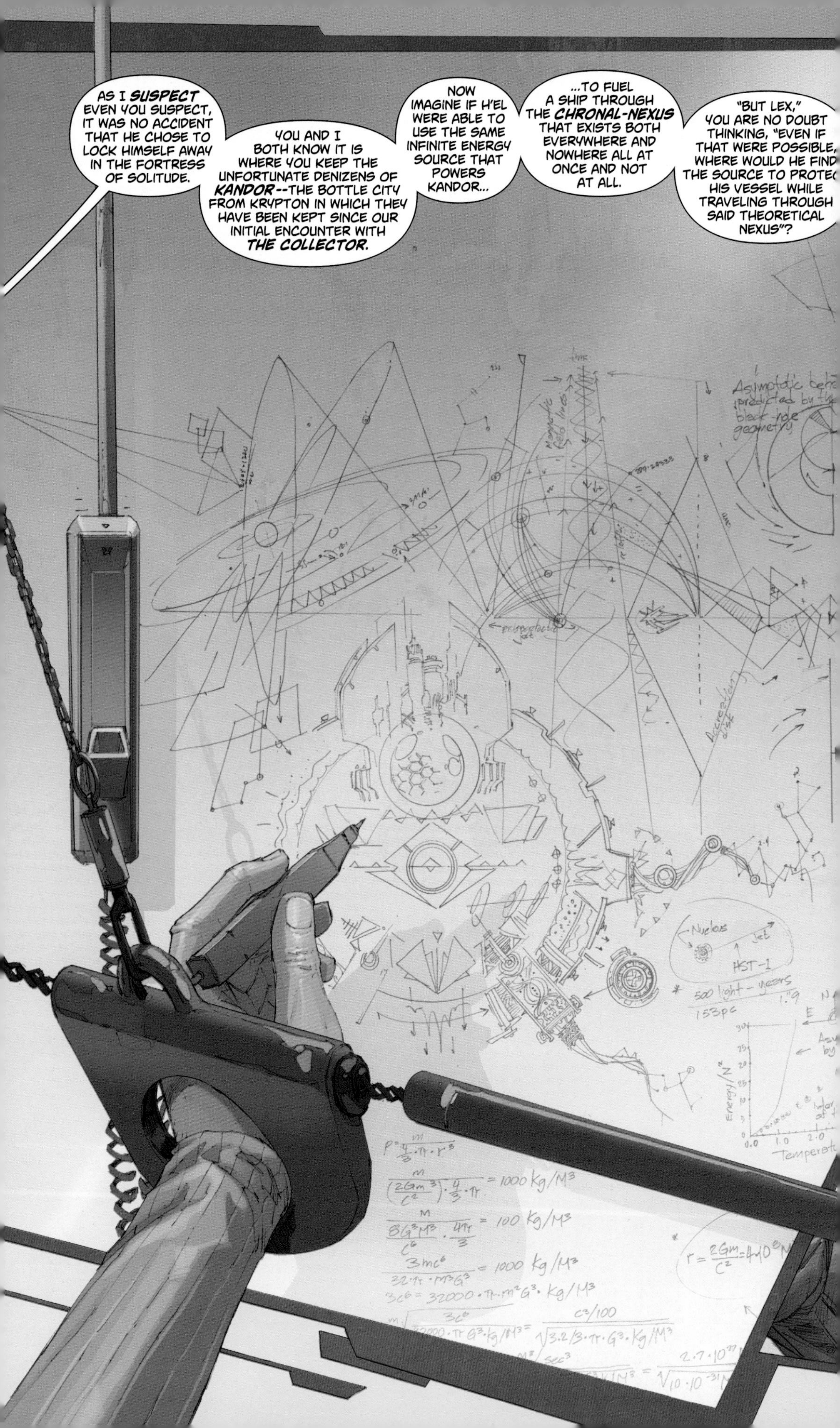
AS I SUSPECT EVEN YOU SUSPECT, IT WAS NO ACCIDENT THAT HE CHOSE TO LOCK HIMSELF AWAY IN THE FORTRESS OF SOLITUDE.
YOU AND I BOTH KNOW IT IS WHERE YOU KEEP THE UNFORTUNATE DENIZENS OF KANDOR--THE BOTTLE CITY FROM KRYPTON IN WHICH THEY HAVE BEEN KEPT SINCE OUR INITIAL ENCOUNTER WITH THE COLLECTOR.
NOW IMAGINE IF H'EL WERE ABLE TO USE THE SAME INFINITE ENERGY SOURCE THAT POWERS KANDOR...
...TO FUEL A SHIP THROUGH THE CHRONAL-NEXUS THAT EXISTS BOTH EVERYWHERE AND NOWHERE ALL AT ONCE AND NOT AT ALL.
"BUT LEX," YOU ARE NO DOUBT THINKING, "EVEN IF THAT WERE POSSIBLE, WHERE WOULD HE FIND THE SOURCE TO PROTEC HIS VESSEL WHILE TRAVELING THROUGH SAID THEORETICAL NEXUS"?

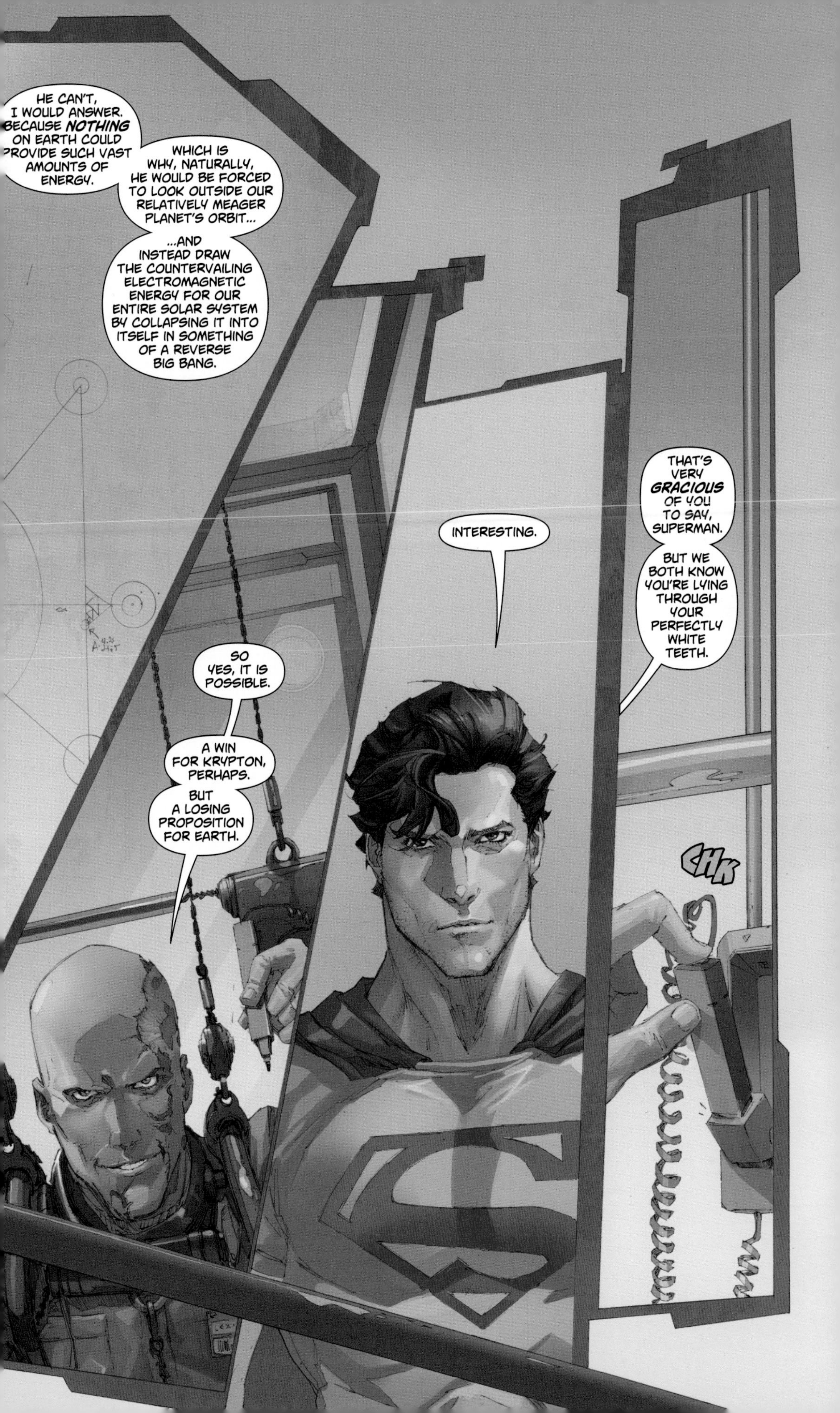
HE CAN'T, I WOULD ANSWER. BECAUSE NOTHING ON EARTH COULD PROVIDE SUCH VAST AMOUNTS OF ENERGY.
WHICH IS WHY, NATURALLY, HE WOULD BE FORCED TO LOOK OUTSIDE OUR RELATIVELY MEAGER PLANET'S ORBIT...
...AND INSTEAD DRAW THE COUNTERVAILING ELECTROMAGNETIC ENERGY FOR OUR ENTIRE SOLAR SYSTEM BY COLLAPSING IT INTO ITSELF IN SOMETHING OF A REVERSE BIG BANG.
SO YES, IT IS POSSIBLE.
A WIN FOR KRYPTON, PERHAPS.
BUT A LOSING PROPOSITION FOR EARTH.
INTERESTING.
THAT'S VERY GRACIOUS OF YOU TO SAY, SUPERMAN.
BUT WE BOTH KNOW YOU'RE LYING THROUGH YOUR PERFECTLY WHITE TEETH.
CHK

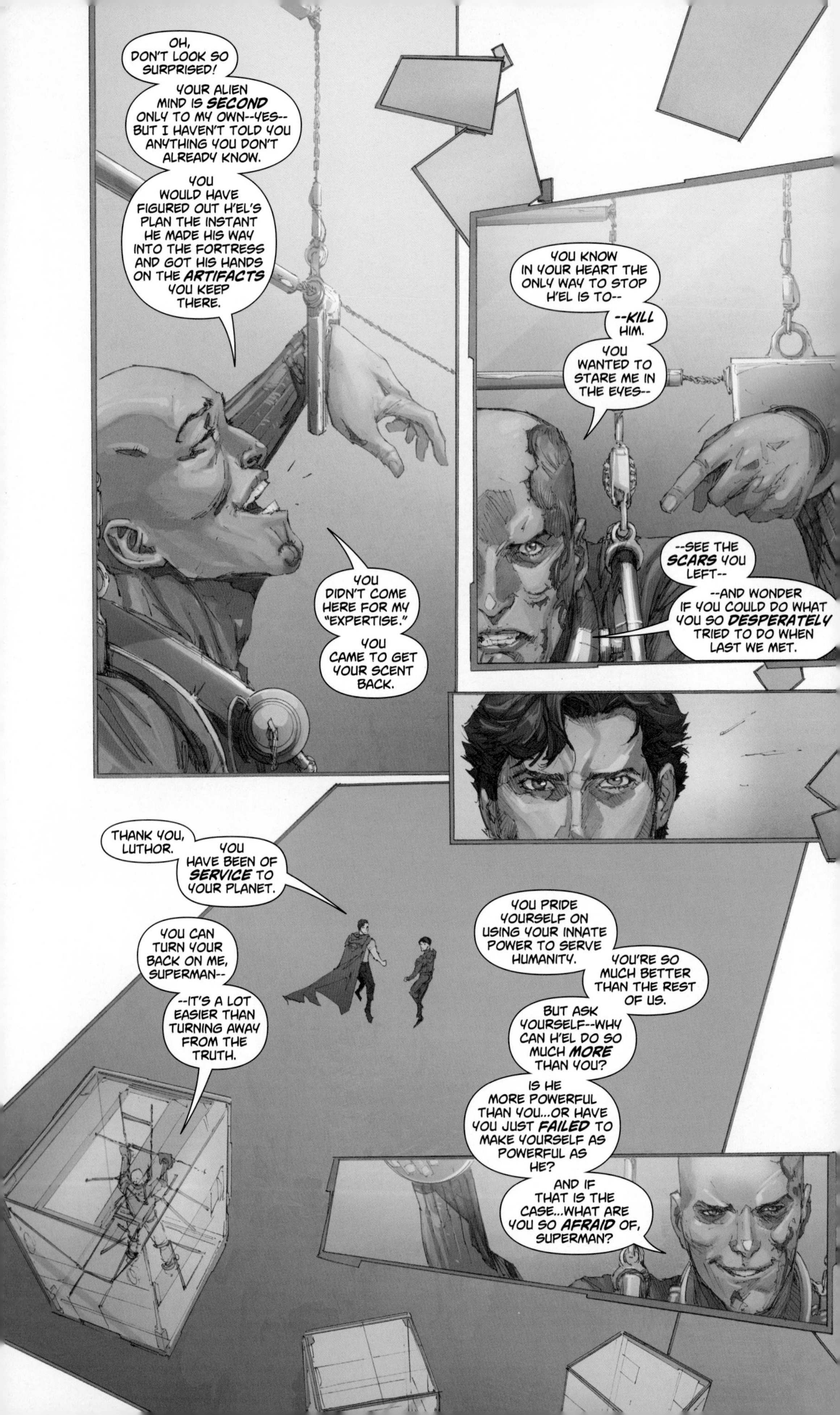

OH, DON'T LOOK SO SURPRISED!
YOUR ALIEN MIND IS SECOND ONLY TO MY OWN--YES--BUT I HAVEN'T TOLD YOU ANYTHING YOU DON'T ALREADY KNOW.
YOU WOULD HAVE FIGURED OUT H'EL'S PLAN THE INSTANT HE MADE HIS WAY INTO THE FORTRESS AND GOT HIS HANDS ON THE ARTIFACTS YOU KEEP THERE.
YOU DIDN'T COME HERE FOR MY "EXPERTISE."
YOU CAME TO GET YOUR SCENT BACK.
YOU KNOW IN YOUR HEART THE ONLY WAY TO STOP H'EL IS TO--
--KILL HIM.
YOU WANTED TO STARE ME IN THE EYES--
--SEE THE SCARS YOU LEFT--
--AND WONDER IF YOU COULD DO WHAT YOU SO DESPERATELY TRIED TO DO WHEN LAST WE MET.
THANK YOU, LUTHOR.
YOU HAVE BEEN OF SERVICE TO YOUR PLANET.
YOU CAN TURN YOUR BACK ON ME, SUPERMAN--
--IT'S A LOT EASIER THAN TURNING AWAY FROM THE TRUTH.
YOU PRIDE YOURSELF ON USING YOUR INNATE POWER TO SERVE HUMANITY.
YOU'RE SO MUCH BETTER THAN THE REST OF US.
BUT ASK YOURSELF--WHY CAN H'EL DO SO MUCH MORE THAN YOU?
IS HE MORE POWERFUL THAN YOU...OR HAVE YOU JUST FAILED TO MAKE YOURSELF AS POWERFUL AS HE?
AND IF THAT IS THE CASE...WHAT ARE YOU SO AFRAID OF, SUPERMAN?

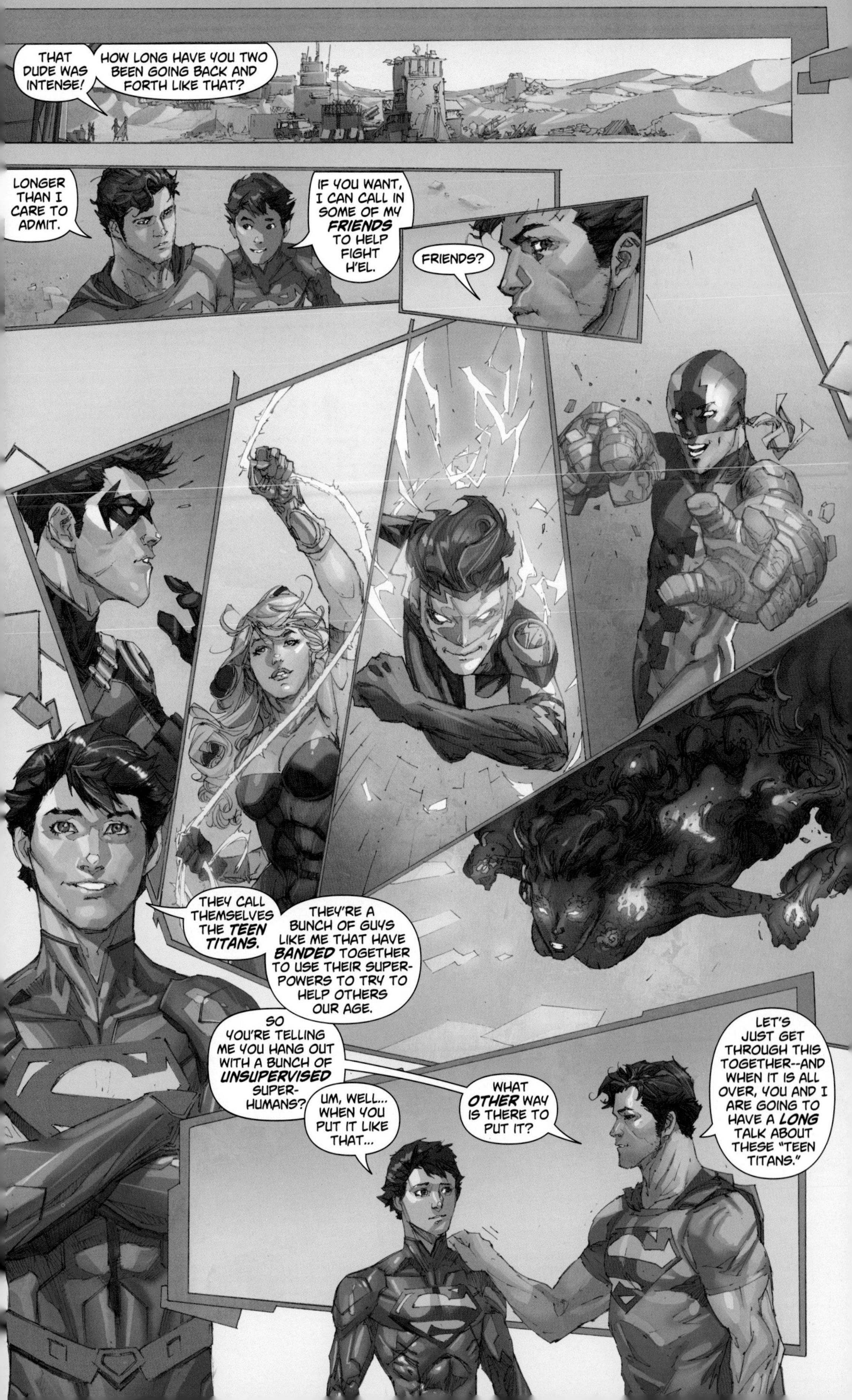
THAT DUDE WAS INTENSE!
HOW LONG HAVE YOU TWO BEEN GOING BACK AND FORTH LIKE THAT?
LONGER THAN I CARE TO ADMIT.
IF YOU WANT, I CAN CALL IN SOME OF MY *FRIENDS* TO HELP FIGHT H'EL.
FRIENDS?
THEY CALL THEMSELVES THE *TEEN TITANS.*
THEY'RE A BUNCH OF GUYS LIKE ME THAT HAVE *BANDED* TOGETHER TO USE THEIR SUPER-POWERS TO TRY TO HELP OTHERS OUR AGE.
SO YOU'RE TELLING ME YOU HANG OUT WITH A BUNCH OF *UNSUPERVISED* SUPER-HUMANS?
UM, WELL... WHEN YOU PUT IT LIKE THAT...
WHAT *OTHER* WAY IS THERE TO PUT IT?
LET'S JUST GET THROUGH THIS TOGETHER--AND WHEN IT IS ALL OVER, YOU AND I ARE GOING TO HAVE A *LONG* TALK ABOUT THESE "TEEN TITANS."

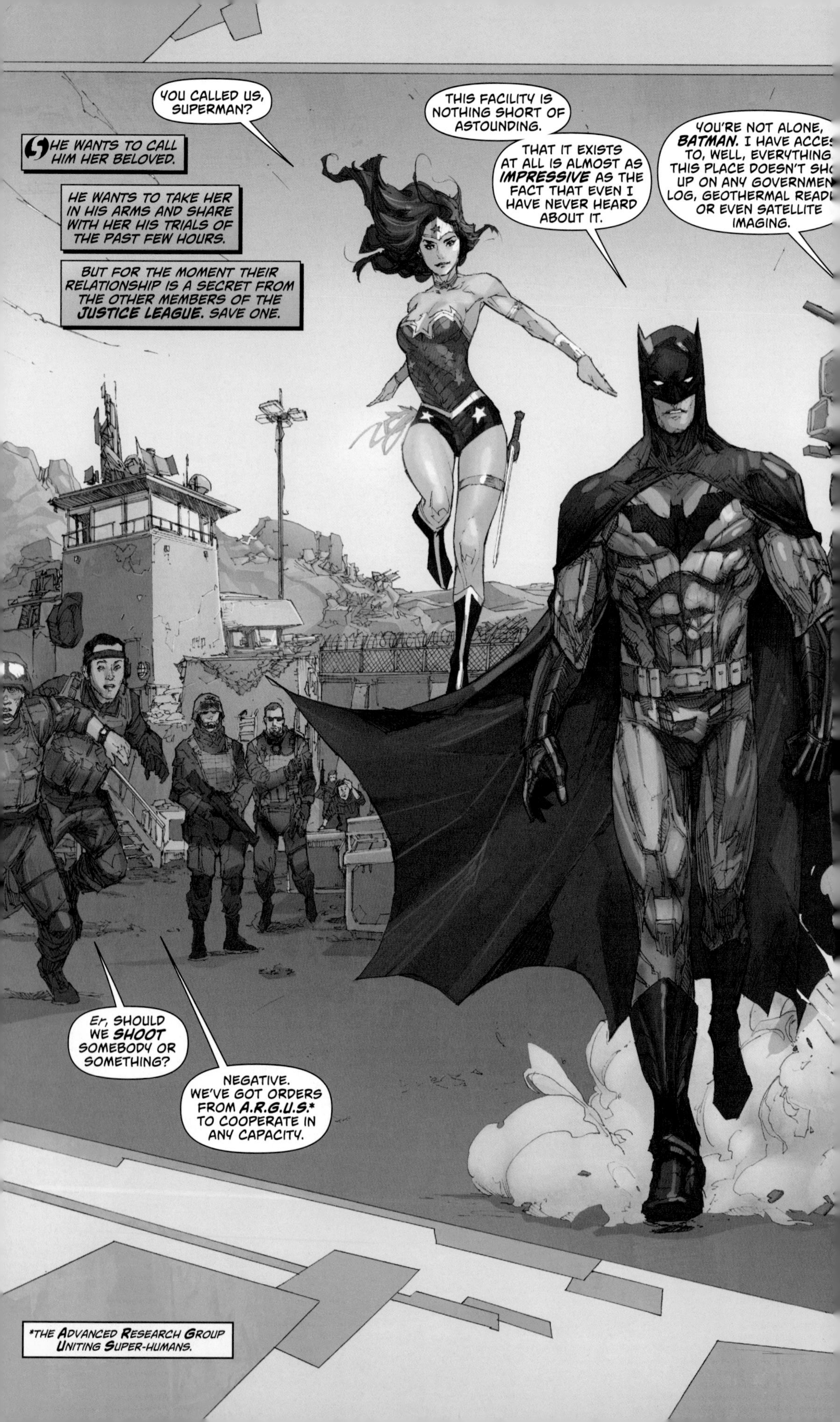

SHE WANTS TO CALL HIM HER BELOVED.
HE WANTS TO TAKE HER IN HIS ARMS AND SHARE WITH HER HIS TRIALS OF THE PAST FEW HOURS.
BUT FOR THE MOMENT THEIR RELATIONSHIP IS A SECRET FROM THE OTHER MEMBERS OF THE JUSTICE LEAGUE. SAVE ONE.
YOU CALLED US, SUPERMAN?
THIS FACILITY IS NOTHING SHORT OF ASTOUNDING.
THAT IT EXISTS AT ALL IS ALMOST AS IMPRESSIVE AS THE FACT THAT EVEN I HAVE NEVER HEARD ABOUT IT.
YOU'RE NOT ALONE, BATMAN. I HAVE ACCES TO, WELL, EVERYTHING THIS PLACE DOESN'T SHO UP ON ANY GOVERNMEN LOG, GEOTHERMAL READI OR EVEN SATELLITE IMAGING.
Er, SHOULD WE SHOOT SOMEBODY OR SOMETHING?
NEGATIVE. WE'VE GOT ORDERS FROM A.R.G.U.S.* TO COOPERATE IN ANY CAPACITY.
*THE ADVANCED RESEARCH GROUP UNITING SUPER-HUMANS.

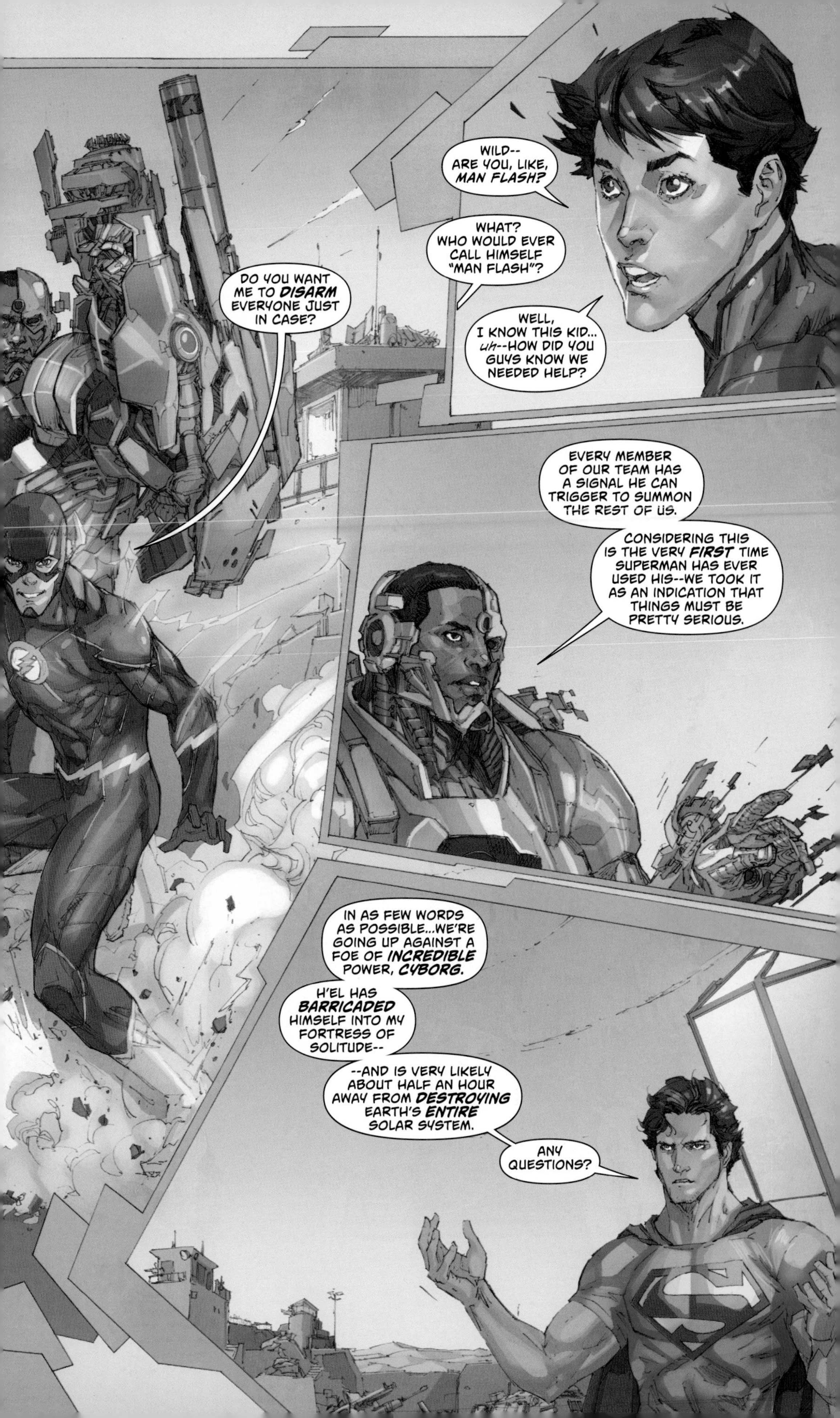
WILD-- ARE YOU, LIKE, MAN FLASH?
WHAT? WHO WOULD EVER CALL HIMSELF "MAN FLASH"?
DO YOU WANT ME TO DISARM EVERYONE JUST IN CASE?
WELL, I KNOW THIS KID... uh--HOW DID YOU GUYS KNOW WE NEEDED HELP?
EVERY MEMBER OF OUR TEAM HAS A SIGNAL HE CAN TRIGGER TO SUMMON THE REST OF US.
CONSIDERING THIS IS THE VERY FIRST TIME SUPERMAN HAS EVER USED HIS--WE TOOK IT AS AN INDICATION THAT THINGS MUST BE PRETTY SERIOUS.
IN AS FEW WORDS AS POSSIBLE...WE'RE GOING UP AGAINST A FOE OF INCREDIBLE POWER, CYBORG.
H'EL HAS BARRICADED HIMSELF INTO MY FORTRESS OF SOLITUDE--
--AND IS VERY LIKELY ABOUT HALF AN HOUR AWAY FROM DESTROYING EARTH'S ENTIRE SOLAR SYSTEM.
ANY QUESTIONS?

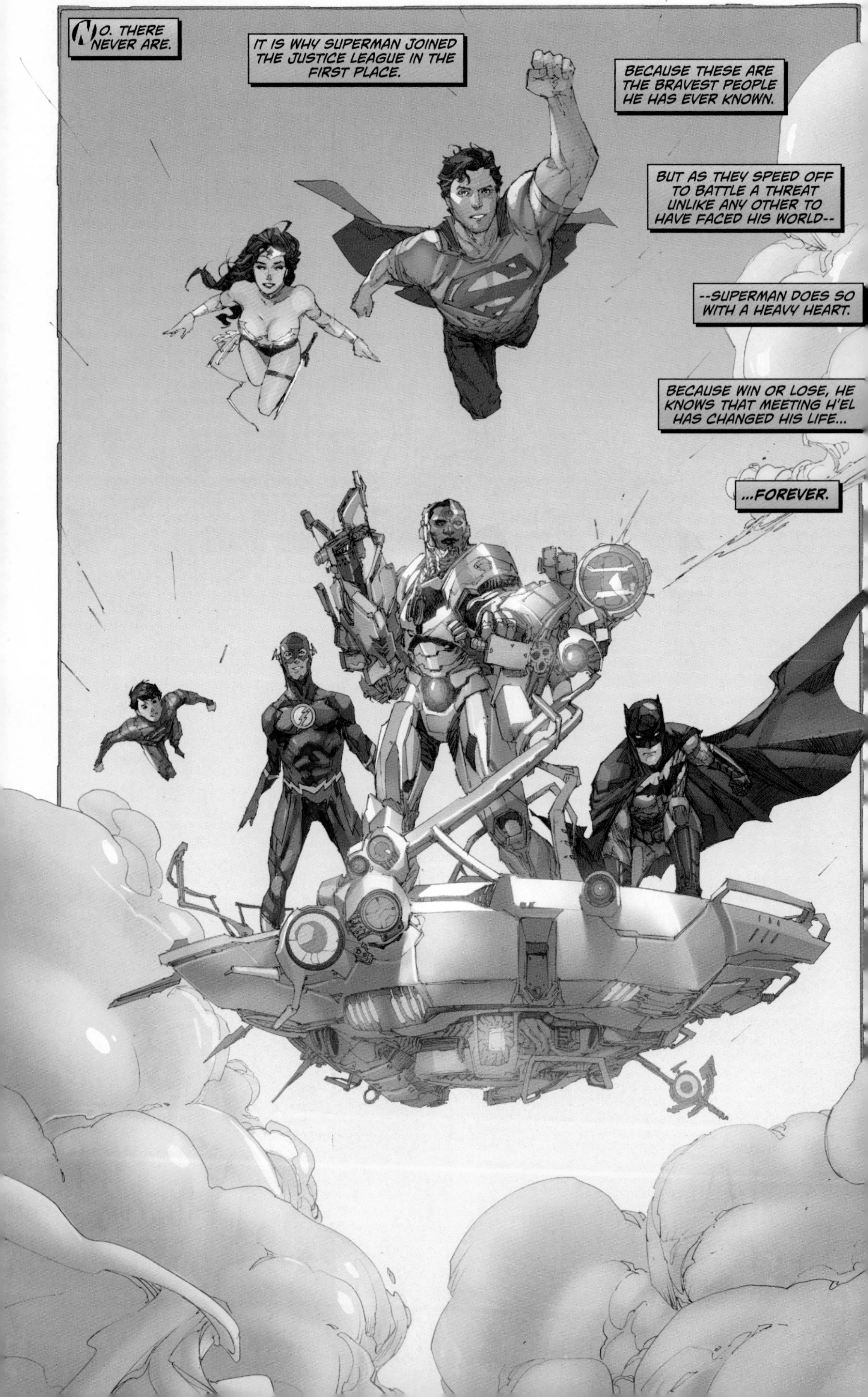
NO. THERE NEVER ARE.
IT IS WHY SUPERMAN JOINED THE JUSTICE LEAGUE IN THE FIRST PLACE.
BECAUSE THESE ARE THE BRAVEST PEOPLE HE HAS EVER KNOWN.
BUT AS THEY SPEED OFF TO BATTLE A THREAT UNLIKE ANY OTHER TO HAVE FACED HIS WORLD--
--SUPERMAN DOES SO WITH A HEAVY HEART.
BECAUSE WIN OR LOSE, HE KNOWS THAT MEETING H'EL HAS CHANGED HIS LIFE...
...FOREVER.

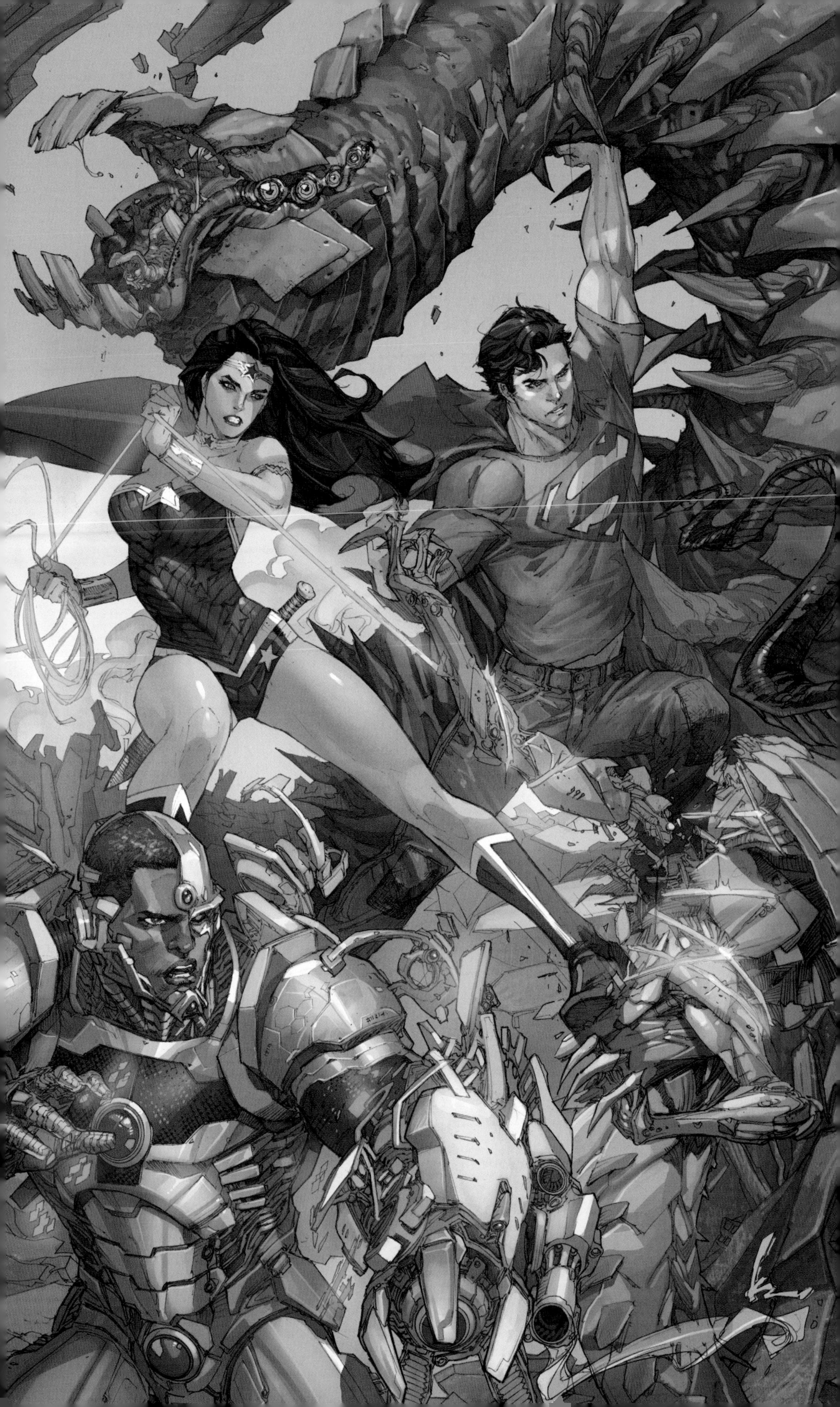

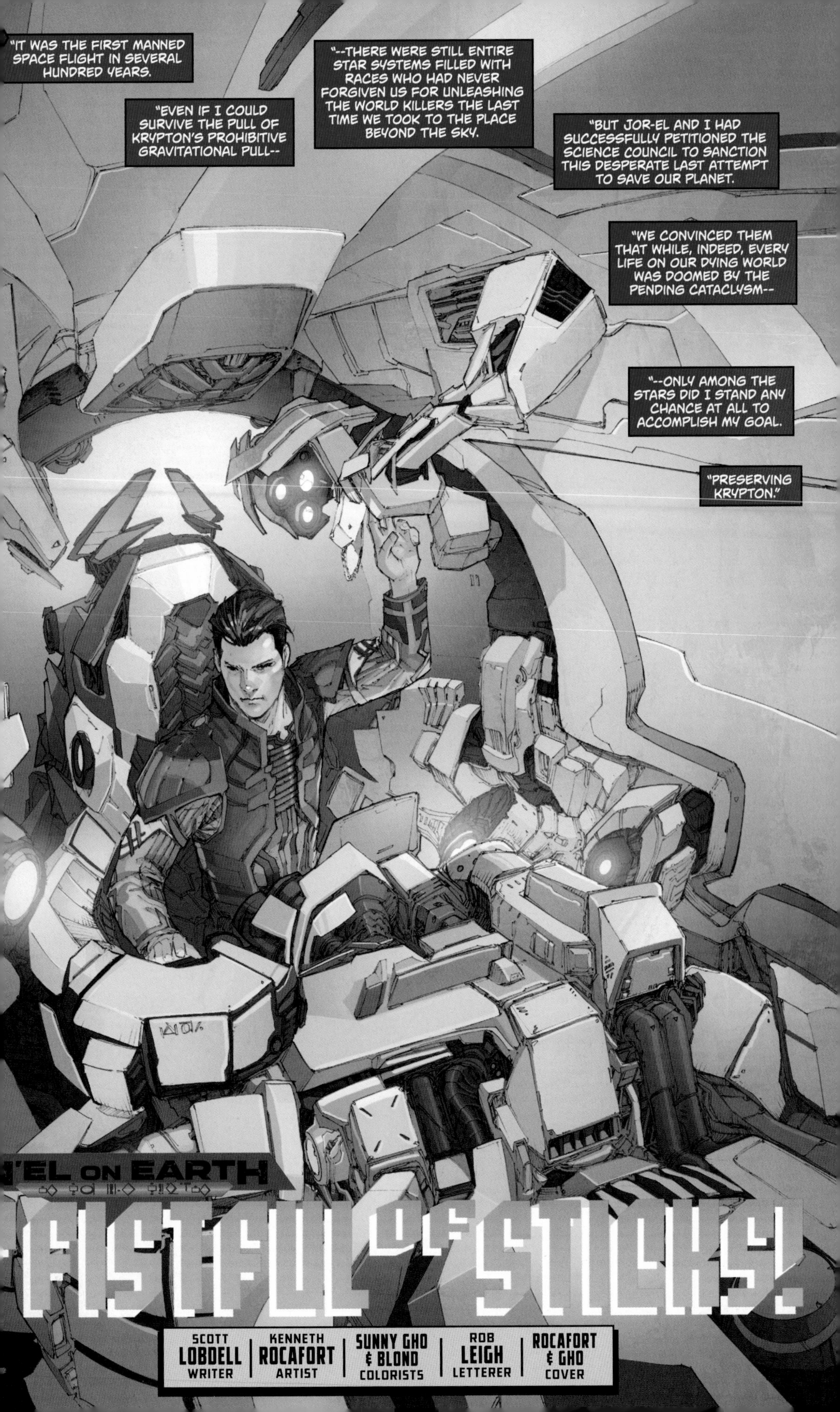
"IT WAS THE FIRST MANNED SPACE FLIGHT IN SEVERAL HUNDRED YEARS.
"EVEN IF I COULD SURVIVE THE PULL OF KRYPTON'S PROHIBITIVE GRAVITATIONAL PULL--
"--THERE WERE STILL ENTIRE STAR SYSTEMS FILLED WITH RACES WHO HAD NEVER FORGIVEN US FOR UNLEASHING THE WORLD KILLERS THE LAST TIME WE TOOK TO THE PLACE BEYOND THE SKY.
"BUT JOR-EL AND I HAD SUCCESSFULLY PETITIONED THE SCIENCE COUNCIL TO SANCTION THIS DESPERATE LAST ATTEMPT TO SAVE OUR PLANET.
"WE CONVINCED THEM THAT WHILE, INDEED, EVERY LIFE ON OUR DYING WORLD WAS DOOMED BY THE PENDING CATACLYSM--
"--ONLY AMONG THE STARS DID I STAND ANY CHANCE AT ALL TO ACCOMPLISH MY GOAL.
"PRESERVING KRYPTON."
'EL ON EARTH
FISTFUL OF STICKS!
SCOTT LOBDELL WRITER
KENNETH ROCAFORT ARTIST
SUNNY GHO & BLOND COLORISTS
ROB LEIGH LETTERER
ROCAFORT & GHO COVER

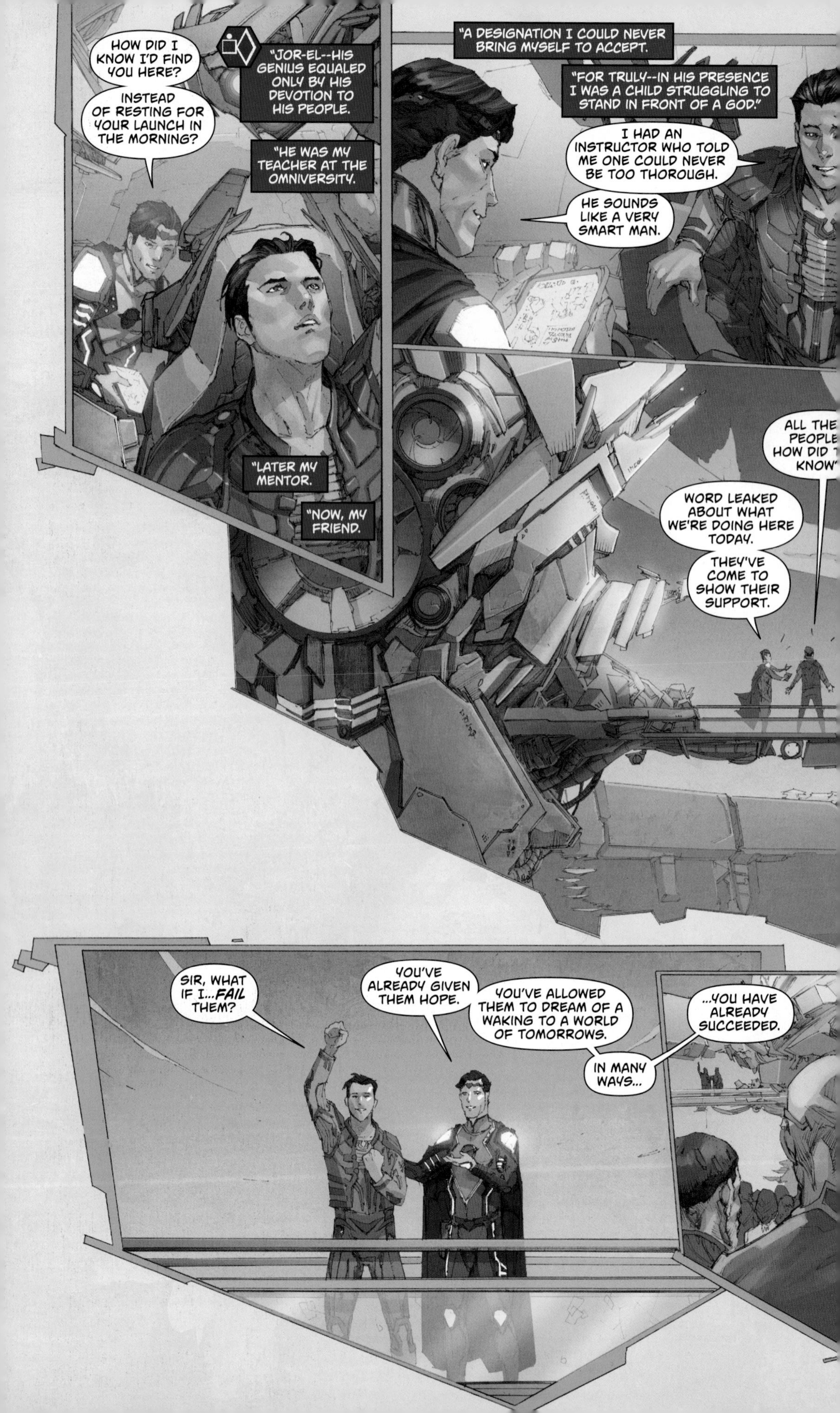
HOW DID I KNOW I'D FIND YOU HERE?
INSTEAD OF RESTING FOR YOUR LAUNCH IN THE MORNING?
"JOR-EL--HIS GENIUS EQUALED ONLY BY HIS DEVOTION TO HIS PEOPLE.
"HE WAS MY TEACHER AT THE OMNIVERSITY.
"LATER MY MENTOR.
"NOW, MY FRIEND.
"A DESIGNATION I COULD NEVER BRING MYSELF TO ACCEPT.
"FOR TRULY--IN HIS PRESENCE I WAS A CHILD STRUGGLING TO STAND IN FRONT OF A GOD."
I HAD AN INSTRUCTOR WHO TOLD ME ONE COULD NEVER BE TOO THOROUGH.
HE SOUNDS LIKE A VERY SMART MAN.
WORD LEAKED ABOUT WHAT WE'RE DOING HERE TODAY.
THEY'VE COME TO SHOW THEIR SUPPORT.
SIR, WHAT IF I...FAIL THEM?
YOU'VE ALREADY GIVEN THEM HOPE.
YOU'VE ALLOWED THEM TO DREAM OF A WAKING TO A WORLD OF TOMORROWS.
IN MANY WAYS...
...YOU HAVE ALREADY SUCCEEDED.

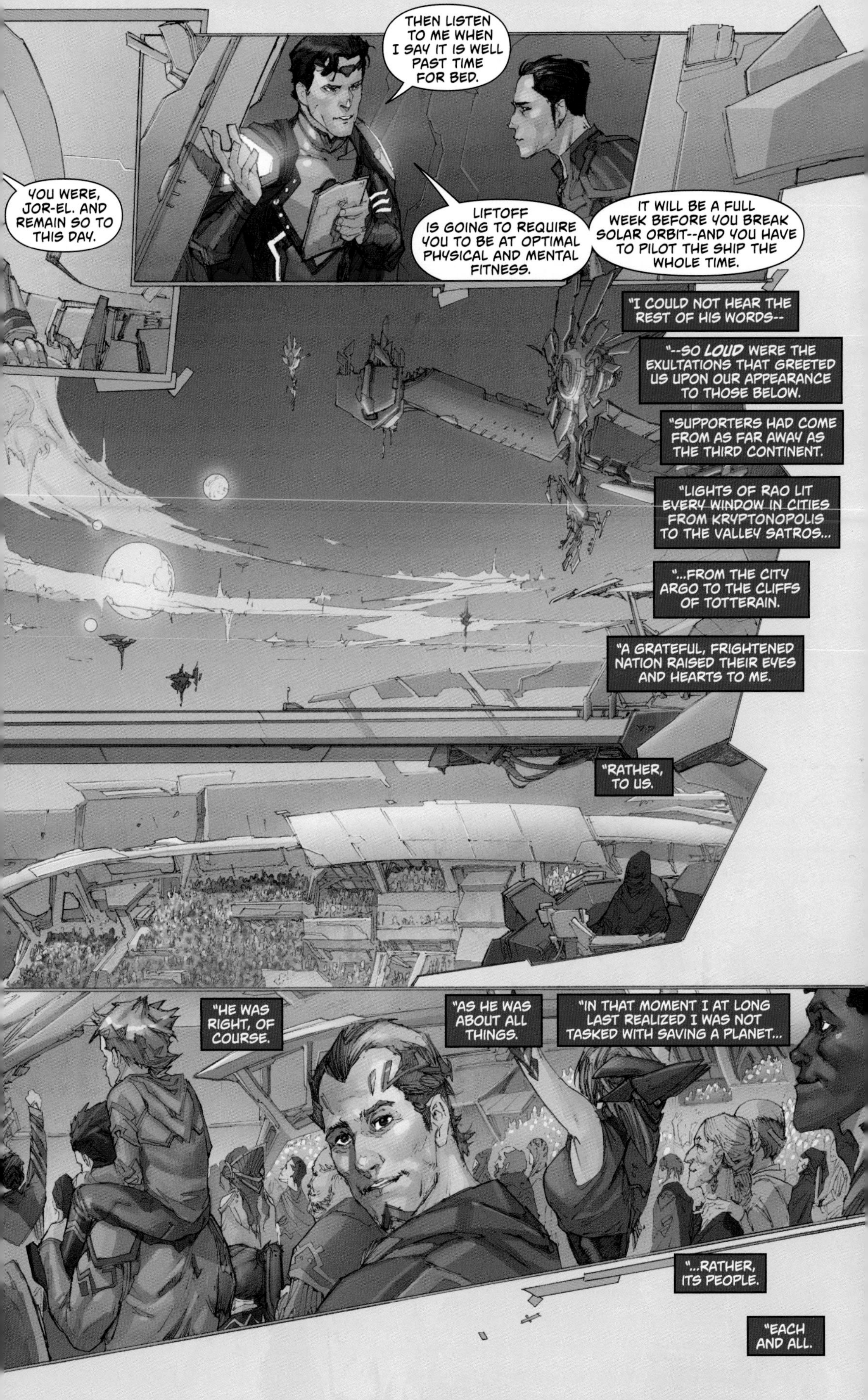
THEN LISTEN TO ME WHEN I SAY IT IS WELL PAST TIME FOR BED.
YOU WERE, JOR-EL. AND REMAIN SO TO THIS DAY.
LIFTOFF IS GOING TO REQUIRE YOU TO BE AT OPTIMAL PHYSICAL AND MENTAL FITNESS.
IT WILL BE A FULL WEEK BEFORE YOU BREAK SOLAR ORBIT--AND YOU HAVE TO PILOT THE SHIP THE WHOLE TIME.
"I COULD NOT HEAR THE REST OF HIS WORDS--
"--SO LOUD WERE THE EXULTATIONS THAT GREETED US UPON OUR APPEARANCE TO THOSE BELOW.
"SUPPORTERS HAD COME FROM AS FAR AWAY AS THE THIRD CONTINENT.
"LIGHTS OF RAO LIT EVERY WINDOW IN CITIES FROM KRYPTONOPOLIS TO THE VALLEY SATROS...
"...FROM THE CITY ARGO TO THE CLIFFS OF TOTTERAIN.
"A GRATEFUL, FRIGHTENED NATION RAISED THEIR EYES AND HEARTS TO ME.
"RATHER, TO US.
"HE WAS RIGHT, OF COURSE.
"AS HE WAS ABOUT ALL THINGS.
"IN THAT MOMENT I AT LONG LAST REALIZED I WAS NOT TASKED WITH SAVING A PLANET...
"...RATHER, ITS PEOPLE.
"EACH AND ALL.

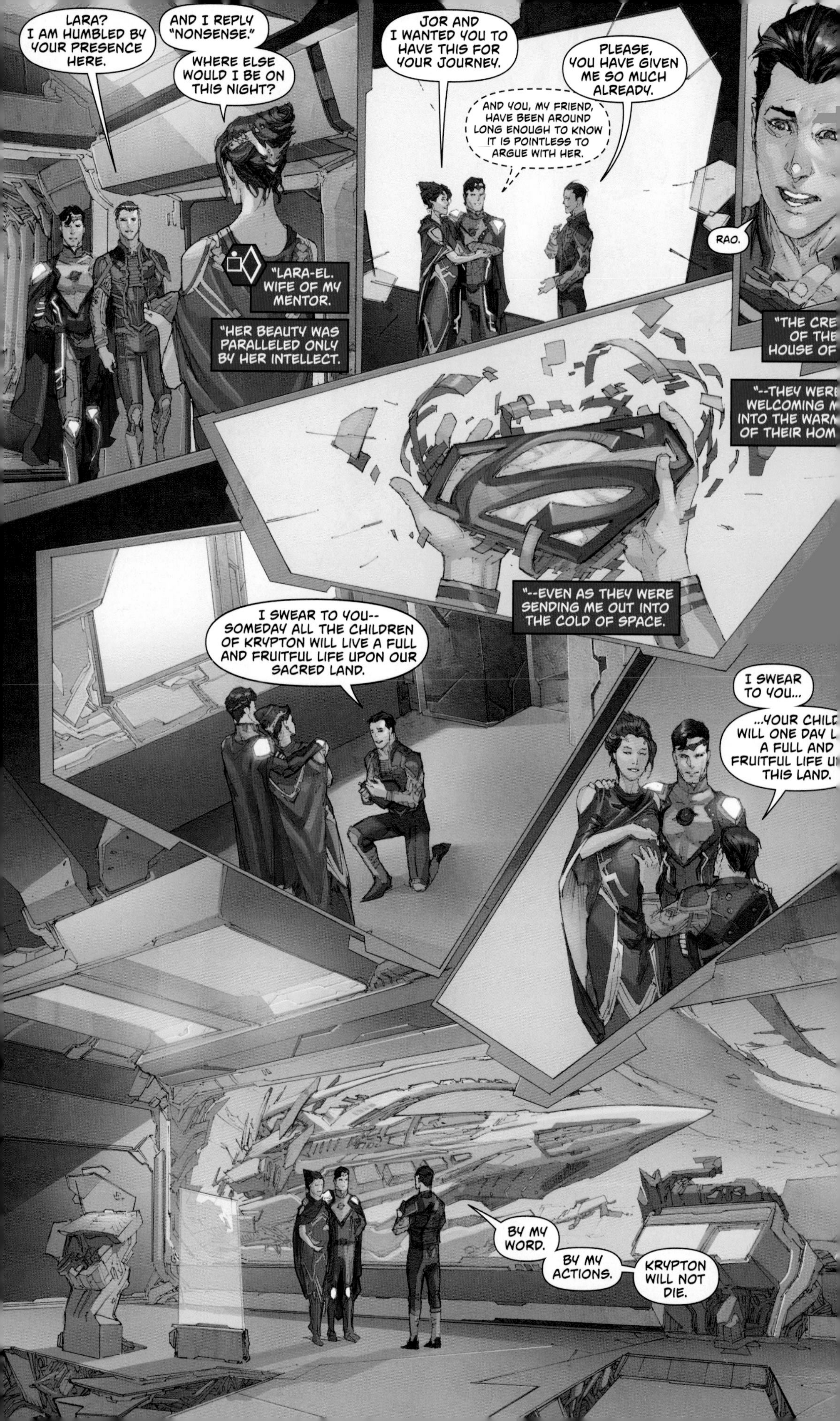
LARA? I AM HUMBLED BY YOUR PRESENCE HERE.
AND I REPLY "NONSENSE."
WHERE ELSE WOULD I BE ON THIS NIGHT?
"LARA-EL. WIFE OF MY MENTOR.
"HER BEAUTY WAS PARALLELED ONLY BY HER INTELLECT.
JOR AND I WANTED YOU TO HAVE THIS FOR YOUR JOURNEY.
PLEASE, YOU HAVE GIVEN ME SO MUCH ALREADY.
AND YOU, MY FRIEND, HAVE BEEN AROUND LONG ENOUGH TO KNOW IT IS POINTLESS TO ARGUE WITH HER.
RAO.
"--THEY WER
INTO THE WARM
OF THEIR HOM
"--EVEN AS THEY WERE SENDING ME OUT INTO THE COLD OF SPACE.
I SWEAR TO YOU-- SOMEDAY ALL THE CHILDREN OF KRYPTON WILL LIVE A FULL AND FRUITFUL LIFE UPON OUR SACRED LAND.
I SWEAR TO YOU...
...YOUR CHILD WILL ONE DAY L A FULL AND FRUITFUL LIFE U THIS LAND.
BY MY WORD.
BY MY ACTIONS.
KRYPTON WILL NOT DIE.

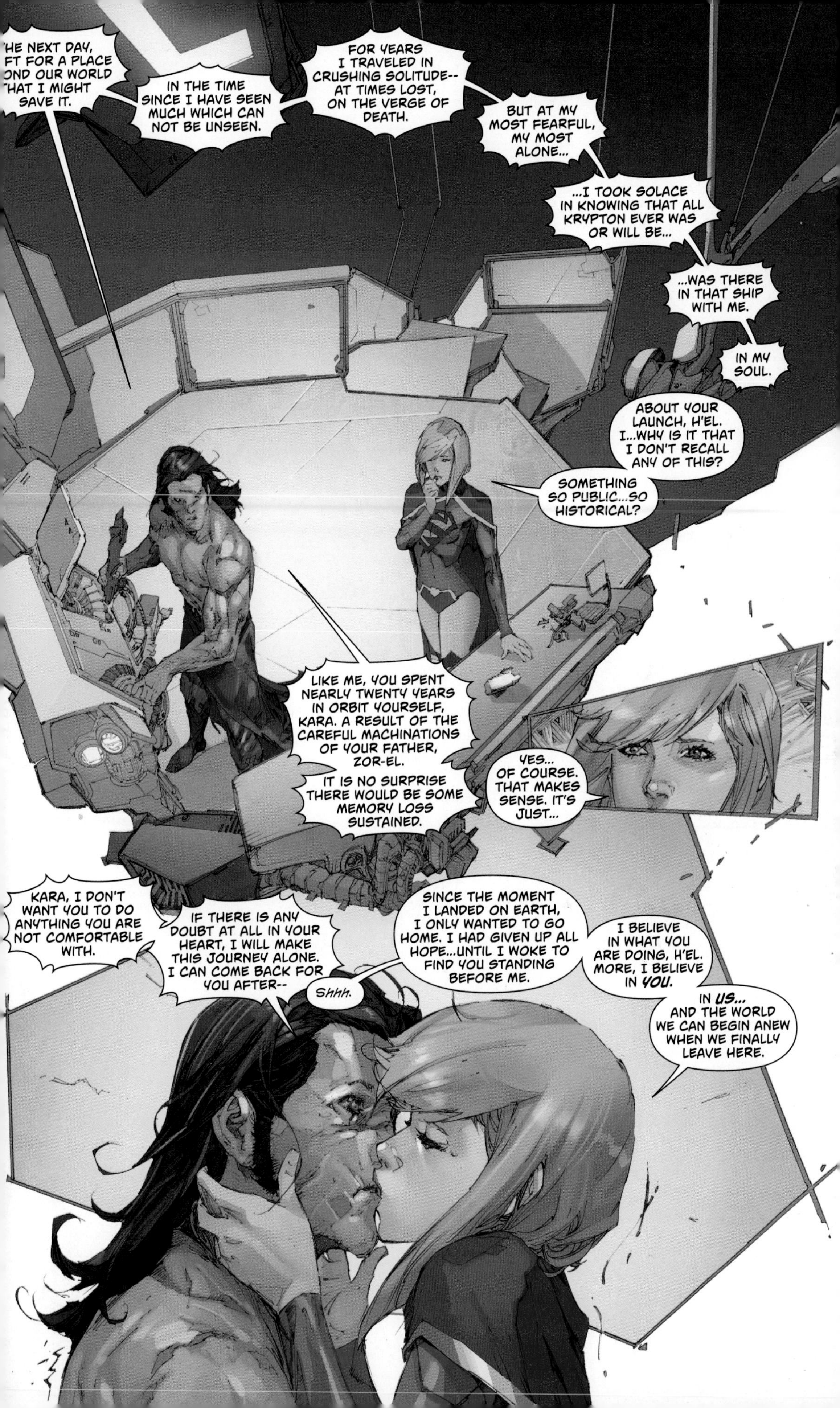

HE NEXT DAY, FT FOR A PLACE OND OUR WORLD THAT I MIGHT SAVE IT.
IN THE TIME SINCE I HAVE SEEN MUCH WHICH CAN NOT BE UNSEEN.
FOR YEARS I TRAVELED IN CRUSHING SOLITUDE-- AT TIMES LOST, ON THE VERGE OF DEATH.
BUT AT MY MOST FEARFUL, MY MOST ALONE...
...I TOOK SOLACE IN KNOWING THAT ALL KRYPTON EVER WAS OR WILL BE...
...WAS THERE IN THAT SHIP WITH ME.
IN MY SOUL.
ABOUT YOUR LAUNCH, H'EL. I...WHY IS IT THAT I DON'T RECALL ANY OF THIS?
SOMETHING SO PUBLIC...SO HISTORICAL?
LIKE ME, YOU SPENT NEARLY TWENTY YEARS IN ORBIT YOURSELF, KARA. A RESULT OF THE CAREFUL MACHINATIONS OF YOUR FATHER, ZOR-EL.
IT IS NO SURPRISE THERE WOULD BE SOME MEMORY LOSS SUSTAINED.
YES... OF COURSE. THAT MAKES SENSE. IT'S JUST...
KARA, I DON'T WANT YOU TO DO ANYTHING YOU ARE NOT COMFORTABLE WITH.
IF THERE IS ANY DOUBT AT ALL IN YOUR HEART, I WILL MAKE THIS JOURNEY ALONE. I CAN COME BACK FOR YOU AFTER--
Shhh.
SINCE THE MOMENT I LANDED ON EARTH, I ONLY WANTED TO GO HOME. I HAD GIVEN UP ALL HOPE...UNTIL I WOKE TO FIND YOU STANDING BEFORE ME.
I BELIEVE IN WHAT YOU ARE DOING, H'EL. MORE, I BELIEVE IN YOU.
IN US... AND THE WORLD WE CAN BEGIN ANEW WHEN WE FINALLY LEAVE HERE.

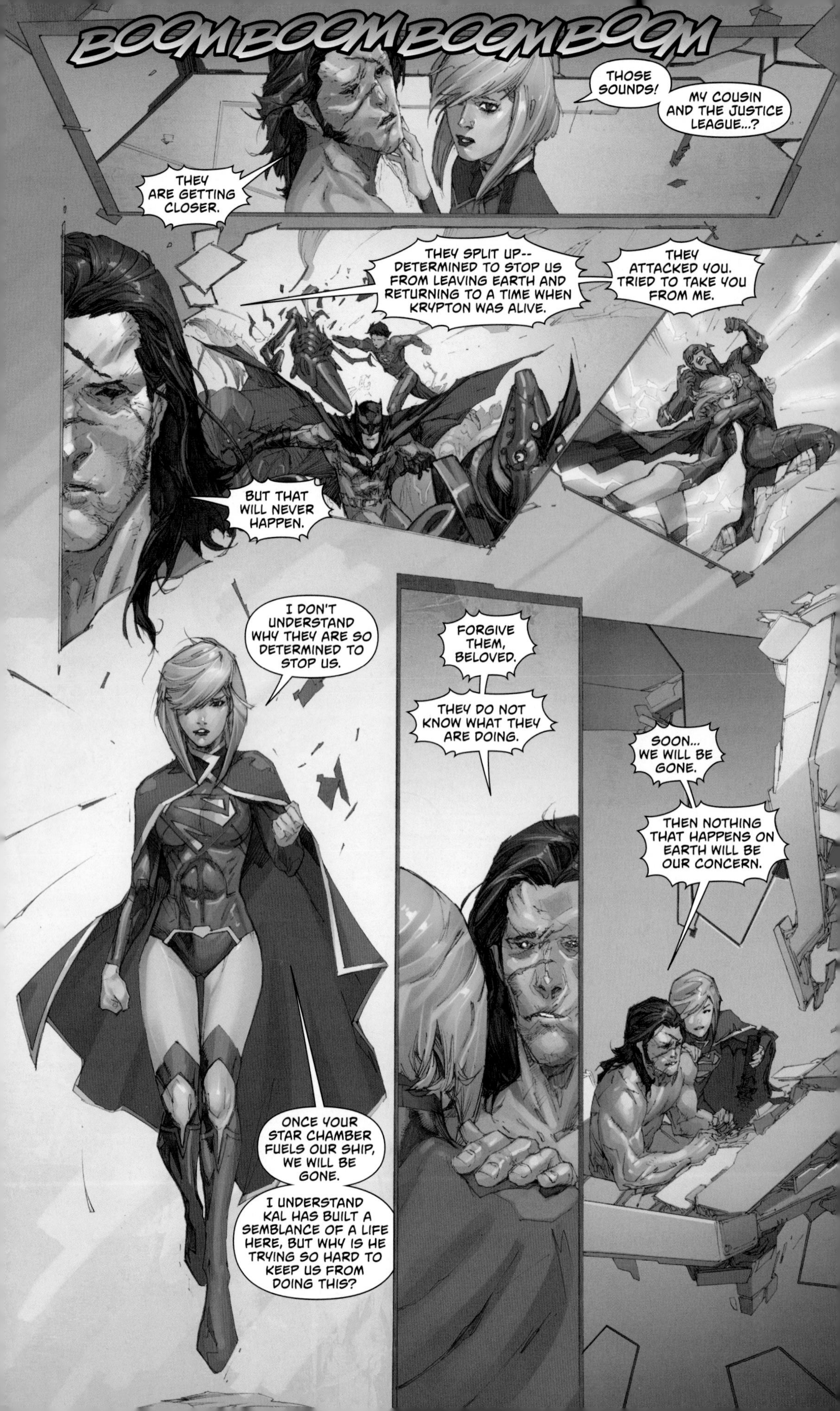
BOOM BOOM BOOM BOOM
THOSE SOUNDS!
MY COUSIN AND THE JUSTICE LEAGUE...?
THEY ARE GETTING CLOSER.
THEY SPLIT UP-- DETERMINED TO STOP US FROM LEAVING EARTH AND RETURNING TO A TIME WHEN KRYPTON WAS ALIVE.
THEY ATTACKED YOU. TRIED TO TAKE YOU FROM ME.
BUT THAT WILL NEVER HAPPEN.
I DON'T UNDERSTAND WHY THEY ARE SO DETERMINED TO STOP US.
ONCE YOUR STAR CHAMBER FUELS OUR SHIP, WE WILL BE GONE.
I UNDERSTAND KAL HAS BUILT A SEMBLANCE OF A LIFE HERE, BUT WHY IS HE TRYING SO HARD TO KEEP US FROM DOING THIS?
FORGIVE THEM, BELOVED.
THEY DO NOT KNOW WHAT THEY ARE DOING.
SOON... WE WILL BE GONE.
THEN NOTHING THAT HAPPENS ON EARTH WILL BE OUR CONCERN.

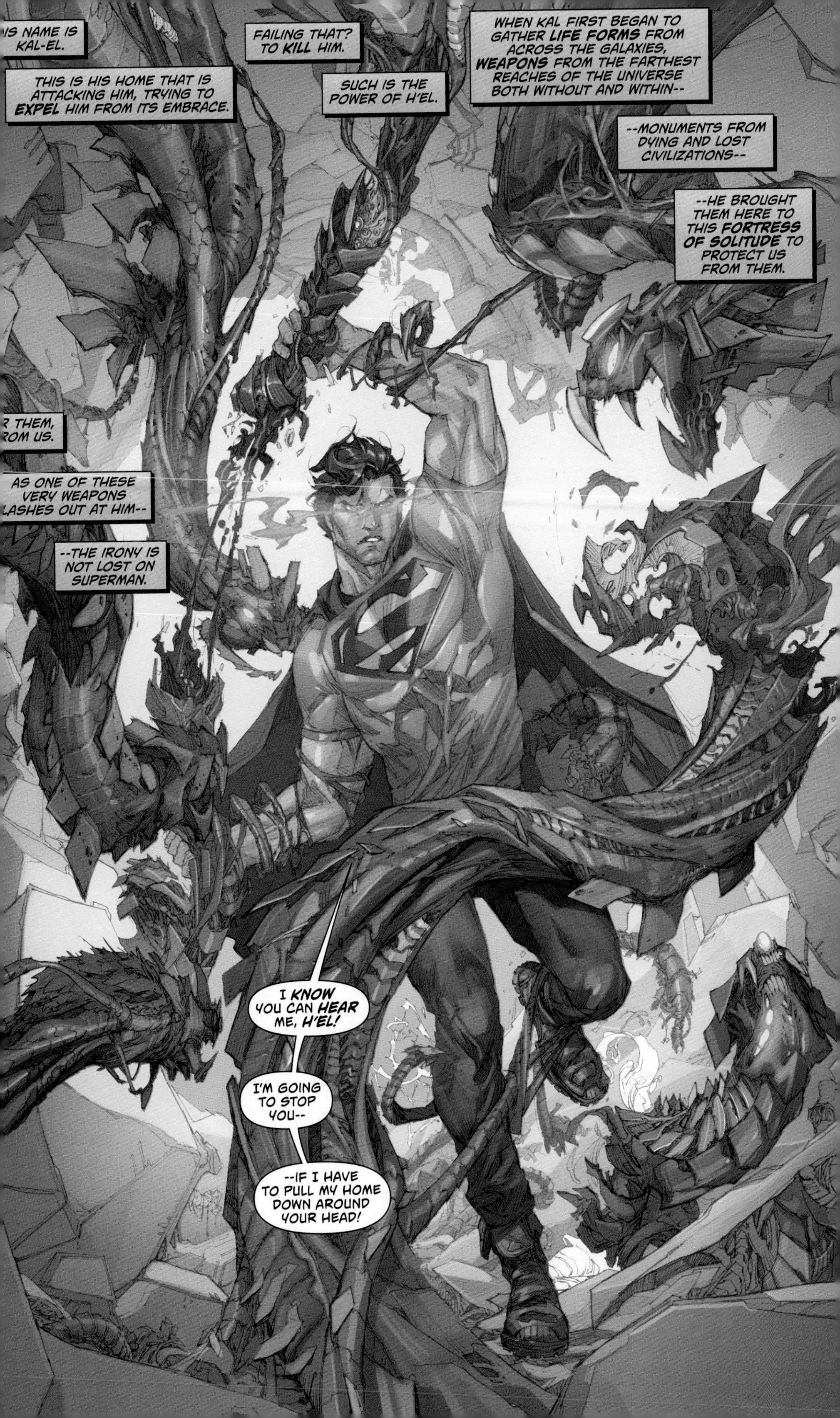
IS NAME IS KAL-EL.
THIS IS HIS HOME THAT IS ATTACKING HIM, TRYING TO EXPEL HIM FROM ITS EMBRACE.
FAILING THAT? TO KILL HIM.
SUCH IS THE POWER OF H'EL.
WHEN KAL FIRST BEGAN TO GATHER LIFE FORMS FROM ACROSS THE GALAXIES, WEAPONS FROM THE FARTHEST REACHES OF THE UNIVERSE BOTH WITHOUT AND WITHIN--
--MONUMENTS FROM DYING AND LOST CIVILIZATIONS--
--HE BROUGHT THEM HERE TO THIS FORTRESS OF SOLITUDE TO PROTECT US FROM THEM.
R THEM, ROM US.
AS ONE OF THESE VERY WEAPONS LASHES OUT AT HIM--
--THE IRONY IS NOT LOST ON SUPERMAN.
I KNOW YOU CAN HEAR ME, H'EL!
I'M GOING TO STOP YOU--
--IF I HAVE TO PULL MY HOME DOWN AROUND YOUR HEAD!

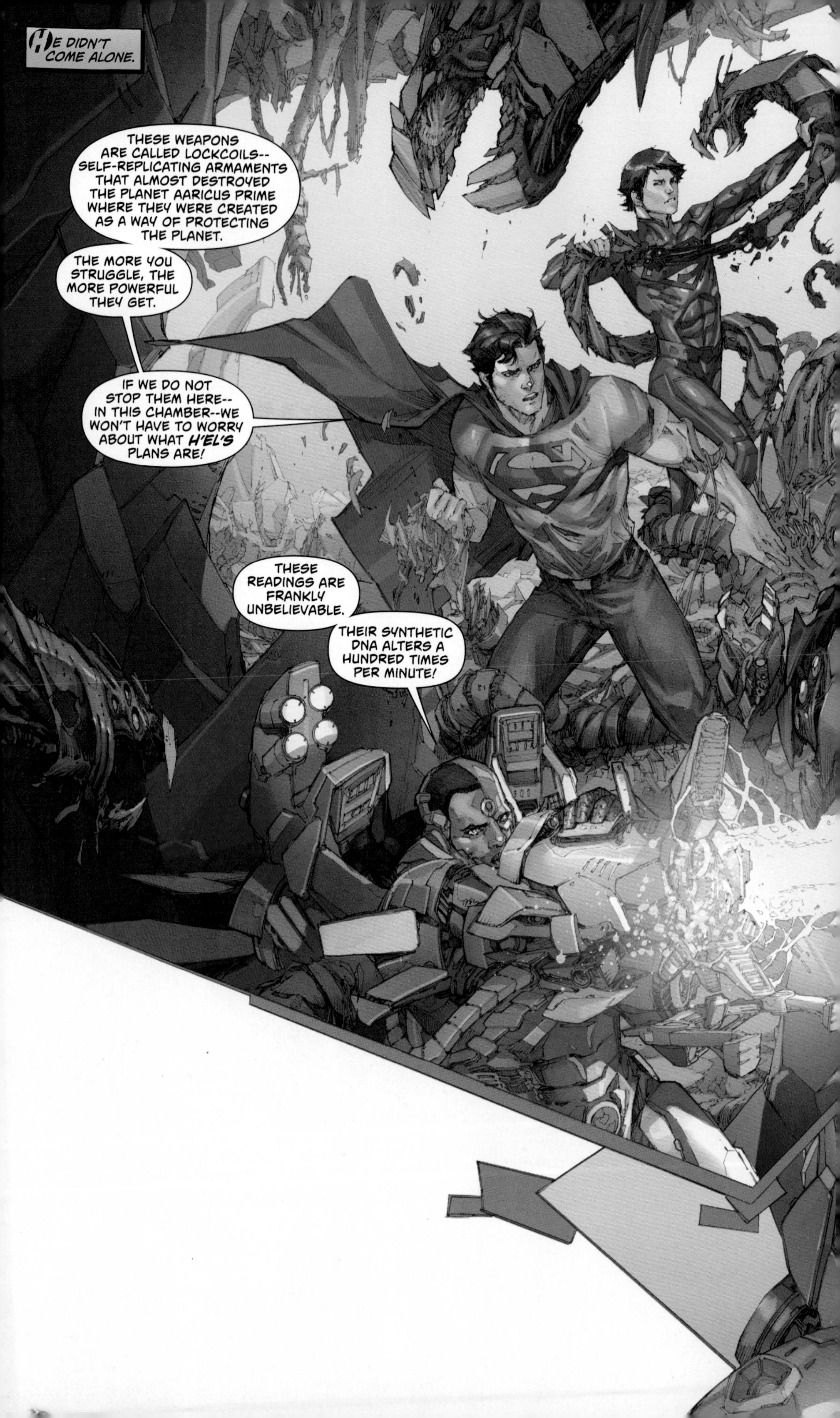

HE DIDN'T COME ALONE.
THESE WEAPONS ARE CALLED LOCKCOILS-- SELF-REPLICATING ARMAMENTS THAT ALMOST DESTROYED THE PLANET AARICUS PRIME WHERE THEY WERE CREATED AS A WAY OF PROTECTING THE PLANET.
THE MORE YOU STRUGGLE, THE MORE POWERFUL THEY GET.
IF WE DO NOT STOP THEM HERE-- IN THIS CHAMBER--WE WON'T HAVE TO WORRY ABOUT WHAT H'EL'S PLANS ARE!
THESE READINGS ARE FRANKLY UNBELIEVABLE.
THEIR SYNTHETIC DNA ALTERS A HUNDRED TIMES PER MINUTE!

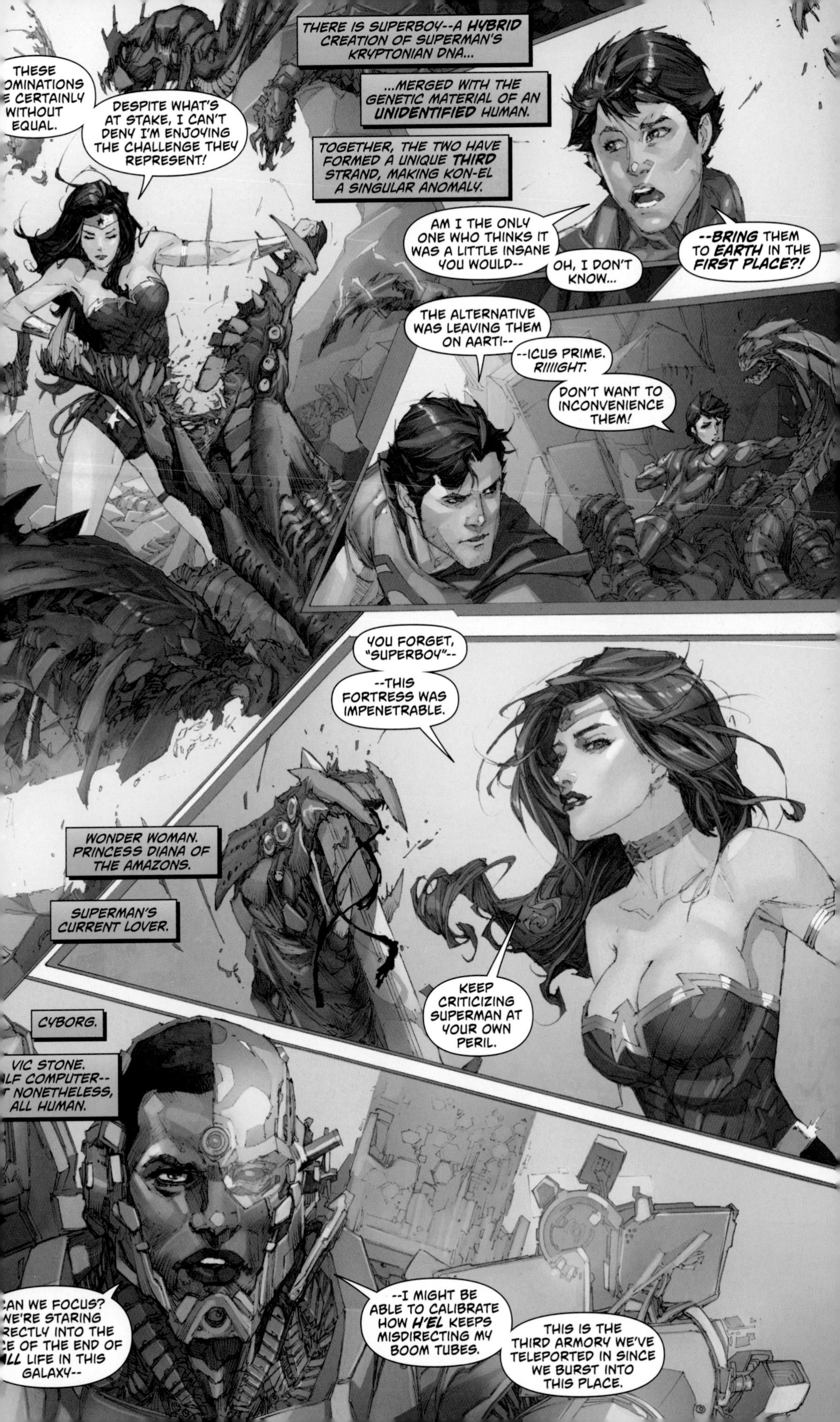
THERE IS SUPERBOY--A HYBRID CREATION OF SUPERMAN'S KRYPTONIAN DNA...
THESE OMINATIONS E CERTAINLY WITHOUT EQUAL.
DESPITE WHAT'S AT STAKE, I CAN'T DENY I'M ENJOYING THE CHALLENGE THEY REPRESENT!
...MERGED WITH THE GENETIC MATERIAL OF AN UNIDENTIFIED HUMAN.
TOGETHER, THE TWO HAVE FORMED A UNIQUE THIRD STRAND, MAKING KON-EL A SINGULAR ANOMALY.
AM I THE ONLY ONE WHO THINKS IT WAS A LITTLE INSANE YOU WOULD--
OH, I DON'T KNOW...
--BRING THEM TO EARTH IN THE FIRST PLACE?!
THE ALTERNATIVE WAS LEAVING THEM ON AARTI--
--ICUS PRIME. RIIIIGHT.
DON'T WANT TO INCONVENIENCE THEM!
YOU FORGET, "SUPERBOY"--
--THIS FORTRESS WAS IMPENETRABLE.
WONDER WOMAN. PRINCESS DIANA OF THE AMAZONS.
SUPERMAN'S CURRENT LOVER.
KEEP CRITICIZING SUPERMAN AT YOUR OWN PERIL.
CYBORG.
VIC STONE. LF COMPUTER-- NONETHELESS, ALL HUMAN.
CAN WE FOCUS? WE'RE STARING RECTLY INTO THE CE OF THE END OF LL LIFE IN THIS GALAXY--
--I MIGHT BE ABLE TO CALIBRATE HOW H'EL KEEPS MISDIRECTING MY BOOM TUBES.
THIS IS THE THIRD ARMORY WE'VE TELEPORTED IN SINCE WE BURST INTO THIS PLACE.

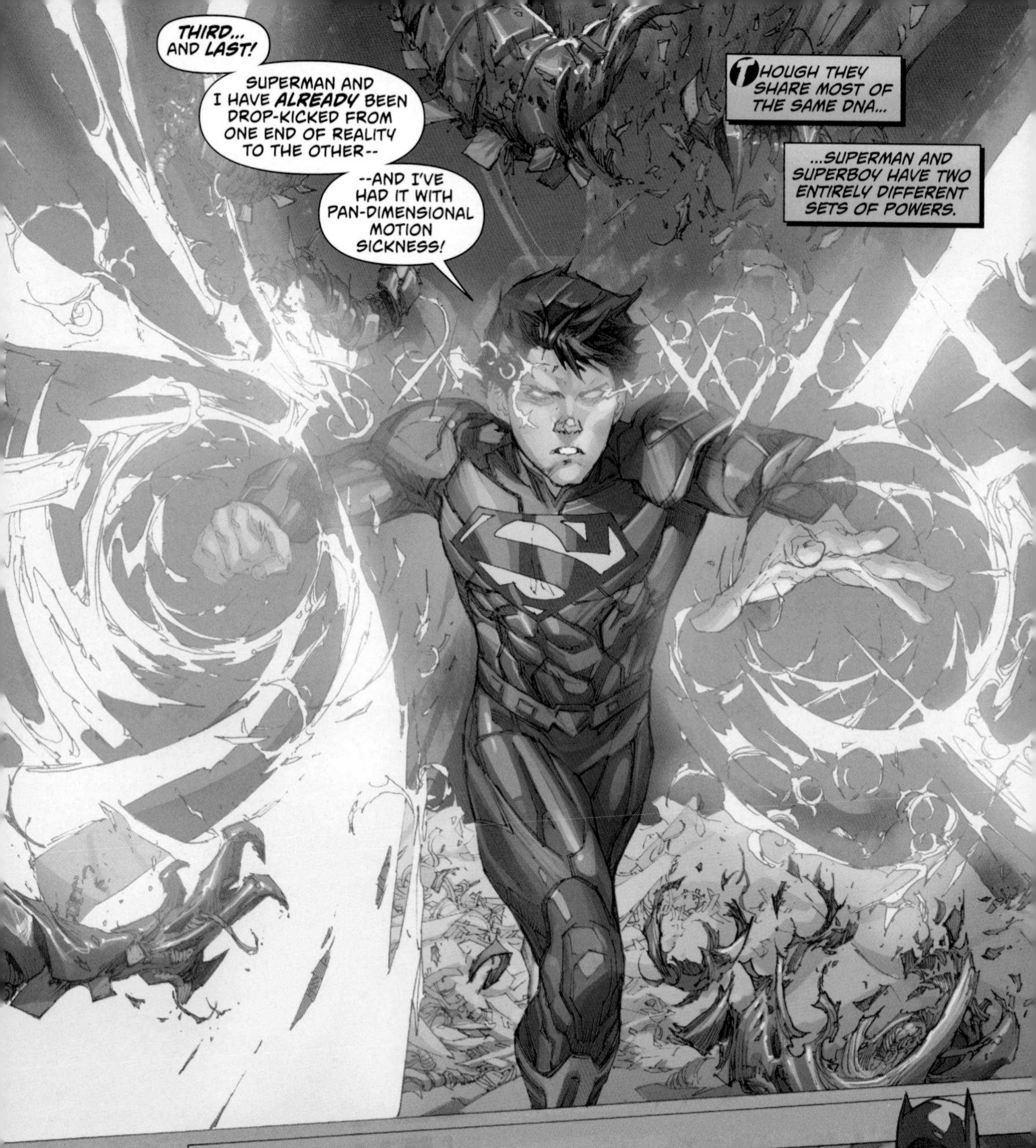
THIRD... AND LAST!
SUPERMAN AND I HAVE ALREADY BEEN DROP-KICKED FROM ONE END OF REALITY TO THE OTHER--
--AND I'VE HAD IT WITH PAN-DIMENSIONAL MOTION SICKNESS!
THOUGH THEY SHARE MOST OF THE SAME DNA...
...SUPERMAN AND SUPERBOY HAVE TWO ENTIRELY DIFFERENT SETS OF POWERS.
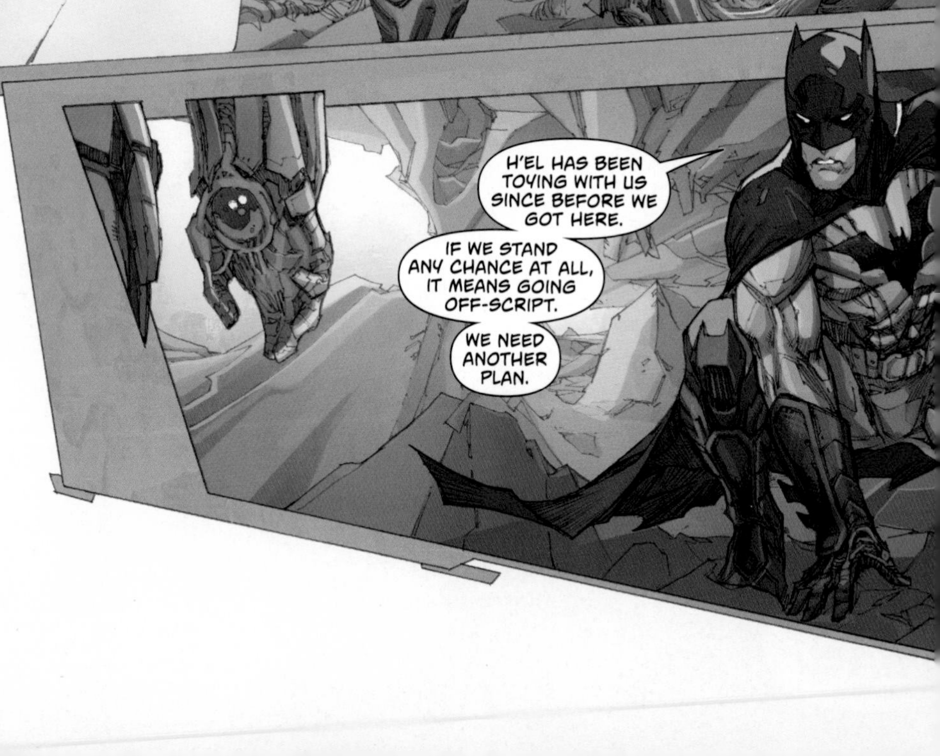
H'EL HAS BEEN TOYING WITH US SINCE BEFORE WE GOT HERE.
IF WE STAND ANY CHANCE AT ALL, IT MEANS GOING OFF-SCRIPT.
WE NEED ANOTHER PLAN.

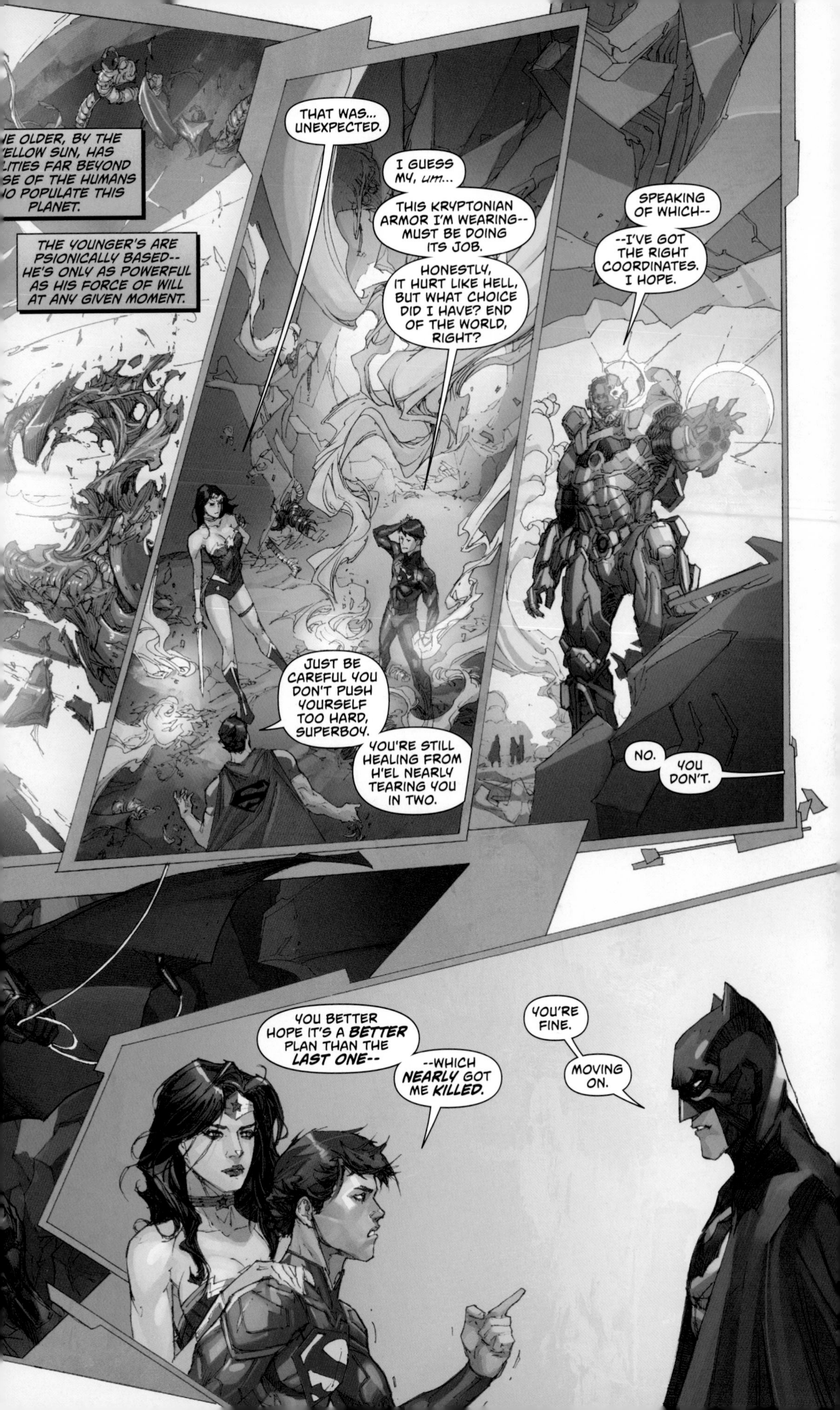

HE OLDER, BY THE YELLOW SUN, HAS LITIES FAR BEYOND SE OF THE HUMANS O POPULATE THIS PLANET.
THE YOUNGER'S ARE PSIONICALLY BASED-- HE'S ONLY AS POWERFUL AS HIS FORCE OF WILL AT ANY GIVEN MOMENT.
THAT WAS... UNEXPECTED.
I GUESS MY, *um*...
THIS KRYPTONIAN ARMOR I'M WEARING-- MUST BE DOING ITS JOB.
HONESTLY, IT HURT LIKE HELL, BUT WHAT CHOICE DID I HAVE? END OF THE WORLD, RIGHT?
JUST BE CAREFUL YOU DON'T PUSH YOURSELF TOO HARD, SUPERBOY.
YOU'RE STILL HEALING FROM H'EL NEARLY TEARING YOU IN TWO.
SPEAKING OF WHICH--
--I'VE GOT THE RIGHT COORDINATES. I HOPE.
NO.
YOU DON'T.
YOU BETTER HOPE IT'S A ***BETTER*** PLAN THAN THE ***LAST ONE--***
--WHICH ***NEARLY*** GOT ME ***KILLED.***
YOU'RE FINE.
MOVING ON.

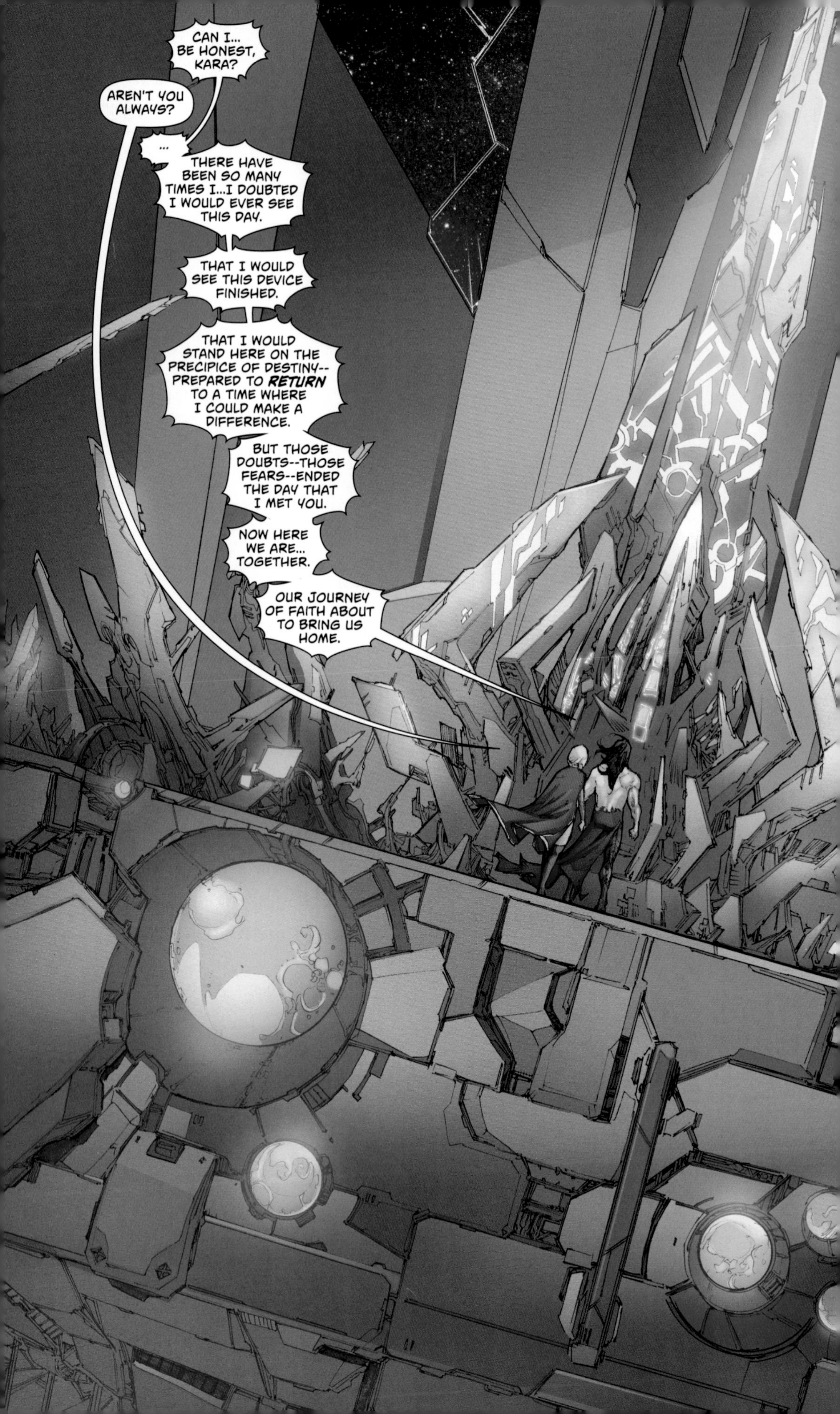
CAN I... BE HONEST, KARA?
AREN'T YOU ALWAYS?
...
THERE HAVE BEEN SO MANY TIMES I...I DOUBTED I WOULD EVER SEE THIS DAY.
THAT I WOULD SEE THIS DEVICE FINISHED.
THAT I WOULD STAND HERE ON THE PRECIPICE OF DESTINY-- --PREPARED TO RETURN TO A TIME WHERE I COULD MAKE A DIFFERENCE.
BUT THOSE DOUBTS--THOSE FEARS--ENDED THE DAY THAT I MET YOU.
NOW HERE WE ARE... TOGETHER.
OUR JOURNEY OF FAITH ABOUT TO BRING US HOME.

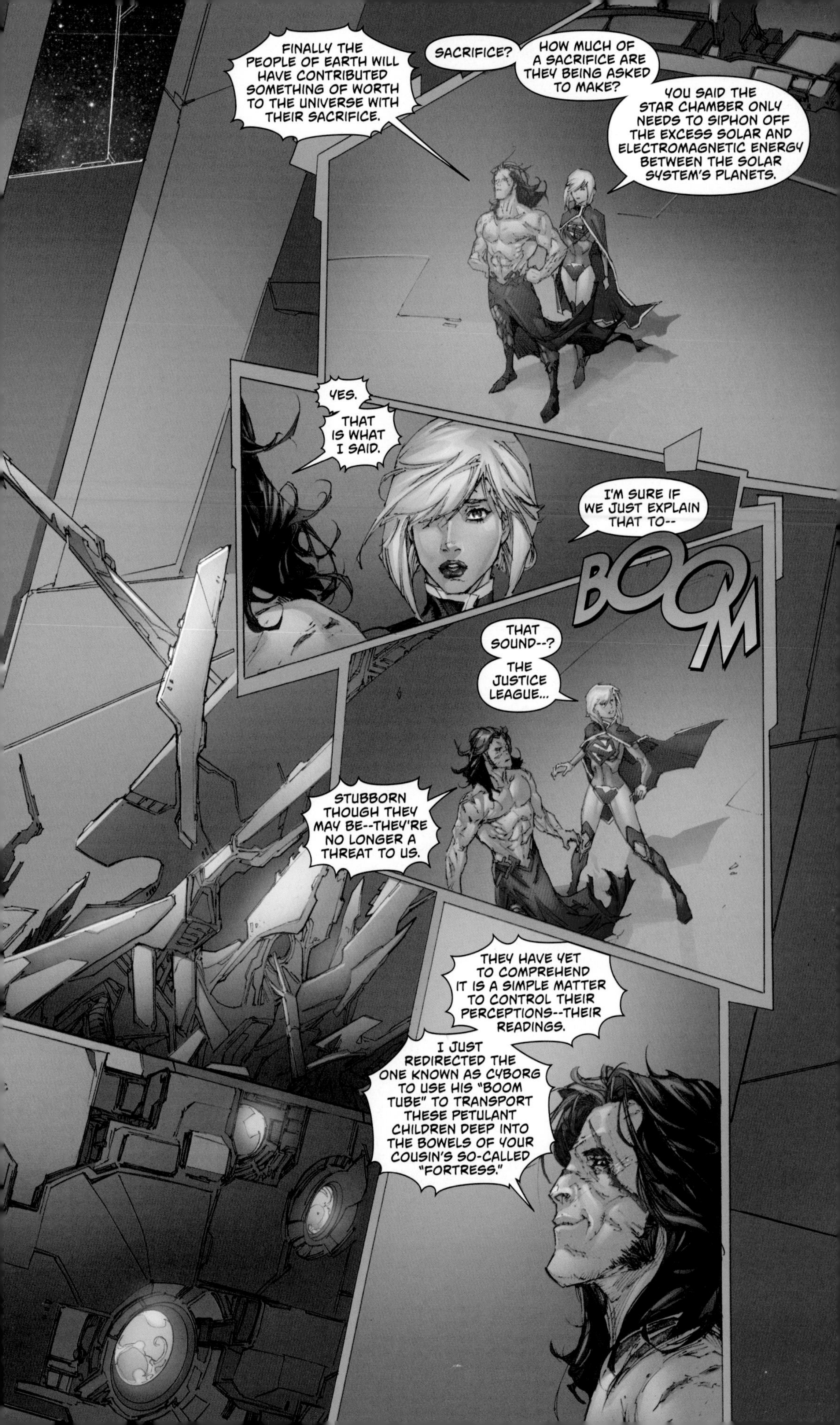

FINALLY THE PEOPLE OF EARTH WILL HAVE CONTRIBUTED SOMETHING OF WORTH TO THE UNIVERSE WITH THEIR SACRIFICE.
SACRIFICE?
HOW MUCH OF A SACRIFICE ARE THEY BEING ASKED TO MAKE?
YOU SAID THE STAR CHAMBER ONLY NEEDS TO SIPHON OFF THE EXCESS SOLAR AND ELECTROMAGNETIC ENERGY BETWEEN THE SOLAR SYSTEM'S PLANETS.
YES.
THAT IS WHAT I SAID.
I'M SURE IF WE JUST EXPLAIN THAT TO--
BOOM
THAT SOUND--?
THE JUSTICE LEAGUE...
STUBBORN THOUGH THEY MAY BE--THEY'RE NO LONGER A THREAT TO US.
THEY HAVE YET TO COMPREHEND IT IS A SIMPLE MATTER TO CONTROL THEIR PERCEPTIONS--THEIR READINGS.
I JUST REDIRECTED THE ONE KNOWN AS CYBORG TO USE HIS "BOOM TUBE" TO TRANSPORT THESE PETULANT CHILDREN DEEP INTO THE BOWELS OF YOUR COUSIN'S SO-CALLED "FORTRESS."

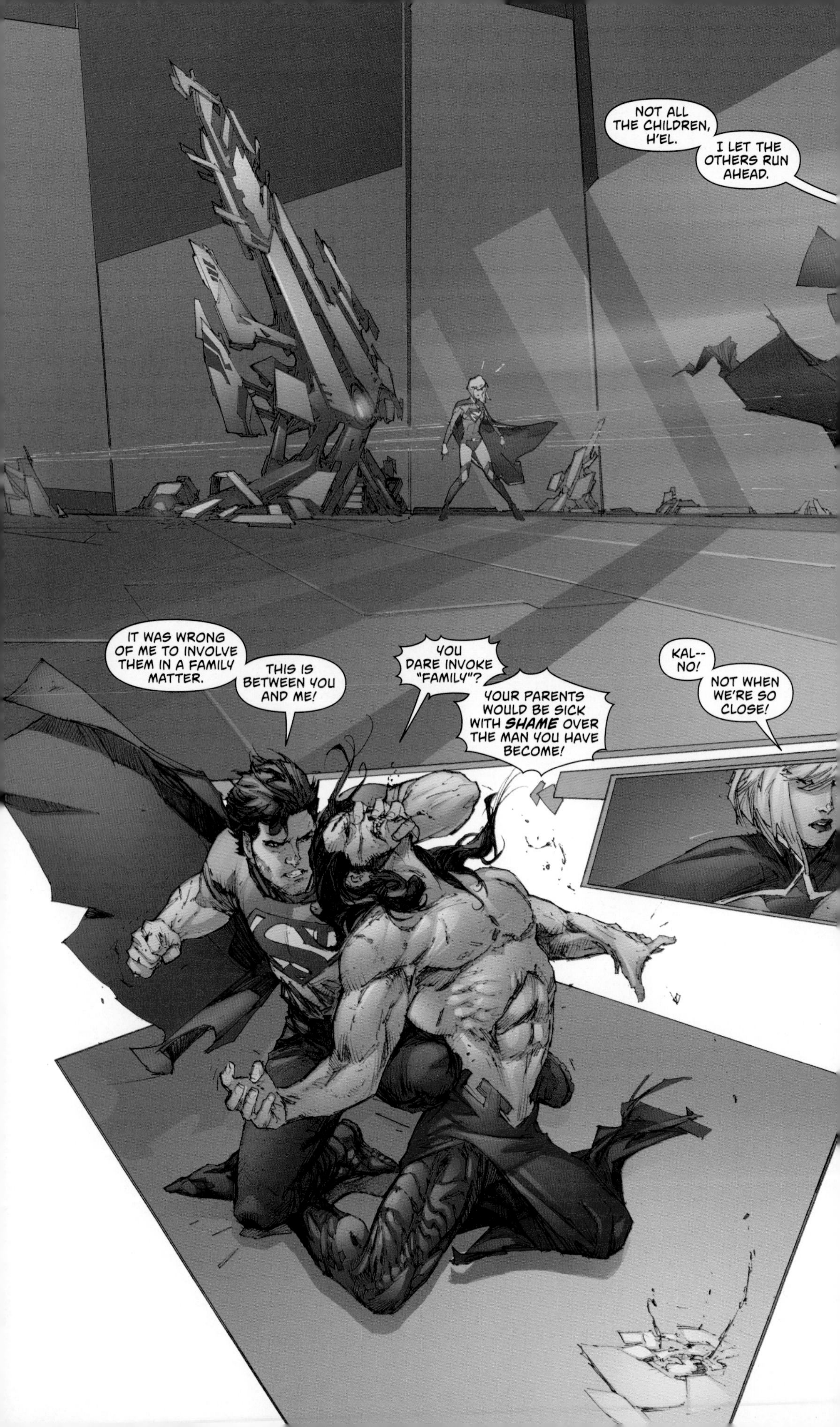
NOT ALL THE CHILDREN, H'EL.
I LET THE OTHERS RUN AHEAD.
IT WAS WRONG OF ME TO INVOLVE THEM IN A FAMILY MATTER.
THIS IS BETWEEN YOU AND ME!
YOU DARE INVOKE "FAMILY"?
YOUR PARENTS WOULD BE SICK WITH SHAME OVER THE MAN YOU HAVE BECOME!
KAL-- NO!
NOT WHEN WE'RE SO CLOSE!

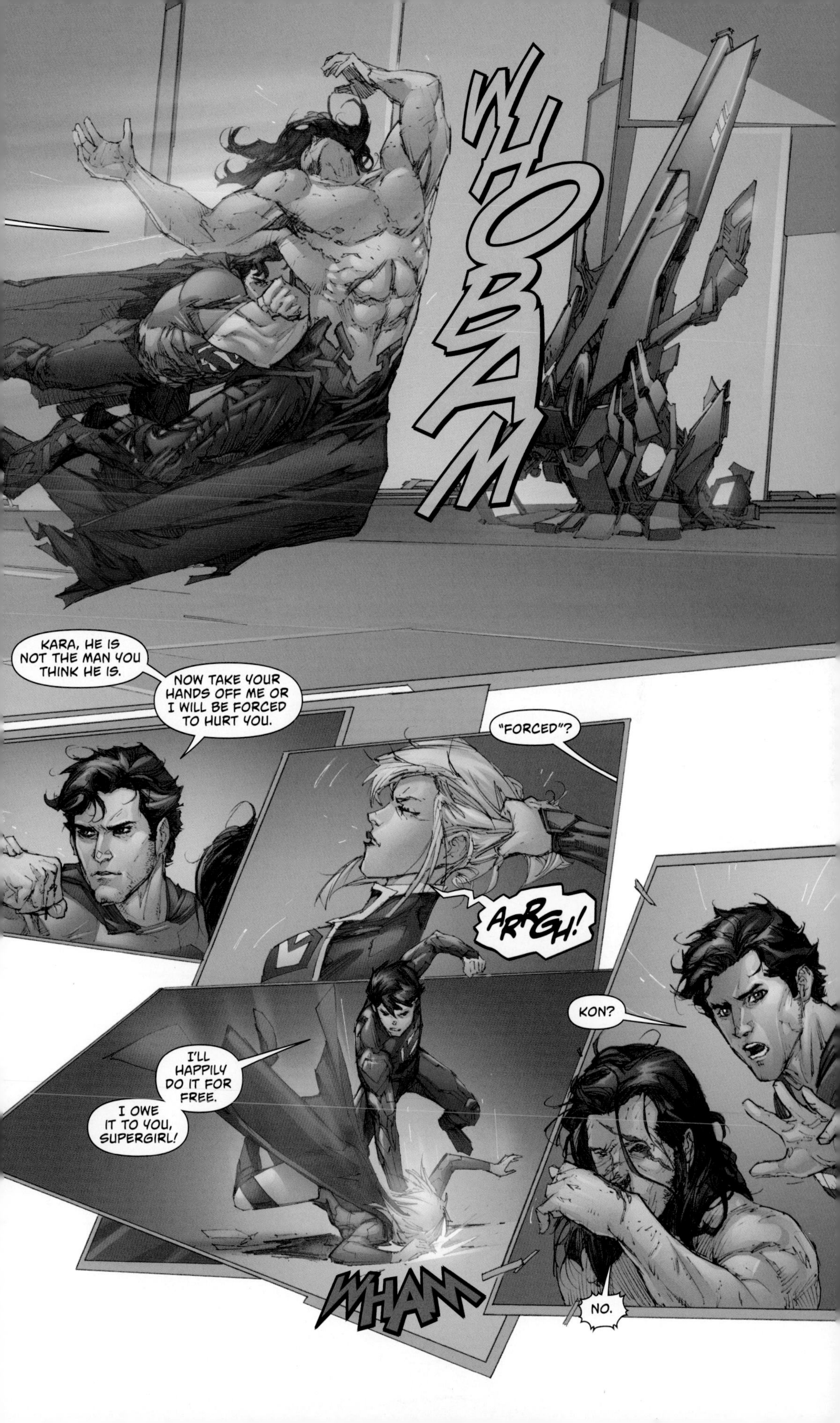
WHOBAM
KARA, HE IS NOT THE MAN YOU THINK HE IS.
NOW TAKE YOUR HANDS OFF ME OR I WILL BE FORCED TO HURT YOU.
"FORCED"?
ARRGH!
I'LL HAPPILY DO IT FOR FREE.
I OWE IT TO YOU, SUPERGIRL!
WHAM
KON?
NO.

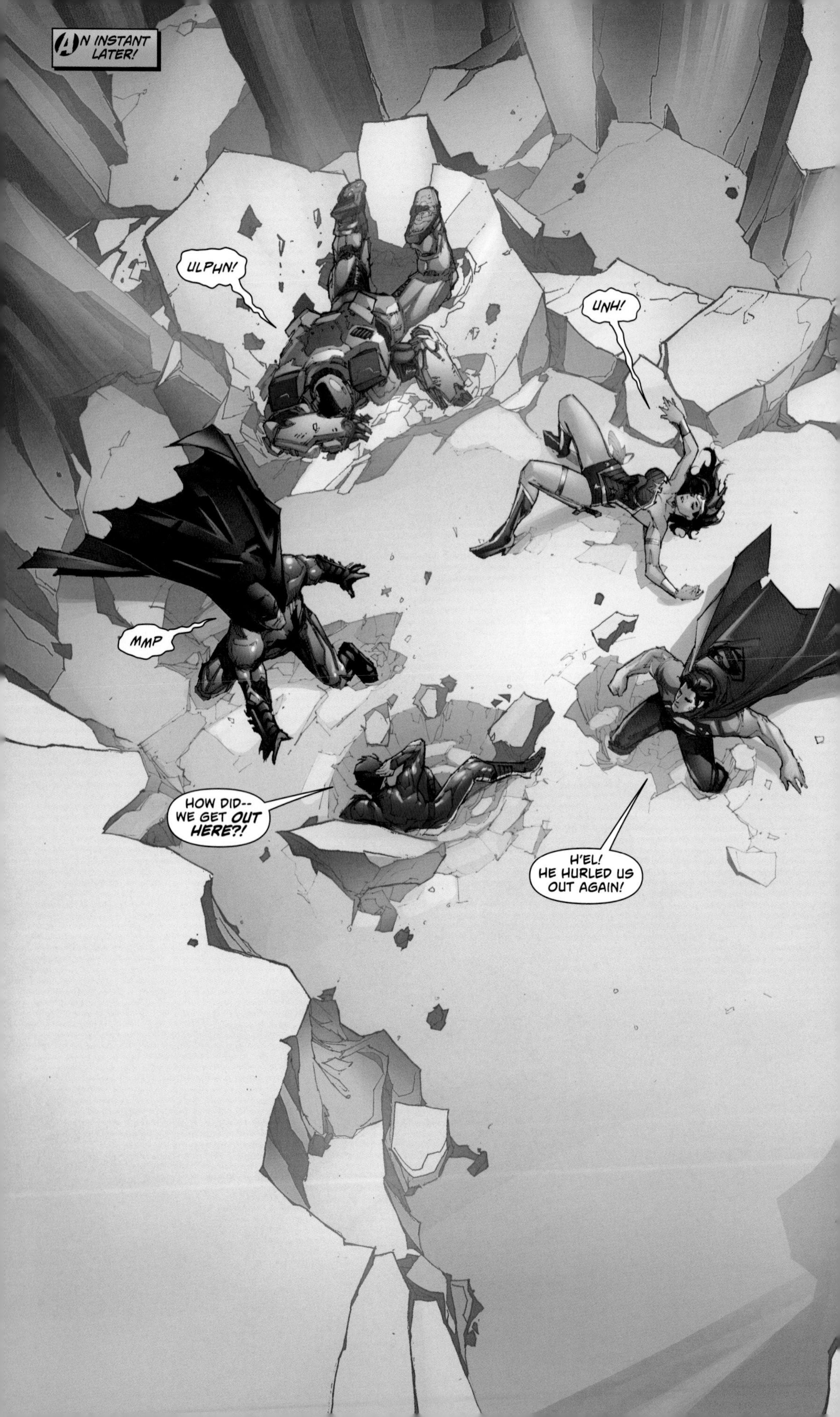
AN INSTANT LATER!
ULPHN!
UNH!
MMP
HOW DID-- WE GET OUT HERE?!
H'EL! HE HURLED US OUT AGAIN!

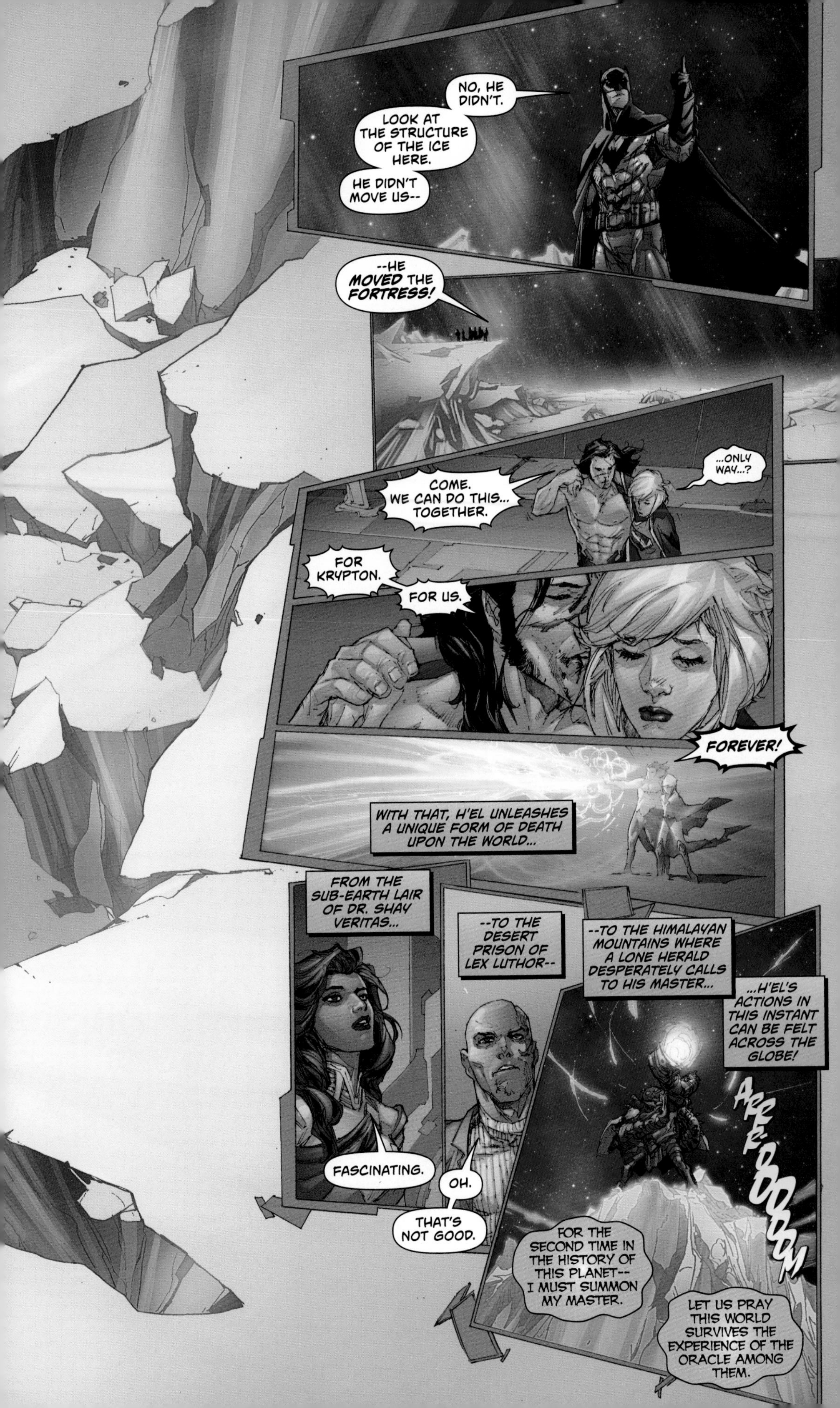
NO, HE DIDN'T.
LOOK AT THE STRUCTURE OF THE ICE HERE.
HE DIDN'T MOVE US--
--HE MOVED THE FORTRESS!
COME. WE CAN DO THIS... TOGETHER.
...ONLY WAY...?
FOR KRYPTON.
FOR US.
FOREVER!
WITH THAT, H'EL UNLEASHES A UNIQUE FORM OF DEATH UPON THE WORLD...
FROM THE SUB-EARTH LAIR OF DR. SHAY VERITAS...
FASCINATING.
--TO THE DESERT PRISON OF LEX LUTHOR--
OH.
THAT'S NOT GOOD.
--TO THE HIMALAYAN MOUNTAINS WHERE A LONE HERALD DESPERATELY CALLS TO HIS MASTER...
...H'EL'S ACTIONS IN THIS INSTANT CAN BE FELT ACROSS THE GLOBE!
ARR-BOOOM
FOR THE SECOND TIME IN THE HISTORY OF THIS PLANET-- I MUST SUMMON MY MASTER.
LET US PRAY THIS WORLD SURVIVES THE EXPERIENCE OF THE ORACLE AMONG THEM.

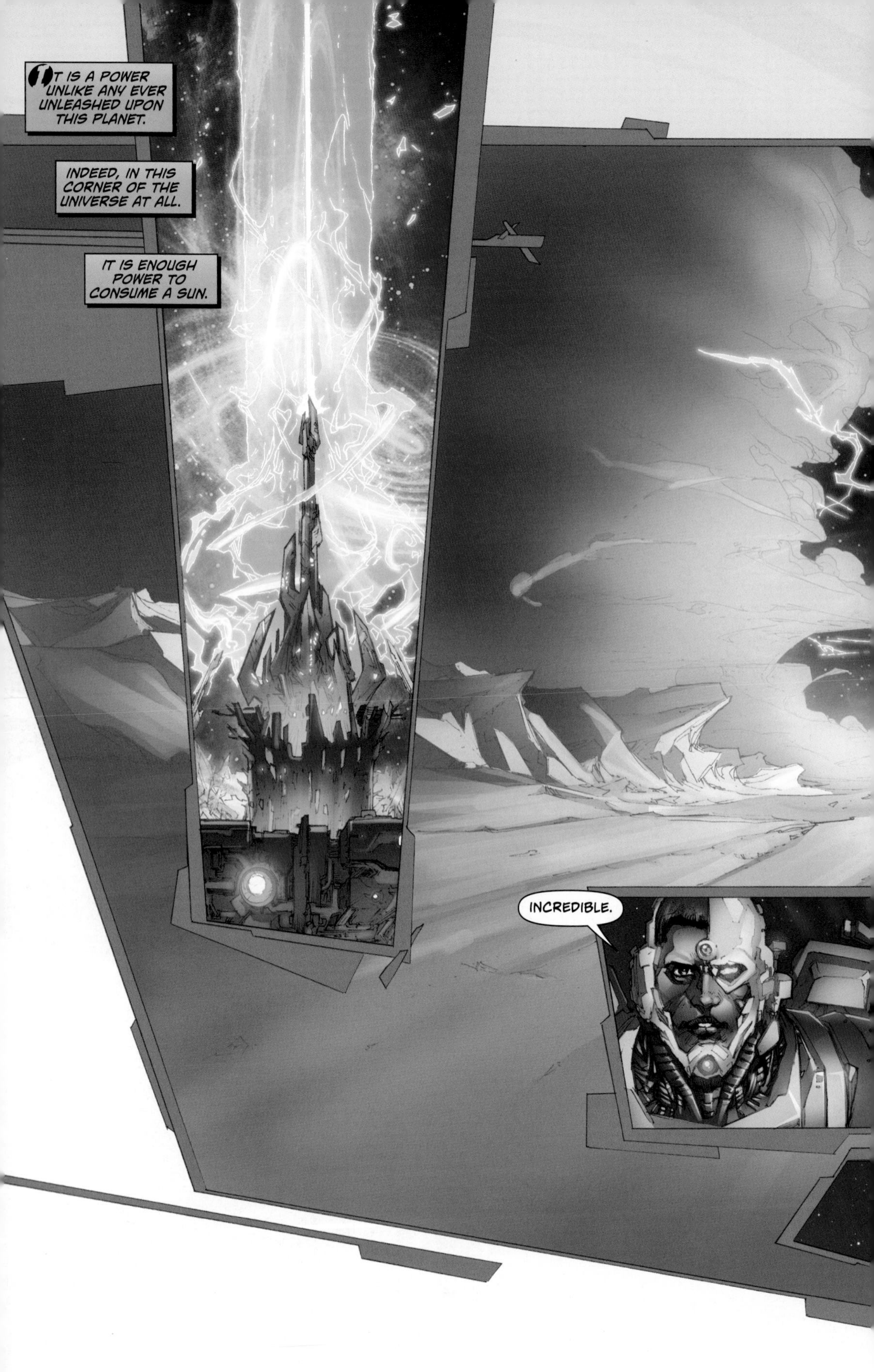
IT IS A POWER UNLIKE ANY EVER UNLEASHED UPON THIS PLANET.
INDEED, IN THIS CORNER OF THE UNIVERSE AT ALL.
IT IS ENOUGH POWER TO CONSUME A SUN.
INCREDIBLE.

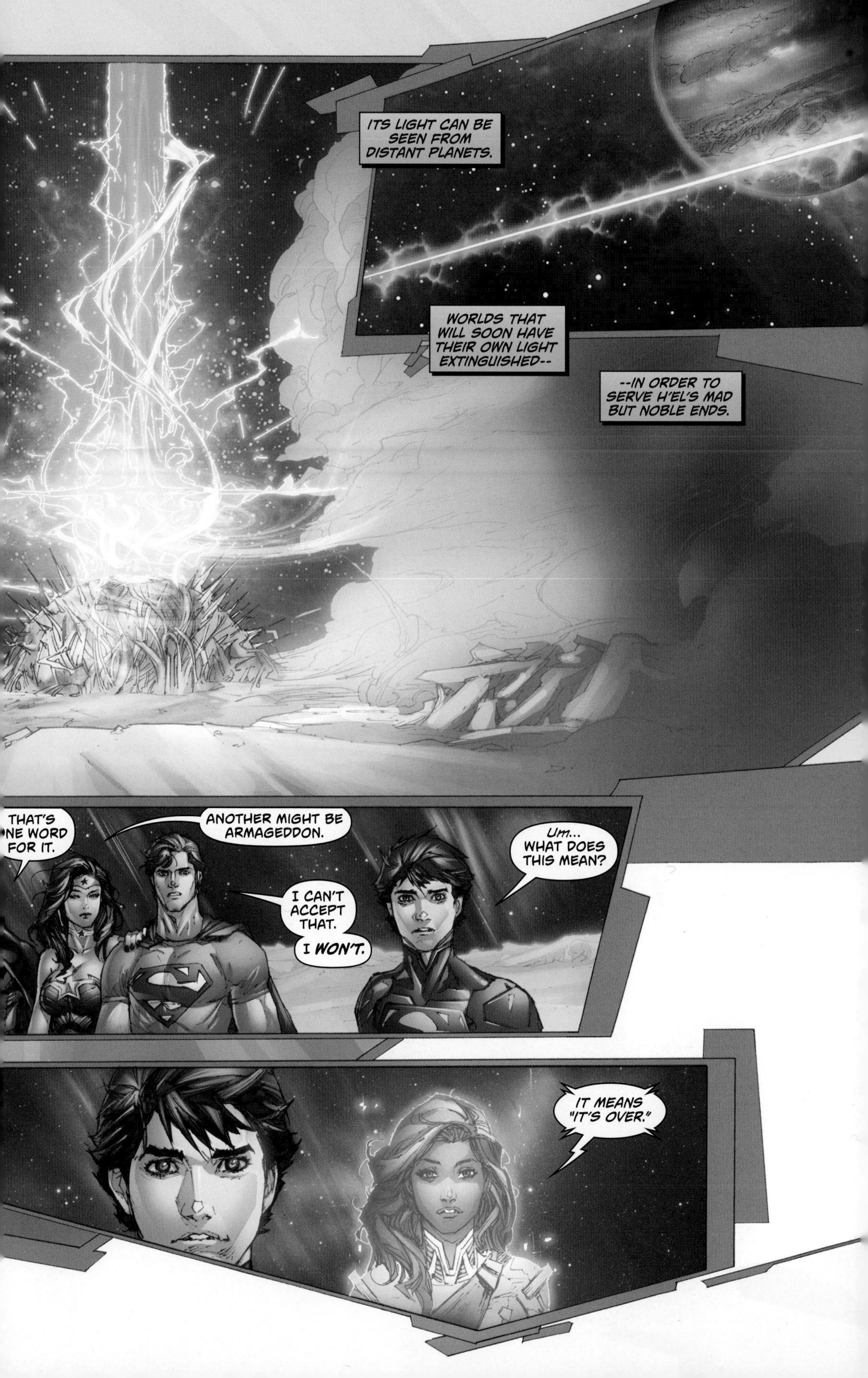
ITS LIGHT CAN BE SEEN FROM DISTANT PLANETS.
WORLDS THAT WILL SOON HAVE THEIR OWN LIGHT EXTINGUISHED--
--IN ORDER TO SERVE H'EL'S MAD BUT NOBLE ENDS.
THAT'S NE WORD FOR IT.
ANOTHER MIGHT BE ARMAGEDDON.
I CAN'T ACCEPT THAT.
I WON'T.
Um... WHAT DOES THIS MEAN?
IT MEANS "IT'S OVER."

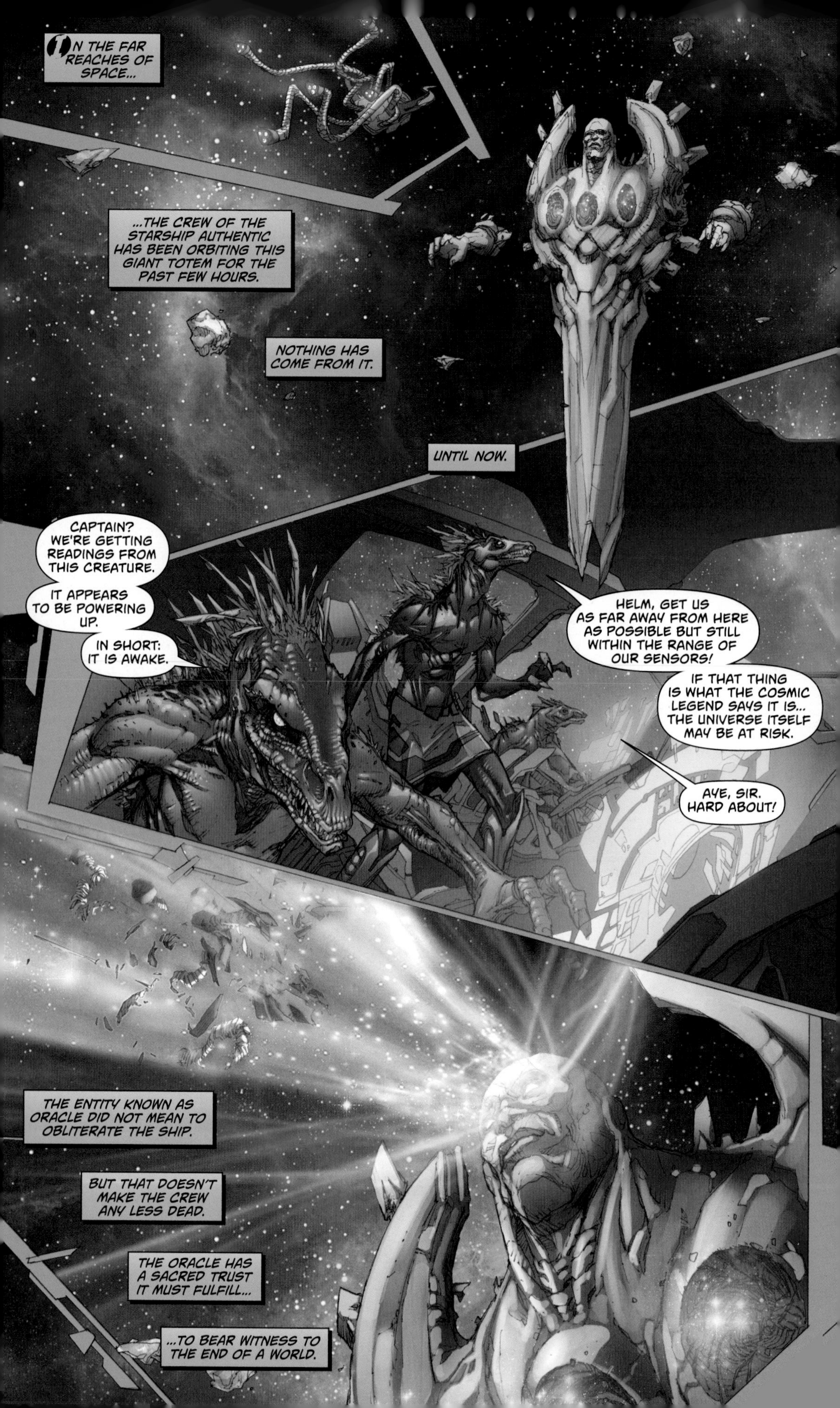
IN THE FAR REACHES OF SPACE...
...THE CREW OF THE STARSHIP AUTHENTIC HAS BEEN ORBITING THIS GIANT TOTEM FOR THE PAST FEW HOURS.
NOTHING HAS COME FROM IT.
UNTIL NOW.
CAPTAIN? WE'RE GETTING READINGS FROM THIS CREATURE.
IT APPEARS TO BE POWERING UP.
IN SHORT: IT IS AWAKE.
HELM, GET US AS FAR AWAY FROM HERE AS POSSIBLE BUT STILL WITHIN THE RANGE OF OUR SENSORS!
IF THAT THING IS WHAT THE COSMIC LEGEND SAYS IT IS... THE UNIVERSE ITSELF MAY BE AT RISK.
AYE, SIR. HARD ABOUT!
THE ENTITY KNOWN AS ORACLE DID NOT MEAN TO OBLITERATE THE SHIP.
BUT THAT DOESN'T MAKE THE CREW ANY LESS DEAD.
THE ORACLE HAS A SACRED TRUST IT MUST FULFILL...
...TO BEAR WITNESS TO THE END OF A WORLD.

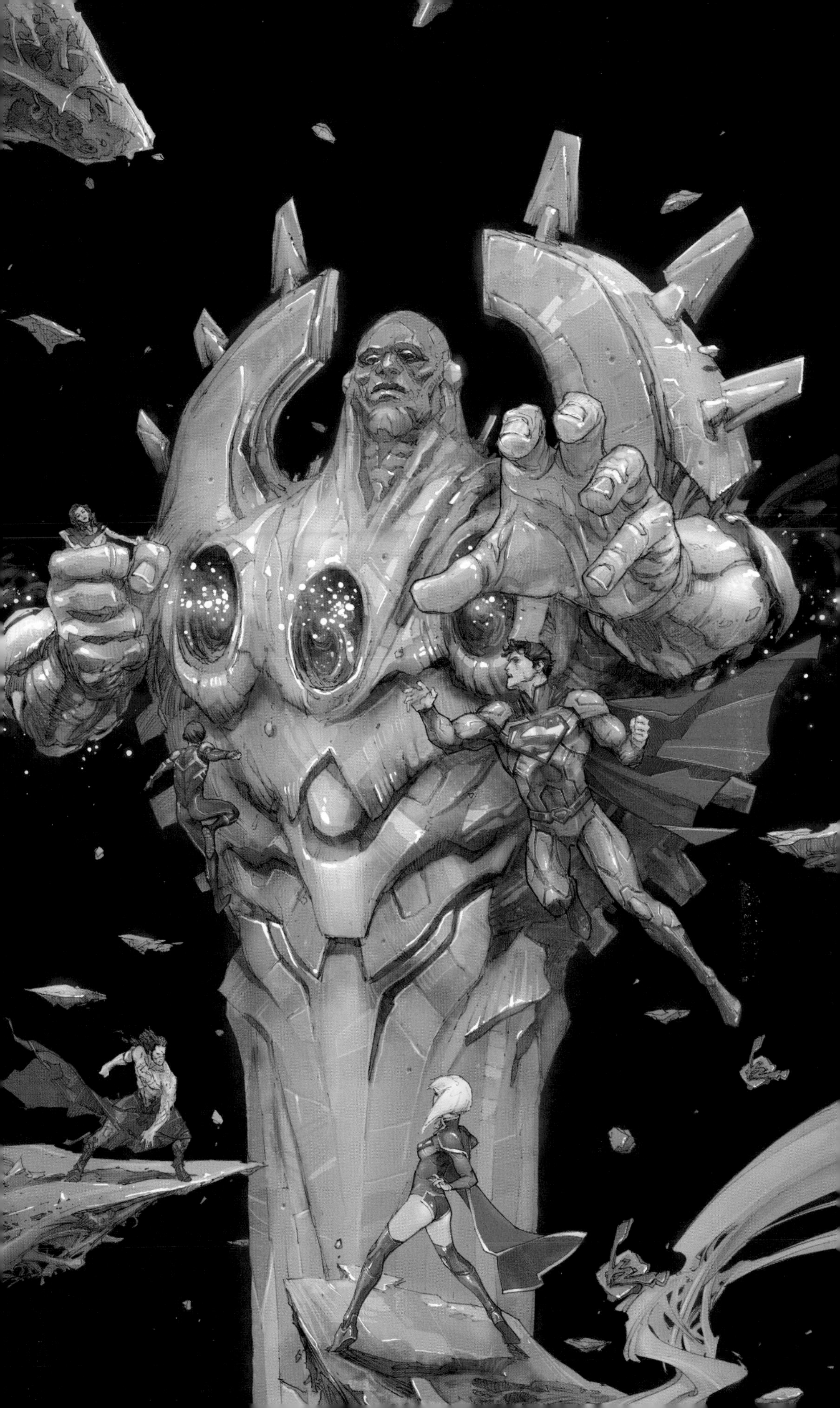

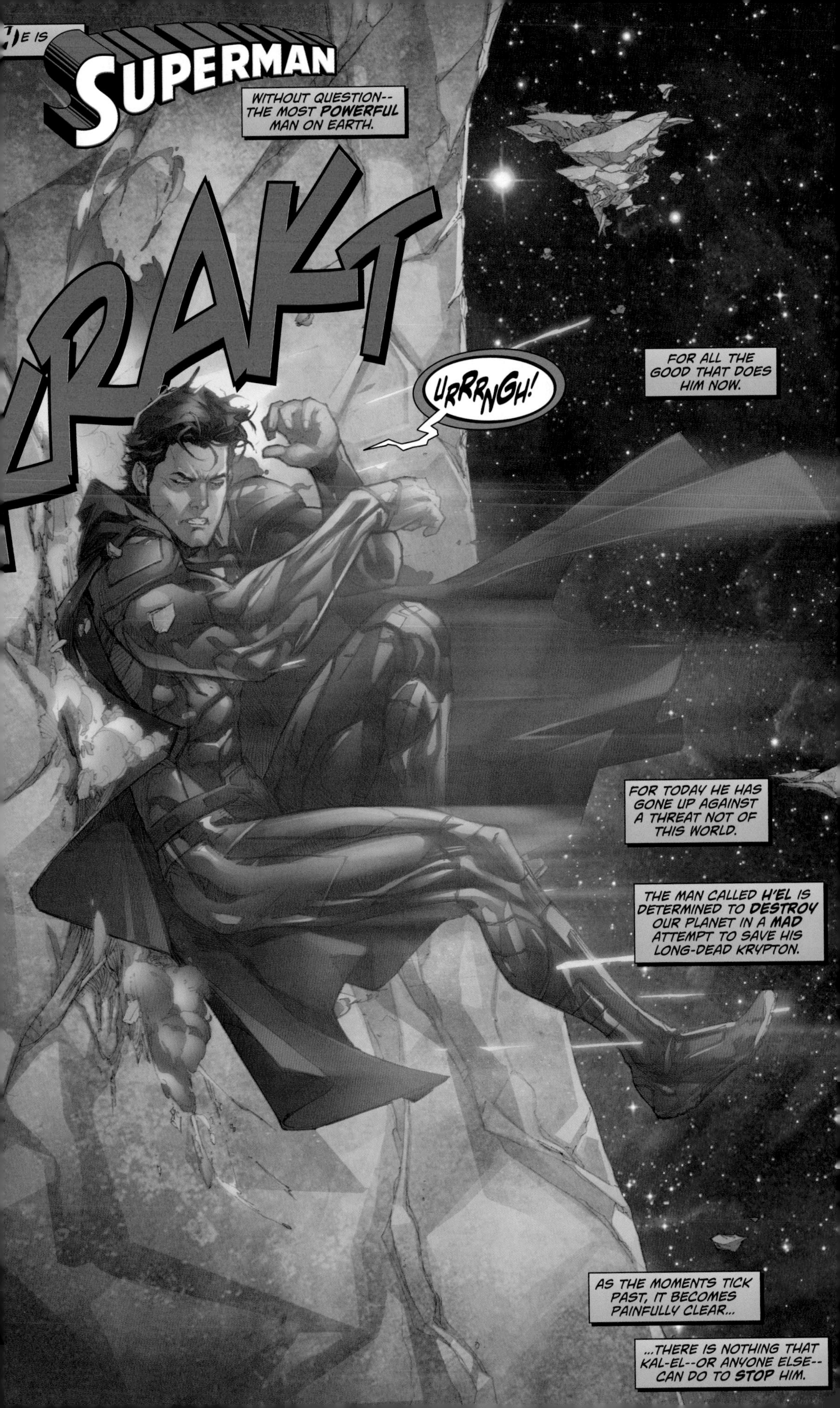
HE IS
SUPERMAN
WITHOUT QUESTION-- THE MOST POWERFUL MAN ON EARTH.
KRAKT
URRRNGH!
FOR ALL THE GOOD THAT DOES HIM NOW.
FOR TODAY HE HAS GONE UP AGAINST A THREAT NOT OF THIS WORLD.
THE MAN CALLED H'EL IS DETERMINED TO DESTROY OUR PLANET IN A MAD ATTEMPT TO SAVE HIS LONG-DEAD KRYPTON.
AS THE MOMENTS TICK PAST, IT BECOMES PAINFULLY CLEAR...
...THERE IS NOTHING THAT KAL-EL--OR ANYONE ELSE-- CAN DO TO STOP HIM.

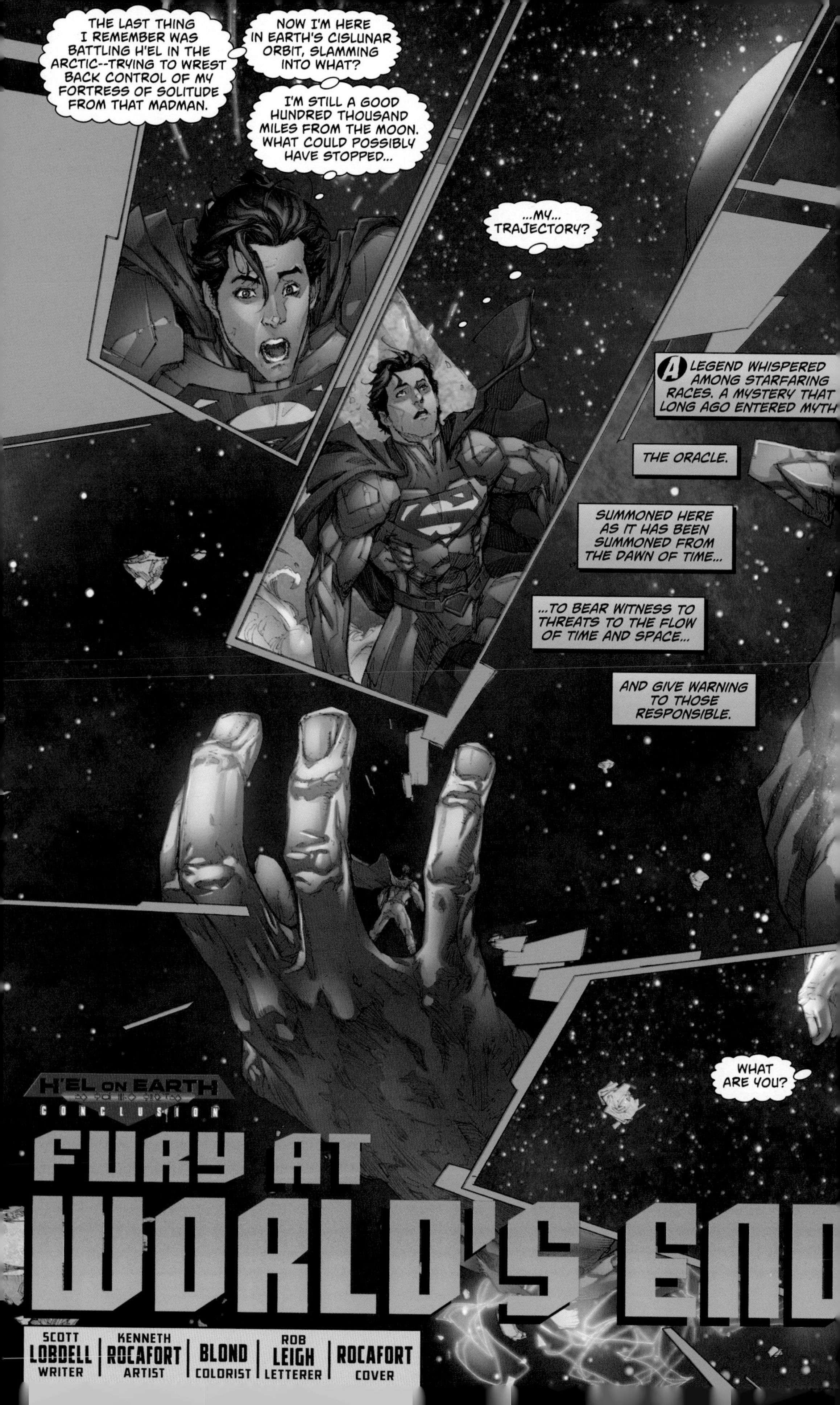
THE LAST THING I REMEMBER WAS BATTLING H'EL IN THE ARCTIC--TRYING TO WREST BACK CONTROL OF MY FORTRESS OF SOLITUDE FROM THAT MADMAN.
NOW I'M HERE IN EARTH'S CISLUNAR ORBIT, SLAMMING INTO WHAT?
I'M STILL A GOOD HUNDRED THOUSAND MILES FROM THE MOON. WHAT COULD POSSIBLY HAVE STOPPED...
...MY... TRAJECTORY?
A LEGEND WHISPERED AMONG STARFARING RACES. A MYSTERY THAT LONG AGO ENTERED MYTH.
THE ORACLE.
SUMMONED HERE AS IT HAS BEEN SUMMONED FROM THE DAWN OF TIME...
...TO BEAR WITNESS TO THREATS TO THE FLOW OF TIME AND SPACE...
AND GIVE WARNING TO THOSE RESPONSIBLE.
WHAT ARE YOU?
H'EL ON EARTH
CONCLUSION
FURY AT WORLD'S END
SCOTT LOBDELL WRITER
KENNETH ROCAFORT ARTIST
BLOND COLORIST
ROB LEIGH LETTERER
ROCAFORT COVER

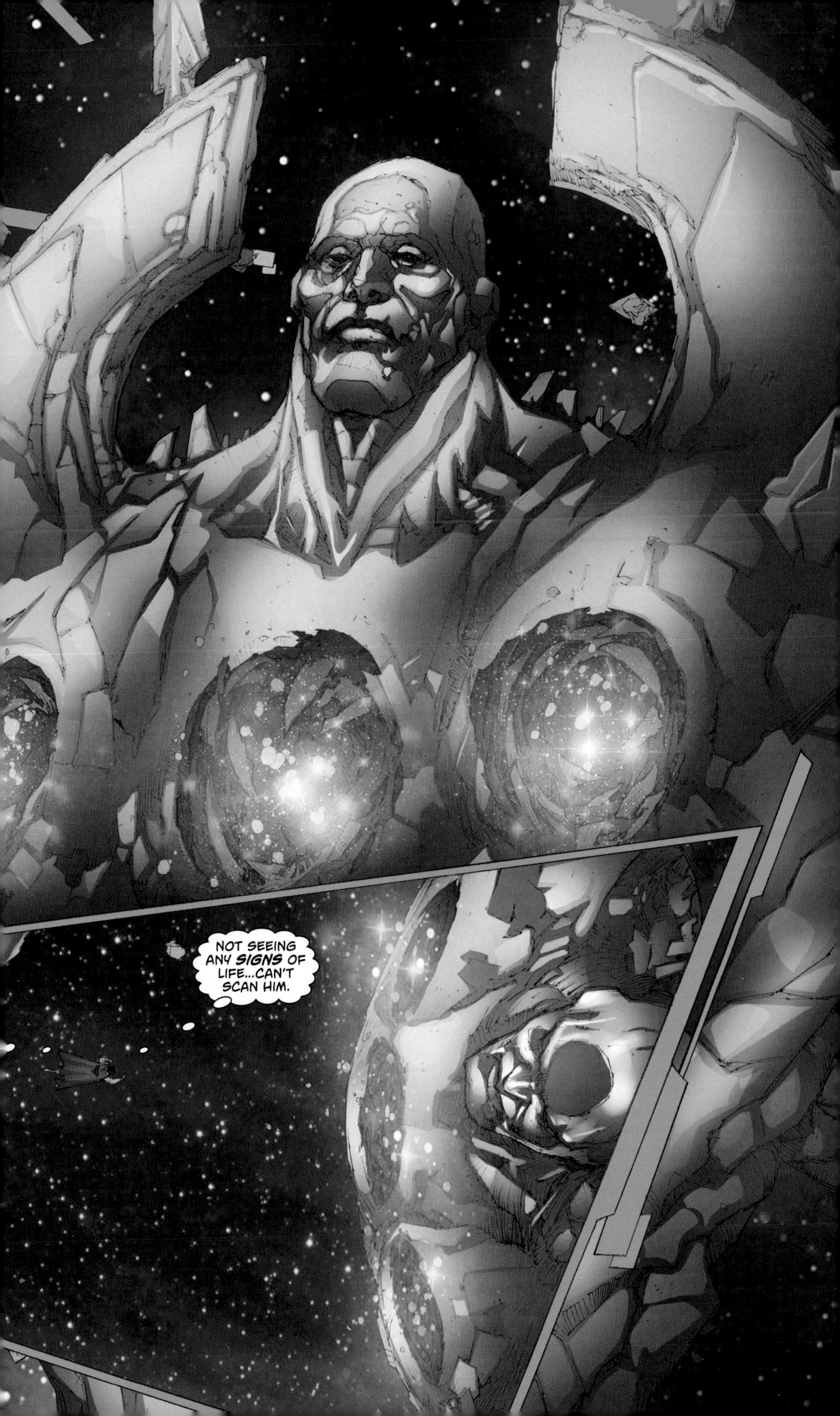
NOT SEEING ANY SIGNS OF LIFE...CAN'T SCAN HIM.

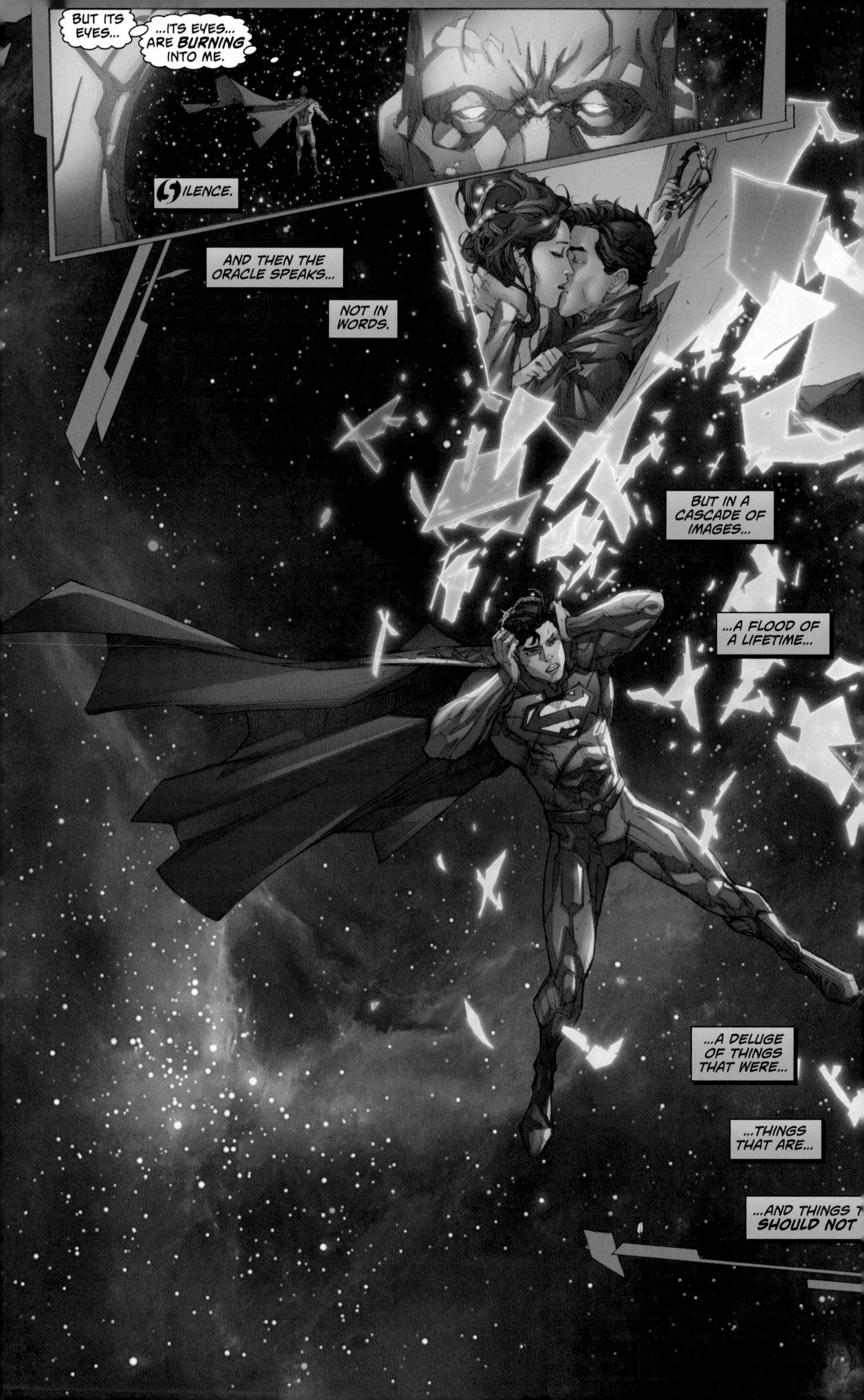
BUT ITS EYES...
...ITS EYES... ARE BURNING INTO ME.
SILENCE.
AND THEN THE ORACLE SPEAKS...
NOT IN WORDS.
BUT IN A CASCADE OF IMAGES...
...A FLOOD OF A LIFETIME...
...A DELUGE OF THINGS THAT WERE...
...THINGS THAT ARE...
...AND THINGS T
SHOULD NOT

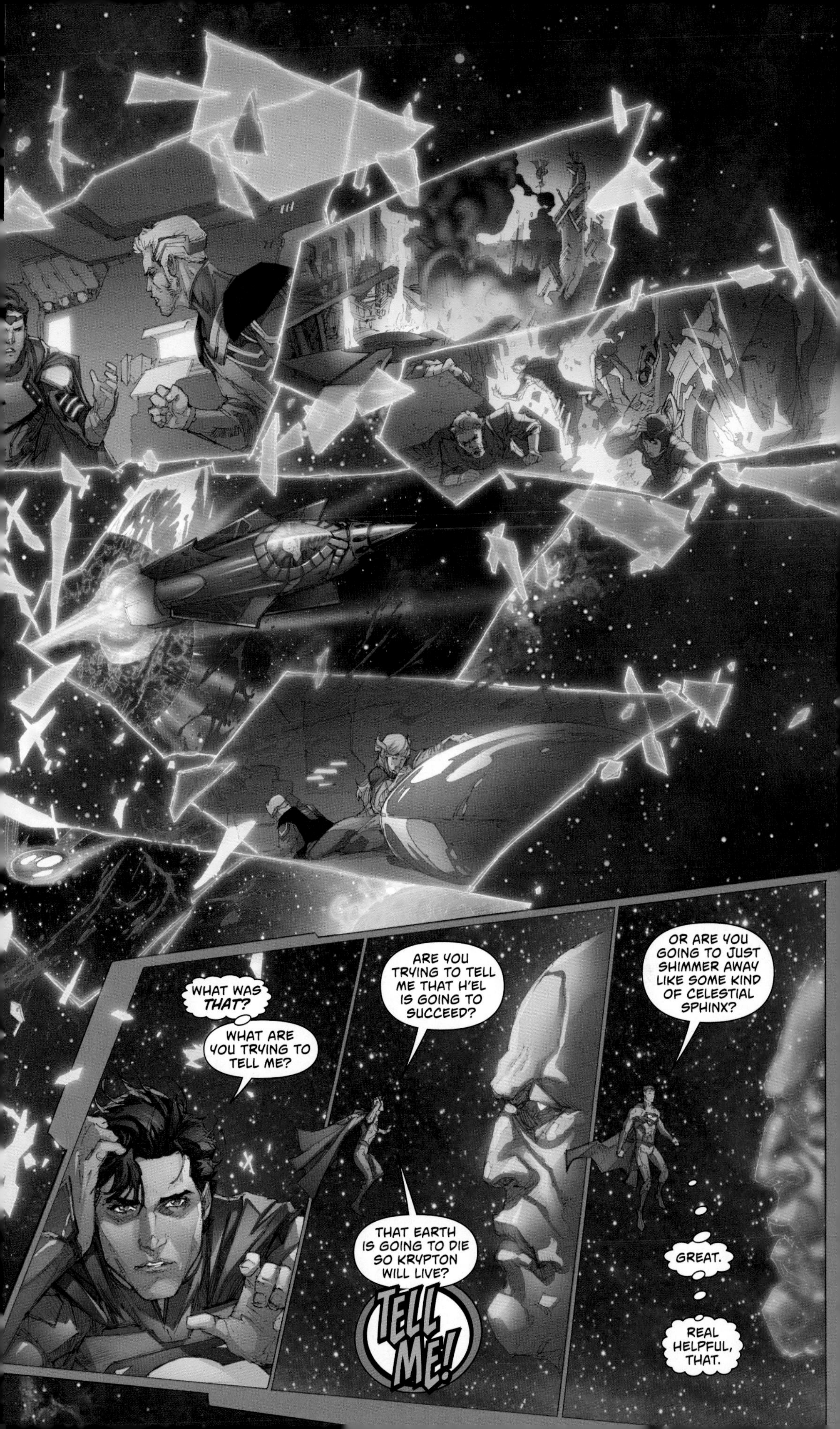
WHAT WAS THAT?
WHAT ARE YOU TRYING TO TELL ME?
ARE YOU TRYING TO TELL ME THAT H'EL IS GOING TO SUCCEED?
THAT EARTH IS GOING TO DIE SO KRYPTON WILL LIVE?
TELL ME!
OR ARE YOU GOING TO JUST SHIMMER AWAY LIKE SOME KIND OF CELESTIAL SPHINX?
GREAT.
REAL HELPFUL, THAT.

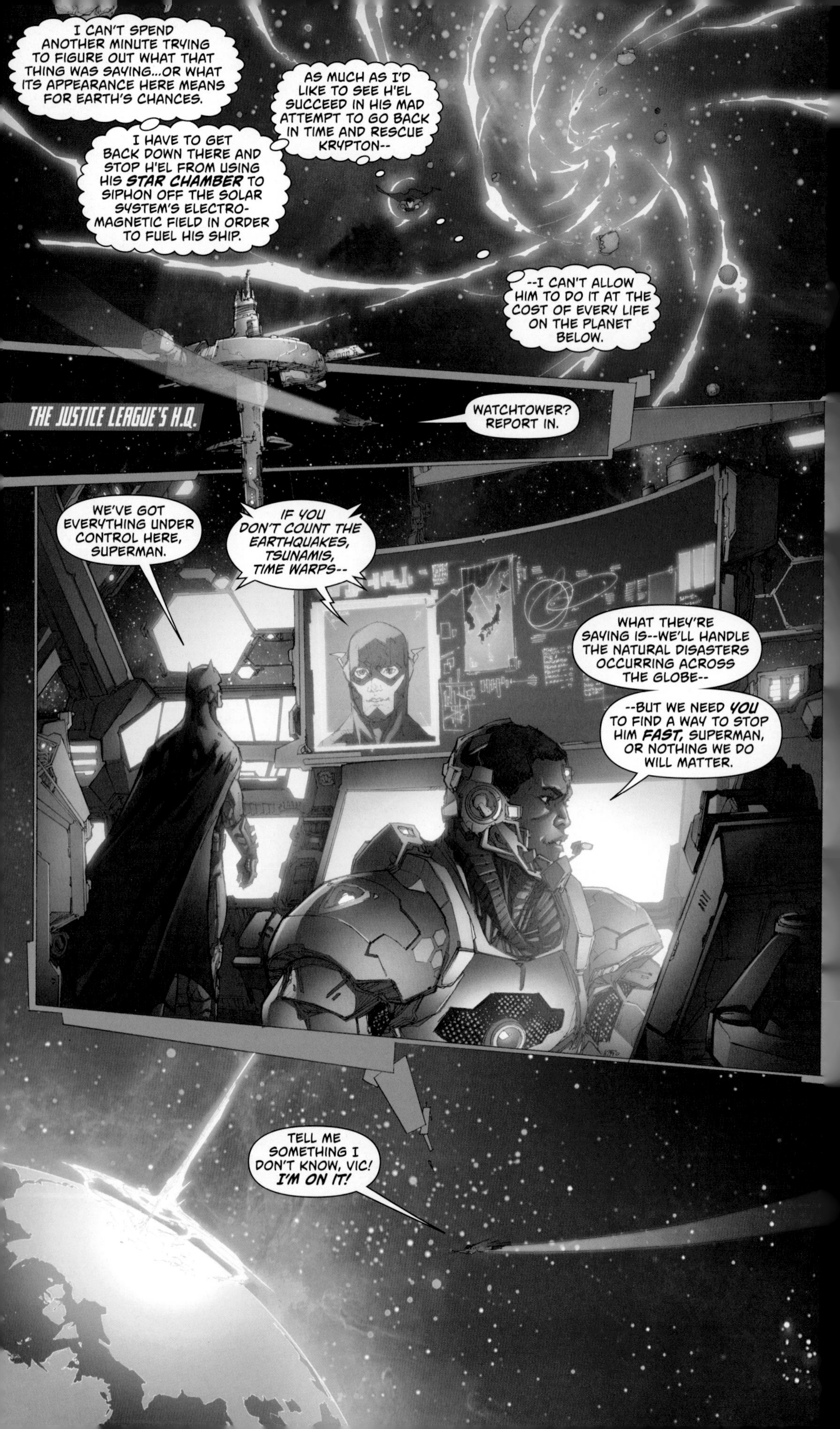

I CAN'T SPEND ANOTHER MINUTE TRYING TO FIGURE OUT WHAT THAT THING WAS SAYING...OR WHAT ITS APPEARANCE HERE MEANS FOR EARTH'S CHANCES.
I HAVE TO GET BACK DOWN THERE AND STOP H'EL FROM USING HIS STAR CHAMBER TO SIPHON OFF THE SOLAR SYSTEM'S ELECTRO-MAGNETIC FIELD IN ORDER TO FUEL HIS SHIP.
AS MUCH AS I'D LIKE TO SEE H'EL SUCCEED IN HIS MAD ATTEMPT TO GO BACK IN TIME AND RESCUE KRYPTON--
--I CAN'T ALLOW HIM TO DO IT AT THE COST OF EVERY LIFE ON THE PLANET BELOW.
THE JUSTICE LEAGUE'S H.Q.
WATCHTOWER? REPORT IN.
WE'VE GOT EVERYTHING UNDER CONTROL HERE, SUPERMAN.
IF YOU DON'T COUNT THE EARTHQUAKES, TSUNAMIS, TIME WARPS--
WHAT THEY'RE SAYING IS--WE'LL HANDLE THE NATURAL DISASTERS OCCURRING ACROSS THE GLOBE--
--BUT WE NEED YOU TO FIND A WAY TO STOP HIM FAST, SUPERMAN, OR NOTHING WE DO WILL MATTER.
TELL ME SOMETHING I DON'T KNOW, VIC! I'M ON IT!

THE ARCTIC...

...SUPERMAN'S FORMERLY IMPENETRABLE HOME NESTLED HIGH ATOP THE WORLD.

IT IS HERE THAT H'EL ERECTED HIS STAR CHAMBER--

--USING KRYPTONIAN TECHNOLOGY STOLEN FROM THE BOTTLE CITY OF KANDOR--

--TO FUEL HIS SHIP ON A JOURNEY THROUGH TIME IN ORDER TO STOP THE IMMINENT DESTRUCTION OF KRYPTON.

THIS IS HOW YOU **HONOR** OUR LOVE, KARA?

I GAVE YOU A CHOICE TO STAND WITH ME--TO COME WITH ME--AND YOU STAB ME IN THE HEART BY SIDING WITH THESE... THESE INSECTS?

"LOVE"?!

WE **NEVER** HAD LOVE, H'EL!

WE HAD YOUR **LIES**--

--AND MY **HOPELESS, DESPERATE** DREAM I COULD MY PARENTS LIVE AGAIN!

BUT WHEN I SUCCEED, KRYPTON WILL NOT DIE AND I'LL NEVER HAVE TO COME TO EARTH TO SACRIFICE IT AT ALL!

"IF" YOU SUCCEED!

WE--YOU-- CAN'T **RISK** THE LIVES OF EVERYONE ON THIS PLANET ON AN "IF!"

WONDER WOMAN, I JUST NEED A FEW MORE MOMENTS OF COVER--

--UNTIL I CAN USE MY T.K. POWER TO PULL THIS STAR CHAMBER DOWN AROUND H'EL'S LONG, UNKEMPT HAIR.

THEN CONCENTRATE ON THE TASK AT HAND, SUPERBOY!

WITH SUPERMAN GONE AND THE JUSTICE LEAGUE OTHERWISE ENGAGED, IT'S ALL UP TO US!

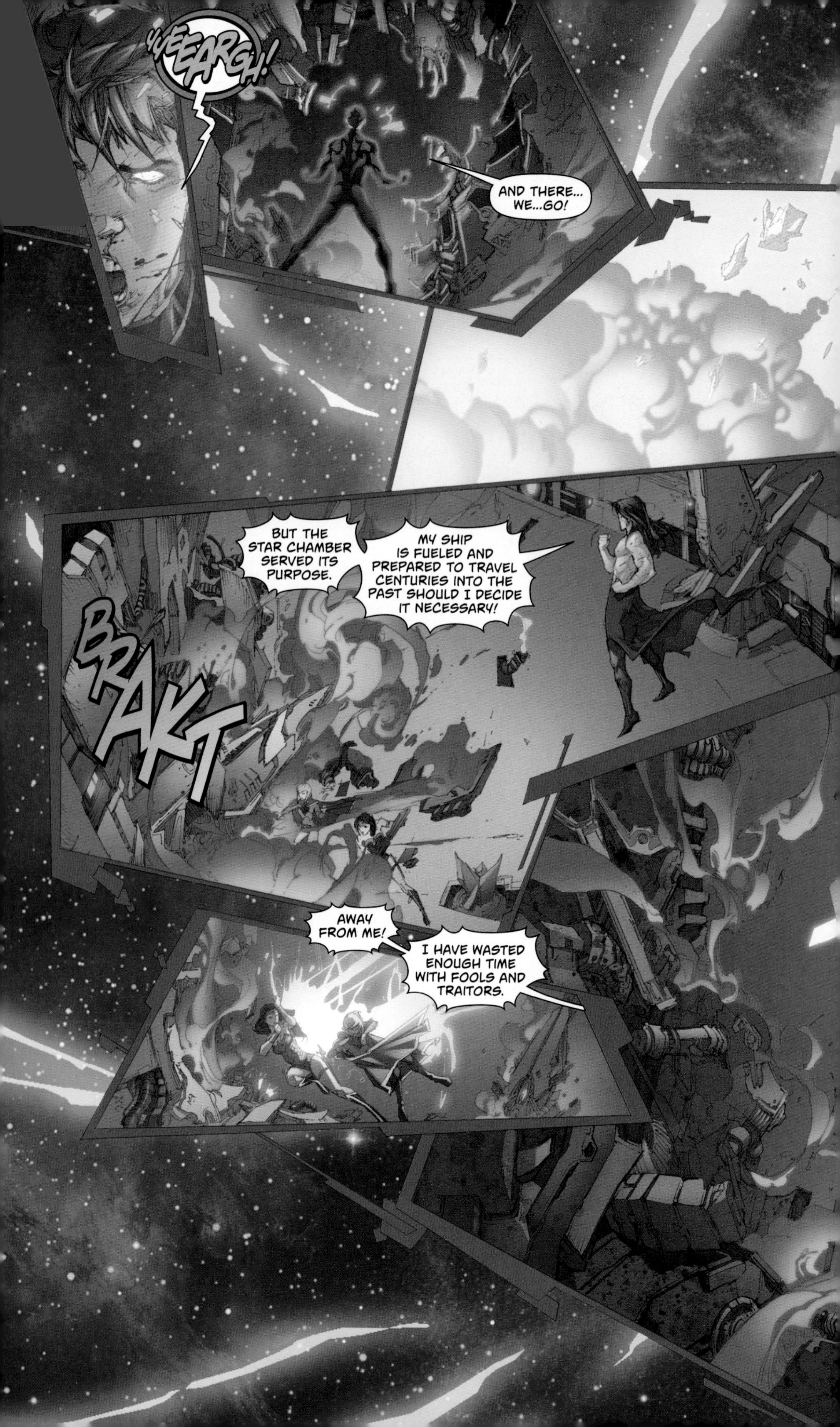
YYEEEARGH!
AND THERE... WE...GO!
BUT THE STAR CHAMBER SERVED ITS PURPOSE.
MY SHIP IS FUELED AND PREPARED TO TRAVEL CENTURIES INTO THE PAST SHOULD I DECIDE IT NECESSARY!
BRAKT
AWAY FROM ME!
I HAVE WASTED ENOUGH TIME WITH FOOLS AND TRAITORS.

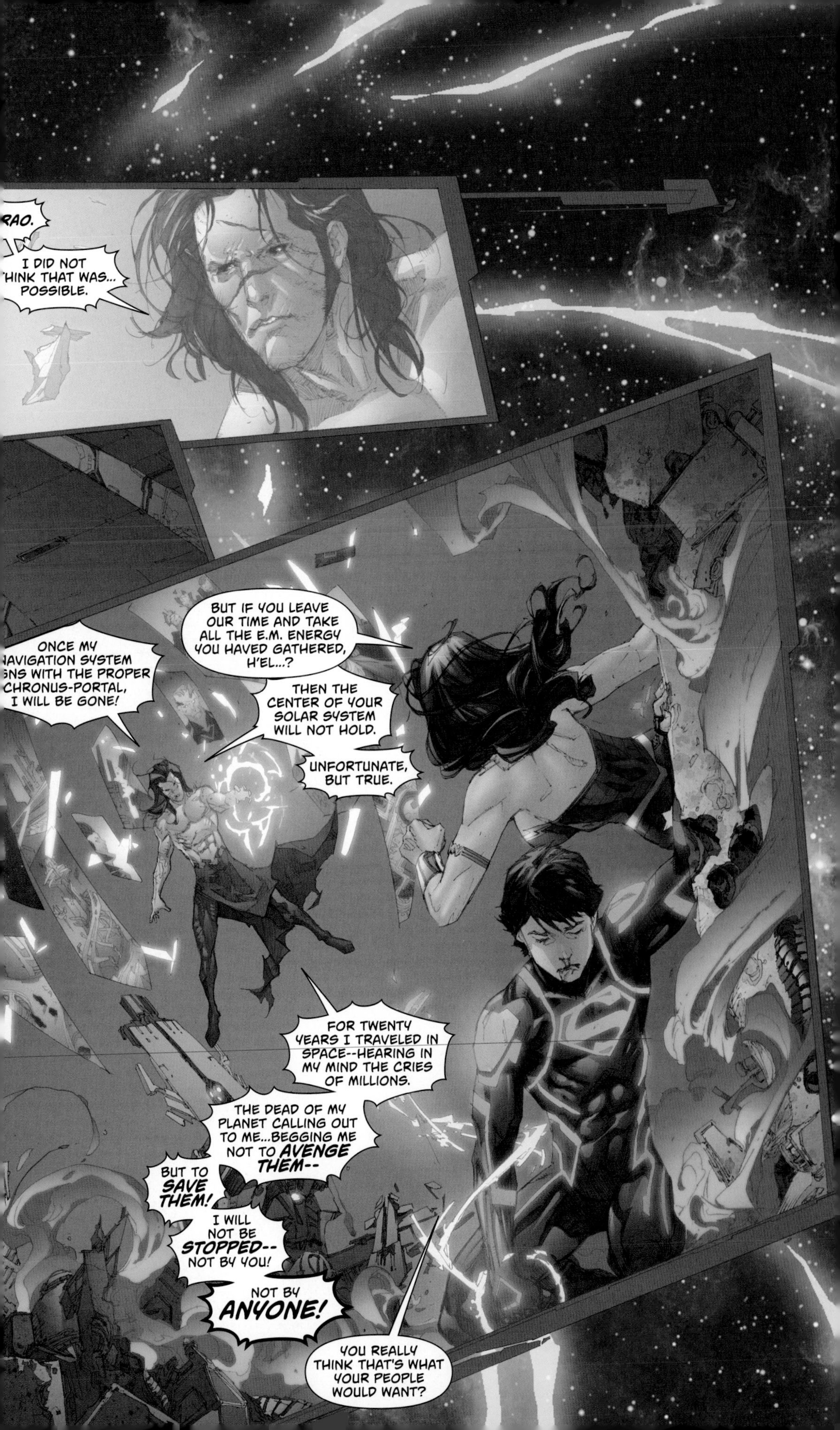
RAO.
I DID NOT HINK THAT WAS... POSSIBLE.
ONCE MY AVIGATION SYSTEM GNS WITH THE PROPER CHRONUS-PORTAL, I WILL BE GONE!
BUT IF YOU LEAVE OUR TIME AND TAKE ALL THE E.M. ENERGY YOU HAVED GATHERED, H'EL...?
THEN THE CENTER OF YOUR SOLAR SYSTEM WILL NOT HOLD.
UNFORTUNATE, BUT TRUE.
FOR TWENTY YEARS I TRAVELED IN SPACE--HEARING IN MY MIND THE CRIES OF MILLIONS.
THE DEAD OF MY PLANET CALLING OUT TO ME...BEGGING ME NOT TO AVENGE THEM--
BUT TO SAVE THEM!
I WILL NOT BE STOPPED-- NOT BY YOU!
NOT BY ANYONE!
YOU REALLY THINK THAT'S WHAT YOUR PEOPLE WOULD WANT?

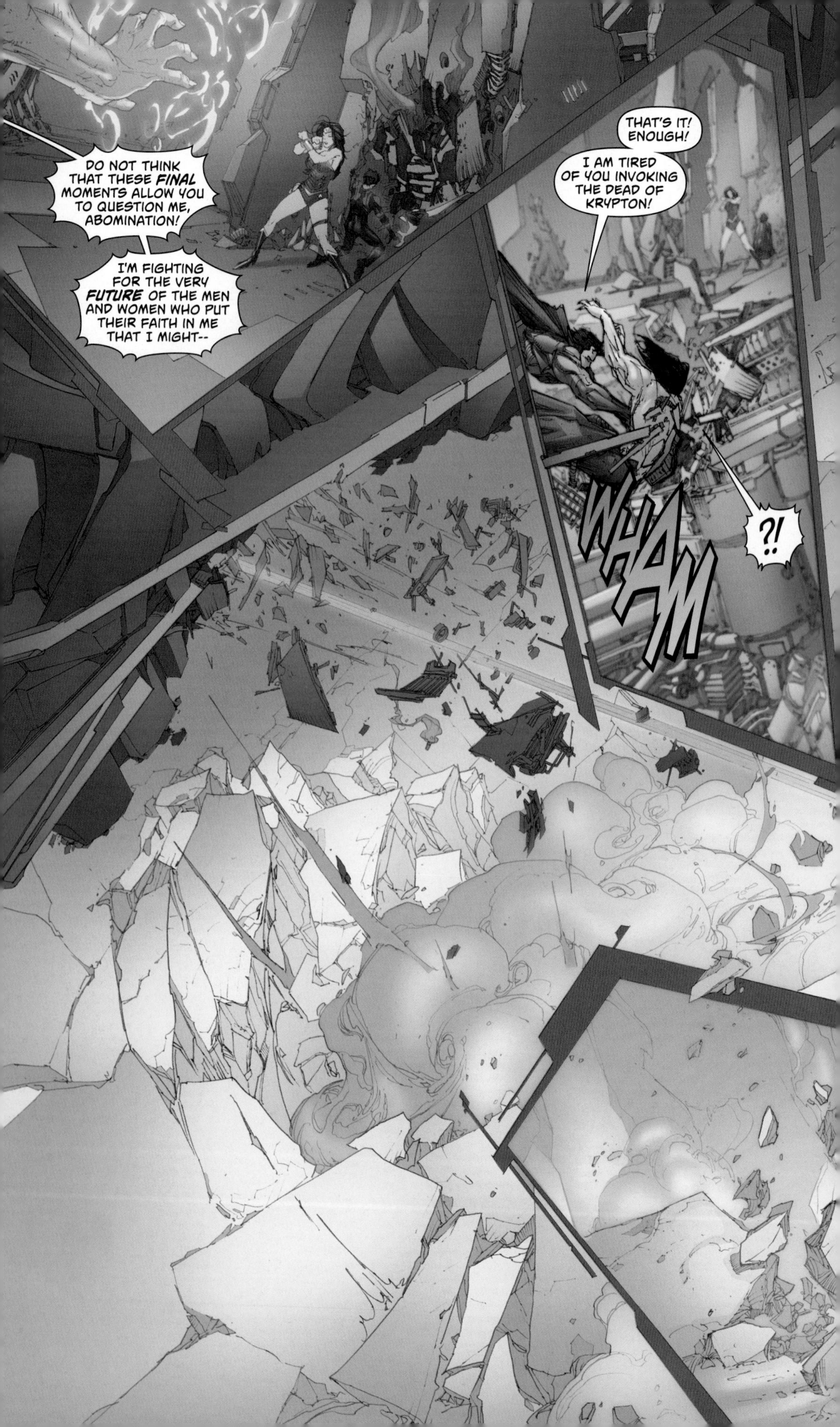
DO NOT THINK THAT THESE FINAL MOMENTS ALLOW YOU TO QUESTION ME, ABOMINATION!
I'M FIGHTING FOR THE VERY FUTURE OF THE MEN AND WOMEN WHO PUT THEIR FAITH IN ME THAT I MIGHT--
THAT'S IT! ENOUGH!
I AM TIRED OF YOU INVOKING THE DEAD OF KRYPTON!
WHAM
?!

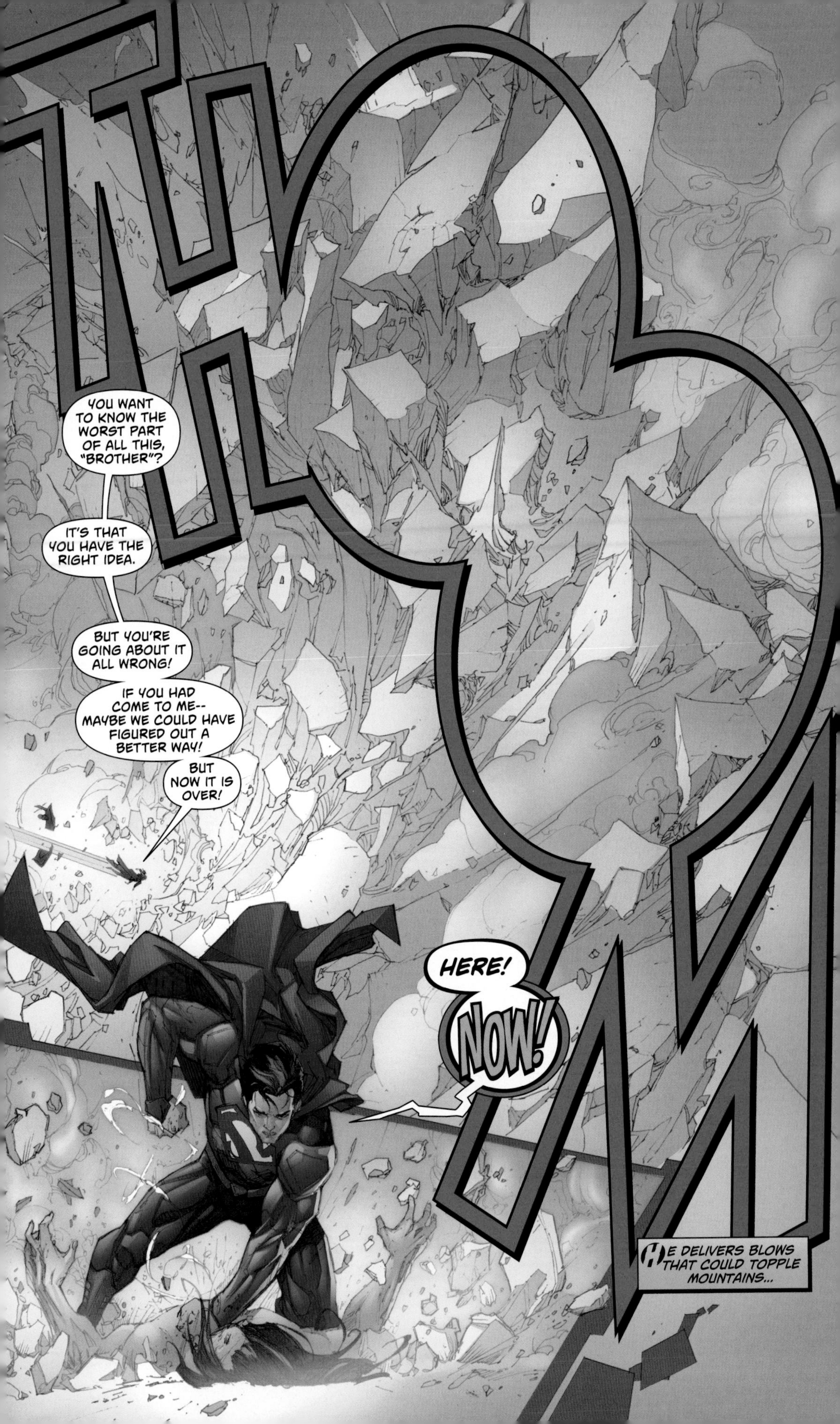

THOOM
YOU WANT TO KNOW THE WORST PART OF ALL THIS, "BROTHER"?
IT'S THAT YOU HAVE THE RIGHT IDEA.
BUT YOU'RE GOING ABOUT IT ALL WRONG!
IF YOU HAD COME TO ME-- MAYBE WE COULD HAVE FIGURED OUT A BETTER WAY!
BUT NOW IT IS OVER!
HERE!
NOW!
HE DELIVERS BLOWS THAT COULD TOPPLE MOUNTAINS...

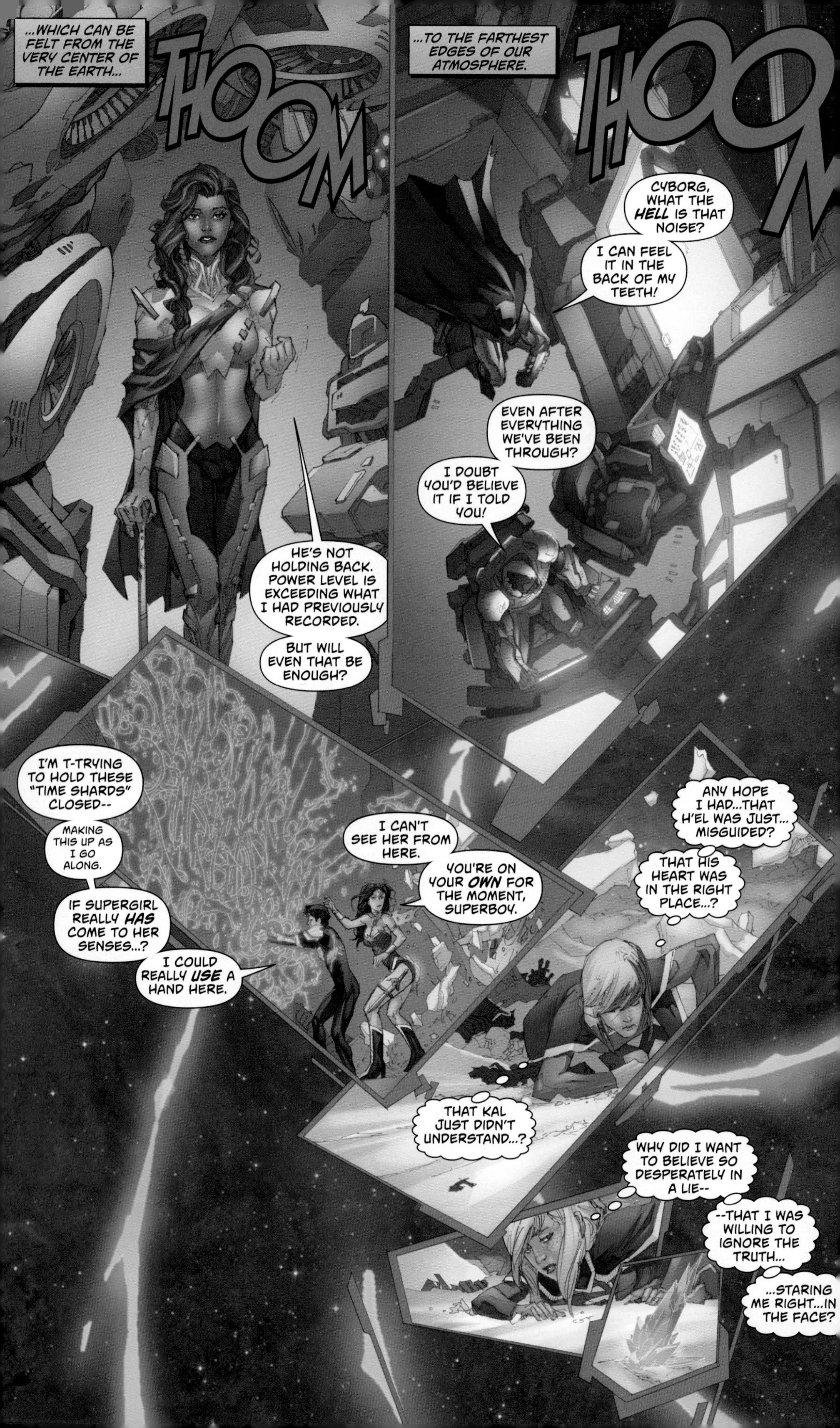
...WHICH CAN BE FELT FROM THE VERY CENTER OF THE EARTH...
THOOM
HE'S NOT HOLDING BACK. POWER LEVEL IS EXCEEDING WHAT I HAD PREVIOUSLY RECORDED.
BUT WILL EVEN THAT BE ENOUGH?
...TO THE FARTHEST EDGES OF OUR ATMOSPHERE.
THOOM
CYBORG, WHAT THE HELL IS THAT NOISE?
I CAN FEEL IT IN THE BACK OF MY TEETH!
EVEN AFTER EVERYTHING WE'VE BEEN THROUGH?
I DOUBT YOU'D BELIEVE IT IF I TOLD YOU!
I'M T-TRYING TO HOLD THESE "TIME SHARDS" CLOSED--
MAKING THIS UP AS I GO ALONG.
IF SUPERGIRL REALLY HAS COME TO HER SENSES...?
I COULD REALLY USE A HAND HERE.
I CAN'T SEE HER FROM HERE.
YOU'RE ON YOUR OWN FOR THE MOMENT, SUPERBOY.
ANY HOPE I HAD...THAT H'EL WAS JUST... MISGUIDED?
THAT HIS HEART WAS IN THE RIGHT PLACE...?
THAT KAL JUST DIDN'T UNDERSTAND...?
WHY DID I WANT TO BELIEVE SO DESPERATELY IN A LIE--
--THAT I WAS WILLING TO IGNORE THE TRUTH...
...STARING ME RIGHT...IN THE FACE?

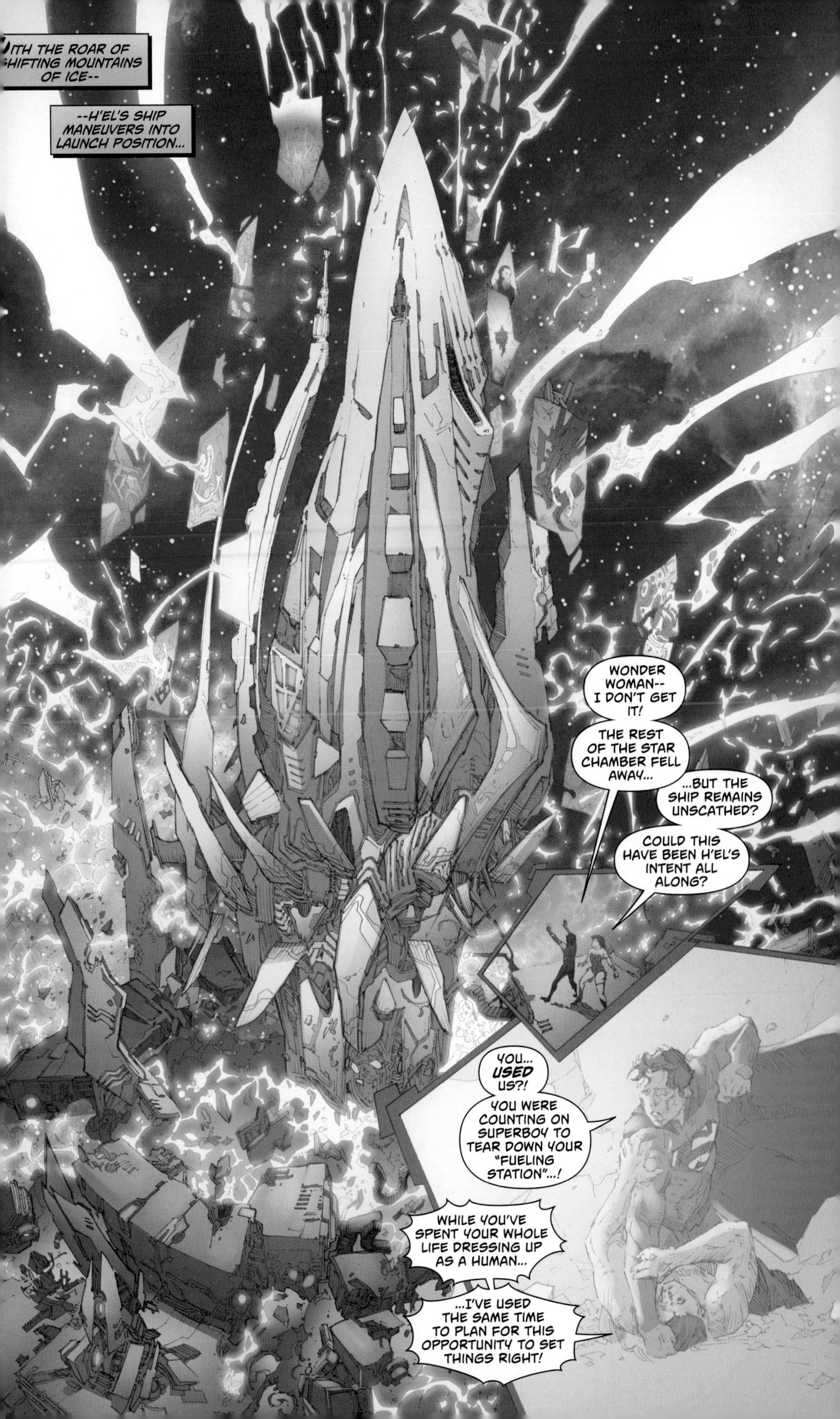

ITH THE ROAR OF HIFTING MOUNTAINS OF ICE--
--H'EL'S SHIP MANEUVERS INTO LAUNCH POSITION...
WONDER WOMAN-- I DON'T GET IT!
THE REST OF THE STAR CHAMBER FELL AWAY...
...BUT THE SHIP REMAINS UNSCATHED?
COULD THIS HAVE BEEN H'EL'S INTENT ALL ALONG?
YOU... USED US?!
YOU WERE COUNTING ON SUPERBOY TO TEAR DOWN YOUR "FUELING STATION"...!
WHILE YOU'VE SPENT YOUR WHOLE LIFE DRESSING UP AS A HUMAN...
...I'VE USED THE SAME TIME TO PLAN FOR THIS OPPORTUNITY TO SET THINGS RIGHT!

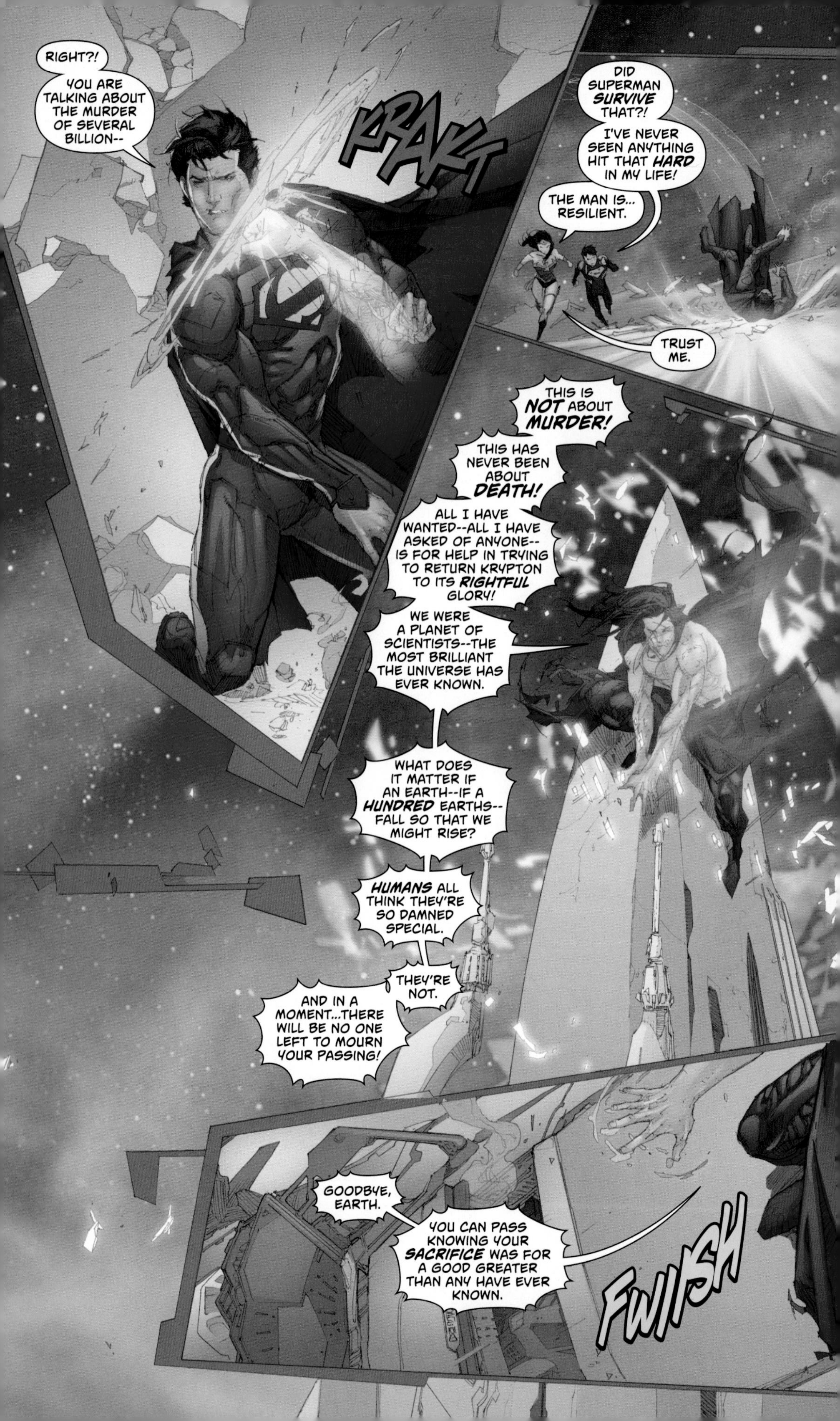
RIGHT?!
YOU ARE TALKING ABOUT THE MURDER OF SEVERAL BILLION--
KRAKT
DID SUPERMAN SURVIVE THAT?!
I'VE NEVER SEEN ANYTHING HIT THAT HARD IN MY LIFE!
THE MAN IS... RESILIENT.
TRUST ME.
THIS IS NOT ABOUT MURDER!
THIS HAS NEVER BEEN ABOUT DEATH!
ALL I HAVE WANTED--ALL I HAVE ASKED OF ANYONE--IS FOR HELP IN TRYING TO RETURN KRYPTON TO ITS RIGHTFUL GLORY!
WE WERE A PLANET OF SCIENTISTS--THE MOST BRILLIANT THE UNIVERSE HAS EVER KNOWN.
WHAT DOES IT MATTER IF AN EARTH--IF A HUNDRED EARTHS--FALL SO THAT WE MIGHT RISE?
HUMANS ALL THINK THEY'RE SO DAMNED SPECIAL.
THEY'RE NOT.
AND IN A MOMENT...THERE WILL BE NO ONE LEFT TO MOURN YOUR PASSING!
GOODBYE, EARTH.
YOU CAN PASS KNOWING YOUR SACRIFICE WAS FOR A GOOD GREATER THAN ANY HAVE EVER KNOWN.
FWISH

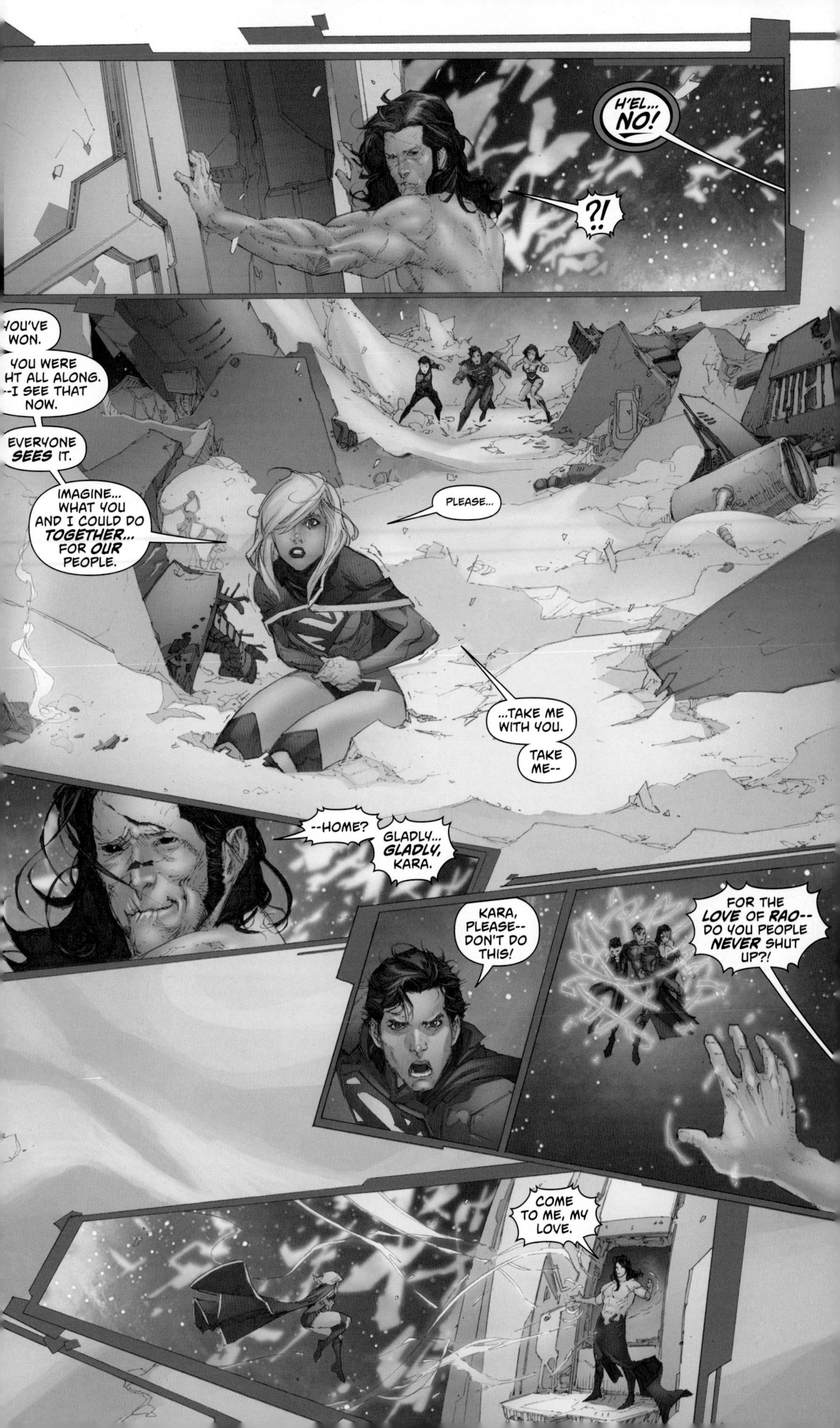

H'EL... NO!
?!
YOU'VE WON.
YOU WERE
HT ALL ALONG.
--I SEE THAT NOW.
EVERYONE SEES IT.
IMAGINE... WHAT YOU AND I COULD DO TOGETHER... FOR OUR PEOPLE.
PLEASE...
...TAKE ME WITH YOU.
TAKE ME--
--HOME?
GLADLY... GLADLY, KARA.
KARA, PLEASE-- DON'T DO THIS!
FOR THE LOVE OF RAO-- DO YOU PEOPLE NEVER SHUT UP?!
COME TO ME, MY LOVE.

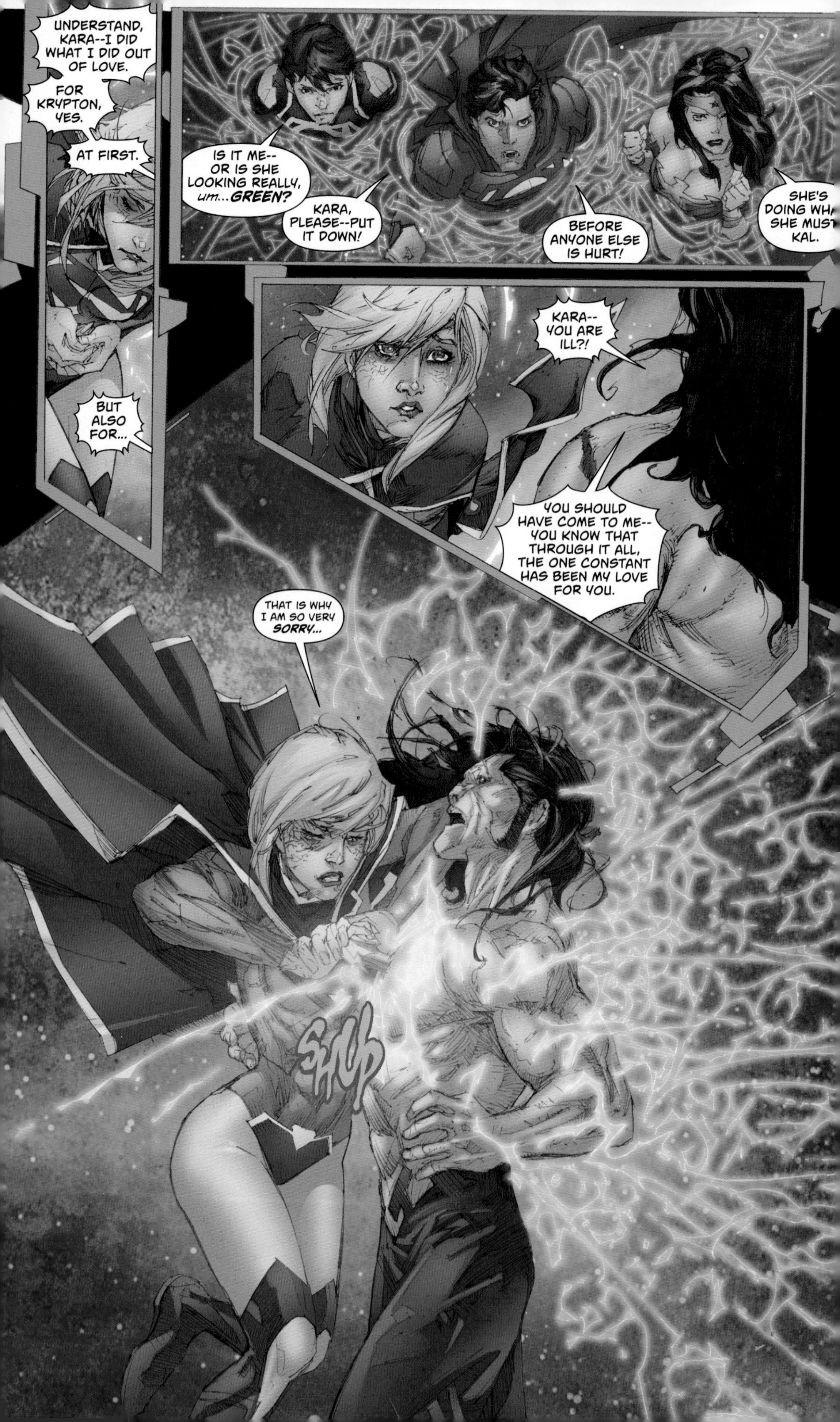

UNDERSTAND, KARA--I DID WHAT I DID OUT OF LOVE.
FOR KRYPTON, YES.
AT FIRST.
BUT ALSO FOR...
IS IT ME-- OR IS SHE LOOKING REALLY, *um*...**GREEN?**
KARA, PLEASE--PUT IT DOWN!
BEFORE ANYONE ELSE IS HURT!
SHE'S DOING WHA SHE MUST KAL.
KARA-- YOU ARE ILL?!
YOU SHOULD HAVE COME TO ME-- YOU KNOW THAT THROUGH IT ALL, THE ONE CONSTANT HAS BEEN MY LOVE FOR YOU.
THAT IS WHY I AM SO VERY **SORRY...**
SHUP

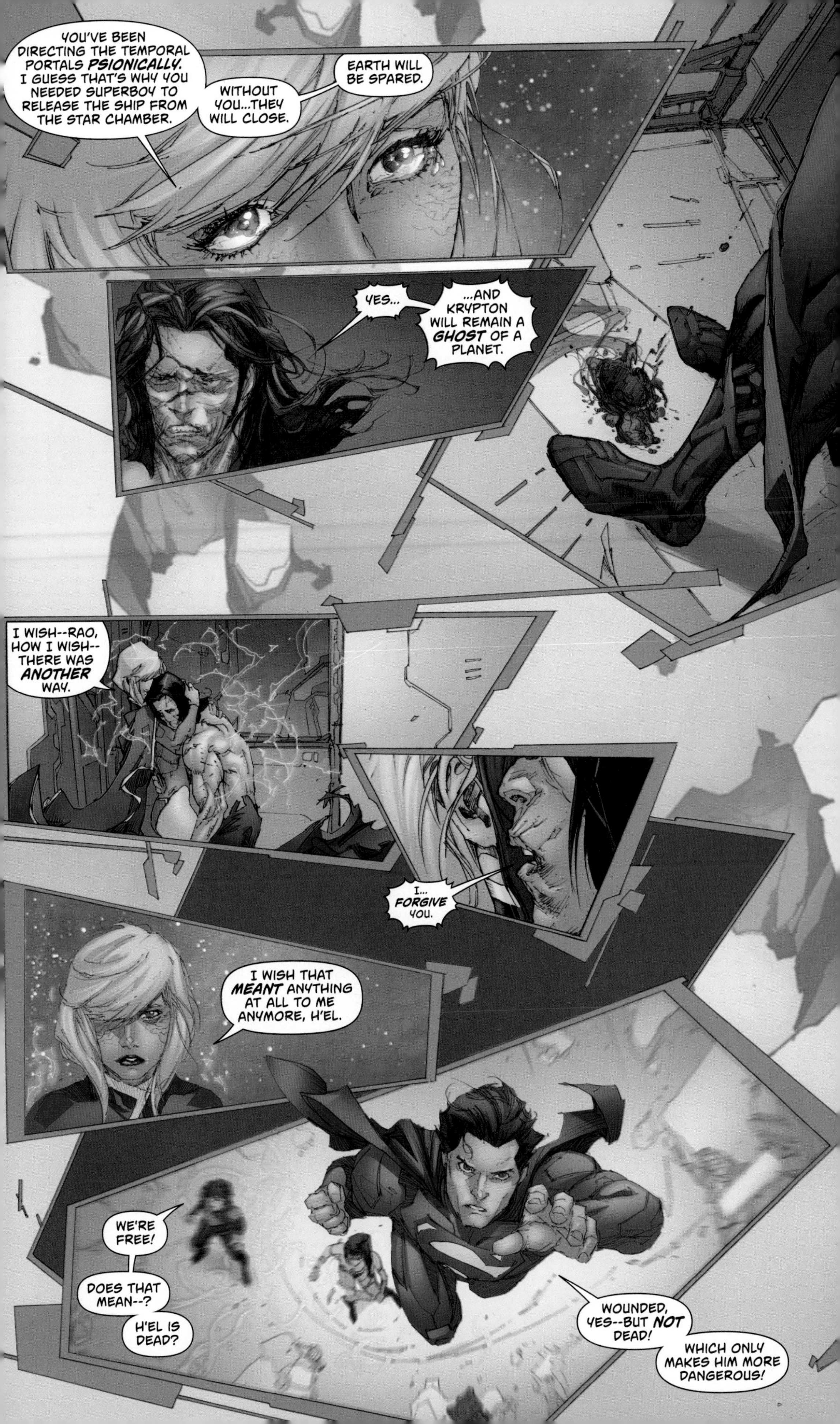
YOU'VE BEEN DIRECTING THE TEMPORAL PORTALS PSIONICALLY. I GUESS THAT'S WHY YOU NEEDED SUPERBOY TO RELEASE THE SHIP FROM THE STAR CHAMBER.
WITHOUT YOU...THEY WILL CLOSE.
EARTH WILL BE SPARED.
YES...
...AND KRYPTON WILL REMAIN A GHOST OF A PLANET.
I WISH--RAO, HOW I WISH--THERE WAS ANOTHER WAY.
I... FORGIVE YOU.
I WISH THAT MEANT ANYTHING AT ALL TO ME ANYMORE, H'EL.
WE'RE FREE!
DOES THAT MEAN--?
H'EL IS DEAD?
WOUNDED, YES--BUT NOT DEAD!
WHICH ONLY MAKES HIM MORE DANGEROUS!

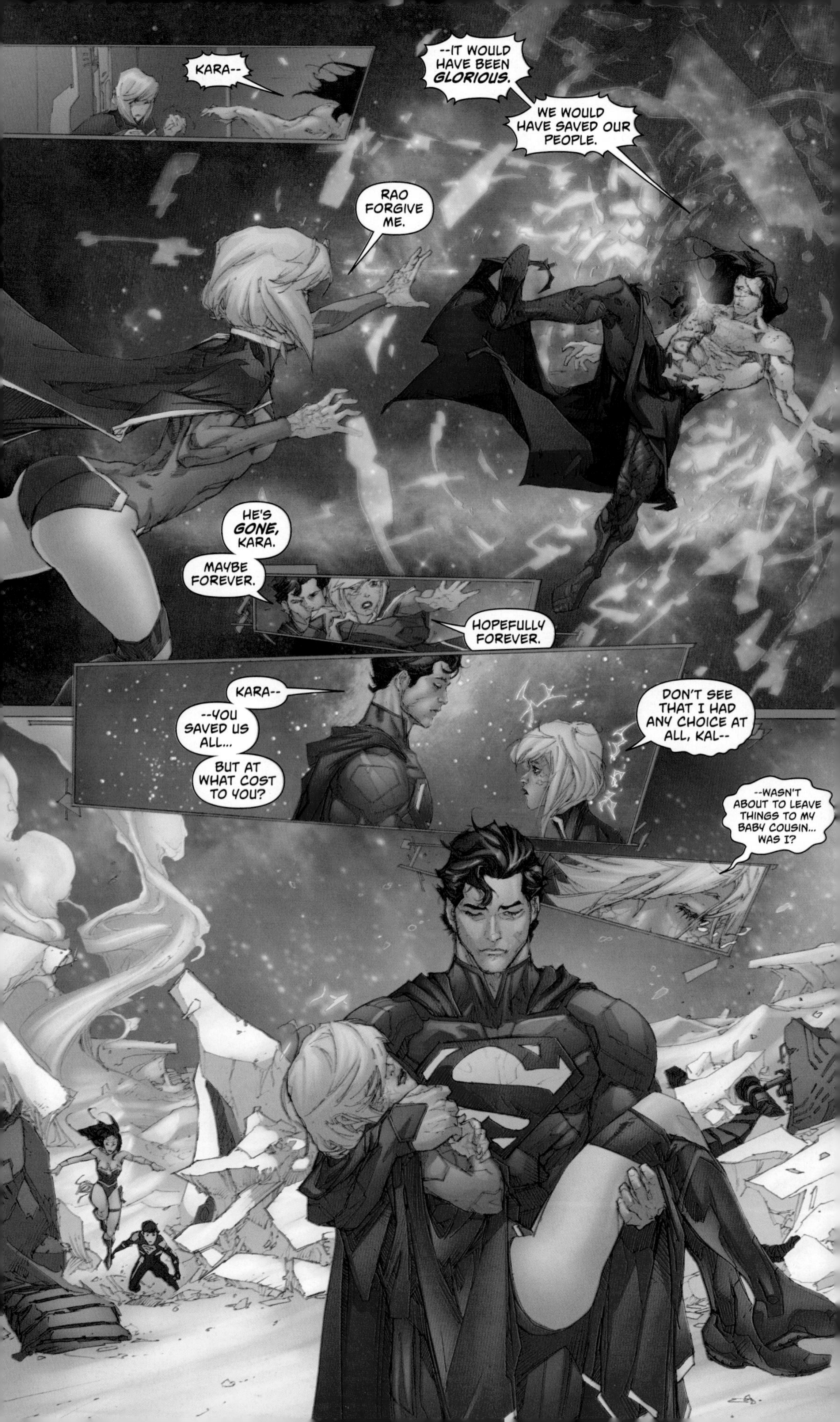
KARA--
--IT WOULD HAVE BEEN GLORIOUS.
WE WOULD HAVE SAVED OUR PEOPLE.
RAO FORGIVE ME.
HE'S GONE, KARA.
MAYBE FOREVER.
HOPEFULLY FOREVER.
KARA--
--YOU SAVED US ALL...
BUT AT WHAT COST TO YOU?
DON'T SEE THAT I HAD ANY CHOICE AT ALL, KAL--
--WASN'T ABOUT TO LEAVE THINGS TO MY BABY COUSIN... WAS I?

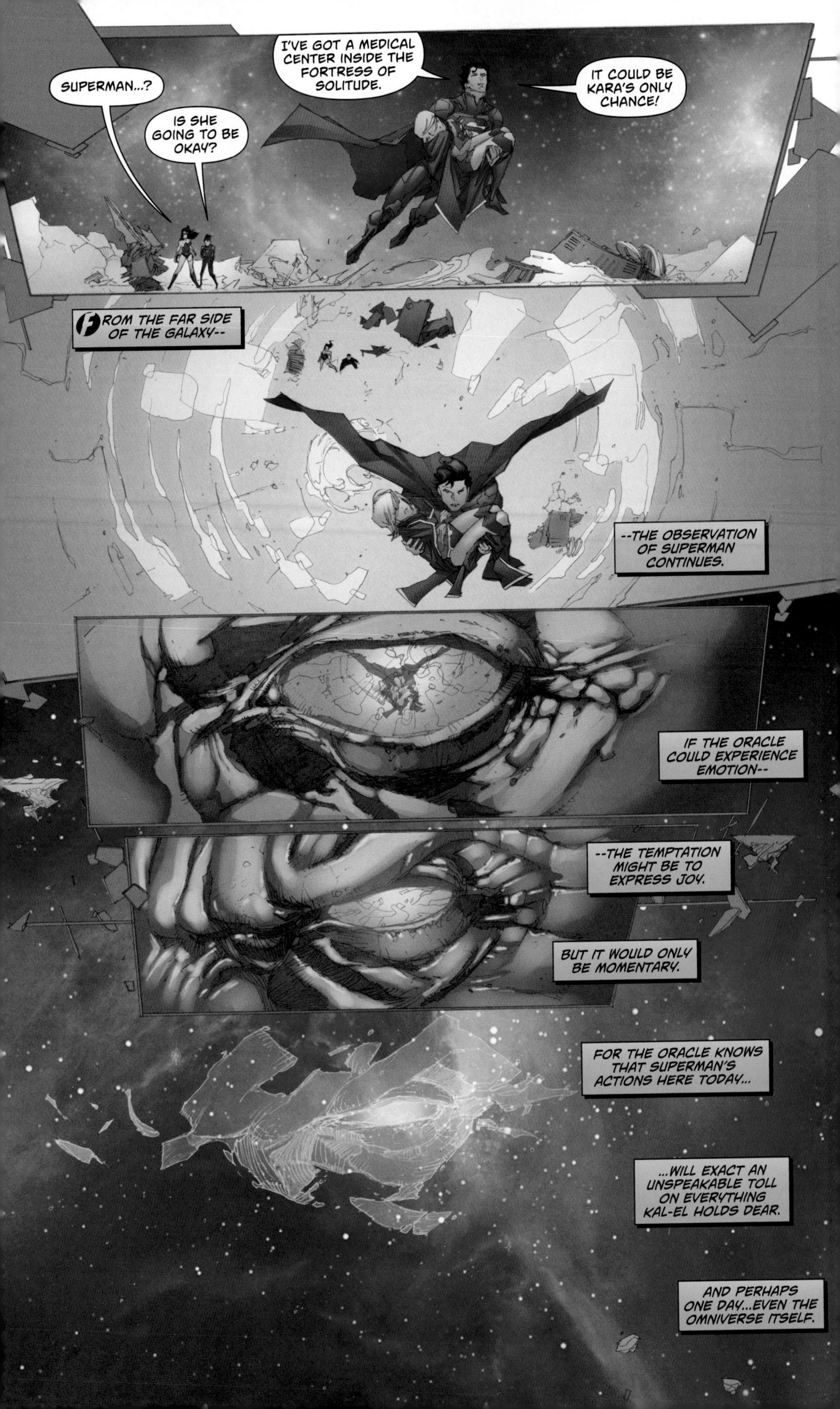
SUPERMAN...?
IS SHE GOING TO BE OKAY?
I'VE GOT A MEDICAL CENTER INSIDE THE FORTRESS OF SOLITUDE.
IT COULD BE KARA'S ONLY CHANCE!
FROM THE FAR SIDE OF THE GALAXY--
--THE OBSERVATION OF SUPERMAN CONTINUES.
IF THE ORACLE COULD EXPERIENCE EMOTION--
--THE TEMPTATION MIGHT BE TO EXPRESS JOY.
BUT IT WOULD ONLY BE MOMENTARY.
FOR THE ORACLE KNOWS THAT SUPERMAN'S ACTIONS HERE TODAY...
...WILL EXACT AN UNSPEAKABLE TOLL ON EVERYTHING KAL-EL HOLDS DEAR.
AND PERHAPS ONE DAY...EVEN THE OMNIVERSE ITSELF.

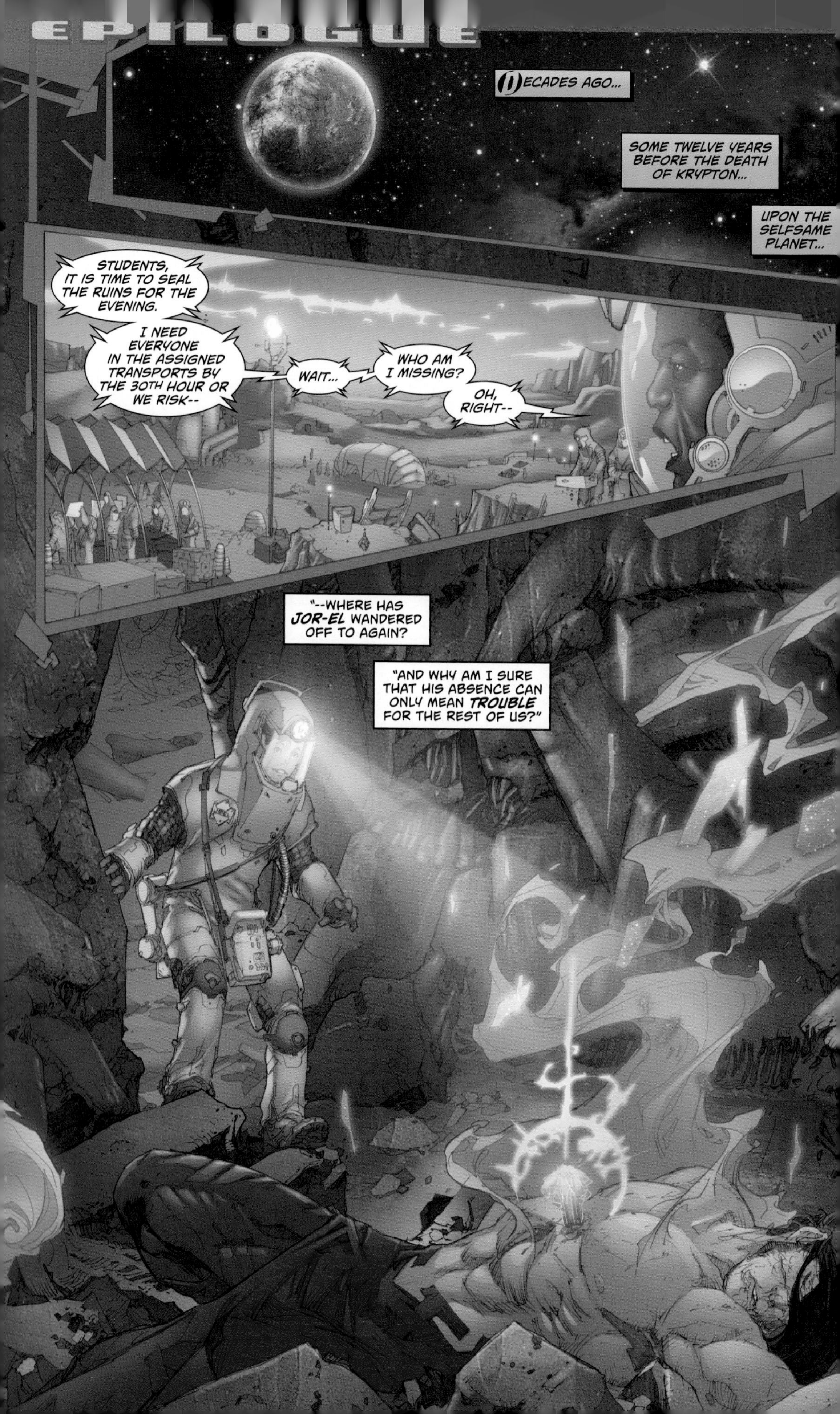
EPILOGUE
DECADES AGO...
SOME TWELVE YEARS BEFORE THE DEATH OF KRYPTON...
UPON THE SELFSAME PLANET...
STUDENTS, IT IS TIME TO SEAL THE RUINS FOR THE EVENING.
I NEED EVERYONE IN THE ASSIGNED TRANSPORTS BY THE 30TH HOUR OR WE RISK--
WAIT...
WHO AM I MISSING?
OH, RIGHT--
"--WHERE HAS JOR-EL WANDERED OFF TO AGAIN?
"AND WHY AM I SURE THAT HIS ABSENCE CAN ONLY MEAN TROUBLE FOR THE REST OF US?"

From issue #0

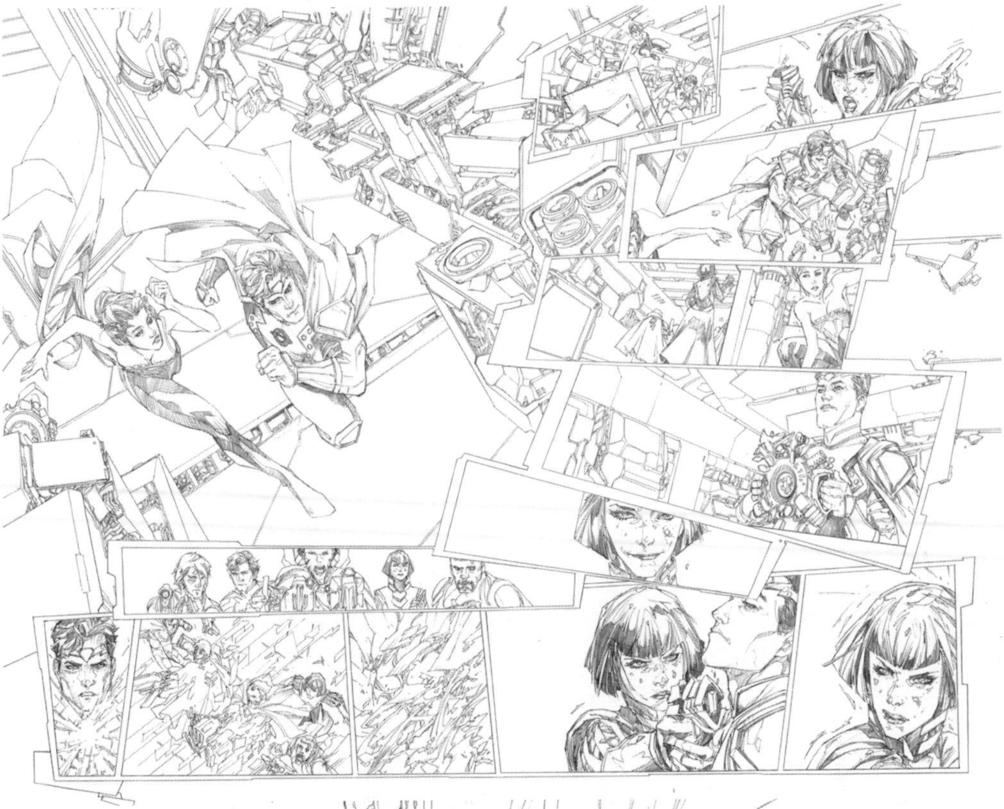

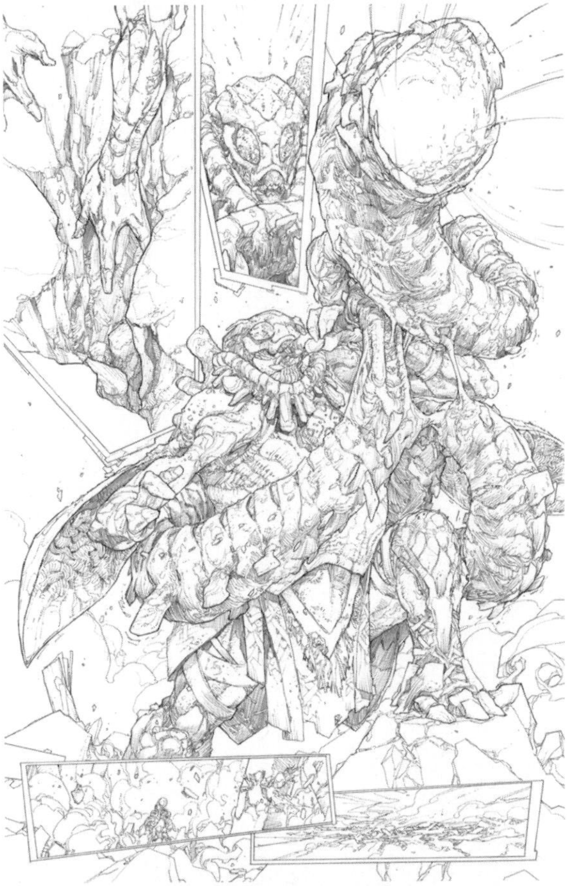

From issue #13

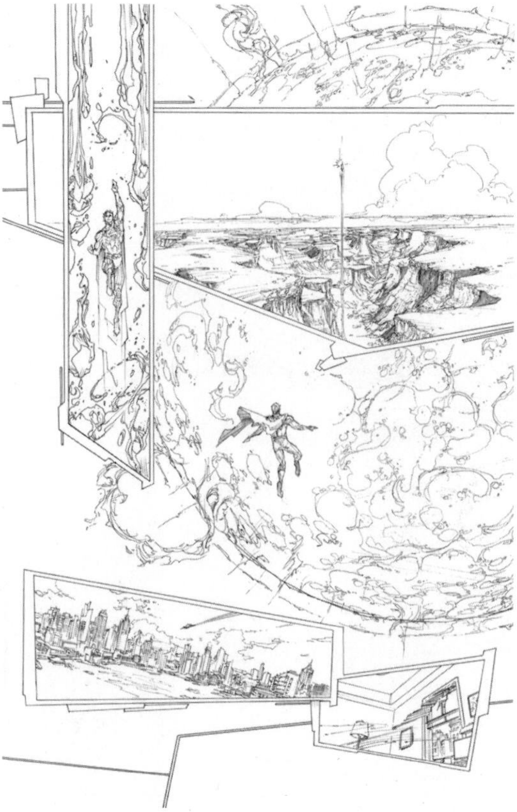

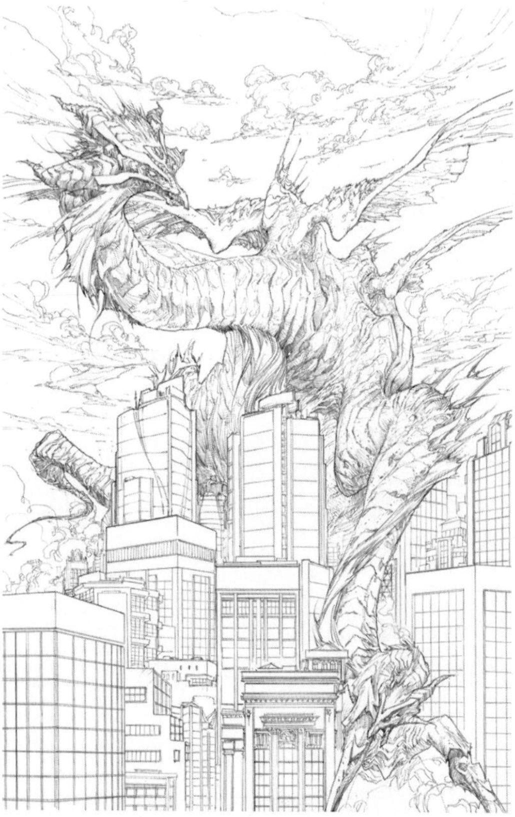

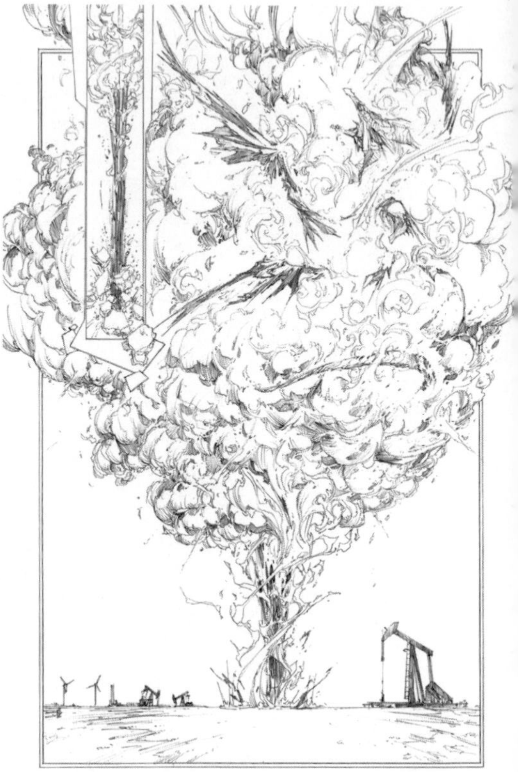

From issue #14

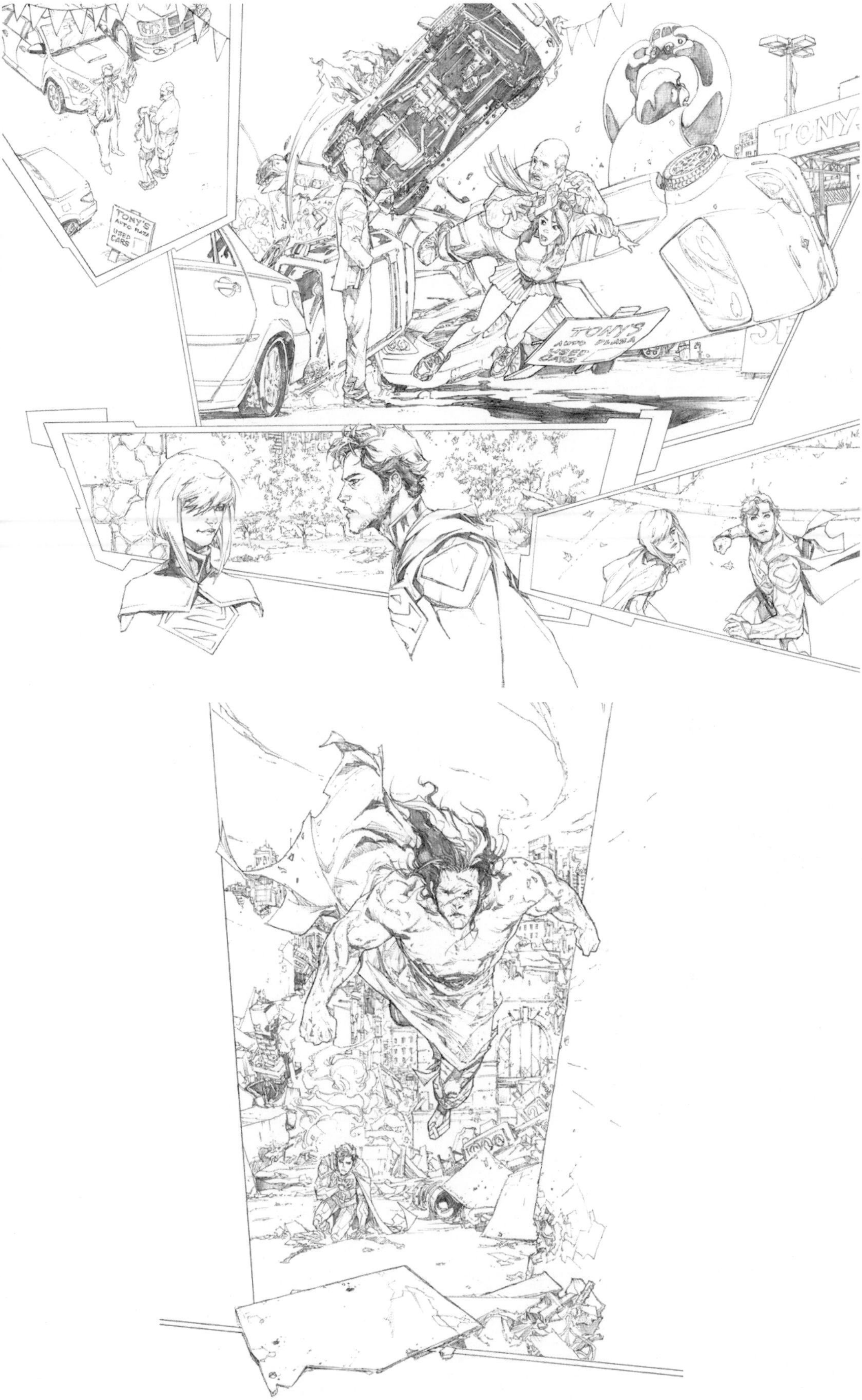
TONY'S AUTO PLAZA USED CARS
TONY'S AUTO PLAZA USED CARS

From issue #15

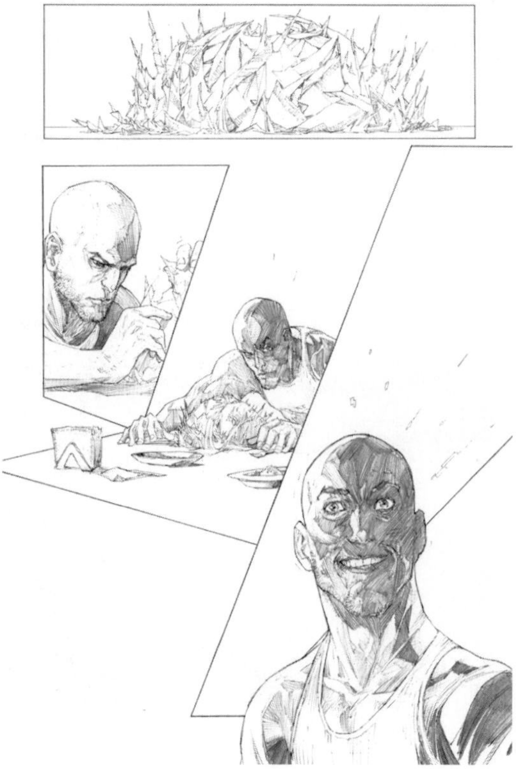

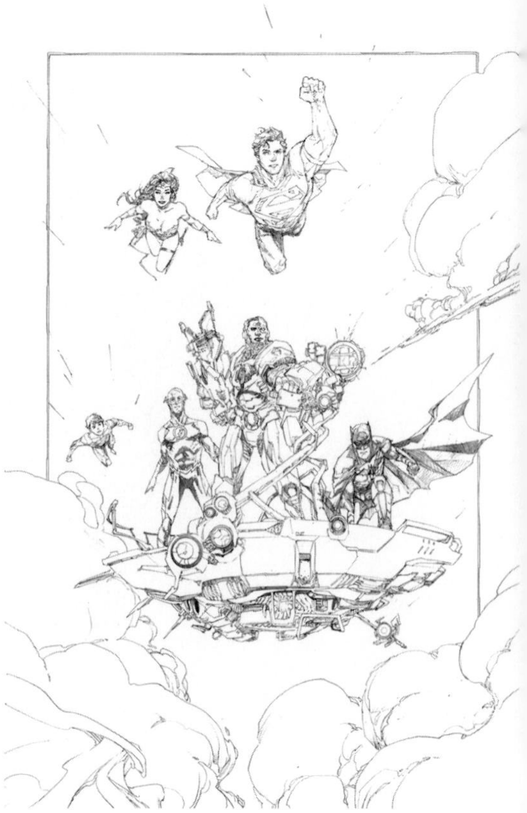

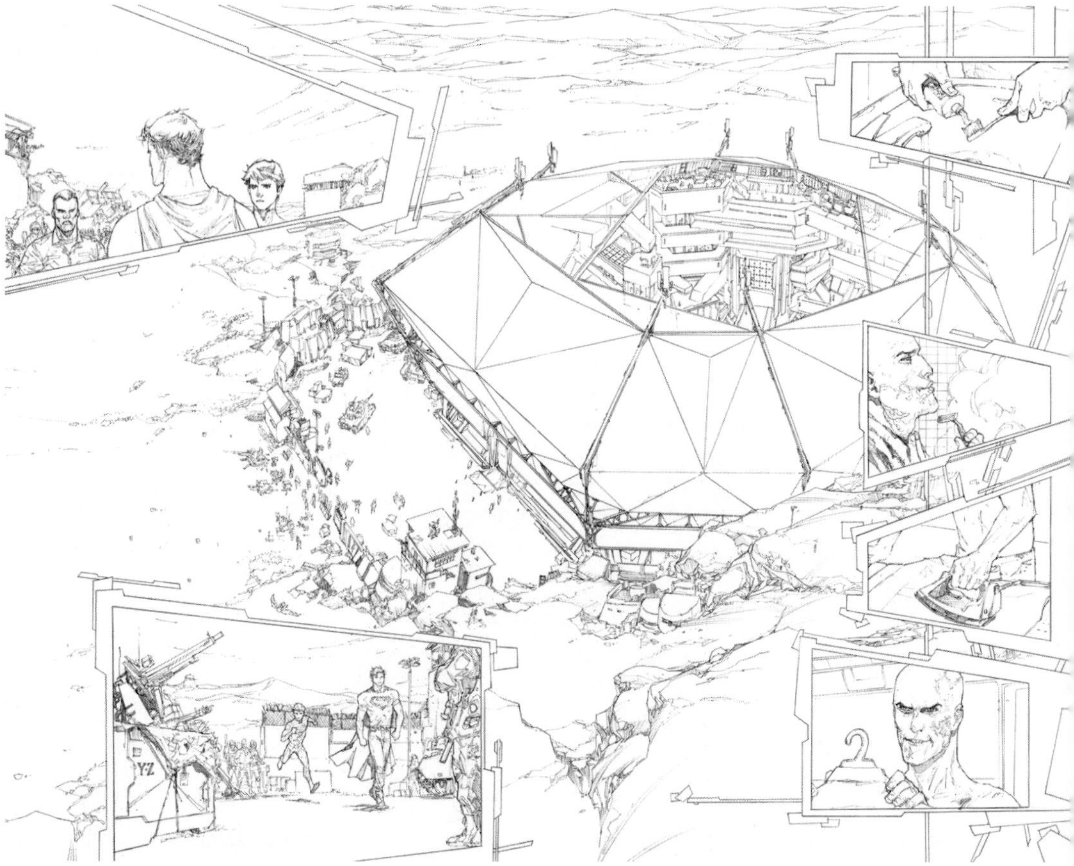

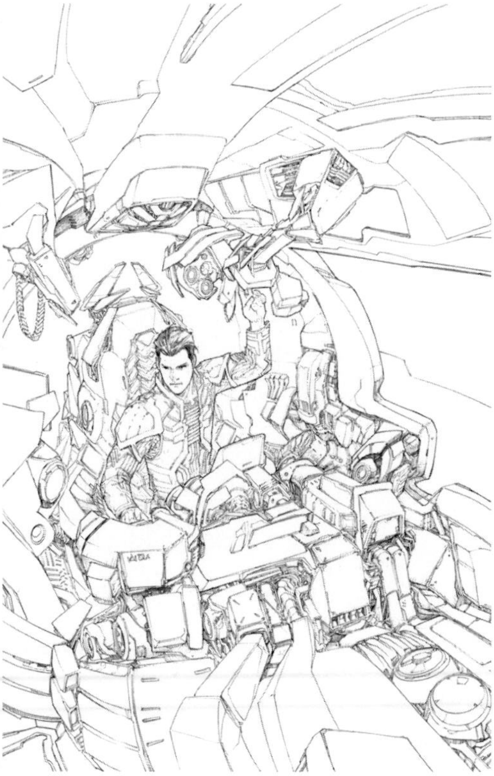

From issue #16

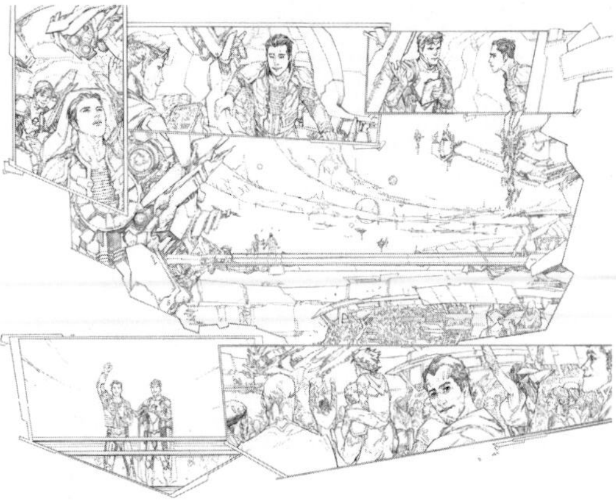

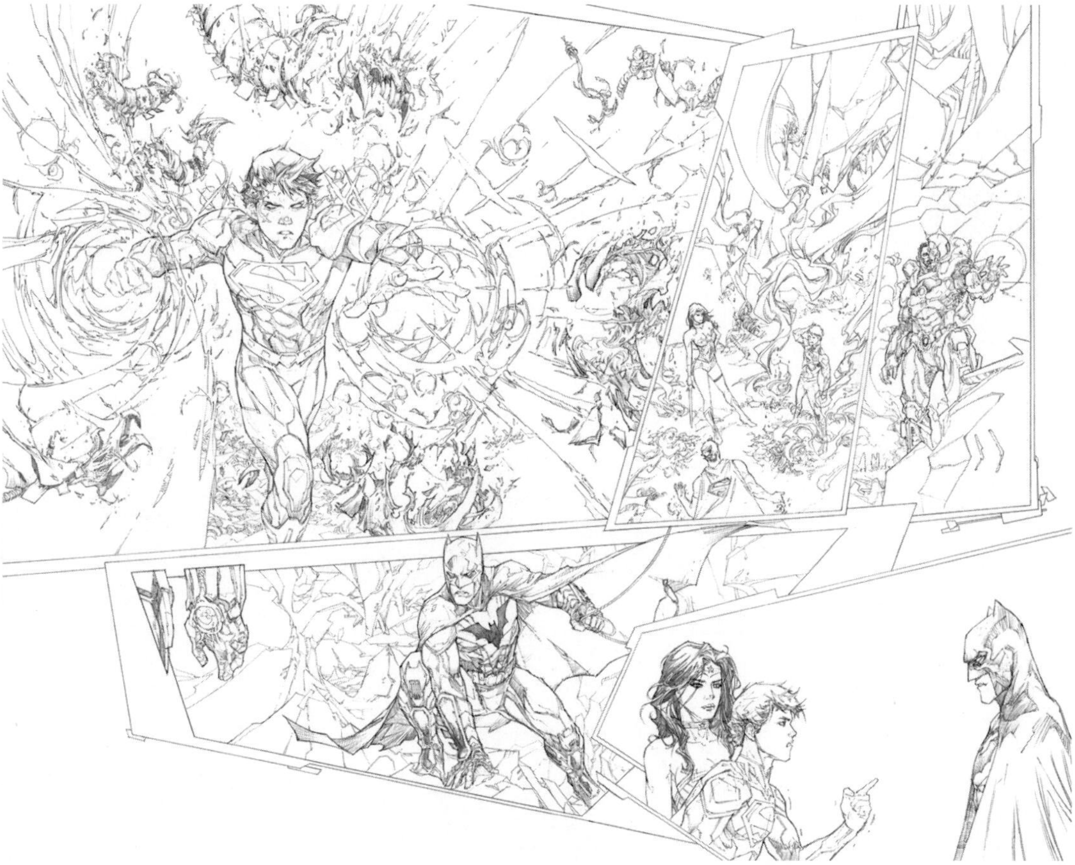

From issue #17

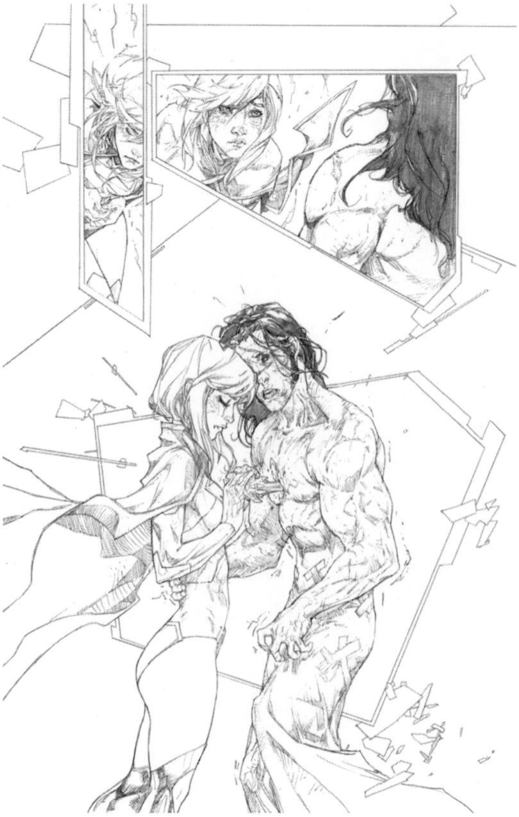

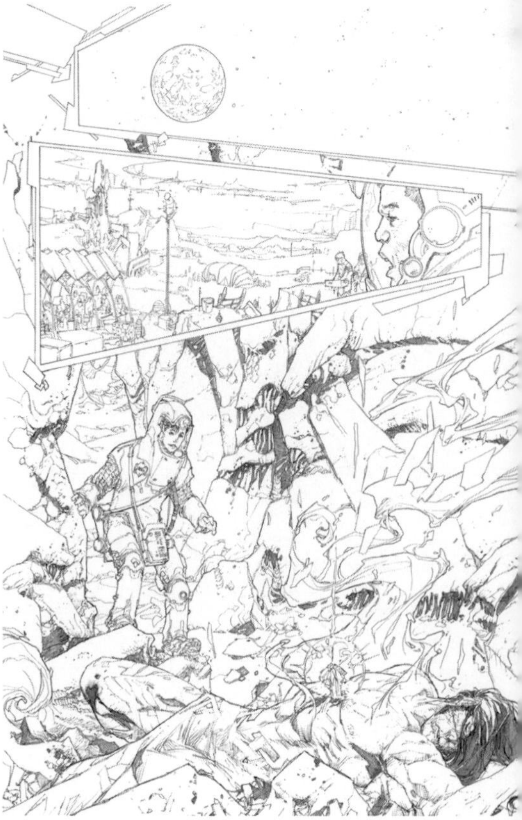

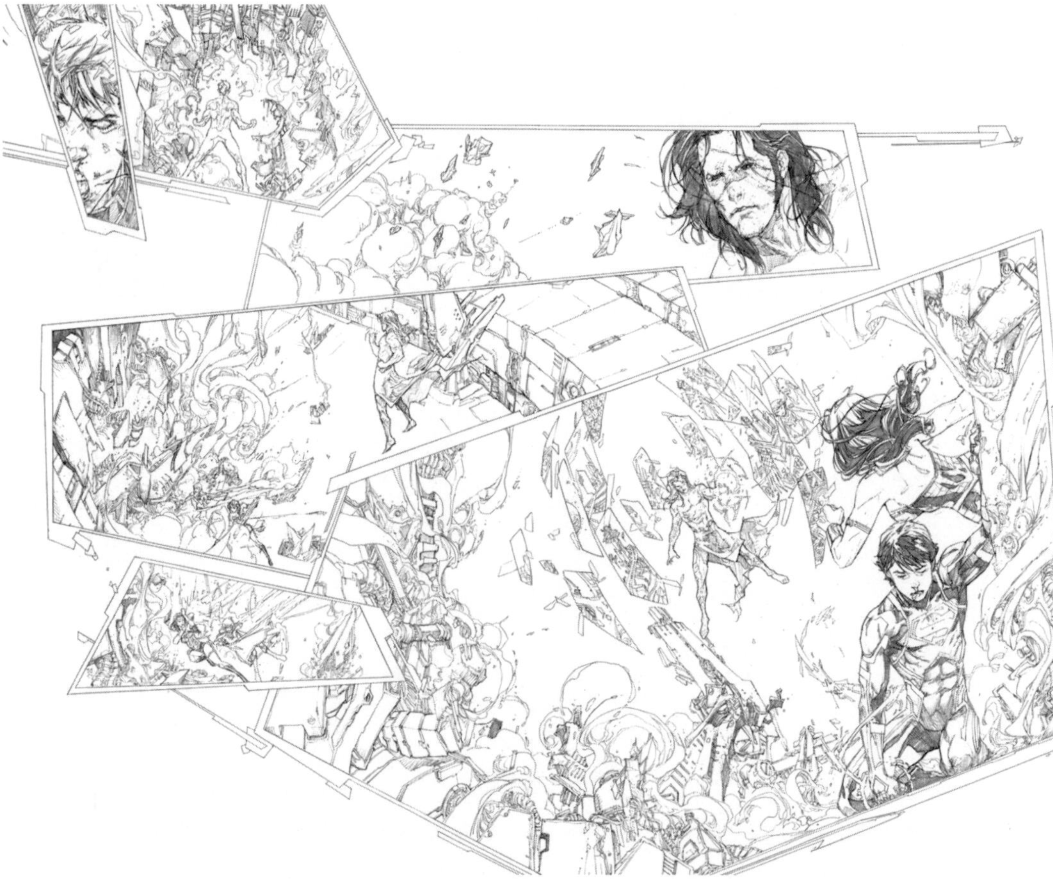

SUPERMAN

COVER PENCILS FOR ISSUE #15 BY KENNETH ROCAFORT

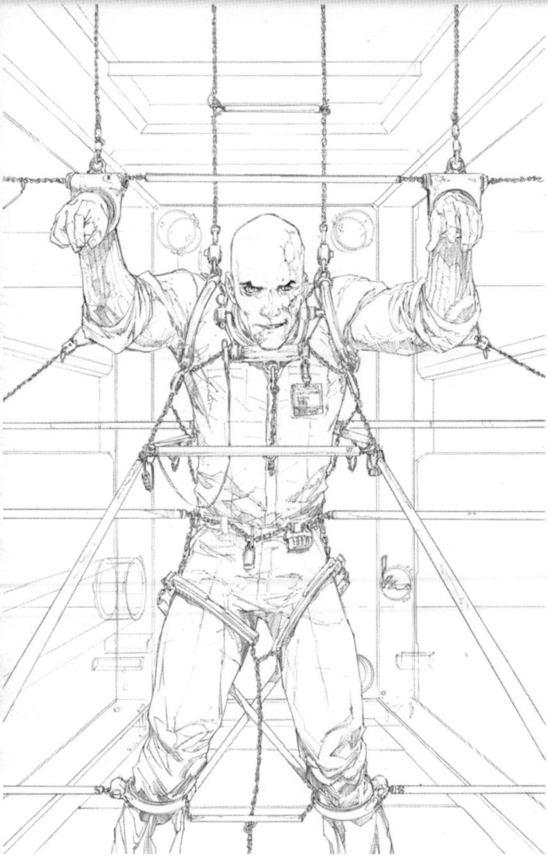

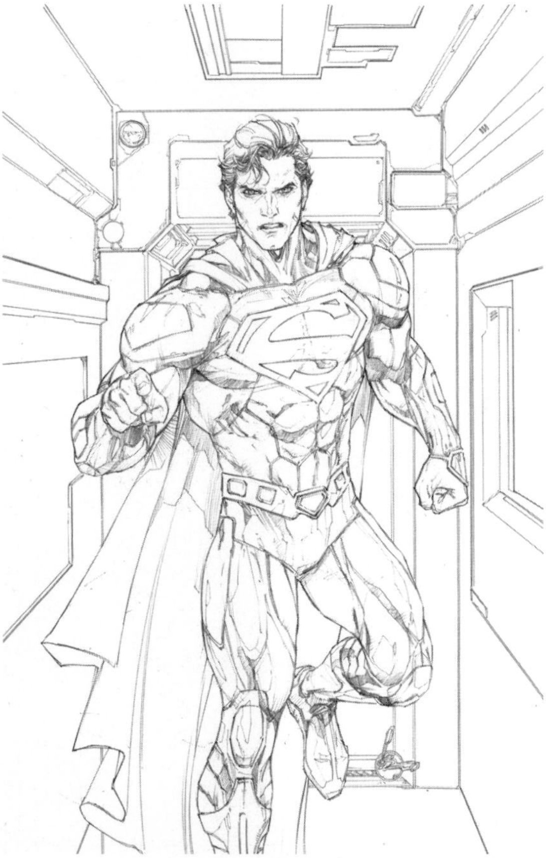

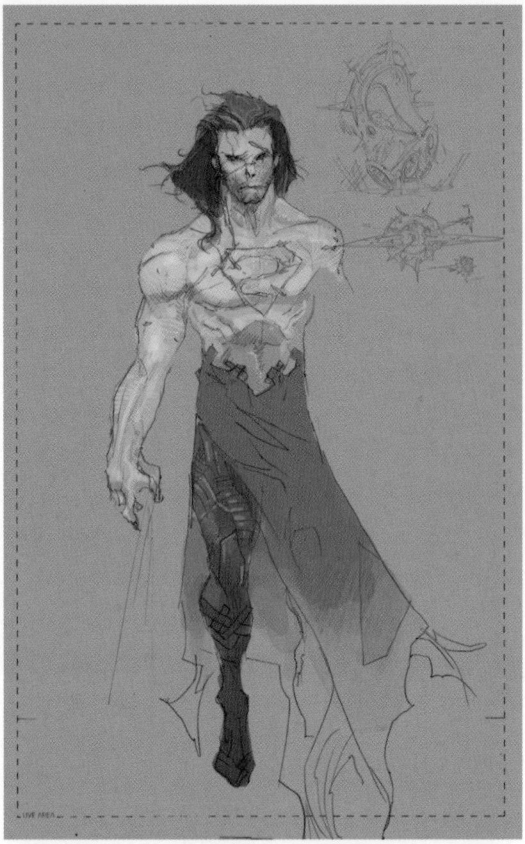

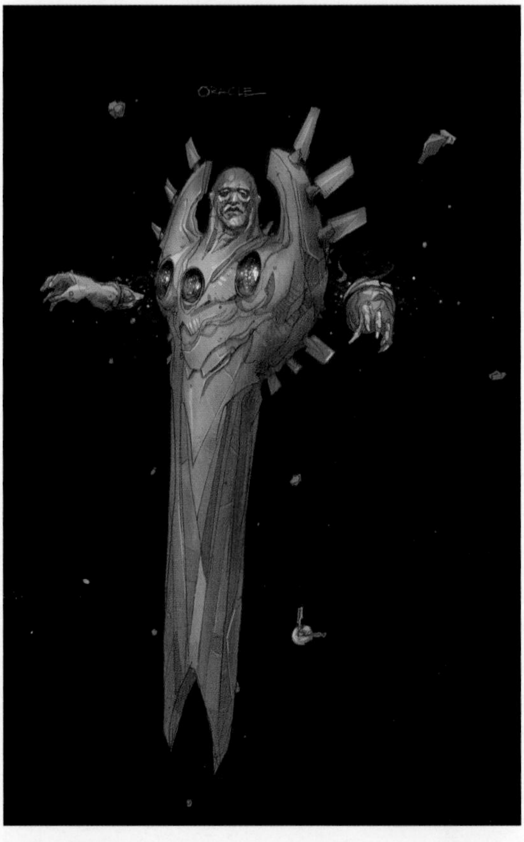
ORACLE